Entire Sanctification

Entire Sanctification:
Holiness of Heart and Life

This book is most emphatically **not** copyrighted. I give full and free permission to anybody to copy as much of it as they please, subject to only two conditions: (A), do not alter the meaning, and (B), do not lie about the authorship. I did not write it for pleasure, or for monetary gain, but because I saw a need for education on this subject within the Church. I wrote this for the benefit of God's people. I believe and sincerely hope that God has, at least to some small degree, influenced or perhaps even inspired my thoughts. As such, to claim ownership (as opposed to authorship) of this book would be well-nigh blasphemy. The mistakes are mine. Everything else belongs to God.

Published 2018 by Daniel Tapio; Colorado Springs
Printed by Tewell Warren

ISBN 978-1-7322699-0-3

Dedication

I dedicate this book to the memory of two people:
My paternal grandmother, Fay Tapio. She taught me more than anybody else what it means to be a Christian. She told me stories about Holiness preachers of by-gone years, and taught me to appreciate my Christian heritage in general, and more specifically, my Holiness heritage. She taught me to "search the Scriptures." She delighted in the way of God, and always attended church services unless illness or some unusual event hindered.
Harlie Smith, who my grandmother became acquainted with when she was a girl, close to 80 years ago. He was a preacher, writer, missionary supporter, prayer-warrior, and friend of God. I never knew him well; I was too young when he died. But I knew him enough to know that very few other Christians have come close to matching his walk with God. He lived and breathed "holiness unto the Lord" like virtually nobody else.

Contents

Note to the Reader

The common practice we have today in the English language of capitalizing words referring to God is actually a fairly recent practice, historically speaking. Therefore old documents and translations do not conform to modern practice in this matter, unless they have specifically been edited with that in mind.

"Think, if you want stirring motives for serving God, what it cost to provide a salvation for your soul. Think how the Son of God left heaven and became Man, suffered on the cross, and lay in the grave, to pay your debt to God, and work out for you a complete redemption. Think of all this and learn that it is no light matter to possess an immortal soul. It is worthwhile to take some trouble about one's soul" (J. C. Ryle).

"My people are destroyed for lack of knowledge" (Hosea 4:6a).

"And yet shew I unto you a more excellent way" (I Cor. 12:31b).

Preface

To the reader who has never heard of this doctrine before: I hope that you will find this book a blessing to your soul. I further hope that you will seek after entire sanctification until you get it.

To the reader who has heard of the doctrine, but opposes it or perhaps misunderstands it: I hope that this book corrects any misunderstandings you might have. I hope that you will be convinced of the Scriptural backing behind this doctrine. I also hope that you will seek after entire sanctification until you get it.

To the reader who has grown up in Holiness circles: I did too, but did not fully understand the doctrine until I studied it for myself. Unfortunately, many Holiness preachers do not explain the doctrine as they should. I hope that this book will leave you with a greater understanding of and deeper appreciation for this doctrine.

I welcome any comments or follow-up questions.

I can be reached at daniel624@gmail.com. I plan to keep this email indefinitely.

I also run a blog, commenting on various things from a Holiness perspective, at: https://holinesscorner.wordpress.com.

Chapter 1

Introduction and Overview

I grew up in Holiness churches, but over the years, I have known several Christians who either had never heard about the doctrine of entire sanctification, or else had heard of it but did not understand it. I have come to realize that both sides need a better understanding of the doctrine and its history, for very few Holiness churches teach the doctrine in the way that it ought to be taught. Many Holiness people (and all of the people outside of the Holiness movement) do not understand how thoroughly the doctrine of Holiness is woven throughout the Bible.

This used to include myself. I thought for many years that I understood the doctrine. However, I came to realize that my knowledge of the doctrine was sorely lacking. Looking back at my memories, I was astonished to realize that many of the Holiness preachers that I had heard over the years did a remarkably poor job of explaining the doctrine. I searched for books on the subject (and there were several). However, a great many of those books were long on poems and anecdotes, but short on theology. I finally came to realize that if I wanted to really understand the doctrine, I would have to turn to the source—the Bible—and study the doctrine from the ground up, from the foundation stone of Scripture. This led to an interesting phenomenon. There were numerous times—I lost track of how many, but several—when during my Bible study I would realize something, and then find out later that a writer from decades or centuries past had made the same point. I also did quite a bit of historical research, and again, I would sometimes read an author from the earlier centuries, only to find out at a later date that that author influenced John Wesley.

This series of "coincidences" shows how Divine truth is independent of any one person or group. It shows how multiple people who study the Bible with an open heart and mind will independently arrive at the same conclusion. God tells us that He does not change, and the fact that people in different cultures, speaking different languages, and separated by hundreds of years, can find the exact same truth in His Word—this is further evidence that the doctrine of Holiness is true and correct.

I had done a lot of study and research for this book, when a friend reminded me of the importance of making sure that Bible study is done correctly. I got to thinking about it, and I realized that while I was almost certain that I was on the right track, and drawing the right conclusions, I wasn't quite absolutely certain. So I prepared to do another, completely separate, round of Bible study.

Before I began this second round, I wanted to make sure that I would not be hampered by any preconceptions that I might have on this subject. I have seen, both in my own life, and in other people's lives, that preconceptions can be tremendously powerful things. They can blind us to truths that should be readily apparent. Therefore, I prayed that God would give me an open mind and open heart to see past any preconceptions that I might have. I wanted to have a truly open mind on the subject, even if by doing so I would learn things that would contradict what I had been taught all my life. It can be very painful when the Bible contradicts what we have been taught by people we love and respect, but Truth should be paramount. I had intended to pray this prayer every day for a week before even beginning this second round of Bible study: like Gideon, I wanted to be absolutely, crystal clear that I knew God's will and truth. But on the fourth day, as I knelt to pray, I felt a definite, surprisingly-strong check of the Spirit. God told me, "You've prayed enough; you're ready now."

The results: I found several more Bible verses that support the doctrine of a second work of grace; verses that I had missed the first time around.

The idea of a second work of grace, and the terminology used to describe it, has caused a great deal of confusion and controversy over the centuries. This doctrine is closely associated with John Wesley, which has caused a fair bit of confusion all on its own; because of this close association, many people have gotten the impression that he came up with the doctrine. In my research for this book, I came across one particular person who had that idea, and he rejected the concept of the second work, precisely because he thought it was a man-made doctrine.

Man-made or not, Wesley did not invent it. The concepts that Wesley popularized go back much farther than many people realize—indeed, to the very earliest days of Church history. I did a great deal of historical research on this, the results of which are in the next section.

I use the KJV throughout this book, for two reasons. Firstly, I strongly prefer it for the vast majority of cases; and secondly, this is the version that Wesley and his contemporaries and his immediate successors used. Thus, when we are talking about the history of the Holiness movement, it is, quite simply, historically accurate to use the KJV.

This doctrine has the potential to be confusing in several respects. For one, many non-Holiness people use the term "sanctification," but they use it in a different manner than Holiness people do. There is a sub-set of non-Holiness people who use the term in a way similar to what we do, but they mean by it something different than what Holiness people do.

When I was in college, I learned in my philosophy classes the importance of defining one's terms. I have seen discussions of various types degenerate into confusion because neither side bothered to properly define the terms being used. So before we go any farther, here is the Holiness movement's definition of "sanctification."

Short definition:

It is a second, definite, instantaneous work of grace that removes every trace of the sin nature that remains after a person gets saved.

Long definition and description:

It is a second, definite, instantaneous work of grace that removes every trace of the sin nature that remains after a person gets saved. A common analogy is to think of sin as a tree—salvation cuts down the tree, but leaves the roots. Sanctification removes the roots. The first recorded instance of this work was on the Day of Pentecost, when the Holy Ghost descended from Heaven, and indwelt the believers in the Upper Room. This indwelling, or filling, by the Spirit is entirely separate from the gift of tongues. The work of sanctification is separate and distinct from the work of regeneration. It is also separate and distinct from the process of growing in grace. It must be sought after just as sincerely and as strongly as salvation is sought after. It is called by several different names—each name usually refers to some specific aspect, and people sometimes choose what name to call it based on a certain aspect that they wish to emphasize. Some of the more common names are "the death-route"; "the second blessing"; "heart holiness"; "the higher life"; "the baptism of the Spirit"; "Christian perfection"; and "sinless perfection." There is no fixed length of time after salvation before a person can be sanctified. A handful of people have gotten sanctified just a few hours after getting saved. It more commonly takes months, or sometimes years. This is partly because it is common for people to be saved for a while before feeling a need to be sanctified. The process by which God leads a person to this work is highly variable, depending on each person, their knowledge, the closeness of their walk with God, their besetting sin, and other factors. When it is received, the most common reaction is great, overwhelming joy; but some people feel nothing but a great, quiet peace. Strictly speaking, the experience of sanctification is not necessary to get to Heaven (salvation takes care of that), although it is tremendously helpful in that regard. There may, however, be individuals who will not get to Heaven without its stabilizing influence. The work of sanctification makes resisting temptation much easier, because there is no longer a "fifth column" of sin in the heart. It helps a Christian remain separate from the world, and live a life that is victorious over the world. It is not, however, a "be-all, end-all" thing. Sanctification is not the final word in Christian living, but rather a deeper, steadier foundation, from which a Christian should continue to grow in grace.

By contrast, when non-Holiness people talk of "sanctification," they almost always mean it in the Old Testament sense. Every major doctrine is found, in some form, in both the Old and New Testaments. But when the Old Testament talks about sanctification, it often means "consecration" or "separation"—sometimes literally, sometimes figuratively. There is certainly an element of that in the New Testament definition, but it encompasses so much more. Actually, the word "sanctification" itself is found exclusively in the New Testament, whereas the verb "sanctify" is found in both. Here are some examples of how the Old Testament often uses the concept.

"Sanctify unto me all the firstborn, whatsoever openeth the womb among the children of Israel, both of man and of beast: it is mine" (Exodus 13:2).

"And thou shalt offer every day a bullock for a sin offering for atonement: and thou shalt cleanse the altar, when thou hast made an atonement for it, and thou shalt anoint it, to sanctify it" (Exodus 29:36).

"And when a man shall sanctify his house to be holy unto the LORD, then the priest shall estimate it, whether it be good or bad: as the priest shall estimate it, so shall it stand" (Lev. 27:14).

"Keep the sabbath day to sanctify it, as the LORD thy God hath commanded thee" (Deut. 5:12).

Notice that the Old Testament talks of beasts and inanimate objects being sanctified. But only people can be sanctified in the New Testament sense.

Far too many Christians think of sanctification only in the Old Testament sense. They say that every Christian is sanctified. In that limited sense, yes, they are correct. But if separation and/or dedication were ALL that sanctification entailed, then monks and nuns would be the holiest people on earth.

Indeed, the early Lutherans protested against people who thought exactly that. And in doing so, they used the type of language that Holiness people use—200 years before John Wesley. "Also condemned are those who teach that Christian perfection requires the forsaking of house and home, wife and child, and the renunciation of such [other] activities as are mentioned above" (Augsberg Confession of 1530, Article 16).

Here are several other words that have a bearing on this subject. All of these definitions come from Webster's 1828 Dictionary. Other than sanctification, which I have already defined, these will be the controlling definitions throughout this book, unless otherwise noted.

Blemish (noun): "Any mark of deformity; any scar or defect that diminishes beauty, or renders imperfect that which is well formed."

Blemished: "Injured or marred by any mark of deformity; tarnished; soiled."

Defile: "1. To make unclean; to render foul or dirty. 2. To make impure. 3. To soil or sully. 6. To taint, in a moral sense; to corrupt; to vitiate; to render impure with sin." (Vitiate: "To injure the substance or qualities of a thing.")

Defilement: "Foulness; dirtiness; uncleanness. 2. Corruption of morals, principles or character; impurity; pollution by sin."

Holy: "Properly, whole, entire or perfect, in a moral sense. Hence, pure in heart, temper or dispositions; free from sin and sinful affections... Man is more or less holy, as his heart is more or less sanctified, or purified from evil dispositions."

Perfect: "1. Finished; complete; consummate; not defective. 3. Complete in moral excellencies."

Perfectness: "2. The highest degree of goodness or holiness of which man is capable in this life."

Purification: "3. A cleansing from guilt or the pollution of sin; the extinction of sinful desires, appetites and inclinations."

Purify: "1. To make pure or clear; to free from extraneous admixture. 2. To free from pollution ceremonially; to remove whatever renders unclean and unfit for sacred services. 3. To free from guilt or the defilement of sin; as, to purify the heart."

Purity: "1. Freedom from foreign admixture or heterogeneous matter. 2. Cleanness; freedom from foulness or dirt. 3. Freedom from guilt or the defilement of sin; innocence; as purity of heart or life."

Righteous: "Just; accordant to the divine law. Applied to persons, it denotes one who is holy in heart, and observant of the divine commands in practice."

Sanctification: "1. The act of making holy. In an evangelical sense, the act of God's grace by which the affections of men are purifed or alienated from sin and the world, and exalted to a supreme love to God."

Sanctified: "Made holy; consecrated; set apart for sacred services. 2. Affectedly holy."

Sanctify: "(Low L. *sanctifico*; from *sanctus*, holy, and *facio*, to make.) 1. In a general sense, to cleanse, purify or make holy. 2. To separate, set apart or appoint to a holy, sacred or religous use. 5. To cleanse from corruption; to purify from sin; to make holy by detaching the affections from the world and its defilements, and exalting them to a supreme love to God."

Sin (noun): "The voluntary departure of a moral agent from a known rule of rectitude or duty, prescribed by God; any voluntary transgression of the divine law, or violation of a divine command; a wicked act; iniquity. Sin is either a positive act in which a known divine law is violated, or it is the voluntary neglect to obey a positive divine command, or a rule of duty clearly implied in such command. Sin comprehends not actions only, but neglect of known duty, all evil thoughts, purposes, words and desires, whatever is contrary to God's commands or law."

John Wesley is often thought of as the founder of the Holiness movement, and in a large sense, he was. He was probably the first to put the doctrine on a truly systematic basis. It is certainly fair to view him as the founder of the **organized** Holiness movement. As I said, some well-intentioned people have drawn the wrong conclusion from this, and believe that Holiness is a man-made doctrine.

In some respects, this is a reasonable conclusion. After all, one would think that if a doctrine could be found in the Bible, that it wouldn't take 1700 years before it was preached for the first time. However, what a lot of people do not realize is that Wesley was not actually the first to preach it. He did not invent the doctrine, but rather helped revive it after a very long period of dormancy and obscurity.

It is instructive to compare John Wesley with Martin Luther. Would we say that salvation by faith was a man-made doctrine, just because Luther rescued it from obscurity in relatively recent times? What Luther did for regeneration (the first work of grace), Wesley did for sanctification (the second work of grace).

"How shall they hear without a preacher?" (Romans 10:14c). God does sometimes deal with people directly—witness Sammy Morris. But that type or level of Divine intervention is really quite rare. It is much more common for God to work through preachers, which means that somebody has to be the first to preach any given doctrine— or, in this case, the first to rediscover and/or popularize it. If you have been taught all your life that a Christian has nothing better to look forward to in this life than a continual battle with his carnal nature, then it may be very difficult at first to understand this doctrine. But an honest, open study of the Bible will show, sooner or later, beyond the shadow of any doubt that entire sanctification is not a man-made doctrine.

I grew up in the Holiness movement. I have heard sermons on this doctrine all my life. And yet, once I began studying the subject, I was greatly astonished at the sheer number of Bible verses that support it, either directly or indirectly.

Mind you, I shouldn't have been surprised. After all, God is holy, and therefore His Word is permeated with the same. With the benefit of hindsight, it would be infinitely more surprising if the Bible *didn't* support the doctrine.

It took me about a month of study to assemble the bulk of the verses that I will quote. And even after that, as I read various books on the subject, I would come across an occasional verse here and there that I hadn't noticed before. Some authors on the subject quote or reference several verses. But to the best of my knowledge, nobody has pulled together such an extensive list before.

For reasons of space, it would be better to simply reference the verses, rather than actually quote them. But, as I studied this subject, I read some books that did just that, and it quickly became one of my pet peeves. It is incredibly inconvenient to have to keep flipping back and forth between the Bible and another book. I do reference a few passages, but the vast majority I actually quote.

But why did it take so long to establish an "official" doctrine of Holiness?

When I started this book, I thought (like most people) that John Wesley was the first person to, in essence, come up with this doctrine of Holiness. As I researched the issue, I discovered that this popular view is incorrect. The pieces were already there—both in Scripture, and in other, earlier writers. A great many of the early Church Fathers wrote about some aspect of Holiness doctrine, although often briefly, and not necessarily in theological terms. It is true that Wesley was probably the first person to fit all the pieces together into a coherent whole.

But why did it take so long to put all the pieces together? After all, the earlier writers, not to mention untold thousands of preachers, had access to the same Bible. I really don't know why it took so long. However, I believe that important clues can be found in the story of the doctrine of the Trinity.

I call it a story, because these things took time—much longer than most people today realize. The writings that we call the Canon did not magically spring forth fully formed—it took discussion by many people over several decades to figure out which books were Divinely inspired and which ones were not. In exactly the same way, the doctrines that we have today did not spring forth in a single body. The story of the doctrine of the Trinity provides some interesting similarities to the doctrine of Holiness.

There are many references to the Trinity throughout the Bible. Indeed, one could almost say that the doctrine was baked into the Hebrew portion of the Bible, due to the grammar that was used. But the first successors to the apostles didn't seem to think it necessary to assemble those references together into a coherent, concise package of doctrine. Perhaps as a result of this, there arose an impressive assortment of heresies, misunderstandings, miscommunications, and errors of judgment concerning the Trinity. There were a great many people who denied that Jesus had ever come in the flesh, but was some kind of spirit; some people claimed that the God of the Old Testament was different from the God of the New Testament; others claimed that Jesus was only partly Divine; still others claimed that He was all Divine and therefore not fully human; and so forth. And to add to the confusion, the Greek-speaking world had its own disagreement over which of two related words best described Jesus—but both of those translated into the same word in Latin. As a result, the Latin-speaking world looked on in some bemusement at an argument which they could not fully understand. Things came to a head with Arius, who maintained that Jesus was a created being who had certain Divine attributes, but was not actually Divine. The Council of Nicaea in 325 was the first attempt to hammer out acceptable doctrine on the matter, and that ended up being incomplete.

Even then, the battle was not yet won. There were several very influential people who championed false doctrine. Speaking of the situation several years after the Council of Nicaea, Jerome said something to the effect that "the whole world groaned to find itself Arian." Indeed, I rather suspect that only Divine intervention kept the orthodox doctrine of the Trinity from being at least temporarily lost. It wasn't until the Council of Constantinople in 381 – 350 years after Pentecost! – that the Church came up with a coherent, concise statement on the Trinity that could be considered "official" doctrine.

Furthermore, it was manifestly necessary that the most fundamental doctrines and key points, such as the Trinity, would need to be settled before moving on to things like Holiness doctrine; things that are still important, but not the most important.

Now, taking all that into account, and also considering that Christendom went into a centuries-long eclipse of Divine truth, I have gained a new perspective on the doctrine of Holiness. I am no longer surprised that it took until the days of the Wesley brothers to assemble all the various pieces of the doctrine into a coherent whole.

The discussion of this topic involves certain words that sometimes seem to mean something different to every person that uses them. "Sanctification" is such a word. There are four different schools of thought regarding it. One holds that sanctification is a gradual, life-long process. Another holds that we get everything at salvation, and therefore a brand-new Christian is as sanctified as he is ever going to be. The third—and the topic of this book—is that sanctification is an instantaneous work of grace, much like the work of salvation, but received at some point after salvation. The fourth holds that regardless of whatever may or may not happen here on earth, sanctification will not be complete until we reach Heaven.

The first conflates sanctification with growing in grace. The second conflates sanctification with justification. And the fourth conflates sanctification with glorification.

The associated topics also cause confusion and controversy. One of the biggest ones is the idea of perfection, which is a result of receiving the second work. But not just any perfection. You see, there are at least five different types of perfection: Divine perfection, angelic perfection, heavenly perfection, human perfection, and Christian perfection. The vast amount of confusion on the subject stems largely from the fact that when discussing it, many people utterly fail to specify which type of perfection they are talking about. Proponents of this doctrine claim Christian perfection (also called sinless perfection)—we do not lay claim to any other type. This distinction is vitally important, and I will discuss it in more detail later on.

On the other hand, many people claim that perfection of any sort is absolutely impossible here on earth. They believe that the taint of sin over the physical creation precludes the possibility of perfection; that we won't be perfect in any way until we get to Heaven. Some of the people who oppose the idea of perfection—but only some—do so because they believe in good faith that the Bible does not support it. There are several Bible verses that talk about perfection, but our opponents have their own way of explaining those verses. Others oppose the idea simply because it takes away a favorite excuse for sinning. Those who oppose it in good faith, regardless of the reason, tend to view John Wesley as a good man, a well-intentioned man, and one who did a great deal of good for God's cause, but terribly mistaken in certain of his ideas.

18 wish we didn't think of other Christians as opponents, even if they disagree doctrinally

This is one point where history is very instructive. As it turns out—and I was very surprised by this myself—the idea of perfection is a constant theme all throughout Church history. I have already given one example from the Lutherans. This is not to say that every theologian or commentator talks about it, but it is far more common than most people today suppose. Various writers seem to have different ideas as to what it means: many of them, unfortunately, do not specifically define it; but a truly astonishing number of writers talk about it in one way or another.

It is true, in terms of formal doctrine, that we have a very long blank space, from the closing of the Canon up until the early Quakers. (Surprise, surprise! You thought I was going to say John Wesley, didn't you? But the Quakers were the ones who started the process of establishing formal doctrine on this point.) However, scattered throughout this time, there are several writers who give us hints of Holiness doctrine. There is an impressive number of writers well before Wesley's time who wrote about some aspect of Holiness theology—perfection, renouncing self, purity of heart, and so forth. Their work is all the more impressive, because many of them were severely hampered by Catholic dogma. Yet somehow they managed to grasp a portion of what would become known as Holiness theology. Some of the early Church Fathers wrote as if they were well acquainted with the doctrine. However, much of their time and energy was spent in combating the various heresies that were already springing up. Furthermore, many of the earliest writings have been lost. In some cases, we have only a reference or two to show that certain writings ever existed at all. Later on, as Divine truth in general suffered an eclipse, the writers get fewer. The later writers in this period certainly did not have any formal point of doctrine relating to Holiness; nevertheless, their writings show that they had, at the very least, an inkling of the doctrine of heart-holiness. The theme of perfection makes an occasional appearance throughout that period.

As I did research, I grew to really love and appreciate the early writers. The Church has done itself a great disservice by largely ignoring their works.

I was surprised at how closely they mirror Holiness teaching on several points: Christian perfection; the extreme importance of a holy, pure life; general standards of dress; and various others. Holiness preachers and teachers down through the years have been echoing (often unknowingly) the early writers. Here is a specific example: Holiness people have generally been pacifists and conscientious objectors. We believe that the military is no place for a Christian. Now here's a quote from one of the early writers.

"It is altogether contrary to the rules of the Church to return to military service in the world after doing penance, as the Apostle says, 'No soldier in God's service entangles himself in the affairs of the world.' Hence he is not free from the snares of the devil who wishes to entangle himself in the military service of the world."

19

This is a letter from Pope Leo the Great to a bishop named Rusticus. This letter was written around AD 450-455. It is an excellent example of how the general teaching of the Holiness movement is much older than the "official" movement itself.

Generally speaking, people who believe in a second work of grace belong to what is called the Holiness movement. This is not a denomination; it includes several denominations, and it cuts across denominational lines. The book *Scriptural Sanctification*, by John Brooks, includes an Introduction by John Tigert, who quotes the Jan. 1899 *London Quarterly Review*:

"And the doctrine of Christian perfection which Wesley calmly maintained in the face of almost universal contempt and derision has been welcomed in these latter days by devout souls in all communions. At any ordinary holiness convention the Episcopalian, the Presbyterian, the Baptist, the Congregationalist, and the Methodist will be found together witnessing to the reality and blessedness of the doctrine of perfect purity and perfect love. These representatives of the several Churches may differ in their definitions of entire sanctification, but the differences are merely verbal; substantially they unanimously witness to the great doctrine for which Wesley contended, viz., that the infinite grace of the sovereign Spirit can renew and perfect the soul here and now. No distinctive doctrine of primitive Methodism puts modern Methodism at a disadvantage. The truths that were once special to her are ceasing to be special, not because she discovers that those truths were partial or misconceived, but because they are becoming the recognized doctrines of the universal Protestant Church."

This is not to say that all of those denominations ever officially embraced the doctrine of Holiness, or the concept of a second work of grace. In some cases, individuals were able to rise up above what they had been taught, and they embraced entire sanctification in defiance of their denomination's official position. Historically, the doctrine is identified primarily with the Methodist Church and its off-shoots, and also with various groups that describe themselves as "Wesleyan." However, this also is a source of confusion for some people. Just like a person can call himself a Christian without actually being one, so too can groups or denominations call themselves "Holiness" without actually being that. The Methodist Church still pays a certain amount of lip-service to the ideas of John Wesley, but has long ago abandoned them in practice. Thus, it is no longer part of the Holiness movement. (Not only that, but the Methodist Church as an organization has been spiritually dead for several decades.) Both the theology and the practical, everyday application of that theology are necessary for a group to be a Holiness group. Certain groups that use "Wesleyan" in their name or description also claim to be Holiness, and used to be Holiness, but are no longer such.

There are also certain groups that occupy somewhat of a middle ground, or a gray area. These still retain the main theology of Holiness teaching, but they have lost some of the ancillary points, and are therefore more liberal in their outlook. I grew up in the conservative, old-fashioned wing of the Holiness movement, and this book is from that perspective.

What is meant by practical, everyday application of theology? There are two things that distinguish Holiness groups from non-Holiness groups. One is the actual theology; the insistence that a second work of grace exists, and various related ideas that grow out of that. The other distinguishing mark is outward. There is a saying that I have heard all my life; I tried to find an actual historical source for this, but so far have not been able to. I have heard it said that the early Methodists could be spotted as far away as the eye could see, because they dressed so differently from the world. (However, I did find a similar statement in Peter Cartwright's *Autobiography*.) We believe in a clear, sharp line of separation from the world. We believe that a Christian should dress and act in a way that shows very clearly and distinctly that he is a Christian, rather than a worldling. We are in the world, but not part of the world. Non-Holiness Christians sometimes talk about such things, but for some reason they generally don't seem to grasp what the concept actually means, at least not altogether. Holiness people almost always dress in a much plainer, more modest manner than other Christians, although there are a handful of other very conservative groups that come quite close to Holiness standards of dress and conduct, including some Pentecostals.

This is another area where the study of Church history turns out to be illuminating. Some of the Church Fathers wrote about such things, and almost invariably those writers laid down certain ideas and principles that are almost exactly (sometimes virtually word for word) what Holiness people teach on the subjects of dress, behavior, and general separation from the world. If a person repeated in his own words to non-Holiness Christians certain things that the early writers said about these subjects, I daresay that such a person would likely be considered a fanatic and a nutcase.

The second work of grace is not a magical thing. There is a process that is necessary to receive it. The details vary from person to person, but it always includes in some form the concept of dying to the world, dying to self, etc. This concept is an integral part of Holiness doctrine. This is another thing that distinguishes Holiness people from non-Holiness. In my experience, it is fairly rare for non-Holiness people to talk about this; and when they do, it is usually in the context of a daily battle that **has** to be fought daily, because it never stays won. Now certainly, we have to fight the good fight daily, but at the same time, there are certain things that we can settle so deeply, so thoroughly, that we never have to go over the same ground again.

Dying out to everything of the world and the flesh makes something else much easier: living without sin. We believe that it is possible to live without sinning. Non-Holiness people, almost unanimously, do not believe this. They often accuse us of redefining "sin" into "mistakes." They say that this redefining is the only way that we can claim to live without sin.

On the other hand, I have noticed that such people often redefine "mistakes" into "sin." This is perhaps the predominant reason for the belief that a sinless life is impossible.

All these things will be dealt with in more detail throughout the book.

I occasionally say things in this book that some people likely will take offense at. It is emphatically NOT my intention to offend anybody. Many times, especially when we grow up with a belief (of any sort), we do not stop and really think about it; it's just simply "always been there" for us, and it's part of our mental/theological/philosophical "wallpaper," so to speak. Whenever I say something potentially offensive, my goal is to shock people into stopping and actually THINKING about a particular thing and its ramifications.

The very first priority that we should have is to make sure that we are in fact saved. The second priority (which is, or at least should be, a natural consequence of the first) is to lead a truly HOLY life—separated from sin, from the world, and from the Devil, and separated unto God.

Having said that, I believe that the third priority should be to understand theology, at least to some extent. Knowing at least a little bit about theology can be very helpful a great deal of the time, and can guard against certain errors.

The purpose of this book is to delve deeply into both history and theology, and to show that the doctrine of entire sanctification has a firm footing on both fronts. I deal with the history first; human experiences, and human writings, are certainly very suggestive, and in many cases can corroborate Scripture; but a doctrine cannot be built on such things alone. Therefore, since the history is the weakest part of the support for this doctrine, we will go through that first, and leave the best for last.

I am very much aware that this book will not convince everybody. I hope that such people will at least give me a fair hearing, and soberly consider what I have to say, instead of simply and reflexively dismissing it. All theological schools of thought have people who have let their zeal run away with their brotherly love. If Satan cannot get a Christian to give up his faith, he will often attack the person's usefulness by trying to push him into the ditch of one extreme or another, and turn him into a crank who leaves no room for "agreeing to disagree." There is a saying that has been attributed to several people; I believe it was first said by Rupertus Meldenius (1582-1651), a Lutheran theologian and educator: "In Essentials Unity, In Non-Essentials Liberty, In All Things Charity."

However, there is much in this book that I believe everybody can appreciate.

"Let the word of Christ dwell in you richly in all wisdom" (Col. 3:16a).

History

Chapter 2

The Apostolic Age: AD 30/33-95

As a preface to the history section, I would like to lay out the way that I have arranged things for the purpose of this book. I have divided Church history into five segments. The years that I chose for the dividing points are somewhat arbitrary, but they do take into account events that I felt marked, or at least symbolized, turning points of one sort or another.

The Apostolic Age: AD 30/33-95

This is the period when the apostles were alive. We do not know for sure what year the Crucifixion, Resurrection, and Day of Pentecost took place. Some people claim to know, but I very seriously doubt whether any of those claims take into account ALL the available evidence. I also somewhat doubt whether it is possible to know the exact year. However, it is very likely indeed that it was either 30 or 33.

The Early Church: 95-400

We do not know when John died, but it was almost certainly within a few years of 95. He may have written Revelation in 95; the earliest non-Canonical writing that we know of was also written about this time. The two things together mark a good spot to consider the Apostolic Age closed, and the next age begun.

The Darkness Descends: 400-1500

The institution of the Papacy more or less got going right around 400. Very few or perhaps none of the "Popes" before this date could be considered Popes in anything remotely resembling the modern sense. For this reason, along with some others, this date is approximately when Christendom really began sliding into the spiritual Dark Ages.

The Darkness Lifts: 1500-1725

Martin Luther posted his Theses in 1517. But Reformation thinking was afoot in a few quarters before that date.

Full Flower of Light: 1725-Modern Times

Now we come to the time of John Wesley and his associates. Now at last we see a full, coherent body of doctrine regarding entire sanctification.

I decided to start our walk through history in a rather unusual fashion. We will start with the writings of the apostles; writings that became part of the Canon. However, we will not at this point delve into the actual scriptures behind Holiness doctrine. That will come later, in the theology section. Opponents of this doctrine rely heavily on certain Bible passages that they believe refute the doctrine. However, the passages they cite are contradicted (so to speak) by other passages. Therefore, any honest person—regardless of which side of the fence he is on in this debate—must figure out a way to reconcile the differences.

I decided to start the history section in this fashion in order to show that the apostolic Church spoke with one voice on the important matters of doctrine. This will lay the foundation for later reconciling the opposing passages. And, after all, the apostles are part of Church history.

1. Love fulfills the law.

Paul...

"Owe no man any thing, but to love one another: for he that loveth another hath fulfilled the law. For this, Thou shalt not commit adultery, Thou shalt not kill, Thou shalt not steal, Thou shalt not bear false witness, Thou shalt not covet; and if there be any other commandment, it is briefly comprehended in this saying, namely, Thou shalt love thy neighbour as thyself. Love worketh no ill to his neighbour: therefore love is the fulfilling of the law" (Romans 13:8-10).

"For all the law is fulfilled in one word, even in this; Thou shalt love thy neighbour as thyself" (Gal. 5:14).

... and James.

"If ye fulfil the royal law according to the scripture, Thou shalt love thy neighbour as thyself, ye do well" (James 2:8).

2. God's longsuffering.

Paul...

"And thinkest thou this, O man, that judgest them which do such things, and doest the same, that thou shalt escape the judgment of God? Or despisest thou the riches of his goodness and forbearance and longsuffering; not knowing that the goodness of God leadeth thee to repentance?" (Romans 2:3, 4).

... and Peter.

"The Lord is not slack concerning his promise, as some men count slackness; but is longsuffering to us-ward, not willing that any should perish, but that all should come to repentance. And account that the longsuffering of our Lord is salvation; even as our beloved brother Paul also according to the wisdom given unto him hath written unto you" (II Peter 3:9, 15).

3. Divinity of Jesus.

Peter...

"The God of Abraham, and of Isaac, and of Jacob, the God of our fathers, hath glorified his Son Jesus; whom ye delivered up, and denied him in the presence of Pilate, when he was determined to let him go" (Acts 3:13).

"For we have not followed cunningly devised fables, when we made known unto you the power and coming of our Lord Jesus Christ, but were eyewitnesses of his majesty. For he received from God the Father honour and glory, when there came such a voice to him from the excellent glory, This is my beloved Son, in whom I am well pleased" (II Peter 1:16, 17).

... and Paul...

"But when the fulness of the time was come, God sent forth his Son, made of a woman, made under the law, to redeem them that were under the law, that we might receive the adoption of sons" (Gal. 4:4, 5).

... and John.

"That which we have seen and heard declare we unto you, that ye also may have fellowship with us: and truly our fellowship is with the Father, and with his Son Jesus Christ" (I John 1:3).

"Who is a liar but he that denieth that Jesus is the Christ? He is antichrist, that denieth the Father and the Son" (I John 2:22).

4. Jesus fulfilled prophecy.

Peter...

"But those things, which God before had shewed by the mouth of all his prophets, that Christ should suffer, he hath so fulfilled" (Acts 3:18).

... and Philip.

"And Philip ran thither to him, and heard him read the prophet Esaias, and said, Understandest thou what thou readest? And he said, How can I, except some man should guide me? And he desired Philip that he would come up and sit with him. The place of the scripture which he read was this, He was led as a sheep to the slaughter; and like a lamb dumb before his shearer, so opened he not his mouth: in his humiliation his judgment was taken away: and who shall declare his generation? for his life is taken from the earth. And the eunuch answered Philip, and said, I pray thee, of whom speaketh the prophet this? of himself, or of some other man? Then Philip opened his mouth, and began at the same scripture, and preached unto him Jesus" (Acts 8:30-35).

5. The Crucifixion and Resurrection.

Peter...

"The God of our fathers raised up Jesus, whom ye slew and hanged on a tree" (Acts 5:30).

"And we are witnesses of all things which he did both in the land of the Jews, and in Jerusalem; whom they slew and hanged on a tree: him God raised up the third day, and shewed him openly" (Acts 10:39, 40).

... and Paul.

"Christ hath redeemed us from the curse of the law, being made a curse for us: for it is written, Cursed is every one that hangeth on a tree" (Gal. 3:13).

"And though they found no cause of death in him, yet desired they Pilate that he should be slain. And when they had fulfilled all that was written of him, they took him down from the tree, and laid him in a sepulchre. But God raised him from the dead: and he was seen many days of them which came up with him from Galilee to Jerusalem, who are his witnesses unto the people" (Acts 13:28-31).

6. The resurrection of the saints.

Paul...

"Behold, I shew you a mystery; We shall not all sleep, but we shall all be changed, in a moment, in the twinkling of an eye, at the last trump: for the trumpet shall sound, and the dead shall be raised incorruptible, and we shall be changed" (I Cor. 15:51, 52).

... and John.

"And I saw thrones, and they sat upon them, and judgment was given unto them: and I saw the souls of them that were beheaded for the witness of Jesus, and for the word of God, and which had not worshipped the beast, neither his image, neither had received his mark upon their foreheads, or in their hands; and they lived and reigned with Christ a thousand years. But the rest of the dead lived not again until the thousand years were finished. This is the first resurrection. Blessed and holy is he that hath part in the first resurrection: on such the second death hath no power, but they shall be priests of God and of Christ, and shall reign with him a thousand years" (Rev. 20:4-6).

7. Separation from the world.

James...

"Ye adulterers and adulteresses, know ye not that the friendship of the world is enmity with God? whosoever therefore will be a friend of the world is the enemy of God" (James 4:4).

... and John...

"Love not the world, neither the things that are in the world. If any man love the world, the love of the Father is not in him. For all that is in the world, the lust of the flesh, and the lust of the eyes, and the pride of life, is not of the Father, but is of the world" (I John 2:15, 16).

... and Peter.

"Dearly beloved, I beseech you as strangers and pilgrims, abstain from fleshly lusts, which war against the soul; having your conversation honest among the Gentiles: that, whereas they speak against you as evildoers, they may by your good works, which they shall behold, glorify God in the day of visitation" (I Peter 2:11, 12).

As you can see, the apostles and other preachers of the Church agreed with each other. Paul was at a disadvantage, compared to the others, in the sense that he had never actually talked with Jesus during those years of training and teaching. However, Paul declares in various places that he got his theology directly from God. Moreover, he was in communication with various of the other apostles at multiple points during his ministry (one example is Gal. 1:18). And later on, as mentioned in II Peter 3:15 under point 2, Peter knew very well what Paul had written to the various churches.

And Paul declares at various points that he was preaching exactly the same Gospel as the other apostles.

"Therefore whether it were I or they, so we preach, and so ye believed" (I Cor. 15:11).

"Then fourteen years after I went up again to Jerusalem with Barnabas, and took Titus with me also. And I went up by revelation, and communicated unto them that gospel which I preach among the Gentiles, but privately to them which were of reputation, lest by any means I should run, or had run, in vain. But of these who seemed to be somewhat, (whatsoever they were, it maketh no matter to me: God accepteth no man's person:) for they who seemed to be somewhat in conference added nothing to me: but contrariwise, when they saw that the gospel of the uncircumcision was committed unto me, as the gospel of the circumcision was unto Peter; (for he that wrought effectually in Peter to the apostleship of the circumcision, the same was mighty in me toward the Gentiles:) and when James, Cephas, and John, who seemed to be pillars, perceived the grace that was given unto me, they gave to me and Barnabas the right hands of fellowship; that we should go unto the heathen, and they unto the circumcision" (Gal. 2:1, 2, 6-9).

It is very difficult to say for sure, but this is likely Paul's account, from his viewpoint, of the great council in Jerusalem in c. AD 50. More details of this council and the story behind it can be found in Acts 15. At any rate, we know from multiple writers—Luke, Peter, and Paul himself—that the apostles met with each other at various times and places, and were well aware of what the others were doing.

As we will see in the theology section, they also agreed with each other regarding the issue of living a truly *holy* life. But before we get to that section, we will see what their successors taught. The apostles are the foundation of the Church (Rev. 21:14); and later writers built on what the apostles wrote.

Chapter 3

The Early Church: 95-400 (Part 1)

As I studied the historical writings of the Church, especially the earliest ones, I came to love and appreciate the early Church Fathers more and more. I had been familiar with some of their names before this, but I didn't know much at all about most of them. They fought mightily to uphold the truth. They explained and defended the new religion to pagans; hurled rhetorical thunderbolts against heretics; and told us which of the many books that were floating around should be considered the inspired Word of God. Every Christian since then owes those men an enormous debt of gratitude.

The idea of Christian perfection is in many respects the central theme of Holiness doctrine. But there are several other aspects to the doctrine. People who reject the idea of a second work of grace don't necessarily reject all the other aspects, but these others are very often ignored, or at best very ill-defined. I have chosen quotes that illustrate various aspects of the doctrine. This is not intended to be a comprehensive list: for reasons of space, I left out several quotes that I would have preferred to include, and I shortened others. Also, there were a few of the early writers that for reasons of time I never got around to looking at.

The reader should be advised that most of the dates in this chapter (and many in the following chapters) are approximate. There is a fair bit of uncertainty regarding the timing of many events of the period. For some people who lived so long ago, you can check three different sources and find three different birth/death dates.

Like the Bible, there are several translations of many of the ancient writings, some using traditional language, and some using modern language. Some of the writings are also known by more than one name. However, I have provided fairly specific citations, so that anybody who wants to can look up the passage for themselves without too much trouble.

Clement of Rome (AD 30-100)

Clement was either the second or third Bishop of Rome. Several people have speculated that he was the Clement mentioned in Phil. 4:3. There is no hard evidence of that, but it is certainly a possibility. Several of the other ancient writers held that opinion.

He wrote one letter that survives, traditionally called *I Clement* to distinguish it from other writings that used to be attributed to him. The church at Corinth had once again fallen into schism. There was nobody at Corinth who seemed capable of healing the breach. So the Corinthians turned to Clement, who, whether or not he is mentioned in the Bible, was almost certainly well acquainted with both Paul and Peter. Other early writers tell us that he was ordained by Peter, and he presumably would have met Paul during that period as well. It is clear that the Corinthian church had learned from Paul the benefit of having an outside authority to turn to in cases such as this, to impose order on an unruly congregation. And since Paul was now dead, Clement was the next best thing. His letter, in response to their plea, was probably written in AD 95 or 96; very close to the same time, possibly even the same year, that John was writing Revelation. This is how early our Church history outside of the Bible starts.

I Clement

"Let your children be partakers of true Christian training; let them learn of how great avail humility is with God—how much the spirit of pure affection can prevail with Him— how excellent and great His fear is, and how it saves all those who walk in it with a pure mind" (chapter 21).

He talks about two different aspects of our inward life—the affections, and the mind—and how they should both be pure. This leaves no room for anger, envy, etc.

"Let us then draw near to Him with holiness of spirit, lifting up pure and undefiled hands unto Him, loving our gracious and merciful Father, who has made us partakers in the blessings of His elect" (ch. 29).

Now he switches to the outward aspect, and talks about how our hands, or works, should be pure. There is a remarkable parallel here between Clement and a development many centuries later. There is a concept in English common law called the "clean hands" doctrine. It means that a person is innocent of wrong-doing. If somebody has done something unfair or illegal, for example in regard to a contract, he is said to have unclean hands. If he then sues the other party involved, the person who is sued can use this doctrine as a defense. Clement uses the same symbolism.

"Seeing, therefore, that we are the portion of the Holy One, let us do all those things which pertain to holiness, avoiding all evil-speaking, all abominable and impure embraces, together with all drunkenness, seeking after change, all abominable lusts, detestable adultery, and execrable pride. 'For God,' saith [the Scripture], 'resisteth the proud, but giveth grace to the humble.' Let us cleave, then, to those to whom grace has been given by God. Let us clothe ourselves with concord and humility, ever exercising self-control, standing far off from all whispering and evil-speaking, being justified by our works, and not our words" (ch. 30).

When I read Clement's epistle in its entirety, one of the things I noticed was how often he sounds very similar to the Bible. Given his history, this should not be a surprise. Just as the apostles entreated their readers to embrace good, and flee from evil, Clement does the same thing. One thing that is a little different, however, is his specific mention of general self-control. Many outward sins would be avoided if people heeded that advice.

My grandma told me how she had temper tantrums as a child. Her mother held her head underneath the water pump. She told my grandma, "You might get angry, but you don't have to show it."

"Let us therefore earnestly strive to be found in the number of those that wait for Him, in order that we may share in His promised gifts. But how, beloved, shall this be done? If our understanding be fixed by faith towards God; if we earnestly seek the things which are pleasing and acceptable to Him; if we do the things which are in harmony with His blameless will; and if we follow the way of truth, casting away from us all unrighteousness and iniquity, along with all covetousness, strife, evil practices, deceit, whispering, and evil-speaking, all hatred of God, pride and haughtiness, vainglory and ambition" (ch. 35).

He lays out a standard of conduct, both inward and outward, that leaves no room whatsoever for sin. He exhorts his readers to cast away ALL unrighteousness from their lives. He presents a stunning contrast to all the people today who claim that they can't get rid of sin in their lives, no matter what they do.

"Let a man be faithful: let him be powerful in the utterance of knowledge; let him be wise in judging of words; let him be pure in all his deeds; yet the more he seems to be superior to others [in these respects], the more humble-minded ought he to be, and to seek the common good of all, and not merely his own advantage" (ch. 48).

Here he does the same thing, but on the positive side. If a person is "pure in all his deeds" it logically follows that there is no room for evil deeds.

"Ye see, beloved, how great and wonderful a thing is love, and that there is no declaring its perfection. Who is fit to be found in it, except such as God has vouchsafed to render so? Let us pray, therefore, and implore of His mercy, that we may live blameless in love, free from all human partialities for one above another. All the generations from Adam even unto this day have passed away; but those who, through the grace of God, have been made perfect in love, now possess a place among the godly, and shall be made manifest at the revelation of the kingdom of Christ" (ch. 50).

Remember in the first chapter that I talked about the concept of perfection running through Church history? And here, in the very first non-Biblical writing of the Church, written perhaps the same year as John wrote Revelation, the idea of perfection makes its first appearance outside the Bible. Wow! That was quick!

Notice, as well, the <u>manner</u> in which Clement talks about it. He talks as if he is <u>personally acquainted</u> with people who are perfect and blameless in love. He clearly regards some form of perfection as <u>eminently</u> <u>achievable in this life.</u>

"Joy and gladness will ye afford us, if ye become obedient to the words written by us and through the Holy Spirit root out the lawless wrath of your jealousy according to the intercession which we have made for peace and unity in this letter. We have sent men faithful and discreet, whose conversation from youth to old age has been blameless amongst us,—the same shall be witnesses between you and us" (ch. 63).

Here we see that the very early Church put theory into practice. Clement declares that <u>he knew people</u> who had lived <u>blameless lives since youth.</u> This is a far cry from the sort of thing that one often hears in modern churches, when people report that they got angry, or broke the law, or cheated somebody, and thereby seriously impaired their Christian testimony. I have heard several people (almost exclusively in non-Holiness churches) report that they did these things. They admit that they knew better, but somehow that just didn't seem to matter in the heat of the moment.

* * * * *

Ignatius (35-107)

Ignatius was the second or possibly the third Bishop of Antioch. He was a disciple of the Apostle John. Thus, like Clement, his writings are tremendously important, as a direct link between the Bible and the succeeding generations of Church leaders. Ignatius is the first person, outside of the Bible, who we know for sure was martyred for his faith. Like Paul, he was arrested, and sent to Rome by ship. The following letters are among the ones that he wrote to various churches during the voyage.

"Let not then any one deceive you, as indeed ye are not deceived; for ye are wholly devoted to God. For when there is no evil desire within you, which might defile and torment you, then do ye live in accordance with the will of God, and are [the servants] of Christ... But ye, being full of the Holy Spirit, do nothing according to the flesh, but all things according to the Spirit" (*Epistle to the Ephesians*, ch. 8).

Notice how he defines living in accordance with God's will—no evil desires within a person; i.e., no carnality remaining in the heart. Not only must we avoid evil actions, but evil desires as well. He is not talking about temptations here. Temptations are inevitable. A person who learned his theology from the apostles would not make such a

33

mistake as to think that we can avoid temptation. Notice as well how he links "being full of the Holy Spirit" to a very definite statement about doing **nothing** "according to the flesh." This is a theology that leaves no room for sin in a believer's life.

"And pray ye without ceasing in behalf of other men. For there is in them hope of repentance that they may attain to God. See, then, that they be instructed by your works, if in no other way. Be ye meek in response to their wrath, humble in opposition to their boasting: to their blasphemies return your prayers; in contrast to their error, be ye stedfast in the faith; and for their cruelty, manifest your gentleness. While we take care not to imitate their conduct, let us be found their brethren in all true kindness; and let us seek to be followers of the Lord (who ever more unjustly treated, more destitute, more condemned?), that so no plant of the devil may be found in you, but ye may remain in all holiness and sobriety in Jesus Christ, both with respect to the flesh and spirit" (*Epistle to the Ephesians*, ch. 10).

He continues laying down a very high, strict standard for how Christians should behave. Our behavior is a powerful testimony. It is very unlikely that somebody who is still a carnal Christian could meet all these requirements; probably only somebody who is perfect in love can meet these. Inward purity will manifest itself in good works.

"None of these things is hid from you, if ye perfectly possess that faith and love towards Christ Jesus which are the beginning and the end of life. For the beginning is faith, and the end is love. Now these two, being inseparably connected together, are of God, while all other things which are requisite for a holy life follow after them. No man [truly] making a profession of faith sinneth; nor does he that possesses love hate any one. The tree is made manifest by its fruit; so those that profess themselves to be Christians shall be recognised by their conduct. For there is not now a demand for mere profession, but that a man be found continuing in the power of faith to the end" (*Epistle to the Ephesians*, ch. 14).

Many people, especially those who oppose the doctrine of a second work of grace, will undoubtedly find this quote very surprising, even shocking. We have here a statement of what we today often call "sinless perfection."

Many people who believe that sinless perfection is impossible in this life often point to the Greek tense in this passage and in I John 3:6, which is essentially a parallel passage to this quote. (More on this verse later.) They say that a more accurate translation would be something like, "No man making a profession of faith keeps on sinning." They don't seem to understand that translating it in that fashion really doesn't change anything. Obviously, a person is going to "keep on sinning" BEFORE he gets saved; this quote, and I John 3:6, are both talking about what happens AFTER a person gets saved. No matter how you translate it, Ignatius is saying here that sinning is supposed to stop once a person gets saved, never to be resumed!

"Do not speak of Jesus Christ, and yet set your desires on the world... For though I am alive while I write to you, yet I am eager to die. My love has been crucified, and there is no fire in me desiring to be fed; but there is within me a water that liveth and speaketh, saying to me inwardly, Come to the Father. I have no delight in corruptible food, nor in the pleasures of this life. I desire the bread of God, the heavenly bread, the bread of life, which is the flesh of Jesus Christ, the Son of God, who became afterwards of the seed of David and Abraham; and I desire the drink of God, namely His blood, which is incorruptible love and eternal life" (*Epistle to the Romans*, ch. 7).

One of the reasons he wrote to the Roman church was because he was afraid that they would try to somehow stop his martyrdom. But he also included some hefty exhortation as well. He tells them that it's pointless to speak of belonging to Christ if you still have your thoughts and desires on earthly things. This sentiment of a sharp, "either/or" division in a person's affections is not exclusive to the Holiness movement, but it's one of the things that we teach. It's also something that a great many non-Holiness churches don't seem to talk about much, if at all.

"Keep yourselves from those evil plants which Jesus Christ does not tend, because they are not the planting of the Father. Not that I have found any division among you, but exceeding purity. For as many as are of God and of Jesus Christ are also with the bishop. And as many as shall, in the exercise of repentance, return into the unity of the Church, these, too, shall belong to God, that they may live according to Jesus Christ. Do not err, my brethren. If any man follows him that makes a schism in the Church, he shall not inherit the kingdom of God. If any one walks according to a strange [heretical] opinion, he agrees not with the passion [of Christ]" (*Epistle to the Philadelphians*, ch. 3).

Here he gives an exhortation to unity, as well as a solemn warning against turning from the things of God.

"I glorify God, even Jesus Christ, who has given you such wisdom. For I have observed that ye are perfected in an immoveable faith, as if ye were nailed to the cross of our Lord Jesus Christ, both in the flesh and in the spirit, and are established in love through the blood of Christ" (*Epistle to the Smyrnaeans*, ch. 1).

In this quote, and in the following one, he returns to the subject of Christian perfection. He speaks of their "immoveable faith"; a tremendous example for us to follow.

"As persons who are perfect, ye should also aim at those things which are perfect. For when ye are desirous to do well, God is also ready to assist you" (*Epistle to the Smyrnaeans*, ch. 11).

Again, many people are likely going to be surprised or shocked by this quote. Ignatius speaks confidently of their perfection as an accomplished state.

* * * * *

Didache (roughly 120)

The *Didache*, sometimes known as the *Teaching of the Twelve Apostles*, is an early, rather simplistic collection of Christian instruction. It is a composite document, apparently a group effort of some kind. Efforts to date its composition have been rather unfruitful. It was most likely written somewhere around 120, give or take a few decades. It employs, as a literary device, the conceit that it is a collection of writings by all twelve apostles.

"See that no one cause thee to err from this way of the Teaching, since apart from God it teacheth thee. For if thou art able to bear all the yoke of the Lord, thou wilt be perfect; but if thou art not able, what thou art able that do" (ch. 6).

Here is yet another reference to Christian perfection. It also implies that there are different types of Christians; some are perfect, and some are not.

* * * * *

Aristides of Athens (dates unknown, but possibly died 133/134)

In the popular conception of Church history, it is thought that Justin Martyr was the first Christian apologist. However, this is not quite true. But for the most part, only a few scholars have ever heard of Aristides. For a long time, his writing was thought lost forever, but it was rediscovered in 1889. Aristides is still so obscure that many lists of the early Fathers do not include him. His *Apology* was written by 125, because that is when he presented it to Hadrian, when the emperor visited Athens.

"And these [Christians] are they who more than all the nations on the earth have found the truth. For they know God, the Creator and Fashioner of all things through the only-begotten Son and the Holy Spirit; and beside Him they worship no other God. They have the commands of the Lord Jesus Christ Himself graven upon their hearts; and they observe them, looking forward to the resurrection of the dead and life in the world to come. They do not commit adultery nor fornication, nor bear false witness, nor covet the things of others; they honour father and mother, and love their neighbours; they judge justly, and they never do to others what they would not wish to happen to themselves; they appeal to those who injure them, and try to win them as friends; they are eager to do good to their enemies; they are gentle and easy to be entreated; they abstain from all unlawful conversation and from all impurity; they despise not the widow, nor oppress the orphan; and he that has, gives ungrudgingly for the maintenance of him who has not" (*Apology*, sec. 15).

Aristides does not talk about theology here, or of what Christians ought to do; he reports what Christians of his day <u>actually do</u>. His description is notable for the list of good deeds, and the reported absence of bad deeds.

36

I've heard Christians in non-Holiness circles talk as if it's terrifically hard work to live as they ought; but we have a first-hand witness in Aristides that it can be done, and was done. It isn't nearly as hard as some people make it out to be—**as long as** a person lives sufficiently close to God. This is one of the big benefits of the second work of grace.

* * * * *

Polycarp (69-155)

He was Bishop of Smyrna. Like Ignatius, he was also a disciple of John, and was ordained by John. He was also martyred. Polycarp was an old man when he was arrested—at least eighty-six, and possibly older. His letter to the Philippians is the only one of his writings that survives.

"May the God and Father of our Lord Jesus Christ, and Jesus Christ Himself, who is the Son of God, and our everlasting High Priest, build you up in faith and truth, and in all meekness, gentleness, patience, longsuffering, forbearance, and purity; and may He bestow on you a lot and portion among His saints, and on us with you, and on all that are under heaven, who shall believe in our Lord Jesus Christ, and in His Father, who 'raised Him from the dead.' Pray for all the saints. Pray also for kings, and potentates, and princes, and for those that persecute and hate you, and for the enemies of the cross, that your fruit may be manifest to all, and that ye may be perfect in Him" (ch. 12).

Here we find the idea of Christian perfection linked to showing all the fruits of the Spirit. A Christian who is jerked around by the tuggings of the carnal nature is not going to match this description very well.

* * * * *

Shepherd of Hermas (140-155)

Here we find the first piece of Christian fiction. It is essentially an instruction and ethics manual in allegorical form. It is sometimes called the *Pastor of Hermas*, especially in older sources. We do not know for sure who wrote it, or when. However, it was probably written by a man named Hermas, who was the brother of Pius, ninth Bishop of Rome. Pius was in office during the period 140-155, and it is likely that the book was written during that period. Even though it is fiction, it is a window into Christian thoughts and viewpoints of the time.

From the Translator's Note: "The Pastor of Hermas was one of the most popular books, if not the most popular book, in the Christian Church during the second, third, and fourth centuries. It occupied a position analogous in some respects to that of Bunyan's *Pilgrim's Progress* in modern times; and critics have frequently compared the two works."

" 'Is it not your opinion that a righteous man commits sin when an evil desire arises in his heart? There is sin in such a case, and the sin is great,' said she; 'for the thoughts

37

of a righteous man should be righteous. For by thinking righteously his character is established in the heavens, and he has the Lord merciful to him in every business. But such as entertain wicked thoughts in their minds are bringing upon themselves death and captivity' " (Book First, Vision First, ch. 1).

I would draw your attention to the last sentence. The author is saying here that anybody who allows wicked thoughts to dwell unchecked in his mind is drawing upon himself the wages of sin. Our inward life must be righteous, or everything else is in vain.

"First of all, believe that there is one God who created and finished all things, and made all things out of nothing. He alone is able to contain the whole, but Himself cannot be contained. Have faith therefore in Him, and fear Him; and fearing Him, exercise self control. Keep these commands, and you will cast away from you all wickedness, and put on the strength of righteousness, and live to God, if you keep this commandment" (Book Second, Commandment First).

Here we find another mention of self-control. We also find a link between keeping God's commands and casting away all wickedness. The author seems to take it for granted that somebody who fully obeys God will not commit sin.

We can already see a pattern in the very early Church of striving for complete purity of life in every respect. I strongly suspect that these writers would have been horrified by the claim made by so many people today, that Christians can't avoid sinning.

"He who has received remission of his sins ought not to sin any more, but to live in purity" (Book Second, Commandment Fourth, ch. 3).

The author recognizes that sin and purity are opposites. There are many commands in the Bible about living a pure life.

" 'Be patient,' said he, 'and of good understanding, and you will rule over every wicked work, and you will work all righteousness. For if you be patient, the Holy Spirit that dwells in you will be pure. He will not be darkened by any evil spirit, but, dwelling in a broad region, he will rejoice and be glad; and with the vessel in which he dwells he will serve God in gladness, having great peace within himself. But if any outburst of anger take place, forthwith the Holy Spirit, who is tender, is straitened, not having a pure place, and He seeks to depart. For he is choked by the vile spirit, and cannot attend on the Lord as he wishes, for anger pollutes him. For the Lord dwells in long-suffering, but the devil in anger. The two spirits, then, when dwelling in the same habitation, are at discord with each other, and are troublesome to that man in whom they dwell' " (Book Second, Commandment Fifth, ch. 1).

This is an interesting description of how sin grieves and drives away God. It puts an obstacle between us and God. But this problem will not arise if we continue to follow God and thereby conquer sin. Notice how he clearly says that it is possible to "rule over," or conquer, EVERY wicked work.

" 'Hear now,' said he, 'how wicked is the action of anger, and in what way it over-throws the servants of God by its action, and turns them from righteousness. But it does not turn away those who are full of faith, nor does it act on them, for the power of the Lord is with them' " (Book Second, Commandment Fifth, ch. 2).

This is a very interesting passage. Allowing ourselves to get angry turns us away *not all anger* from righteousness—which is logical, since anger is a sin. But notice that he also men-tions two classes of Christians. Those who are not yet perfect in their walk with God are much more susceptible to temptation. This is at least in part because they do not have the full power of God in their lives that they could have.

"Do no evil in your life, and serve the Lord with a pure heart: keep His command-ments, walking in His precepts, and let no evil desire arise in your heart; and believe in God. If you do these things, and fear Him, and abstain from every evil thing, you will live unto God" (Book Third, Similitude Fifth, ch. 1).

Here we see a link between doing no evil, and having a pure heart. The reverse is also true: if we do evil, we no longer have a pure heart, and we no longer "live unto God." The author clearly believes that living without doing evil is an attainable goal. Otherwise, what would be the point in making such an exhortation?

* * * * *

Justin Martyr (100-165)

In general church circles, Justin is perhaps the best-known writer from this period. He was born in or near Shechem (Roman name Flavia Neapolis, modern name Nab-lus). He was converted about 130. He marks the rise of a school of thought which was to be very influential in Christian circles for some years afterward—that Christianity is the best and purest philosophy, and only a Christian can be a true philosopher. He praised the pagan philosophers for the glimpses of Divine truth that they showed in their writings, while rejecting what was false in their writings. His *First Apology* was written somewhere around 150, and the *Dialogue with Trypho* probably about 160. The *Dialogue* is based on an actual conversation that Justin had with a Rabbi.

"And reckon ye that it is for your sakes we have been saying these things; for it is in our power, when we are examined, to deny that we are Christians; but we would not live by telling a lie. For, impelled by the desire of the eternal and pure life, we seek the abode that is with God, the Father and Creator of all, and hasten to confess our faith, persuaded and convinced as we are that they who have proved to God by their works that they followed Him, and loved to abide with Him where there is no sin to cause disturbance, can obtain these things. This, then, to speak shortly, is what we expect and have learned from Christ, and teach" (*First Apology*, ch. 8).

He is not talking about sin that a person sees around him in society; everybody who lives close to God is disturbed and saddened by what he sees around him. Rather, Justin is saying that a person can live so close to God that there exists no sin in his own life to cause disturbance.

Dialogue with Trypho

"By reason, therefore, of this laver of repentance and knowledge of God, which has been ordained on account of the transgression of God's people, as Isaiah cries, we have believed, and testify that that very baptism which he announced is alone able to purify those who have repented; and this is the water of life. But the cisterns which you have dug for yourselves are broken and profitless to you. For what is the use of that baptism which cleanses the flesh and body alone? Baptize the soul from wrath and from covetousness, from envy, and from hatred; and, lo! the body is pure. For this is the symbolic significance of unleavened bread, that you do not commit the old deeds of wicked leaven" (ch. 14).

I find this to be a very interesting passage. Justin links the ancient symbolism of unleavened bread to living a life free from sin.

"You deceive yourselves while you fancy that, because you are the seed of Abraham after the flesh, therefore you shall fully inherit the good things announced to be bestowed by God through Christ. For no one, not even of them, has anything to look for, but only those who in mind are assimilated to the faith of Abraham... So that it becomes you to eradicate this hope from your souls, and hasten to know in what way forgiveness of sins, and a hope of inheriting the promised good things, shall be yours. But there is no other [way] than this,—to become acquainted with this Christ, to be washed in the fountain spoken of by Isaiah for the remission of sins; and for the rest, to live sinless lives" (ch. 44).

And here he states much the same thing in even starker terms. It should be becoming evident by now that the very early Church preached a far higher standard of purity and sinlessness than most churches do today, especially non-Holiness churches. Justin leaves no room for any type of sin in a believer's life.

"For the goodness and the lovingkindness of God, and His boundless riches, hold righteous and sinless the man who, as Ezekiel tells, repents of sins; and reckons sinful, unrighteous, and impious the man who fails away from piety and righteousness to unrighteousness and ungodliness" (ch. 47).

Salvation is only half the battle. We must continue to live righteously. We find here a warning against backsliding. Justin is saying that the supreme righteousness of God cuts both ways: it's a help to the sinner who repents, but it leads to eternal punishment

40

for the unrepentant backslider. Note also that he did not come up with this concept; he is merely repeating what Ezekiel says in Ez. 18:20-28 & 33:11-19.

"I affirm that He announced beforehand the future salvation for the human race through the blood of Christ. For the sign of the scarlet thread, which the spies, sent to Jericho by Joshua, son of Nave (Nun), gave to Rahab the harlot, telling her to bind it to the window through which she let them down to escape from their enemies, also manifested the symbol of the blood of Christ, by which those who were at one time harlots and unrighteous persons out of all nations are saved, receiving remission of sins, and continuing no longer in sin" (ch. 111).

We see here that the idea of living a pure life—one free from sin—is a recurring theme in Justin's thoughts. A person's lifestyle is supposed to be different after salvation. But preachers in non-Holiness churches often talk at great length about "accepting Christ"—and never say one single word about repentance; i.e., turning away from sin.

* * * * *

Tatian (120-173/180)

He was born in Syria. He was a disciple of Justin Martyr; but after Justin died, he drifted away from the Church, and fell into Gnosticism late in life. Only two of his works survive, both of which were written at some point while he was still orthodox in his views. His *Address to the Greeks* was likely written around 155. There is considerable disagreement over when he died.

"But with us there is no desire of vainglory, nor do we indulge in a variety of opinions. For having renounced the popular and earthly, and obeying the commands of God, and following the law of the Father of immortality, we reject everything which rests upon human opinion" (*Address to the Greeks*, ch. 32).

We see here the concepts of renouncing and dying out to earthly things, and dying out to the opinions of people. "What will people think?" is a powerful tool that Satan uses against us, to try to prevent us from obeying God's commands. A weak, unstable Christian is sometimes terribly afraid of being thought a fanatic. Once a person receives the second work of grace, this attack is robbed of its power.

* * * * *

Athenagoras of Athens (133-190)

Other than his approximate birth and death dates, we know very little about Athenagoras. He was a Christian apologist, and he was able to present his work to the emperor Marcus Aurelius (in many respects one of the best emperors) and his son, Commodus. This was probably in 177. He describes Christian beliefs, and various aspects of the Christian life. He also wrote a separate book specifically defending the doctrine of the Resurrection.

"Therefore the kiss, or rather the salutation, should be given with the greatest care, since, if there be mixed with it the least defilement of thought, it excludes us from eternal life" (*A Plea for the Christians*, ch. 32).

This is from a chapter describing in more detail how Christians have a higher sense of morality than other people. The holy kiss, or kiss of love, that Paul mentions at the end of some of his epistles was a wide-spread practice that continued in the Church for the first few centuries. Make no mistake; Paul was speaking of a literal, physical kiss. This is something that very few congregations today practice, partly for the practical reasons mentioned in this quote from Athenagoras. We see here that a good action done with wrong intentions is a sin. We also see how careful a Christian should be to avoid sin: it would be a terrible tragedy to start out well on the road to Heaven, and then miss the goal because of unforgiven sin in our lives.

* * * * *

Theophilus of Antioch (115-181/188)

He was the seventh Bishop of Antioch. Only one of his writings survives, but it is an important one, partly because it is the first extant work from any writer to use the word "Trinity." This work was addressed to a pagan friend of his, by the name of Autolycus, and was written around 180. Theophilus was born a pagan, and was converted after studying the Scriptures. This is about all we know of him.

"But God at least, the Father and Creator of the universe, did not abandon mankind, but gave a law, and sent holy prophets to declare and teach the race of men, that each one of us might awake and understand that there is one God. And they also taught us to refrain from unlawful idolatry, and adultery, and murder, fornication, theft, avarice, false swearing, wrath, and every incontinence and uncleanness; and that whatever a man would not wish to be done to himself, he should not do to another; and thus he who acts righteously shall escape the eternal punishments, and be thought worthy of the eternal life from God" (*Theophilus to Autolycus*, Book 2, ch. 34).

See here the high standard that we should follow. Someone who wishes to escape eternal damnation must put away **all** uncleanness, and follow after righteousness wholeheartedly. He says that we must be righteous in every aspect of our lives, or else we will face eternal punishment.

"And concerning chastity, the holy word teaches us not only not to sin in act, but not even in thought, not even in the heart to think of any evil, nor look on another man's wife with our eyes to lust after her. Solomon, accordingly, who was a king and a prophet, said: 'Let thine eyes look right on, and let thine eyelids look straight before thee: make straight paths for your feet' " (*Theophilus to Autolycus*, Book 3, ch. 13).

If anything, the standard is even higher here. Many people, upon reading this, may wonder how it's possible to adhere to such a standard. Only with the help and power of God; there is no other way. Yes, it's a high standard; but it is God's standard. We ignore it, or make excuses why we can't follow it, at our eternal peril.

The quote that he gives here is a part quote, part paraphrase of Prov. 4:25-27.

* * * * *

Irenaeus (120-202)

Irenaeus was born in Asia Minor; he became Bishop of Lugdunum in Gaul (now Lyons, France). In his youth, he was a disciple of Polycarp, who you will remember had been a disciple of the Apostle John. His primary effort, and the one for which he is best known, is his book explaining the errors of the Gnostics, *Against Heresies*. This was a massive book for those times.

The Gnostics were a major heretical sect. We can see a dim reflection of their beginnings in some of the warnings in the Bible, notably in Jude, and a few other places. There were several different sub-groups, each with somewhat different beliefs. However, they all rejected the God of the Bible as the supreme ruler of the universe. They also believed that physical matter is inherently sinful. Thus, in their view, Jesus could not have had a human body, because then He would have no longer been perfectly sinless. It follows that the Crucifixion and Resurrection could not have happened.

For a long time, virtually all that was known about the Gnostics came from Irenaeus' descriptions in *Against Heresies*. In recent decades, their own writings have been discovered. The results are almost humorous, in a way. It turns out that the various historians and other researchers—not Christians—evidently didn't believe the power of Christian testimony and living: they were shocked to discover that a Christian would actually tell the truth about his opponents! The actual writings of the Gnostics line up quite well with what Irenaeus said about them.

Irenaeus wrote *Against Heresies* around 180. Fairly shortly thereafter, he wrote a much shorter book called *The Demonstration of the Apostolic Preaching*. This one was aimed at Christians; it is more of a guide or teaching tool for Christians to learn about the faith in more depth. It is addressed to Marcianus, who was apparently a friend of Irenaeus.

Against Heresies

"For, after our Lord rose from the dead, [the apostles] were invested with power from on high when the Holy Spirit came down [upon them], were filled from all [His gifts], and had perfect knowledge: they departed to the ends of the earth, preaching the glad tidings of the good things [sent] from God to us, and proclaiming the peace of heaven to men, who indeed do all equally and individually possess the Gospel of God" (Book 3, ch. 1)

He recounts one of the benefits of entire sanctification: more power for God's service.

I don't believe that he meant the apostles had perfect knowledge in a human sense,

43

but rather in a spiritual sense. Jesus, speaking to the Twelve in John 14:26, told them that the Holy Ghost would remind them of what He had said.

"But that both the apostles and their disciples thus taught as the Church preaches, and thus teaching were perfected, wherefore also they were called away to that which is perfect—Stephen, teaching these truths, when he was yet on earth, saw the glory of God, and Jesus on His right hand, and exclaimed, 'Behold, I see the heavens opened, and the Son of man standing on the right hand of God.' These words he said, and was stoned; and thus did he fulfil the perfect doctrine, copying in every respect the Leader of martyrdom, and praying for those who were slaying him, in these words: 'Lord, lay not this sin to their charge' " (Book 3, ch. 12).

It is very unlikely that any carnal Christian could come anywhere close to following Stephen's example: the carnal nature has too much influence. Stephen is a case study on how perfect love allows a person to follow Jesus' example.

"For as, in the New Testament, that faith of men [to be placed] in God has been increased, receiving in addition [to what was already revealed] the Son of God, that man too might be a partaker of God; so is also our walk in life required to be more circumspect, when we are directed not merely to abstain from evil actions, but even from evil thoughts, and from idle words, and empty talk, and scurrilous language" (Book 4, ch. 28).

Again, a very high standard of conduct, and one that leaves no room for sin. Notice how he mentions idle words in the same breath as evil thoughts. This is an aspect of doctrine that has almost been lost to the Church. Far too many people forget that we will have to give an account for every single thing that we say. Very few preachers preach on this point.

"True knowledge is [that which consists in] the doctrine of the apostles, and the ancient constitution of the Church throughout all the world, and the distinctive manifestation of the body of Christ according to the successions of the bishops, by which they have handed down that Church which exists in every place, and has come even unto us, being guarded and preserved without any forging of Scriptures, by a very complete system of doctrine" (Book 4, ch. 33).

This is very important testimony. Remember, Irenaeus was close enough to the time of the apostles that long-lived people he knew, personally knew the apostles. Many of the churches then in existence were founded by the apostles; the apostles then appointed successors; those in turn appointed other successors. Thus the Church in general not only taught the same body of doctrine everywhere, but also knew that what they were teaching at that time was the same as what the apostles taught. This is the true "apostolic succession"—not overarching authority of one leader in one city, but the assurance that the teachings of the Church remained pure. The early Christians took great pains to obey II Thess. 2:15.

"And on this account does Paul declare to the Corinthians, 'I have fed you with milk, not with meat, for hitherto ye were not able to bear it.' That is, ye have indeed learned the advent of our Lord as a man; nevertheless, because of your infirmity, the Spirit of the Father has not as yet rested upon you. 'For when envying and strife,' he says, 'and dissensions are among you, are ye not carnal, and walk as men?' That is, that the Spirit of the Father was not yet with them, on account of their imperfection and shortcomings of their walk in life. As, therefore, the apostle had the power to give them strong meat— for those upon whom the apostles laid hands received the Holy Spirit, who is the food of life [eternal]—but they were not capable of receiving it, because they had the sentient faculties of the soul still feeble and undisciplined in the practice of things pertaining to God; so, in like manner, God had power at the beginning to grant perfection to man; but as the latter was only recently created, he could not possibly have received it, or even if he had received it, could he have contained it, or containing it, could he have retained it. It was for this reason that the Son of God, although He was perfect, passed through the state of infancy in common with the rest of mankind, partaking of it thus not for His own benefit, but for that of the infantile stage of man's existence, in order that man might be able to receive Him" (Book 4, ch. 38).

He talks here about two kinds of Christians: one type carnal and as yet imperfect; the other type perfect and no longer carnal, having received the Holy Ghost. It is clear, from this and other sources (including the Bible itself), that the apostles had the power to somehow help a person receive the second work by the laying on of hands. This was not a necessary step, but it was apparently quite common.

Why do we lay on hands? Was it a special power? Or an encouragement to seek for? Or?

"And for this cause does the apostle, explaining himself, make it clear that the saved man is a complete man as well as a spiritual man; saying thus in the first Epistle to the Thessalonians, 'Now the God of peace sanctify you perfect; and may your spirit, and soul, and body be preserved whole without complaint to the coming of the Lord Jesus Christ.' Now what was his object in praying that these three—that is, soul, body, and spirit—might be preserved to the coming of the Lord, unless he was aware of the [future] reintegration and union of the three, and [that they should be heirs of] one and the same salvation? For this cause also he declares that those are 'the perfect' who present unto the Lord the three [component parts] without offence. Those, then, are the perfect who have had the Spirit of God remaining in them, and have preserved their souls and bodies blameless, holding fast the faith of God, that is, that faith which is [directed] towards God, and maintaining righteous dealings with respect to their neighbours" (Book 5, ch. 6).

We see here a form of spiritual equation: perfect = spiritually whole = righteous =

giving no offense to God = being blameless = being pure = without sin.

The Demonstration of the Apostolic Preaching

"The apostles, who after (receiving) the power of the Holy Spirit were sent forth by Him into all the world, and wrought the calling of the Gentiles, showing to mankind the way of life, to turn them from idols and fornication and covetousness, cleansing their souls and bodies by the baptism of water and of the Holy Spirit... And they counseled them by the word of truth to keep their flesh undefiled unto the resurrection and their soul unstained.

"For such is the state of those who have believed, since in them continually abides the Holy Spirit, who was given by Him in baptism, and is retained by the receiver, if he walks in truth and holiness and righteousness and patient endurance" (Sections [Paragraphs] 41, 42).

Unlike the Gnostics, a Christian recognizes that the body can be morally pure. Regarding the inward part of man, a person who possesses godliness will see that godliness ruined if he sins. There is nothing other than sin that can pollute the soul. Notice the condition that we have to meet, in order to retain God in our lives.

"Since, then, by this calling life has been given [us], and God has summed up again for Himself in us the faith of Abraham, we ought not to turn back any more—I mean, to the first legislation. For we have received the Lord of the Law, the Son of God; and by faith in Him we learn to love God with all our heart, and our neighbour as ourselves. Now the love of God is far from all sin, and love to the neighbour worketh no ill to the neighbour.

"Wherefore also we need not the Law as a tutor. Behold, with the Father we speak, and in His presence we stand, being *children in malice,** and grown strong in all righteousness and soberness. For no longer shall the Law say, *Do not commit adultery*, to him who has no desire at all for another's wife; and *Thou shalt not kill*, to him who has put away from himself all anger and enmity; [and] *Thou shalt not covet thy neighbor's field or ox or ass*, to those who have no care at all for earthly things, but store up the heavenly fruits: nor *An eye for an eye, and a tooth for a tooth*, to him who counts no man his enemy, but all men his neighbors, and therefore cannot stretch out his hand at all for vengeance. It will not require tithes of him who consecrates all his possessions to God, leaving father and mother and all his kindred, and following the Word of God. And there will be no command to remain idle for one day of rest, to him who perpetually keeps sabbath, that is to say, who in the temple of God, which is man's body, does service to God, and in every hour works righteousness" (Sections 95, 96). *The wording is a little awkward here. He means that we are innocent of malice.

This is the picture of a man who is wholly dedicated to God. He clings so closely to God that there is no space for even the smallest sin to get between them. Or, to use a modern idiom, there is no daylight between such a man and God. We see from Irenaeus that there is nothing new or unusual about the doctrine of sinless perfection.

* * * * *

Clement of Alexandria (150-215)

Clement was probably born in Athens. He eventually found his way to Alexandria. For several years, he served as head of the very influential catechetical school of Alexandria. (Jerome and others believed that the school had been founded by St. Mark.) Clement was the first well-known head of the school. In some respects, it was somewhat analogous to a modern seminary; however it taught various subjects both sacred and profane. He wrote several books; the longest and most important are *The Exhortation to the Heathen*; *The Instructor;* and the *Stromata* ("Miscellanies"). The first is evangelical, aimed at converting the heathen. The second is instructional, aimed at Christians; it goes into great detail regarding various points of how Christians should behave. The third is also for Christians, but is a somewhat disjointed collection of a variety of things. He also wrote an essay that is rather surprising considering the times in which he lived: it dealt with the subject of how a Christian who is wealthy should view and use his money. Christians were vastly more likely to be poor and persecuted than wealthy, in those days. Most of his books were written in the period 180-202. He follows in the footsteps of Justin Martyr in terms of regarding Christianity as the true philosophy.

"The Lord ministers all good and all help, both as man and as God: as God, forgiving our sins; and as man, training us not to sin" (*The Instructor*, Book 1, ch. 3).

Jesus set an example for us to follow. We are expected to follow His example. He lived a sinless life; so should we.

"He enjoins His commands, and at the same time gives them such a character that they may be accomplished... I say, too, that it is requisite to contemplate human nature, and to live as the truth directs, and to admire the Instructor and His injunctions, as suitable and harmonious to each other. According to which image also we ought, conforming ourselves to the Instructor, and making the word and our deeds agree, to live a real life" (*The Instructor*, Book 1, ch. 12).

I like the point he makes, that both Jesus' life and His commands to us were completely compatible with each other. Jesus practised what He preached, and showed us that He was not commanding impossible things.

Stromata

"He, then, who has received the forgiveness of sins ought to sin no more. For, in addition to the first and only repentance from sins (this is from the previous sins in the first and heathen life—I mean that in ignorance), there is forthwith proposed to those

47

who have been called, the repentance which cleanses the seat of the soul from transgressions, that faith may be established" (Book 2, ch. 13).

Here he explicitly talks about two separate works of grace. The innermost corners of the heart should be cleansed from sin. Clement was clearly well-aware of the stabilizing influence that sanctification has on a person's walk with God. If our hearts remain pure, our lives will, too.

"He will bless when under trial, like the noble Job; like Jonas, when swallowed up by the whale, he will pray, and faith will restore him to prophesy to the Ninevites; and though shut up with lions, he will tame the wild beasts; though cast into the fire, he will be besprinkled with dew, but not consumed. He will give his testimony by night; he will testify by day; by word, by life, by conduct, he will testify. Dwelling with the Lord he will continue his familiar friend, sharing the same hearth according to the Spirit; pure in the flesh, pure in heart, sanctified in word. 'The world,' it is said, 'is crucified to him, and he to the world.' He, bearing about the cross of the Saviour, will follow the Lord's footsteps, as God, having become holy of holies...

"Wherefore the divine law appears to me necessarily to menace with fear, that, by caution and attention, the philosopher may acquire and retain absence of anxiety, continuing without fall and without sin in all things. For peace and freedom are not otherwise won, than by ceaseless and unyielding struggles with our lusts" (Book 2, ch. 20).

This is a marvellous description of the perfect Christian. Such a person, by his conduct and imitation of Jesus, unceasingly testifies to the world regarding the power of God to change lives. Such conduct leaves no room for sin. If we take care to always be busy "about our Father's business" there will be no time for sin!

"Here I find perfection apprehended variously in relation to Him who excels in every virtue. Accordingly one is perfected as pious, and as patient, and as continent, and as a worker... But I know no one of men perfect in all things at once, while still human, though according to the mere letter of the law, except Him alone who for us clothed Himself with humanity. Who then is perfect? He who professes abstinence from what is bad...

"We are then to strive to reach manhood as befits [the Christian], and to be as perfect as we can while still abiding in the flesh, making it our study with perfect concord here to concur with the will of God, to the restoration of what is the truly perfect nobleness and relationship, to the fulness of Christ, that which perfectly depends on our perfection" (Book 4, ch. 21).

Here we see a clear distinction drawn between Christian perfection and human perfection. We see that Christian perfection consists of a sin-free life.

"And if, in doing good, he be met with anything adverse, he will let the recompense pass without resentment as if it were good, he being just and good 'to the just and the unjust.' To such the Lord says, 'Be ye [perfect], as your Father is perfect.'

"To him the flesh is dead; but he himself lives alone, having consecrated the sepulchre into a holy temple to the Lord, having turned towards God the old sinful soul...

"Now purity is to think holy thoughts... For sanctity, as I conceive it, is perfect pureness of mind, and deeds, and thoughts, and words too, and in its last degree sinlessness in dreams" (Book 4, ch. 22).

A very high standard indeed!

I do not think it a coincidence that the primitive Church held such a high standard; for the primitive Church was a persecuted Church. But in recent centuries, wherever there has been a lack of persecution, we see preachers and theologians of various stripes relaxing the standards of holy living, and claiming that there is no such thing as a sin-free life.

"And again, as if in eagerness to divulge this knowledge, he [Paul] thus writes: 'Warning every man in all wisdom, that we may present every man (the whole man) perfect in Christ;' not every man simply, since no one would be unbelieving. Nor does he call every man who believes in Christ perfect; but he says all the man, as if he said the whole man, as if purified in body and soul" (Book 5, ch. 10).

Like some of the other early writers, Clement mentions two classes of Christians: those who are perfect, and those who are not.

"And should it be granted that the affections specified above [courage, joy, etc.], when produced rationally, are good, yet they are nevertheless inadmissible in the case of the perfect man, who is incapable of exercising courage: for neither does he meet what inspires fear, as he regards none of the things that occur in life as to be dreaded; nor can aught dislodge him from this—the love he has towards God. Nor does he need cheerfulness of mind; for he does not fall into pain, being persuaded that all things happen well. Nor is he angry; for there is nothing to move him to anger, seeing he ever loves God, and is entirely turned towards Him alone, and therefore hates none of God's creatures. No more does he envy; for nothing is wanting to him, that is requisite to assimilation, in order that he may be excellent and good. Nor does he consequently love any one with this common affection, but loves the Creator in the creatures. Nor, consequently, does he fall into any desire and eagerness; nor does he want, as far as respects his soul, aught appertaining to others, now that he associates through love with the Beloved One, to whom he is allied by free choice, and by the habit which results from training, approaches closer to Him, and is blessed through the abundance of good things" (Book 6, ch. 9).

The Devil wants us to forget how far apart the things of God are from the things of the world. Someone who continually lives close to God, and casts all care upon Him, will have no occasion to sin, for God provides every needed thing.

"But he does not use wordy prayer by his mouth; having learned to ask of the Lord what is requisite. In every place, therefore, but not ostensibly and visibly to the multitude, he will pray. But while engaged in walking, in conversation, while in silence, while engaged in reading and in works according to reason, he in every mood prays" (Book 7, ch. 7).

Here is a description of another aspect of a perfect Christian. Such a man always has the spirit of prayer. This means, for example, that he does not get angry, for it is impossible to have the spirit of prayer while angry. This excludes all other sins as well.

If you don't believe me, run an experiment. Try sinning and praying at the same time. It can't be done!

Prayer is two-way communing with God, and we do it when we love God. Could you hug a person and slap his face at the same time? In much the same way, it is impossible to love God, and yet reject Him by sinning, at the same time.

"Striving, then, to attain to the summit of knowledge; decorous in character; composed in mien; possessing all those advantages which belong to the true [Christian]; fixing his eye on fair models, on the many patriarchs who have lived rightly, and on very many prophets and angels reckoned without number, and above all, on the Lord, who taught and showed it to be possible for him to attain that highest life of all,—he therefore loves not all the good things of the world, which are within his grasp, that he may not remain on the ground, but the things hoped for, or rather already known, being hoped for so as to be apprehended.

"So then he undergoes toils, and trials, and afflictions, not as those among the philosophers who are endowed with manliness, in the hope of present troubles ceasing, and of sharing again in what is pleasant; but knowledge has inspired him with the firmest persuasion of receiving the hopes of the future. Wherefore he contemns not alone the pains of this world, but all its pleasures.

"They say, accordingly, that the blessed Peter, on seeing his wife led to death, rejoiced on account of her call and conveyance home, and called very encouragingly and comfortingly, addressing her by name, 'Remember thou the Lord.' Such was the marriage of the blessed and their perfect disposition towards those dearest to them" (Book 7, ch. 11).

A heart and mind that are fully stayed upon God will not give undue consideration to the things of this world. Viewed in the light of Eternity, such things are so small and trifling that they're simply not worth bothering about.

I don't know if this story about Peter really happened, and I don't think Clement knew. The wording sounds like he was simply repeating a fairly wide-spread story. But I fully believe that Peter had the attitude shown in the story.

* * * * *

Tertullian (155-225/240)

He was born a pagan, in Carthage. Most of his writing was done 197-218. He is another person who started out well, but fell into wrong beliefs later in life. He drifted into Montanism around 206, and formally separated from the Church somewhere around 211/213. Montanism, also called "New Prophecy," is now considered to be an actual heresy, but it took some time before the Church came to that conclusion. It was started by Montanus about 156, but the movement was not officially condemned until roughly 20 years later, and that was by a local council. In the beginning, at least, the problems with Montanism were with their practices, rather than with their theology. Indeed, even after Tertullian joined the movement, many of his writings are completely orthodox in nature; they give no evidence that he had left the mainstream of the Church. It is only in certain documents that we learn his views had changed. One of the appeals of the movement to a lot of people was the fact that it upheld strict standards of morality. Some of the people who joined it did so because they felt that the Church was becoming lax and soft on sin. Its adherents believed that they were given prophecies by God. These prophecies, or at least many of them, eventually turned out to be false. Another major part of the movement was something very similar to modern Pentecostalism.

"The Christian husband has nothing to do with any but his own wife. Democritus, in putting out his eyes, because he could not look on women without lusting after them, and was pained if his passion was not satisfied, owns plainly, by the punishment he inflicts, his incontinence. But a Christian with grace-healed eyes is sightless in this matter; he is mentally blind against the assaults of passion... If equanimity be the contention, you have Lycurgus choosing death by self-starvation, because the Lacons had made some emendation of his laws: the Christian, even when he is condemned, gives thanks... If the matter of sincerity is to be brought to trial, Aristotle basely thrust his friend Hermias from his place: the Christian does no harm even to his foe... But it will be said that some of us, too, depart from the rules of our discipline. In that case, however, we count them no longer Christians; but the philosophers who do such things retain still the name and the honour of wisdom" (*Apology*, ch. 46).

Democritus, Lycurgus, and Aristotle were famous Greeks who lived at various times before the time of Christ. They did much to improve their society, but their improvements were of course confined to outward things. Tertullian contrasts the morality of non-Christians and Christians, and shows the tremendous difference that the power of God makes.

Even the early Church, as pure as it was, had those who turned their backs on God. Notice how the Church viewed such people.

"A state of faith admits no plea of necessity; they are under no necessity to sin, whose

51

one necessity is, that they do not sin. For if one is pressed to the offering of sacrifice [to the Roman gods] and the sheer denial of Christ by the necessity of torture or of punishment, yet discipline does not connive even at that necessity; because there is a higher necessity to dread denying and to undergo martyrdom, than to escape from suffering, and to render the homage required. In fact, an excuse of this sort overturns the entire essence of our sacrament, removing even the obstacle to voluntary sins; for it will be possible also to maintain that inclination is a necessity, as involving in it, forsooth, a sort of compulsion" (*The Chaplet*, ch. 11).

Remember, Tertullian was writing to and about people for whom their religion was literally a matter of life and death. Yet not even torture or death is a sufficient excuse for sinning.

"But if there be any (heresies) which are bold enough to plant themselves in the midst of the apostolic age, that they may thereby seem to have been handed down by the apostles, because they existed in the time of the apostles, we can say: Let them produce the original records of their churches; let them unfold the roll of their bishops, running down in due succession from the beginning in such a manner that [that first bishop of theirs] shall be able to show for his ordainer and predecessor some one of the apostles or of apostolic men,—a man, moreover, who continued stedfast with the apostles. For this is the manner in which the apostolic churches transmit their registers: as the church of Smyrna, which records that Polycarp was placed therein by John; as also the church of Rome, which makes Clement to have been ordained in like manner by Peter. In exactly the same way the other churches likewise exhibit (their several worthies), whom, as having been appointed to their episcopal places by apostles, they regard as transmitters of the apostolic seed" (*The Prescription Against Heretics*, ch. 32).

Like Irenaeus, Tertullian writes about apostolic succession. He prescribes it as an absolute test of truth versus heresy. Truth was what was handed down in an unbroken line from the apostles to their immediate successors, and on down the line. Heresy was what did not have an apostolic pedigree. We have already seen that the ideas of sinless living and Christian perfection were preached by people who were appointed to their positions by the apostles.

"For what I say is this, that the repentance which, being shown us and commanded us through God's grace, recalls us to grace with the Lord, when once learned and undertaken by us ought never afterward to be cancelled by repetition of sin. No pretext of ignorance now remains to plead on your behalf; in that, after acknowledging the Lord, and accepting His precepts—in short, after engaging in repentance of sins—you again betake yourself to sins. Thus, in as far as you are removed from ignorance, in so far are you cemented to contumacy [rebelliousness or insubordination]. For if the ground on which you had repented of having sinned was that you had begun to fear the Lord, why have you preferred to rescind what you did for fear's sake, except because you have ceased to fear?... Since there is no exception which defends from liability to penalty even such as are ignorant of the Lord—because ignorance of God, openly as He is set before men, and comprehensible as He is even on the score of His heavenly benefits, is not possible—how perilous is it for Him to be despised when known? Now, that man does despise Him, who, after attaining by His help to an understanding of things good and evil, offers an affront to his own understanding—that is, to God's gift—by resuming what he understands ought to be shunned, and what he has already shunned: he rejects the Giver in abandoning the gift; he denies the Benefactor in not honouring the benefit... Besides, that man commits no light sin against the Lord, who, after he had by repentance renounced His rival the devil, and had under this appellation subjected him to the Lord, again upraises him by his own return [to the enemy], and makes himself a ground of exultation to him; so that the Evil One, with his prey recovered, rejoices anew against the Lord. Does he not—what is perilous even to say, but must be put forward with a view to edification—place the devil before the Lord? For he seems to have made the comparison who has known each; and to have judicially pronounced him to be the better whose [servant] he has preferred again to be. Thus he who, through repentance for sins, had begun to make satisfaction to the Lord, will, through another repentance of his repentance, make satisfaction to the devil, and will be the more hateful to God in proportion as he will be the more acceptable to His rival" (*On Repentance*, ch. 5).

Tertullian's writing is sometimes rather dense; it may be necessary to read this quote twice to fully understand it.

This is an important quote, because it goes into such detail about how sinning again after salvation cancels repentance. I would like to emphaze this part: "For if the ground on which you had repented of having sinned was that you had begun to fear the Lord, why have you preferred to rescind what you did for fear's sake, except because you have ceased to fear?" There are many people who would, in a sense, almost automatically live more victorious lives if they took this to heart.

Anybody who gives in to temptation has, at least for the moment, ceased to fear the Lord.

"So long, Lord Christ, may the blessing of learning or hearing concerning the discipline of repentance be granted to Thy servants, as is likewise behoves them, while learners, not to sin; in other words, may they thereafter know nothing of repentance, and require nothing of it... We have escaped once: thus far and no farther let us commit ourselves to perils, even if we seem likely to escape a second time. Men in general, after escaping shipwreck, thenceforward declare divorce with ship and sea; and by cherishing the memory of the danger, honour the benefit conferred by God,—their deliverance, namely. I praise their fear, I love their reverence; they are unwilling a second time to be a burden to the divine mercy" (*On Repentance*, ch. 7).

I personally find this to be a very interesting quote, because it brings to mind I Cor. 9:27, where Paul talks about the precautions he took against making shipwreck of his own faith.

"Nor merely from anger, but altogether from all perturbation of mind, ought the exercise of prayer to be free, uttered from a spirit such as the Spirit unto whom it is sent. For a defiled spirit cannot be acknowledged by a holy Spirit, nor a sad by a joyful, nor a fettered by a free. No one grants reception to his adversary: no one grants admittance except to his compeer" (*On Prayer*, ch. 12).

The Bible is very clear that only sin can defile a person's soul. If God will not grant reception to a person with unforgiven sin in his life, how can such a person enter Heaven?

"The will of God is our sanctification, for He wishes His 'image'—us—to become likewise His 'likeness;' that we may be 'holy' just as Himself is 'holy' " (*On Exhortation to Chastity*, ch. 1).

The fact that we were made in God's image is both an honor and a duty. It obligates us to remove **all** sin from our lives, by any means necessary, if we wish to truly be like God.

* * * * *

Hippolytus of Rome (170-236)

Hippolytus is a living example of the apostolic succession mentioned by Irenaeus and Tertullian. To recap: the Apostle John taught Polycarp; Polycarp taught Irenaeus; and Irenaeus taught Hippolytus.

He was probably born in Rome, and he was a bishop somewhere; we don't even know the city. The Catholics call him the first anti-pope; in this particular case, the name is a badge of honor. The church at Rome went through something of a rough patch during this time, with some of the Roman bishops showing distinctly poor judgment in certain points of doctrine. Of course the Papacy did not exist at this time; the Catholics insist on regarding all bishops of Rome, even strictly local ones, as Popes. They were sometimes called "Pope," but that does not strengthen the Catholic position; a little-known historical fact is that it was fairly common up into the 300s for the bishop of any major city to be called "Pope." Hippolytus was a vigorous opponent of heresy, and much of his writing was aimed at combating it.

"The Apostles, having in the first instance received [the Holy Spirit], have transmitted to those who have rightly believed. But we, as being their successors, and as participators in this grace, high-priesthood, and office of teaching, as well as being reputed guardians of the Church, must not be found deficient in vigilance, or disposed to suppress correct doctrine" (*The Refutation of All Heresies*, Book 1, Preface).

As we have seen, there was a great deal of uniformity among the various churches regarding doctrine, even though many of the major churches were far apart, and travel was difficult. It is clear that Hippolytus was very serious about his role in passing on the truth to the next generation.

"Although it may be said that the painful retribution that falls upon those who are by choice wicked comes from God, it would be only in accordance with right reason, to think that ills of that kind find both their beginnings and their causes in ourselves. For to one who lives without sin there is no darkness, no worm, no hell, no fire, nor any other of these words or things of terror" (Commentary on Psalm 78).

Here he shows a seemingly casual acceptance of the idea that it's possible to live without sin. As we have already seen, the idea was very widespread among those who considered themselves guardians of Divine truth.

"Figuratively speaking, he keeps a fire in his breast who permits an impure thought to dwell in his heart. And he walks upon coals who, by sinning in act, destroys his own soul" (Commentary on Proverbs).

Obviously, any kind of sin, whether in act or in thought, will destroy the soul. Hippolytus describes the danger of failing to view sin through God's eyes.

"He who loves truth, and never utters a false word with his mouth, may say, "I have chosen the way of truth" (Commentary on Psalm 119:30).

One of Satan's greatest triumphs was convincing the world that there is such a thing as a "white lie." Even the smallest sin will keep us out of Heaven, unless we repent of it.

* * * * *

Origen (185-254)

Origen was born in or near Alexandria, where he spent approximately the first half of his life. Origen is among the most controversial of the early Fathers, because of his unusual (some would say heretical) beliefs in a few specific areas. For example, he believed that even Satan will eventually be saved. It is also reported that he applied Matt. 19:12 to himself in a very literal manner, although some historians doubt the truth of the story. However, other than a few specific points, he was quite orthodox. He is perhaps the best-known of everybody who headed the catechetical school. He was a prolific writer. His biggest accomplishment was the Hexapla, the first parallel Bible. It had six columns. It was so massive that it was probably never copied in its entirety, which is one reason why only fragments exist today. He is generally regarded as the Church's first true theologian.

About 177, a pagan philosopher named Celsus wrote the first comprehensive attack against Christianity. Roughly seventy years later, Origen write a rebuttal of Celsus.

"To him belongs the rare honour of convincing heretics of their errors, and of leading them back to the Church; a result which must have been due as much to the gentleness and earnestness of his Christian character, as to the prodigious learning, marvellous acuteness, and logical power, which entitle him to be regarded as the greatest of the Fathers. It is singular, indeed, that a charge of heresy should have been brought, not only after his death, but even during his life, against one who rendered such eminent services to the cause of orthodox Christianity" (Dr. Crombie, quoted in *Ante-Nicene Fathers*, vol. 4).

De Principiis ("On First Principles")

"After these points, also, the apostolic teaching is that the soul, having a substance and life of its own, shall, after its departure from the world, be rewarded according to its deserts... This also is clearly defined in the teaching of the Church, that every rational soul is possessed of freewill and volition; that it has a struggle to maintain with the devil and his angels, and opposing influences, because they strive to burden it with sins; but if we live rightly and wisely, we should endeavour to shake ourselves free of a burden of that kind. From which it follows, also, that we understand ourselves not to be subject to necessity, so as to be compelled by all means, even against our will, to do either good or evil. For if we are our own masters, some influences perhaps may impel us to sin, and others help us to salvation; we are not forced, however, by any necessity either to act rightly or wrongly, which those persons think is the case who say that the courses and movements of the stars are the cause of human actions, not only of those which take place beyond the influence of the freedom of the will, but also of those which are placed within our own power" (Preface).

In my research for this book, I have observed that opponents of the second work of grace very often talk as if they didn't have free will; as if they are somehow forced to sin. Origen classes such a belief with superstition.

"He [the Holy Spirit] will take up His dwelling, not in all men, nor in those who are flesh, but in those whose land has been renewed. Lastly, for this reason was the grace and revelation of the Holy Spirit bestowed by the imposition of the apostles' hands after baptism. Our Saviour also, after the resurrection, when old things had already passed away, and all things had become new, Himself a new man, and the first-born from the dead, His apostles also being renewed by faith in His resurrection, says, 'Receive the Holy Spirit.' This is doubtless what the Lord the Saviour meant to convey in the Gospel, when He said that new wine cannot be put into old bottles, but commanded that the bottles should be made new, i.e., that men should walk in newness of life, that they might receive the new wine, i.e., the newness of grace of the Holy Spirit. In this manner, then, is the working of the power of God the Father and of the Son extended without distinction to every creature; but a share in the Holy Spirit we find possessed only by the saints" (Book 1, ch. 3).

Here we see a definite statement of two separate works of grace. The fullness of the Holy Ghost comes only *after* salvation. As Origen says, our "land" must be renewed first.

"It appears to me that the divine mysteries were concealed from the wise and prudent, according to the statement of Scripture, that 'no flesh should glory before God,' and revealed to children—to those, namely, who, after they have become infants and little children, i.e., have returned to the humility and simplicity of children, then make progress; and on arriving at perfection, remember that they have obtained their state of happiness, not by their own merits, but by the grace and compassion of God" (Book 3, ch. 1).

Like so many other early writers, Origen talks about Christian perfection.

"It is quite within our reach, when a malignant power has begun to incite us to evil, to cast away from us the wicked suggestions, and to resist the vile inducements, and to do nothing that is at all deserving of blame. And, on the other hand, it is possible, when a divine power calls us to better things, not to obey the call; our freedom of will being preserved to us in either case" (Book 3, ch. 2).

Here he talks even more clearly and more simply about free will. Jesus could have given in to temptation, but He did not. His life is given to us for an example.

Origen Against Celsus

"God the Word was sent, indeed, as a physician to sinners, but as a teacher of divine mysteries to those who are already pure and who sin no more. But Celsus, unable to see this distinction,—for he had no desire to be animated with a love of truth,—remarks, 'Why was he not sent to those who were without sin? What evil is it not to have committed sin?' To which we reply, that if by those 'who were without sin' he means those who sin no more, then our Saviour Jesus was sent even to such, but not as a physician. While if by those 'who were without sin' he means such as have never at any time sinned,—for he made no distinction in his statement,—we reply that it is impossible for a man thus to be without sin. And this we say, excepting, of course, the man understood to be in Christ Jesus, who 'did no sin.' It is with a malicious intent, indeed, that Celsus says of us that we assert that 'God will receive the unrighteousness man if he humble himself on account of his wickedness, but that He will not receive the righteous man, although he look up to Him, (adorned) with virtue from the beginning.' Now we assert that it is impossible for a man to look up to God (adorned) with virtue from the beginning. For wickedness must necessarily first exist in men. As Paul also says, 'When the commandment came, sin revived, and I died' " (Book 3, ch. 62).

Origen brings out the crucial distinction between having never sinned, and currently being without sin. If we had never sinned, we would not need a Savior. But going forward, in our walk with God, it is indeed possible to live without sin.

"The Jewish prophets, who were enlightened as far as was necessary for their prophetic work by the Spirit of God, were the first to enjoy the benefit of the inspiration; and by the contact—if I may so say—of the Holy Spirit they became clearer in mind, and their souls were filled with a brighter light. And the body no longer served as a hindrance to a virtuous life; for to that which we call 'the lust of the flesh' it was deadened. For we are persuaded that the Divine Spirit 'mortifies the deeds of the body,' and destroys that enmity against God which the carnal passions serve to excite" (Book 7, ch. 4).

Many opponents of the second work seem to regard the physical body as an impenetrable obstacle to living a truly holy life. But the body itself cannot prevent that; if we live a holy life, a pure body will be an inevitable result.

"As Celsus supposes that we uphold the doctrine of the resurrection in order that we may see and know God, he thus follows out his notions on the subject: 'After they have been utterly refuted and vanquished, they still, as if regardless of all objections, come back again to the same question, "How then shall we see and know God? how shall we go to Him?"' Let any, however, who are disposed to hear us observe, that if we have need of a body for other purposes, as for occupying a material locality to which this body must be adapted, and if on that account the 'tabernacle' is clothed in the way we have shown, we have no need of a body in order to know God. For that which sees God is not the eye of the body; it is the mind which is made in the image of the Creator, and which God has in His providence rendered capable of that knowledge. To see God belongs to the pure heart, out of which no longer proceed 'evil thoughts, murders, adulteries, fornications, thefts, false witness, blasphemies, the evil eye,' or any other evil thing. Wherefore it is said, 'Blessed are the pure in heart, for they shall see God.' But as the strength of our will is not sufficient to procure the perfectly pure heart, and as we need that God should create it, he therefore who prays as he ought, offers this petition to God, 'Create in me a clean heart, O God'" (Book 7, ch. 33).

A truly pure heart is one in which there is no trace of sin. It should be abundantly clear by this point that the primitive Church regarded a pure heart and pure life as eminently attainable in this life.

"Let any one who chooses learn how we are taught, that our bodies are the temple of God, and that if any one by lust or sin defiles the temple of God, he will himself be destroyed, as acting impiously towards the true temple" (Book 8, ch. 19).

It is sin, and nothing else, that defiles the body. Origen warns against such defilement in the strongest terms.

"To the perfect Christian, who is ever in his thoughts, words, and deeds serving his natural Lord, God the Word, all his days are the Lord's, and he is always keeping the Lord's day. He also who is unceasingly preparing himself for the true life, and abstaining from the pleasures of this life which lead astray so many,—who is not indulging the lust of the flesh, but 'keeping under his body, and bringing it into subjection,'—such a one is always keeping Preparation-day. Again, he who considers that 'Christ our Passover was sacrificed for us,' and that it is his duty to keep the feast by eating of the flesh of the Word, never ceases to keep the paschal feast; for the *pascha* means a 'passover,' and he is ever striving in all his thoughts, words, and deeds, to pass over from the things of this life to God, and is hastening towards the city of God. And, finally, he who can truly say, 'We are risen with Christ,' and 'He hath exalted us, and made us to sit with Him in heavenly places in Christ,' is always living in the season of Pentecost; and most of all, when going up to the upper chamber, like the apostles of Jesus, he gives himself to sup-plication and prayer, that he may become worthy of receiving 'the mighty wind rushing from heaven,' which is powerful to destroy sin and its fruits among men, and worthy of having some share of the tongue of fire which God sends" (Book 8, ch. 22).

This is a beautiful example of how Christian perfection is a stabilizing, keeping power in the life of the believer. Such a person can always serve God, without ruining his testimony by falling into sin. He also mentions how the second work of grace destroys sin in the heart.

Preparation day is the day before the Sabbath or any other holy day.

* * * * *

Dionysius of Alexandria (190/200-264)

Dionysius was born a pagan; we do not know when he was converted. He studied under Origen, and become head of the catechetical school, as well as later serving as Bishop of Alexandria. Most of his surviving writing is in the form of letters to various people. One of his biggest concerns was preserving unity in the Church. He generally dealt gently and lovingly with people with whom he had theological disputes. Only scat-tered fragments of his writings remain.

"The individual who is not perfectly pure both in soul and in body, shall be interdict-ed from approaching the holy of holies" (Epistle to Bishop Basilides, Canon 2).

This leaves no room for sin. The High Priest was required to be both morally and ceremonially pure in order to enter the Holy of Holies.

Temptation, not holiness

"What difference is there between being tempted, and falling or entering into temp-tation? Well, if one is overcome of evil—and he will be overcome unless he struggles against it himself, and unless God protects him with His shield—that man has entered into temptation, and is in it, and is brought under it like one that is led captive. But if one withstands and endures, that man is indeed tempted; but he has not entered into temptation, or fallen under it" (An Exposition of Luke 22:46).

When we yield to temptation, we are no longer conquerors in Christ, or living a victorious life.

* * * * *

Cyprian (200-258)

Cyprian was born in Carthage. He was a lawyer before his conversion, which occurred in his mid-40s. He shortly thereafter became Bishop of Carthage. He was the main opponent of Novatian (who wrote some very good things, but let his zeal for God run away with his brotherly love). We find time and time again that many of the early leaders were greatly concerned about Christian unity; they tended to come down hard on anything that threatened that unity. At the same time, however, they were zealous for correct doctrine. Sometimes the two things clashed. This latter concern led Cyprian into a dispute with Stephen, Bishop of Rome (254-257). With Stephen we see the first definite stirrings of the attitude of Roman supremacy that would later lead to the institution of the Papacy. Cyprian held the view that Stephen had no special authority outside of his own bishopric. Cyprian ended his life as a martyr.

"Yet I exhort you by our common faith, by the true and simple love of my heart towards you, that, having overcome the adversary in this first encounter, you should hold fast your glory with a brave and persevering virtue. We are still in the world; we are still placed in the battle-field; we fight daily for our lives. Care must be taken, that after such beginnings as these there should also come an increase, and that what you have begun to be with such a blessed commencement should be consummated in you. It is a slight thing to have been able to attain anything; it is more to be able to keep what you have attained; even as faith itself and saving birth makes alive, not by being received, but by being preserved. Nor is it actually the attainment, but the perfecting, that keeps a man for God. The Lord taught this in His instruction when He said, 'Behold, thou art made whole; sin no more, lest a worse thing come unto thee.' Conceive of Him as saying this also to His confessor, 'Lo thou art made a confessor; sin no more, lest a worse thing come unto thee.' Solomon also, and Saul, and many others, so long as they walked in the Lord's ways, were able to keep the grace given to them. When the discipline of the Lord was forsaken by them, grace also forsook them... There ought also to be no contentions and emulations among you, since the Lord left to us His peace, and it is written, 'Thou shalt love thy neighbour as thyself.' 'But if ye bite and find fault with one another, take heed that ye be not consumed one of another.' From abuse and revilings also I entreat you to abstain, for 'revilers do not attain the kingdom of God;' and the tongue which has confessed Christ should be preserved sound and pure with its honour. For he who, according to Christ's precept, speaks things peaceable and good and just, daily confesses Christ" (Epistle 6; to Rogatianus the Presbyter, and the Other Confessors).

Not only is it necessary to get saved, if we want to enter Heaven, but we must take care to live a Christian life from that point forward.

Notice that he also talks about the keeping, stabilizing influence of sanctification. "Nor is it actually the attainment, but the perfecting, that keeps a man for God."

"The highest degree of happiness is, not to sin; the second, to acknowledge our sins. In the former, innocence flows pure and unstained to preserve us; in the latter, there comes a medicine to heal us" (Epistle 54; To Cornelius, Concerning Fortunatus and Felicissimus, or Against the Heretics).

Notice how he links preserving power with not sinning. The preserving power of God is precisely what enables us to live without sin.

"But further, one is not born by the imposition of hands when he receives the Holy Ghost, but in baptism, that so, being already born, he may receive the Holy Spirit, even as it happened in the first man Adam. For first God formed him, and then breathed into his nostrils the breath of life. For the Spirit cannot be received, unless he who receives first have an existence" (Epistle 73; To Pompey, Against the Epistle of Stephen About the Baptism of Heretics).

This quote is likely to be misunderstood without an explanation. It sounds here as if Cyprian thinks that baptism is required for salvation. He is very clear elsewhere that it is not necessary for salvation, but is merely a symbol. Several of the early writers tended to refer to baptism, somewhat carelessly, as a sort of shorthand for being saved. This was at least partly because baptism was treated differently than it often is today. Converts generally were not baptized immediately, but were put on a form of probation for a few months, to make sure that their lives matched their profession.

We see another clear indication here of two separate works of grace. The fullness of the Holy Ghost cannot be received unless a person has already been born into the Christian life.

"An example is given us to avoid the way of the old man, to stand in the footsteps of a conquering Christ, that we may not again be incautiously turned back into the nets of death, but, foreseeing our danger, may possess the immortality that we have received. But how can we possess immortality, unless we keep those commands of Christ whereby death is driven out and overcome, when He Himself warns us, and says, 'If thou wilt enter into life, keep the commandments?' And again: 'If ye do the things that I command you, henceforth I call you not servants, but friends.' Finally, these persons He calls strong and stedfast; these He declares to be founded in robust security upon the rock, established with immoveable and unshaken firmness, in opposition to all the tempests and hurricanes of the world. 'Whosoever,' says He, 'heareth my words, and doeth them, I will liken him unto a wise man, that built his house upon a rock: the rain descended, the floods came, the winds blew, and beat upon that house; and it fell not: for it was founded upon a rock.' We ought therefore to stand fast on His words, to learn and do whatever He both taught and did. But how can a man say that he believes in Christ, who does not do what Christ commanded him to do? Or whence shall he attain to the reward of faith, who will not keep the faith of the commandment? He must of necessity waver and wander, and, caught away by a spirit of error, like dust which is shaken by the wind, be blown about; and he will make no advance in his walk towards salvation, because he

61

does not keep the truth of the way of salvation...

"Let not the tongue which has confessed Christ be evil-speaking; let it not be turbulent, let it not be heard jarring with reproaches and quarrels, let it not after words of praise, dart forth serpents' venom against the brethren and God's priests. But if one shall have subsequently been blameworthy and obnoxious; if he shall have wasted his confession by evil conversation; if he shall have stained his life by disgraceful foulness; if, finally, forsaking the Church in which he has become a confessor, and severing the concord of unity, he shall have exchanged his first faith for a subsequent unbelief, he may not flatter himself on account of his confession that he is elected to the reward of glory, when from this very fact his deserving of punishment has become the greater" (Treatise 1; On the Unity of the Church).

A good beginning should lead to a good ending. If it doesn't, it's our fault. Our life should match our profession. If it doesn't, we're in trouble. We must back up our claim of being God's children by our actions if we wish to see Heaven; otherwise, we have only a dead, empty faith. God's children inherently do different things than the actions of Satan's children.

* * * * *

Gregory Thaumaturgus (213-270)
The name Thaumaturgus means the "Wonder-Worker." This name was given to him because of many miracles and other unusual things that he is alleged to have done and have happened to him. Many of those stories probably did not happen; legends grew up about him after his death, more so than many contemporaries. Gregory was born in Neocaesarea, Pontus (now Niksar, Turkey); he studied under Origen while Origen was in the Holy Land. Interestingly, he became Origen's pupil while still a pagan. The things he learned led him to salvation. Later he became Bishop of Neocaesarea. We don't know very much for sure about his life; it is difficult to separate legend from hard fact.

"There is One Holy Spirit, having His subsistence from God, and being made manifest by the Son, to wit to men: Image of the Son, Perfect Image of the Perfect; Life, the Cause of the living; Holy Fount; Sanctity, the Supplier, or Leader, of Sanctification" (*A Declaration of Faith*).

I'm not sure how he's using "sanctification" here, but it's notable that he credits the Holy Ghost with being its author. It's impossible to be sanctified in the New Testament sense without the Holy Ghost.

"Beginning with this one [the virtue of piety], we shall find all the other virtues grow upon us most readily: if, while for ourselves we earnestly aspire after this grace, which every man, be he only not absolutely impious, or a mere pleasure seeker, ought to acquire for himself, in order to his being a friend of God and a maintainer of His truth, and while we diligently pursue this virtue, we also give heed to the other virtues, in order that we may not approach our God in unworthiness and impurity, but with all virtue and wisdom as our best conductors and most sagacious priests. And the end of all I consider to be nothing but this: By the pure mind make thyself like to God, that thou mayest draw near to Him, and abide in Him" (The Oration and Panegyric Addressed to Origen, Argument 12).

Here we see that it requires a pure mind and heart to be like Jesus.

* * * * *

Methodius of Olympus (?-311)

We know very little about the life of Methodius. He may have been born about 260, although that is essentially a guess. He was probably a bishop, although some researchers are not sure of that. About all we can say for sure is that he was a leader or teacher of some type, and a notable theologian. He combated Origen's incorrect ideas, with some success. He became a martyr during the last persecution, shortly before Constantine became emperor. He was an excellent writer; one of his most important books defended the Resurrection. Another book is *The Banquet*, an allegory about Christian morality and purity. In it he uses physical virginity as a symbol of spiritual virginity and purity. It is based on the parable of the ten virgins.

The Banquet of the Ten Virgins

"It is frequently the case that the Scriptures thus call the assembly and mass of believers by the name of the Church, the more perfect in their progress being led up to be the one person and body of the Church. For those who are the better, and who embrace the truth more clearly, being delivered from the evils of the flesh, become, on account of their perfect purification and faith, a church and help-meet of Christ, betrothed and given in marriage to Him as a virgin, according to the apostle, so that receiving the pure and genuine seed of His doctrine, they may co-operate with Him, helping in preaching for the salvation of others. And those who are still imperfect and beginning their lessons, are born to salvation, and shaped, as by mothers, by those who are more perfect, until they are brought forth and regenerated unto the greatness and beauty of virtue; and so these, in their turn making progress, having become a church, assist in labouring for the birth and nurture of other children, accomplishing in the receptacle of the soul, as in a womb, the blameless will of the Word" (Discourse 3, ch. 8).

Once again we see the recurring theme of Christian perfection. Methodius makes a clear distinction between those Christians who are perfect, and those who are not.

"Now we should consider the case of the renowned Paul, that when he was not yet perfect in Christ, he was first born and suckled, Ananias preaching to him, and renewing him in baptism, as the history in the Acts relates. But when he was grown to a man, and was built up, then being moulded to spiritual perfection, he was made the help-meet and bride of the Word; and receiving and conceiving the seeds of life, he who was before a child, becomes a church and a mother, himself labouring in birth of those who, through him, believed in the Lord, until Christ was formed and born in them also. For he says, 'My little children, of whom I travail in birth again until Christ be formed in you;' and again, 'In Christ Jesus I have begotten you through the Gospel' " (Discourse 3, ch. 9).

As far as I have been able to tell from what I have read of the extant writings, none of the earliest Church Fathers had any conception of the modern idea that Paul fought a losing battle with sin once he was a mature Christian.

"Now, he who watches over and restrains himself in part, and in part is distracted and wandering, is not wholly given up to God. Hence it is necessary that the perfect man offer up all, both the things of the soul and those of the flesh, so that he may be complete and not lacking" (Discourse 5, ch. 2).

Perfection consists in large part in renouncing, in our heart and will, everything of the world, whether good or bad. This does not mean that we must divest ourselves of all possessions, as the rich young ruler was told to do. It means that we must be **willing** to do so, without a single murmur or a moment's hesitation, should God command it.

"For let us say what it is to offer up oneself perfectly to the Lord. If, for instance, I open my mouth on some subjects, and close it upon others; thus, if I open it for the explanation of the Scriptures, for the praise of God, according to my power, in a true faith and with all due honour, and if I close it, putting a door and a watch upon it against foolish discourse, my mouth is kept pure, and is offered up to God... If, too, I accustom my eyes not to lust after the charms of the body, nor to take delight in unseemly sights, but to look up to the things which are above, then my eyes are kept pure, and are offered to the Lord. If I shut my ears against detraction and slanders, and open them to the word of God, having intercourse with wise men, then have I offered up my ears to the Lord. If I keep my hands from dishonourable dealing, from acts of covetousness and of licentiousness, then are my hands kept pure to God. If I withhold my steps from going in perverse ways, then have I offered up my feet, not going to the places of public resort and banquets, where wicked men are found, but into the right way, fulfilling something of the commands. What, then, remains to me, if I also keep the heart pure, offering up all its thoughts to God; if I think no evil, if anger and wrath gain no rule over me, if I meditate in the law of the Lord day and night? And this is to preserve a great chastity, and to vow a great vow" (Discourse 5, ch. 4).

This is a wonderful portrait of Christian perfection. This state leaves no room for sin of any kind.

"Nor is it right, on the one hand, by the use of chastity to keep virginity, and, on the

64

other hand, to pollute the soul by evil deeds and lust; nor here to profess purity and continence, and there to pollute it by indulgence in vices. Nor, again, here to declare that the things of this world bring no care to himself; there to be eager in procuring them, and in concern about them. But all the members are to be preserved intact and free from corruption; not only those which are sexual, but those members also which minister to the service of lusts. For it would be ridiculous to preserve the organs of generation pure, but not the tongue; or to preserve the tongue, but neither the eyesight, the ears, nor the hands; or lastly, to preserve these pure, but not the mind, defiling it with pride and anger" (Discourse 11, ch. 1).

In other words, any type of sin defiles. It does no good in the long run to avoid some sins if we fail to avoid all sin.

Chapter 4

The Early Church: 95-400 (Part 2)

Lactantius (250-325)

With Lactantius we reach the era of Constantine—a time of mixed blessings. After reading about the tremendous persecutions and martyrdoms, it is a relief to come to the point where Christianity becomes legalized. And yet, that legalization, in large measure, paved the way for the fall into the spiritual dark ages that followed. Once the Church no longer had to deal with such a degree of overt opposition, Satan shifted the attack to include a much larger degree of false doctrine, much of which culminated in the Roman Catholic system that we see today.

Lactantius was born a pagan, in North Africa; he was a professor of rhetoric in Nicomedia (now Izmit, Turkey). Most of his writings are from the fairly short period 303-313. Several of his writings have been lost. He had a remarkable second career; in his old age, he was appointed tutor of Constantine's son Crispus.

The Divine Institutes

"But what are the enemies of the soul, but lusts, vices, and sins? And if virtue shall have overcome and put to flight these, the soul will be pure and free from stain... Lusts having been subdued, and the desire of earthly things overcome, our souls, pure and victorious, may return to God" (Book 3, ch. 12).

We can conquer sin by God's power. This renders and keeps the soul pure and spotless.

"But let us grant that the case which the philosopher proposes is possible: what, then, will the just man do, if he shall have met with a wounded man on a horse, or a shipwrecked man on a plank? I am not unwilling to confess he will rather die than put another to death. Nor will justice, which is the chief good of man, on this account receive the name of folly. For what ought to be better and dearer to man than innocence? And this must be the more perfect, the more you bring it to extremity, and choose to die rather than to detract from the character of innocence...

"But who is able to distinguish right from wrong except the wise man? Thus it comes to pass, that he can never be just who is foolish, nor wise who is unjust. And if this is most true, it is plain that he who has not taken away a plank from a shipwrecked man, or a horse from one who is wounded, is not foolish; because it is a sin to do these things, and the wise man abstains from sin... Now a wise man never gives himself to the pursuit of gain, because he despises these earthly advantages: nor does he allow any one to be deceived, because it is the duty of a good man to correct the errors of men, and to bring them back to the right way; since the nature of man is social and beneficent, in which respect alone he bears a relation to God" (Book 5, ch. 18).

Notice a characteristic of the wise man—abstaining from sin. Physical death is to be preferred over spiritual death. One is the doorway to better things; the other, if left unchanged, is a final loss of hope.

"But undoubtedly this is the cause why he appears to be foolish who prefers to be in want, or to die rather than to inflict injury or take away the property of another,—namely, because they think that man is destroyed by death. And from this persuasion all the errors both of the common people and also of the philosophers arise. For if we have no existence after death, assuredly it is the part of the most foolish man not to promote the interests of the present life, that it may be long-continued, and may abound with all advantages. But he who shall act thus must of necessity depart from the rule of justice. But if there remains to man a longer and a better life—and this we learn both from the arguments of great philosophers, and from the answers of seers, and the divine words of prophets—it is the part of the wise man to despise this present life with its advantages, since its entire loss is compensated by immortality" (Book 5, ch. 19).

He shows here the same sort of attitude that Paul showed in Phil. 3:8. Any losses or sufferings that we undergo for the sake of righteousness will be more than compensated for by the reward of righteousness. And yet a lot of people try to hold both God and the world—something that often appears to be working in the short term, but never works in the long term.

"The nature of good and evil things is so fixed, that they always oppose and drive out one another: and thus it comes to pass that vices cannot be removed without virtues, nor can virtues be introduced without the removal of vices" (Book 6, ch. 3).

A man cannot be both a sinner (a partaker in vices) and a Christian (a partaker in virtues) at the same time.

"As, therefore, in undertaking a journey, it is of no profit to know the way, unless we also have the effort and strength for walking, so truly knowledge is of no avail if our virtue fails. For, in general, even they who sin perceive what is good and evil, though not perfectly; and as often as they act improperly, they know that they sin, and therefore endeavour to conceal their actions. But though the nature of good and evil does not escape their notice, they are overpowered by an evil desire to sin, because they are wanting in virtue, that is, the desire of doing right and honourable things...

"It is a virtue to restrain anger, to control desire, to curb lust; for this is to flee from vice. For almost all things which are done unjustly and dishonestly arise from these affections. For if the force of this emotion which is called anger be blunted, all the evil contentions of men will be lulled to rest; no one will plot, no one will rush forth to injure another. Also, if desire be restrained, no one will use violence by land or by sea, no one will lead an army to carry off and lay waste the property of others. Also, if the ardour of lusts be repressed, every age and sex will retain its sanctity; no one will suffer, or do anything disgraceful. Therefore all crimes and disgraceful actions will be taken away from the life and character of men, if these emotions are appeased and calmed by virtue. And this calming of the emotions and affections has this meaning, that we do all things which are right. The whole duty of virtue then is, not to sin. And assuredly he cannot discharge this who is ignorant of God, since ignorance of Him from whom good things proceed must thrust a man unawares into vices. Therefore, that I may more briefly and significantly fix the offices of each subject, knowledge is to know God, virtue is to worship Him: the former implies wisdom, the latter righteousness" (Book 6, ch. 5).

Sinners are represented here as being overpowered by sin. But Christians are different: we have trusted in the power of God to break the chains of sin. Therefore, sin cannot overpower us unless we allow it, or unless we have become careless and are not living close enough to God to have enough of His presence.

"What, therefore, can be so calamitous to a good man, so opposed to his character, as to let loose the reins to anger, which deprives him not only of the title of a good man, but even of a man; since to injure another, as he himself [Cicero] most truly says, is not in accordance with the nature of man? For if you provoke cattle or horses, they turn against you either with their hoof or their horn; and serpents and wild beasts, unless you pursue them that you may kill them, give no trouble. And to return to examples of men, even the inexperienced and the foolish, if at any time they receive an injury, are led by a blind and irrational fury, and endeavour to retaliate upon those who injure them... For he who endeavours to return an injury, desires to imitate that very person by whom he has been injured. Thus he who imitates a bad man can by no means be good" (Book 6, ch. 18).

He says that giving way to anger lowers a person to the level of the animals. Allowing sin to take over means that we are no longer good or holy.

"Nor, however, let any one be disheartened, or despair concerning himself, if, overcome by passion, or impelled by desire, or deceived by error, or compelled by force, he has turned aside to the way of unrighteousness. For it is possible for him to be brought back, and to be set free, if he repents of his actions, and, turning to better things, makes satisfaction to God... For if we think that our children are corrected when we perceive that they repent of their faults, and though we have disinherited and cast them off, we again receive, cherish, and embrace them, why should we despair that the mercy of God our Father may again be appeased by repentance? Therefore He who is at once the Lord and most indulgent Parent promises that He will remit the sins of the penitent, and that He will blot out all the iniquities of him who shall begin afresh to practice righteousness. For as the uprightness of his past life is of no avail to him who lives badly, because the subsequent wickedness has destroyed his works of righteousness, so former sins do not stand in the way of him who has amended his life, because the subsequent righteousness has effaced the stain of his former life... Thus repentance makes a man cautious and diligent to avoid the faults into which he has once fallen through deceit... [God] will quench the ardour of desires, He will root out lusts, He will remove envy, He will mitigate anger. He will give true and lasting health. This remedy should be sought by all, inasmuch as the soul is harassed by greater danger than the body, and a cure should be applied as soon as possible to secret diseases. For if any one has his eyesight clear, all his limbs perfect, and his entire body in the most vigorous health, nevertheless I should not call him sound if he is carried away by anger, swollen and puffed up with pride, the slave of lust, and burning with desires; but I should rather call him sound who does not raise his eyes to the prosperity of another, who does not admire riches, who looks upon another's wife with chaste eye, who covets nothing at all, does not desire that which is another's, envies no one, disdains no one; who is lowly, merciful, bountiful, mild, courteous: peace perpetually dwells in his mind.

"That man is sound, he is just, he is perfect. Whoever, therefore, has obeyed all these heavenly precepts, he is a worshipper of the true God, whose sacrifices are gentleness of spirit, and an innocent life, and good actions. And he who exhibits all these qualities offers a sacrifice as often as he performs any good and pious action. For God does not desire the sacrifice of a dumb animal, nor of death and blood, but of man and life. And to this sacrifice there is neither need of sacred boughs, nor of purifications, nor of sods of turf, which things are plainly most vain, but of those things which are put forth from the innermost breast. Therefore, upon the altar of God, which is truly very great, and which is placed in the heart of man, and cannot be defiled with blood, there is placed righteousness, patience, faith, innocence, chastity, and abstinence" (Book 6, ch. 24).

Notice here how he says that a perfect man is one in whom is no sin. God can and will root out *all* sin from our hearts, if we will let Him. This is the path to Christian perfection. But if we do not let Him do that, we are in danger of losing everything. Lactantius warns us very plainly against returning to sin.

"The chief ceremonial in the worship of God is praise from the mouth of a just man directed towards God. That this, however, may be accepted by God, there is need of humility, and fear, and devotion in the greatest degree, lest any one should chance to place confidence in his integrity and innocence, and thus incur the charge of pride and arrogance, and by this deed lose the recompense of his virtue. But that he may obtain the favour of God, and be free from every stain, let him always implore the mercy of God, and pray for nothing else but pardon for his sins, even though he has none" (Book 6, ch. 25).

This is a subtle danger: the very fact of our righteousness can be used as a weapon against us by Satan. He can tempt us to become proud of our humility. That way lies utter ruin.

"For what is greater in power than God, or more perfect in reason, or brighter in clearness? And since He begat us to wisdom, and produced us to righteousness, it is not allowable for man to forsake God, who is the giver of intelligence and life and to serve earthly and frail things, or, intent upon seeking temporal goods, to turn aside from innocence and piety. Vicious and deadly pleasures do not render a man happy; nor does opulence, which is the inciter of lusts; nor empty ambition; nor frail honours, by which the human soul, being ensnared and enslaved to the body, is condemned to eternal death: but innocence and righteousness alone, the lawful and due reward of which is immortality, which God from the beginning appointed for holy and uncorrupted minds, which keep themselves pure and uncontaminated from vices, and from every earthly impurity" (*A Treatise on the Anger of God*; ch. 23).

Great purity receives great reward. But such reward is dependent on our keeping that purity. God does not participate in the current "feel-good" movement, where a person gets a trophy merely for showing up.

It was not allowable for Adam and Eve to forsake God, and it is not allowable for a person to forsake God after becoming a Christian. The penalty is the same.

* * * * *

Alexander of Alexandria (?-326)

Alexander may have been born around 250; we do not know. He became Bishop of Alexandria in 313. Many of his writings have been lost. He did a great deal while he was Bishop, including work on the dating of Easter. But perhaps his most important service to the Church lay in his mentorship of Athanasius. This relationship was to have permanent effects on history.

"For what progress can the wisdom of God make? What increase can the truth itself and God the Word receive? In what respect can the life and the true light be made better?... But men and angels, who are His creatures, have received His blessing that they might make progress, exercising themselves in virtues and in the commandments of the law, so as not to sin" (Epistle to Alexander, Bishop of Constantinople).

Clearly Alexander felt that it is possible to live without sinning.

* * * * *

Athanasius (296/8-373)

Athanasius' great claim to fame is his tremendous service in combating Arianism. Arius taught that Jesus was a created being (and thus not Divine). This controversy culminated in the Council of Nicaea in 325. Athanasius, as young as he was, and not having much official authority (he was a mere deacon in a council of bishops), was nevertheless the leader of the orthodox forces who championed the Trinity. The Nicene Creed explicitly proclaims the Divinity of Jesus.

Naturally, the bulk of his writings revolved around this issue. However, he did sometimes write about other subjects. He wrote a biography of Antony, one of the first monks.

"An ecumenical council was a new experiment... That the heads of all the Churches of Christendom should meet in free and brotherly deliberation, and should testify to all the world their agreement in the Faith handed down independently but harmoniously from the earliest times in Churches widely remote in situation, and separated by differences of language, race, and civilisation, is a grand and impressive idea, an idea approximately realised at Nicæa as in no other assembly that has ever met. The testimony of such an assembly carries the strongest evidential weight; and the almost unanimous horror of the Nicene Bishops at the novelty and profaneness of Arianism condemns it irrevocably as alien to the immemorial belief of the Churches" (*Nicene and Post-Nicene Fathers*, Series 2, vol. 4).

"In the beginning wickedness did not exist. Nor indeed does it exist even now in those who are holy, nor does it in any way belong to their nature" (*Against the Heathen*, Part 1, sec. 2).

In other words, "holy" does not equal "wicked." This may seem to many people to be self-evident, but a great many people who claim to be Christians also claim that they can do whatever they want, including any type of sin, and still get to Heaven. This quote is a clear statement that a sinless life is a possibility here on earth.

"Why not rather get those things which we can take away with us—to wit, prudence, justice, temperance, courage, understanding, love, kindness to the poor, faith in Christ, freedom from wrath, hospitality? If we possess these, we shall find them of themselves preparing for us a welcome there in the land of the meek-hearted.

"And so from such things let a man persuade himself not to make light of it, especially if he considers that he himself is the servant of the Lord, and ought to serve his Master. Wherefore as a servant would not dare to say, because I worked yesterday, I will not work today; and considering the past will do no work in the future; but, as it is written in the Gospel, daily shows the same readiness to please his master, and to avoid risk: so let us daily abide firm in our discipline, knowing that if we are careless for a single day the Lord will not pardon us, for the sake of the past, but will be wrath against us for our neglect. As also we have heard in Ezekiel; and as Judas because of one night destroyed his previous labour.

"Wherefore, children, let us hold fast our discipline, and let us not be careless. For in it the Lord is our fellow-worker, as it is written, 'to all that choose the good, God worketh with them for good.' But to avoid being heedless, it is good to consider the word of the Apostle, 'I die daily.' For if we too live as though dying daily, we shall not sin. And the meaning of that saying is, that as we rise day by day we should think that we shall not abide till evening; and again, when about to lie down to sleep, we should think that we shall not rise up. For our life is naturally uncertain, and Providence allots it to us daily. But thus ordering our daily life, we shall neither fall into sin, nor have a lust for anything, nor cherish wrath against any, nor shall we heap up treasure upon earth" (*Life of Antony;* sec. 9).

This is taken from one of Antony's discourses. He warns in solemn terms against falling into sin; not because God cannot or will not pardon in such a case, but because some people recklessly assume that their past righteousness will help them in such a case. Once we have been redeemed, it is far better to avoid all sin, rather than needing to ask God for forgiveness once again.

"For what our Lord has now commanded, the same also He spoke by His Saints before His coming in the flesh: and this is the rule which is given unto men to lead them to perfection—what God commands, that to do" (*Defence of his Flight*).

During one period, when the Arians appeared to have the upper hand in the great struggle, Athanasius fled to a safer location. He put forth this defense of his actions in order to counter accusations of cowardice.

We see here that in the midst of this battle for truth, Athanasius still finds time to talk about Christian perfection. The Bible commands us in many places to flee sin, to keep ourselves unspotted, etc. If we fully obey God, we will certainly obey these commands. Therefore, Athanasius' definition of perfection means living without sin.

"For if, as they [the Arians] hold, the Essence of the Word being of created nature, therefore He says, 'The Lord created me,' being a creature, He was not created for us; but if He was not created for us, we are not created in Him; and, if not created in Him, we have Him not in ourselves but externally; as, for instance, as receiving instruction from Him as from a teacher. And it being so with us, sin has not lost its reign over the flesh, being inherent and not cast out of it. But the Apostle opposes such a doctrine a little before, when he says, 'For we are His workmanship, created in Christ Jesus;' and if in Christ we are created, then it is not He who is created, but we in Him; and thus the words 'He created' are for our sake. For because of our need, the Word, though being Creator, endured words which are used of creatures; which are not proper to Him, as being the Word, but are ours who are created in Him... So, when for our need He became man, consistently does He use language, as ourselves, 'The Lord hath created Me,' that, by His dwelling in the flesh, sin might perfectly be expelled from the flesh, and we might have a free mind" (*Against the Arians*, Discourse 2, ch. 20).

It is precisely because Jesus is Divine that He has the power to cast out sin from our lives when we become a new creature. But all too many people let sin back into their lives on the excuse that they can't help sinning.

"And again, since God's work, that is, man, though created perfect, has become wanting through the transgression, and dead by sin, and it was unbecoming that the work of God should remain imperfect... ; therefore the perfect Word of God puts around Him an imperfect body, and is said to be created 'for the works;' that, paying the debt in our stead, He might, by Himself, perfect what was wanting to man... For then, because the works were become imperfect and mutilated from the transgression, He is said in respect to the body to be created; that by perfecting them and making them whole, He might present the Church unto the Father, as the Apostle says, 'not having spot or wrinkle or any such thing, but holy and without blemish.' Mankind then is perfected in Him and restored, as it was made at the beginning, nay, with greater grace. For, on rising from the dead, we shall no longer fear death, but shall ever reign in Christ in the heavens" (*Against the Arians*, Discourse 2, ch. 21).

Like so very many early writers, Athanasius regards perfection as an eminently-attainable goal. In addition, he is careful to distinguish between Christian perfection and human perfection. He also talks a little about Heavenly perfection.

"But since also certain [people] seemed to be contending together concerning the fleshly Economy of the Saviour, we enquired of both parties. And what the one confessed, the others also agreed to, that the Word did not, as it came to the prophets, so dwell in a holy man at the consummation of the ages, but that the Word Himself was made flesh, and being in the Form of God, took the form of a servant, and from Mary after the flesh became man for us, and that thus in Him the human race is perfectly and wholly delivered from sin and quickened from the dead, and given access to the kingdom of the heavens" (Synodal Letter to the People of Antioch).

He is writing here about a dispute that he helped mediate. Notice that both sides of the dispute agreed that complete deliverance from sin is possible. As we have seen, this was a wide-spread view in the early Church.

"The blessed Paul wrote to the Corinthians that he always bore in his body the dying of Jesus, not as though he alone should make that boast, but also they and we too, and in this let us be followers of him, my brethren. And let this be the customary boast of all of us at all times... Now this is becoming in us, especially in the days of the feast, when a commemoration of the death of our Saviour is held. For he who is made like Him in His death, is also diligent in virtuous practices, having mortified his members which are upon the earth, and crucifying the flesh with the affections and lusts, he lives in the Spirit, and is conformed to the Spirit. He is always mindful of God, and forgets Him not, and never does the deeds of death...

"But the saints, and they who truly practise virtue, 'mortify their members which are upon the earth, fornication, uncleanness, passions, evil concupiscence;' and, as the result of this, are pure and without spot, confiding in the promise of our Saviour, who said, 'Blessed are the pure in heart, for they shall see God.' These, having become dead to the world, and renounced the merchandise of the world, gain an honourable death; for, 'precious in the sight of the Lord is the death of His saints.' They are also able, pre-serving the Apostolic likeness, to say, 'I am crucified with Christ, nevertheless I live; yet not I, but Christ liveth in me.' For that is the true life, which a man lives in Christ; for although they are dead to the world, yet they dwell as it were in heaven, minding those things which are above, as he who was a lover of such a habitation said, 'While we walk on earth, our dwelling is in heaven.' Now those who thus live, and are partakers in such virtue, are alone able to give glory to God, and this it is which essentially constitutes a feast and a holiday" (Festal Letter 7, for A.D. 335).

"The variations of practice which had rendered the Paschal Feast a subject of contro-versy from very early times had given rise to the custom of the announcement of Easter at a convenient interval beforehand by circular letters. In the third century the Bishops of Alexandria issued such letters, and at the Council of Nicæa, where the Easter question was dealt with, the Alexandrian see was requested to undertake the duty of announcing the correct date to the principal foreign Churches as well as to its own suffragan sees" (*Nicene and Post-Nicene Fathers*, Series 2, vol. 4).

I would like to draw special attention to the end of the first paragraph: "He is always mindful of God, and forgets Him not, and never does the deeds of death." In other words, somebody who is properly mindful of Divine things does not sin, for only sin brings death.

"The might of man and of all creatures, is weak and poor; but the Might which is above man, and uncreated, is rich and incomprehensible, and has no beginning, but is eternal. He does not then possess one method only of healing, but being rich, He works in divers manners for our salvation by means of His Word, Who is not restricted or hindered in His dealings towards us; but since He is rich and manifold, He varies Himself according to the individual capacity of each soul... To those then who have not yet attained to the perfect way He becomes like a sheep giving milk, and this was administered by Paul: 'I have fed you with milk, not with meat.' To those who have advanced beyond the full stature of childhood, but still are weak as regards perfection, He is their food, according to their capacity, being again administered by Paul, 'Let him that is weak eat herbs.' But as soon as ever a man begins to walk in the perfect way, he is no longer fed with the things before mentioned, but he has the Word for bread, and flesh for food, for it is written, 'Strong meat is for those who are of full age, for those who, by reason of their capacity, have their senses exercised' " (Festal Letter 10, for A.D. 338).

He speaks of a definite progression towards Christian perfection. Furthermore, he regards such perfection as entirely possible here on earth.

* * * * *

Macarius of Egypt (300-391)

Egypt was the birthplace of monasticism, and Macarius was one of the first monks. He became renowned for his great wisdom and humility. There is a collection of sermons entitled *Fifty Spiritual Homilies* that is attributed to him. Some modern scholars believe that these were written significantly later than his time, but in my opinion there is sufficient evidence that the traditional view is correct. He may not have actually written them, but they are an accurate representation of what he said at various times.

Fifty Spiritual Homilies

"A man watches a bird flying, and wishes to fly himself, but he cannot, because he has no wings. Even so the will is present with a man to be pure, and blameless, and without spot, and to have no wickedness in him, but to be always with God; but he has not the power. To fly into the air of God and the liberty of the Holy Ghost may be his wish, but unless wings are given him, he cannot. Let us then beseech God to bestow upon us the wings of a dove, even of the Holy Ghost, that we may fly to Him and be at rest, and that He would separate and make to cease from our souls and bodies, that evil wind, which is the sin that dwelleth in the members of our souls and bodies. None but He can do it. Behold, it says, the Lamb of God, that taketh away the sin of the world. He alone has shewn this mercy to those men who believe Him, redeeming them from sin; and for those who are always waiting for Him, and hope, and seek without ceasing, He achieves this unutterable salvation" (Homily 2).

He talks clearly about living without sin. It is only the power of God in us that enables us to live above sin. We cannot do so outside of God.

"There are some who say thus—that the Lord requires of men only the fruits that

75

are visible, and that it is for God to rectify the things that are hidden. That is not the case. As a man secures himself with regard to the outer man, so ought he to carry on strife and war in his thoughts. The Lord requires of thee to be angry with thyself, and to do battle with thy mind, and neither to consent nor to take pleasure in the thoughts of wickedness.

"Nevertheless, to root out sin and the evil that is ever with us, this can only be accomplished by the divine power. It is not possible or within a man's competence to root out sin by his own power. To wrestle against it, to fight against it, to give and receive blows, is thine; to uproot is God's" (Homily 3).

We must earnestly desire to have the root of sin taken out; otherwise, God will not do it.

"Perfect Christians, who have been permitted to arrive at measures of perfection and to come very near the King, these are continually consecrated to the cross of Christ. As in the days of the prophets the unction was more precious than all things else, since unction made them kings and prophets, so now spiritual men, who are anointed with the heavenly unction, become Christs according to grace, so that they too are kings, and prophets of heavenly mysteries. These are sons, and lords, and gods, made prisoners and captives, plunged deep, crucified, consecrated. If the anointing of oil, which came from a material plant, a visible tree, had such force that those who were anointed received dignity beyond dispute—for it was a fixed rule, so that they were appointed kings; David, for instance, after being anointed, immediately fell into persecutions and was afflicted, and then after seven years became king—how much more do all who are anointed in mind and the inner man with the hallowing and cheering oil of gladness, the heavenly spiritual oil, receive the stamp of that kingdom of the imperishable and everlasting power, the earnest of the Spirit, the Holy Ghost the Comforter. He is called the Comforter, because He comforts and cheers those who are in afflictions.

"These, being anointed from the tree of life, Jesus Christ, the heavenly plant, are privileged to come to measures of perfection, the measures of the kingdom and the adoption, truly sharers of the secrets of the heavenly King, having free access to the Almighty, entering into His palace, where the angels and the spirits of the saints are, even while they are still in this world. Although they have not yet received the perfect inheritance prepared for them in that age, they are sure, from the earnest which they have now received, as if already crowned and reigning; and being about to reign with Christ, they are not surprised at the abundance and freedom of the Spirit. Why? Because while still in the flesh they had that relish of sweetness, and that effectual working of power" (Homily 17).

The language used in the first paragraph, when he says "become Christs," requires an explanation. He is not saying that "ye shall be as gods"; but rather that a Christian imbibes the nature of Christ (see II Peter 1:4). This sort of language was surprisingly common in the early days of the Church.

Macarius follows his predecessors in declaring that a Christian can be perfect here on earth.

"One who has found and has within him this heavenly treasure of the Spirit, effects thereby every righteousness of commandments and every accomplishment of virtues unblameably and purely, without forcing and with ease. Let us therefore beseech God, and seek and beg of Him, to bestow on us the treasure of His Spirit, and that thus we may be able to walk in all His commandments unblameably and purely, and to fulfil all the righteousness of the Spirit purely and perfectly, by means of the heavenly treasure, which is Christ...

"When the soul arrives at the perfection of the Spirit, perfectly cleansed from passion, and united and mingled with the Spirit Paraclete by that unspeakable communion, and is permitted to become spirit itself in mixture with the Spirit, then it is made all light, all eye, all spirit, all joy, all rest, all gladness, all love, all compassion, all goodness and loving-kindness. As in the bottom of the sea a stone is encompassed on every side by water, so these men, mingled in every way with the Spirit, are made like Christ, having in themselves the virtues of the power of the Spirit unalterably, being faultless and spotless and pure within and without" (Homily 18).

When we partake of the purity of God, we also partake of the power of God.

"If outwardly you keep your body from corruption and fornication, but inwardly commit adultery, to God you are an adulterer and a fornicator in your thoughts, and you have gained nothing by the virginity of your body. If there is a young woman and a young man, and he by guile wheedles her till she is corrupted, she then becomes an object of loathing to her spouse, because she has been unfaithful. So the incorporeal soul, if it holds fellowship with the serpent that lurks within, the wicked spirit, goes a-whoring from God, as it is written, Everyone that looketh upon a woman to lust after her hath committed adultery already in his heart. There is a fornication effected in the body, and there is a fornication of the soul, when it holds fellowship with Satan. The same soul is partner and sister either of devils, or of God and the angels; and if it commits adultery with the devil, it is unfit for the heavenly Bridegroom.

"As the Lord put on the body, leaving behind all principality and power, so Christians put on the Holy Ghost, and are at rest. Even if war comes outwardly, Satan may knock, but they are secured within by the power of the Lord, and do not mind Satan. He tempted the Lord in the wilderness forty days, and what harm did it do Him, to approach His body outwardly? Inwardly He was God. So Christians, though outwardly tempted, are inwardly filled with the Godhead, and are in nothing injured. But if any one has reached these measures, he has arrived at the perfect love of Christ, and at the fulness of the Godhead. One that is not so, has still war within. For an hour he is at rest in prayer; at

77

another hour he stands in affliction and at war. Such is the will of the Lord. Because he is still a child, He practises him in the wars; and both things spring up in him, light and darkness, rest and affliction. They rest in prayer, and at another hour they are in distress" (Homily 26).

He shows two classes of Christians here. When the unsanctified Christian is tempted, he must fight a two-front war: without, against Satan; and within, against the tuggings of the carnal nature that respond to the temptation. Jesus was perfectly pure within; we should follow His example. As Macarius mentions, Christian perfection is a stabilizing force.

"In the shadow of the law given by Moses God commanded that every man should rest on the sabbath and do nothing. This was a type and shadow of the true sabbath given to the soul from the Lord. For the soul to which it has been granted to be set free from base and foul thoughts both keeps true sabbath and enjoys true rest, being idle and at leisure so far as the works of darkness are concerned. There, in the typical sabbath, although they rested in bodily fashion, their souls were in bondage to wickednesses and sins. This, the true sabbath, is true rest, the soul being idle and cleansed from the suggestions of Satan, and resting in the eternal rest and joy of the Lord.

As then He enjoined that even the unreasoning animals should rest on the sabbath day, that the ox should not be forced under the yoke of necessity, and that they should not lade the ass—for the animals also were to rest from their heavy works—so when the Lord came and gave the true eternal sabbath, He gave rest to the soul which was burdened and heavy laden with the burdens of the iniquity of unclean imaginations, and labouring perforce at the works of unrighteousness, as being in bondage to bitter masters; and He lightened it of the burdens, hard to be borne, of vain and impure imaginations; and He took away the yoke, the bitter yoke, of the works of unrighteousness, and refreshed the soul when it was wearied with the imaginations of uncleanness.

"The Lord calls man to rest, saying, Come, all ye that labour and are heavy laden, and I will give you rest; and as many souls as are obedient and draw near, He makes them rest from all these heavy, burdensome, unclean thoughts, and they are idle from all iniquity, keeping a true, delicious, holy sabbath, and celebrate a festival of the Spirit, a festival of joy and gladness unspeakable; and they perform a pure service, well pleasing to God, out of a pure heart. This is the true and the holy sabbath. Let us therefore beseech God that we also may enter into this rest, that we may be idle from base and evil and vain imaginations, that thus we may be able to serve God out of a pure heart, and celebrate the feast of the Holy Ghost. Blessed is he who enters into that rest. Glory to Him whose good pleasure it is, Father, Son, and Holy Ghost, for ever. Amen" (Homily 35).

This is a beautiful description of the sanctified state. An unsanctified Christian who keeps falling back into sin on a regular basis can't possibly keep this Sabbath, at least not for any length of time.

"The Christian ought at all times to have God in remembrance; for it is written, Thou shalt love the Lord thy God with all thy heart; that he may love the Lord not only when he goes into the place of prayer, but that in walking, and talking, and eating, he may have the remembrance of God, and love and dutiful affection for Him. It says, Where thy mind is, there also is thy treasure. To whatever thing a man's heart is tied, and where his desire draws him, that is his God. If the heart at all times desires God, He is the Lord of his heart. But if a man after renouncing and making himself without possessions, and without home, and fasting—if this one is still tied to the man that he is, or to worldly affairs, or to house, or to the charm of parents, where his heart is tied and his mind is captive, that is his God, and he is found to have gone out of the world by the front door, but to have entered and thrown himself into the world by the side door.

"As sticks thrown into the fire cannot resist the power of the fire, but are forthwith burned up, so the devils desiring to fight with a man to whom the Spirit has been vouchsafed are burned and consumed by the divine power of the fire, if only the man is at all times cleaving to the Lord, and keeping his trust and his hope towards Him. And even if the devils are strong as strong mountains, they are burned by prayer, like wax by fire. But meantime great is the struggle and the battle against them which awaits the soul. There are rivers of dragons, and mouths of lions. There is fire which flames into the soul. As the perfect evildoer, drunk with the spirit of error, is insatiable to evil, either murdering, or committing adultery, so Christians, when they have been baptized into the Holy Spirit, are without experience of evil; but those who have grace, but are still mingled with sin, these are subject to fear, and travel through fearful places. For as merchants on a voyage, though they find a wind to suit them and the sea calm, but have not yet reached the haven, are always subject to fear, lest suddenly a contrary wind should stir and the sea rise into billows, and the ship be in peril, so Christians, even if they have in themselves a favourable wind of the Holy Spirit blowing, are nevertheless yet subject to fear, lest the wind of the adverse power should rise and blow on them, and stir disturbance and billows for their souls. There is need therefore of great diligence, that we may arrive at the haven of rest, at the perfect world, at the eternal life and pleasure, at the city of the saints, at the heavenly Jerusalem, at the church of the firstborn. Unless a man gets through these measures, he is under much fear, lest in the meantime the evil power should effect some fall.

"As a woman who has conceived carries her babe within in the dark, so to speak, and in covert; but if by and by the child comes forth at the proper time, it sees a new creation, which it never saw before, of sky and earth and sun, and immediately friends and kinsfolk with cheerful countenances receive it into their arms; but if through some derangement it happens that the child is displaced, then the surgeons whose business it is are obliged to use the knife, and the child is thus found to pass from death to death, from darkness to darkness—so think of what happens in the spiritual world. As many as have received the seed of the Godhead, these have it invisibly, and because of sin which dwells there also they conceal it in dark and obscure places. If therefore they make themselves sure, and preserve the seed, these in due time are visibly born again, and then at the dissolution of the body the angels and all the companies above receive them with cheerful countenances. But if after receiving the weapons of Christ to fight manfully a man grows slack, such a one is immediately delivered over to the enemies, and at the dissolution of the body passes from the darkness which now encompasses him to another and a worse darkness, and to perdition" (Homily 43).

Perfect love is a powerful weapon in our fight against the Devil. It casts out fear, and double-mindedness. He talks about the importance of renouncing the world. In the second paragraph, he mentions the two classes of Christians—those that are perfect, and then those that are still carnal.

"He that has chosen the solitary life ought to consider all things that are concerned with this world as alien and strange to himself. One who in truth pursues the cross of Christ, denying all things, yea, and his own life also, ought to have his mind nailed to the love of Christ, esteeming the Lord before parents, brethren, wife, children, kindred, friends, possessions. This Christ set forth, when He said, 'Every one that hath not left father, or mother, or brethren, or wife, or children, or lands, and followeth Me, is not worthy of Me.' In nothing else is salvation and peace found for men, as we have been told" (Homily 45).

There were still many pagan influences in society at this time. This was partly the impetus for the monastic movement. Society was so terribly wicked in those days that many Christians desired to remove themselves from it, not only metaphorically, but also physically. Today we know better. We cannot function as salt and light if we cut off all contact with the world. Nevertheless, the life of a Christian is in many ways a solitary one, and there are many things in society that we cannot participate in. We must be willing to give up everything for God. The choice to abandon our claim on any possession or person is an essential step to reach Christian perfection.

* * * * *

Constitutions of the Twelve Apostles (or, *Apostolic Constitutions*)

This is a collection of eight writings, or books, loosely based on the *Didache*. The compiler is unknown, but it was apparently written in Syria. Like the *Didache*, it purports to be written by the apostles themselves. We don't know for sure when it was written; the first six books are somewhat older than the final two. It is essentially a church manual, touching on points of public worship, instruction of new converts, Christian morality, and so forth. It was compiled into its final form somewhere around 375-380, although parts of it are likely a century or more older than that.

"Let examination also be made whether he be unblameable as to the concerns of this life; for it is written: 'Search diligently for all the faults of him who is to be ordained for the priesthood' " (Book 2, sec. 1).

This is from a section regarding candidates for bishop. Even more so than average Christians, church leaders should live above sin.

"On which account let him [a bishop] also be void of anger; for Wisdom says: 'Anger destroys even the prudent.' Let him also be merciful, of a generous and loving temper; for our Lord says: 'By this shall all men know that ye are my disciples, if ye love one another.' Let him be also ready to give, a lover of the widow and the stranger; ready to serve, and minister, and attend; resolute in his duty; and let him know who is the most worthy of his assistance" (Book 2, sec. 2).

It continues describing how leaders should behave. Giving in to sin is a "luxury" that a church leader cannot afford without serious risk of damaging his influence, and harming the cause of God.

"Beloved, be it known to you that those who are baptized into the death of our Lord Jesus are obliged to go on no longer in sin; for as those who are dead cannot work wickedness any longer, so those who are dead with Christ cannot practice wickedness. We do not therefore believe, brethren, that any one who has received the washing of life continues in the practice of the licentious acts of transgressors. Now he who sins after his baptism, unless he repent and forsake his sins, shall be condemned to hell-fire...

"But if the offender sees that the bishop and deacons are innocent and unblameable, and the flock pure, he will either not venture to despise their authority, and to enter into the Church of God at all, as one smitten by his own conscience: or if he values nothing, and ventures to enter in, either he will be convicted immediately, as Uzza at the ark, when he touched it to support it; and as Achan, when he stole the accursed thing; and as Gehazi, when he coveted the money of Naaman, and so will be immediately punished: or else he will be admonished by the pastor, and drawn to repentance. For when he looks round the whole Church one by one, and can spy no blemish, neither in the bishop nor in the people who are under his care, he will be put to confusion, and pricked at the heart, and in a peaceable manner will go his way with shame and many tears, and the flock will remain pure. He will apply himself to God with tears, and will repent of his sins, and have hope. Nay, the whole flock, at the sight of his tears, will be instructed, because a sinner avoids destruction by repentance" (Book 2, sec. 3).

Here we see that it is not only possible to live a sinless life, but it is a duty. If we fail in that duty, it is imperative that we repent if we wish to regain our blameless standing before God, and thus be fit to enter Heaven. The advantages of living a sinless life are not ours alone, but they extend to people around us; we can testify by our mode of life to the power and purity of God.

"But he that denies himself to be a Christian, that he may not be hated of men, and so loves his own life more than he does the Lord, in whose hand his breath is, is wretched and miserable, as being detestable and abominable, who desires to be the friend of men, but is the enemy of God, having no longer his portion with the saints, but with those that are accursed; choosing instead of the kingdom of the blessed, that eternal fire which is prepared for the devil and his angels: not being any longer hated by men, but rejected by God, and cast out from His presence. For of such a one our Lord declared, saying: 'Whosoever shall deny me before men, and shall be ashamed of my name, I also will deny and be ashamed of him before my Father which is in heaven.'...

"Every one therefore who learns any art, when he sees his master by his diligence and skill perfecting his art, does himself earnestly endeavour to make what he takes in hand like to it. If he is not able, he is not perfected in his work. We therefore who have a Master, our Lord Jesus Christ, why do we not follow His doctrine?—since He renounced repose, pleasure, glory, riches, pride, the power of revenge, His mother and brethren, nay, and moreover His own life, on account of His piety towards His Father, and His love to us the race of mankind; and suffered not only persecution and stripes, reproach and mockery, but also crucifixion, that He might save the penitent, both Jews and Gentiles. If therefore He for our sakes renounced His repose, was not ashamed of the cross, and did not esteem death inglorious, why do not we imitate His sufferings, and renounce on His account even our own life, with that patience which He gives us? For He did all for our sakes, but we do it for our own sakes: for He does not stand in need of us, but we stand in need of His mercy... Let us therefore renounce our parents, and kinsmen, and friends, and wife, and children, and possessions, and all the enjoyments of life, when any of these things become an impediment to piety. For we ought to pray that we may not enter into temptation; but if we be called to martyrdom, with constancy to confess His precious name, and if on this account we be punished, let us rejoice, as hastening to immortality. When we are persecuted, let us not think it strange; let us not love the present world, nor the praises which come from men, nor the glory and honour of rulers, according as some of the Jews wondered at the mighty works of our Lord, yet did not believe on Him, for fear of the high priests and the rest of the rulers: 'For they loved the praise of men more than the praise of God.' But now, by confessing a good confession, we not only save ourselves, but we confirm those who are newly illuminated, and strengthen the faith of the catechumens. But if we remit any part of our confession, and deny godliness by the faintness of our persuasion, and the fear of a very short punishment, we not only deprive ourselves of everlasting glory, but we shall also become the causes of the perdition of others; and shall suffer double punishment, as affording suspicion, by our denial that that truth which we gloried in so much before is an erroneous doctrine" (Book 5, sec. 1).

We know that Jesus was given to us for an example. But I am convinced that for many Christians, this fact is more theoretical than real—they have never stopped to really consider what it means. Jesus was tempted with rewards for wrong-doing; He was tempted to turn aside from God's will by the threat of horrible suffering; yet He never strayed from the path of righteousness.

"Thou shalt hate all hypocrisy; and whatsoever is pleasing to the Lord, that shalt thou do. By no means forsake the commands of the Lord. But thou shalt observe what things thou hast received from Him, neither adding to them nor taking away from them. 'For thou shalt not add unto His words, lest He convict thee, and thou becomest a liar.' Thou shalt confess thy sins unto the Lord thy God; and thou shalt not add unto them, that it may be well with thee from the Lord thy God, who willeth not the death of a sinner, but his repentance" (Book 7, sec. 1).

The way of God is truly a narrow way. To either add to or take away from God's Word leads to damnation. It is possible to misunderstand certain parts of God's Word, and still get to Heaven, as long as we truly love God. But dying with unforgiven sin in our lives will not get us to Heaven, and it is dangerous to live with unforgiven sin, for life is not guaranteed to us. If we do fall into sin, and do not repent immediately, we might never get the chance. Notice what this quote says about not adding to our sins after they have been forgiven.

* * * * *

Gregory of Nyssa (335-395)

Gregory was born in Cappadocia (now central Turkey). He grew up in a Christian family. His grandmother, mother, one of his brothers, and one of his sisters all influenced him deeply in his walk with God. For a while he was a professor of rhetoric; he became Bishop of Nyssa in 372. He was instrumental in the Council of Constantinople in 381, which finalized the Nicene Creed, and marked the final vanquishment of the Arian party. The Council of Nicea was predominantly concerned with the Divinity of Jesus, and barely mentioned the Holy Ghost. The Council of Constantinople corrected that oversight.

On Virginity

"Deep indeed will be the thought necessary to understand the surpassing excellence of this grace. It is comprehended in the idea of the Father incorrupt; and here at the outset is a paradox, viz. that virginity is found in Him, Who has a Son and yet without passion has begotten Him. It is included too in the nature of this Only-begotten God, Who struck the first note of all this moral innocence; it shines forth equally in His pure and passionless generation. Again a paradox; that the Son should be known to us by virginity. It is seen, too, in the inherent and incorruptible purity of the Holy Spirit; for when you have named the pure and incorruptible you have named virginity. It accompanies the whole supramundane existence; because of its passionlessness it is always

83

present with the powers above; never separated from aught that is Divine, it never touches the opposite of this. All whose instinct and will have found their level in virtue are beautified with this perfect purity of the uncorrupted state; all who are ranked in the opposite class of character are what they are, and are called so, by reason of their fall from purity... It is possible to be ever mindful of this gift of God; and our lips may always speak of this blessing; that, though it is the property of spiritual existence and of such singular excellence, yet by the love of God it has been bestowed on those who have received their life from the will of the flesh and from blood; that, when human nature has been based by passionate inclinations, it stretches out its offer of purity like a hand to raise it up again and make it look above. This, I think, was the reason why our Master, Jesus Christ Himself, the Fountain of all innocence, did not come into the world by wedlock. It was, to divulge by the manner of His Incarnation this great secret; that purity is the only complete indication of the presence of God and of His coming, and that no one can in reality secure this for himself, unless he has altogether estranged himself from the passions of the flesh" (ch. 2).

In this book, he uses physical virginity as a symbol for spiritual virginity and purity. Entire sanctification is the best and most efficient way of getting greater measures of purity. God has commanded us to live pure and holy lives: it is our duty to obey, by any means necessary.

"But if we apprehend at last the perfection of this grace, we must understand as well what necessarily follows from it; namely that it is not a single achievement, ending in the subjugation of the body, but that in intention it reaches to and pervades everything that is, or is considered, a right condition of the soul. That soul indeed which in virginity cleaves to the true Bridegroom will not remove herself merely from all bodily defilement; she will make that abstension only the beginning of her purity, and will carry this security from failure equally into everything else upon her path. Fearing lest, from a too partial heart, she should by contact with evil in any one direction give occasion for the least weakness of unfaithfulness (to suppose such a case: but I will begin again what I was going to say), that soul which cleaves to her Master so as to become with Him one spirit, and by the compact of a wedded life has staked the love of all her heart and all her strength on Him alone—that soul will no more commit any other of the offences contrary to salvation, than imperil her union with Him by cleaving to fornication; she knows that between all sins there is a single kinship of impurity, and that if she were to defile herself with but one, she could no longer retain her spotlessness. An illustration will show what we mean. Suppose all the water in a pool remaining smooth and motionless, while no disturbance of any kind comes to mar the peacefulness of the spot; and then a stone thrown into the pool; the movement in that one part will extend to the whole, and while the stone's weight is carrying it to the bottom, the waves that are set in motion round it pass in circles into others, and so through all the intervening commotion are pushed on to the very edge of the water, and the whole surface is ruffled with these circles, feeling the movement of the depths. So is the broad serenity and calm of the soul troubled by one invading passion, and affected by the injury of a single part" (ch. 14).

The smallest sin, if left unforgiven, is big enough to keep us out of Heaven. Notice here how being without spot is the same as being without sin. Notice, too, that he views true purity as a "security from failure." It is always possible to sin after being sanctified, but sanctification makes sinning much less likely.

"Let that which was then said by our Lord be the general maxim for every life; especially let it be the maxim for those who are coming nearer God through the gateway of virginity, that they should never in watching for a perfection in one direction present an unguarded side in another and contrary one; but should in all directions realize the good, so that they may guarantee in all things their holy life against failure. A soldier does not arm himself only on some points, leaving the rest of his body to take its chance unprotected. If he were to receive his death-wound upon that, what would have been the advantage of this partial armour? Again, who would call that feature faultless, which from some accident had lost one of those requisites which go to make up the sum of beauty? The disfigurement of the mutilated part mars the grace of the part untouched. The Gospel implies that he who undertakes the building of a tower, but spends all his labour upon the foundations without ever reaching the completion, is worthy of ridicule; and what else do we learn from the Parable of the Tower, but to strive to come to the finish of every lofty purpose, accomplishing the work of God in all the multiform structures of His commandments? One stone, indeed, is no more the whole edifice of the Tower, than one commandment kept will raise the soul's perfection to the required height" (ch. 17).

The unsanctified Christian may have large protective walls surrounding his heart, but he allows the enemy to retain possession of part of the inner citadel. We see here that Christian perfection consists in keeping **all** of God's commands. One of those commands is that we live a holy life unspotted by sin.

"The master of a private dwelling will not allow any untidiness or unseemliness to be seen in the house, such as a couch upset, or the table littered with rubbish, or vessels of price thrown away into dirty corners, while those which serve ignobler uses are thrust forward for entering guests to see. He has everything arranged neatly and in the proper place, where it stands to most advantage; and then he can welcome his guests, without any misgivings that he need be ashamed of opening the interior of his house to receive them. The same duty, I take it, is incumbent on that master of our 'tabernacle,' the mind; it has to arrange everything within us, and to put each particular faculty of the soul, which the Creator has fashioned to be our implement or our vessel, to fitting and noble uses... Righteousness will be our rule of straightforwardness, guarding us from stumbling either in word or deed, and guiding us in the disposal of the faculties of our soul, as well as in the due consideration for every one we meet... But I must return here to what I said at first; that the perfection of this liberty does not consist only in that one point of abstaining from marriage. Let no one suppose that the prize of virginity is so insignificant and so easily won as that; as if one little observance of the flesh could settle so vital a matter. But we have seen that every man who doeth a sin is the servant of sin; so that a declension towards vice in any act, or in any practice whatever, makes a slave, and still more, a branded slave, of the man, covering him through sin's lashes with bruises and seared spots. Therefore it behoves the man who grasps at the transcend-ent aim of all virginity to be true to himself in every respect, and to manifest his purity equally in every relation of his life. If any of the inspired words are required to aid our pleading, the Truth Itself will be sufficient to corroborate the truth when It inculcates this very kind of teaching in the veiled meaning of a Gospel Parable [Matt. 13:47]: the good and eatable fish are separated by the fishers' skill from the bad and poisonous fish, so that the enjoyment of the good should not be spoilt by any of the bad getting into the 'vessels' with them. The work of true sobriety is the same; from all pursuits and habits to choose that which is pure and improving, rejecting in every case that which does not seem likely to be useful, and letting it go back into the universal and secular life, called 'the sea,' in the imagery of the Parable" (ch. 18).

The Bible is very clear that a person can serve only one master at a time. If our mas-ter is God, then it behooves us to pay attention to all His commands, including the ones to be pure and holy.

"When the Lord invites the blest to their inheritance in the kingdom of heaven, He does not include a pilgrimage to Jerusalem amongst their good deeds; when He an-nounces the Beatitudes, He does not name amongst them that sort of devotion. But as to that which neither makes us blessed nor sets us in the path to the kingdom, for what reason it should be run after, let him that is wise consider. Even if there were some profit in what they do, yet even so, those who are perfect would do best not to be eager in practising it; but since this matter, when closely looked into, is found to inflict upon those who have begun to lead the stricter life a moral mischief, it is so far from being worth an earnest pursuit, that it actually requires the greatest caution to prevent him who has devoted himself to God from being penetrated by any of its hurtful influences" (*On Pilgrimages*).

Notice that he speaks of those who have attained Christian perfection in this life. The closer a person walks to God, the more careful he is that everything in his life should be pleasing to God.

"As they who wash clothes do not pass over some of the dirt and cleanse the rest, but clear the whole cloth from all its stains, from one end to the other, that the cloak by being uniformly brightened from washing may be throughout equal to its own standard of cleanness, in like manner, since the life of man was defiled by sin, in its beginning, end, and all its intermediate states, there needed an abstergent force to penetrate the whole, and not to mend some one part by cleansing, while it left another unattended to" (*The Great Catechism*, ch. 27).

Opponents of the second work don't seem to understand this principle. They claim that there's no such thing as being perfectly cleansed from sin.

"But, as far as what has been already said, the instruction of this Catechism does not seem to me to be yet complete. For we ought, in my opinion, to take into consideration the sequel of this matter; which many of those who come to the grace of baptism overlook, being led astray, and self-deceived, and indeed only seemingly, and not really, regenerate. For that change in our life which takes place through regeneration will not be change, if we continue in the state in which we were... It is evident that when those evil features which mark our nature have been obliterated a change to a better state takes place. If, then, by being 'washed,' as says the Prophet, in that mystic bath we become 'clean' in our wills and 'put away the evil' of our souls, we thus become better men, and are changed to a better state. But if, when the bath has been applied to the body, the soul has not cleansed itself from the stains of its passions and affections, but the life after initiation keeps on a level with the uninitiate life, then, though it may be a bold thing to say, yet I will say it and will not shrink; in these cases the water is but water, for the gift of the Holy Ghost in no ways appears in him who is thus baptismally born; whenever, that is, not only the deformity of anger, or the passion of greed, or the unbridled and unseemly thought, with pride, envy, and arrogance, disfigures the Divine image, but the gains, too, of injustice abide with him, and the woman he has procured by adultery still even after that ministers to his pleasures. If these and the like vices, after, as before, surround the life of the baptized, I cannot see in what respects he has been changed; for I observe him the same man as he was before... Now the child born of any one is entirely of a kindred nature with his parent. If, then, you have received God, if you have become a child of God, make manifest in your disposition the God that is in you, manifest in yourself Him that begot you. By the same marks whereby we recognize God, must this relationship to God of the son so born be exhibited... If you live amidst such things as these, you are a child of God indeed; but if you continue with the characteristic marks of vice in you, it is in vain that you babble to yourself of your birth from above" (*The Great Catechism*, ch. 40).

Note: he is clear elsewhere that baptism is symbolic.

Opponents of Holiness doctrine insist that we have no choice but to continue on after salvation still retaining the "characteristic marks of vice," although possibly to a lesser degree than before. But we see that Gregory questions the salvation of any person whose life does not show a complete change.

*****

John Chrysostom (347-407)

Chrysostom ("Golden-mouthed") posthumously received his popular name because of his eloquence. He was born in Antioch, and started his career as a preacher in that city. In 397, he was called to become Bishop of Constantinople, a position which he accepted with considerable reluctance. Eudoxia, the Empress, quickly became an enemy, because of his fervent preaching against worldliness and extravagance. This enmity eventually lead to his banishment from Constantinople in 404. During the last few years of his life, he wrote many influential letters to the people of Constantinople. Chrysostom is one of the earliest people who has a large body of surviving work; there were others before him who wrote prolifically, but many of their writings have been lost. He did not actually write his sermons, however; they were written down by people who heard him. The following quotes, although many, are only a tiny sampling of his work.

"For the priestly office is indeed discharged on earth, but it ranks amongst heavenly ordinances; and very naturally so: for neither man, nor angel, nor archangel, nor any other created power, but the Paraclete Himself, instituted this vocation, and persuaded men while still abiding in the flesh to represent the ministry of angels. Wherefore the consecrated priest ought to be as pure as if he were standing in the heavens themselves in the midst of those powers" (*Treatise Concerning the Christian Priesthood*, Book 3, sec. 4).

This is a very high standard, but one that Jesus met while on earth. We are citizens of Heaven; we should act like it.

Instructions to Catechumens

"This is not the time for you to hear words about repentance, rather may the time never come for you to fall into the need of these remedies, but may you always remain in preservation of the beauty and the brightness which ye are now about to receive, unsullied. In order, then, that ye may ever remain thus, come and let us discourse to you a little about your manner of life" (First Instruction, sec. 4).

This book was for new converts, while they were under instruction and probation before being baptised. He goes on to talk about watching what we say, etc. Satan wants to make us forget that we will have to give account to God for everything, no matter how small. Notice his desire that the new converts would lead a sinless life, and thereby would not find themselves in need of repentance.

"For not because of the carelessness of thy fellow servants, but from the injunctions of his own laws, will God record his vote against thee. I have commanded, he says, thou oughtest to obey, not to shelter thyself behind such and such a person and concern thyself with other persons' evil. Since the great David sinned a grievous sin, is it then safe for us to sin?" (First Instruction, sec. 5).

Opponents of the second work make this mistake of sheltering behind others' sins. They use the failure of others to fully obey God not only as an excuse why they should not have to fully obey God, but also as an excuse why they *can't* fully obey.

"In order, therefore, that we return not to our former vomit, let us henceforward discipline ourselves. For that we must repent beforehand, and desist from our former evil, and so come forward for grace, hear what John says, and what the leader of the apostles says to those who are about to be baptized. For the one says, 'Bring forth fruit worthy of repentance, and begin not to say within yourselves, we have Abraham to our Father;' and the other says again to those who question him, 'Repent ye and be baptized every one of you in the name of the Lord Jesus Christ.' Now he who repents, no longer touches the same matters of which he repented. On this account, also, we are bidden to say, 'I renounce thee, Satan,' in order that we may never more return to him" (Second Instruction, sec. 3).

We must turn away from sin before salvation can come. This is what repentance means. Someone who is not willing to do this is not sorry for his sin, but merely sorry for being caught. Repentance should be permanent, and not need to be repeated.

"When thou goest forth, then, beware of one thing—that sin does not meet thee. For this it is which trips us up. And without this the devil will be able to do us no harm" (Second Instruction, sec. 5).

It is not temptation in and of itself that we must fear, for mere temptation cannot possibly harm us. Only the yielding to temptation can harm us.

Homilies addressed to the people of Antioch
"This certainly I foretell and testify, that although this cloud [of their trouble] should pass away, and we yet remain in the same condition of listlessness, we shall again have to suffer much heavier evils than those we are now dreading; for I do not so much fear the wrath of the Emperor, as your own listlessness. Surely it is not sufficient by way of apology that we supplicate two or three days, but it is necessary that we should make a change in our whole life, and that whilst abstaining from wickedness we should persevere continually in virtue. For as those who are sickly, unless they keep up a constant regimen, would find no advantage by their observing a two or three days' discipline; so those who are in sin, if they do not exercise sobriety at all times, will find no benefit in two or three days' amendment. For as it is said, that he who is washed, and is again afterwards polluted with the mire, hath gained nothing; so he who has repented for three days, and has again returned to his former state, has accomplished nothing" (Homily 3).

Only faithfulness and perseverance to the end will accomplish the goal; anything else falls short of the mark, and will not get us to Heaven. It's astonishing to me that so many Christians believe that they are destined to return to the mire time and time again.

"For think what a good practice this would be, having dismissed all other matters public or private, to discourse only of the divine laws continually, at the table, in the forum, and in your other meetings. Would we give our attention to these things, we should say nothing of a dangerous or injurious nature, nor should we sin unwittingly" (Homily 6).

Christians would see a great many of their troubles disappear if they sought God's presence moment by moment. The continual spirit of prayer is a great help and benefit to a person. If people followed the advice given here, it would be very difficult to sin.

"For if we would look to this, that we might not merely correct ourselves, but also bring others to the same point, we shall ourselves quickly arrive at the goal; since while we undertake to instruct others, we shall be ashamed and blush, should we in our own case seem to leave those things unperformed, which we enjoin upon them. There is no need to say more; for much has been already spoken on these matters; and these things are now said only by way of remembrance. But may God, who is more sparing of our souls than we are, make us perfect in this, and every good work; that so having completed the whole fruit of righteousness, we may be found worthy of the kingdom of heaven" (Homily 9).

He does not regard Christian perfection as some far-off thing, but as a state that can be reached here on earth.

"On every side then let us search closely into these matters. Often has a wife, often have children, often have friends, often have neighbours, proved a snare to the unheeding! And why, it is asked, are there so many snares? That we may not fly low, but seek the things that are above. For just as birds, as long as they cleave the upper air, are not easily caught; so also thou, as long as thou lookest to things above, wilt not be easily captured, whether by a snare, or by any other device. The devil is a fowler. Soar, then, too high for his arrows. The man who hath mounted aloft will no longer admire any thing in the affairs of this life. But as when we have ascended to the top of the mountains, the city and its walls seem to us to be but small, and the men appear to us to be going along upon the earth like ants; so when thou hast ascended to the heights of spiritual wisdom, nothing upon the earth will be able to fascinate thee; but every thing, yea even riches, and glory, and honour, and whatever else there be of that kind, will appear insignificant when thou regardest heavenly things...

"Let us obey then, and let us think of this continually, that even as to the bird caught in the snare, wings are of no service, but he beats them about vainly, and to no purpose; so also to thee there is no utility in thy reasonings, when once thou art powerfully captivated by wicked lust, but struggle as much as thou mayest, thou art captured! For this reason wings are given to birds; that they may avoid snares. For this reason men have the power of thinking; that they may avoid sin. What pardon then, or what excuse will be ours, when we become more senseless than the brutes? For the bird which has once been captured by the snare, yet afterwards escaped, and the deer which has fallen into the net, but has broken through it, are hard to be captured again with the like; since experience becomes a teacher of caution to every one. But we, though often snared in the same nets, fall into the same again; and though honoured with reason, we do not imitate the forethought and care of the irrational animals!...

"Therefore, let us not only avoid sins, but those things too which seem to be indifferent, yet by degrees lead us into these misdeeds. He, indeed, who walks by the side of a precipice, even though he may not fall over, trembles; and very often he is overset by this same trembling, and falls to the bottom. So also he who does not avoid sins from afar, but walks near them, will live in fear, and will often fall into them" (Homily 15).

He is not exactly flattering here to opponents of the second work. But rather than getting upset, I hope that this will cause some to stop and really think.

Part of being made in God's image is the ability to reason. But someone who falls into sin over and over again is not using what God has given him.

"There is nothing whatever that will be able to afflict one who is well ordered in mind, and careful about his own soul; but he will enjoy a pure and continued pleasure. And that this is true ye have to-day heard from Paul, who exhorts us, saying, 'Rejoice in the Lord always, and again I say, rejoice.' I know indeed that to many this saying seems impossible. 'For how is it possible,' says some one, 'that he who is but a man, can continually rejoice? To rejoice is no hard matter, but to rejoice continually, this seems to me to be impossible.' For many are the causes of sadness, which surround us on all sides. A man has lost either a son, or a wife, or a beloved friend, more necessary to him than all kindred; or he has to sustain the loss of wealth; or he has fallen into sickness; or he has to bear some other change of fortune; or to grieve for contemptuous treatment which he did not deserve; or famine, or pestilence, or some intolerable exaction, or circumstances in his family trouble him;—nay, there is no saying how many circumstances of a public or private nature are accustomed to occasion us grief. How then, he may say, is it possible to 'rejoice always?' Yea, O man! it is possible; and if it were not so, Paul would not have given the exhortation; nor would a man endowed with spiritual wisdom have offered such counsel" (Homily 18).

There are some commands in the Bible that are impossible, or at least extremely difficult, to obey without being sanctified. This is one of them. If this command seems impossible, you may take it as proof that you are not living close enough to God.

Homilies on Matthew
"Forasmuch then as we have partaken of so great a gift [of salvation], let us do everything not to dishonor such a benefit. For if even before this honor, what was done

was worthy of punishment, much more now, after this unspeakable benefit. And this I say not now for no cause, but because I see many after their baptism living more carelessly than the uninitiated, and having nothing peculiar to distinguish them in their way of life... Whereas they ought to be distinguished not by their place, but by their way of life. For as men's outward dignities are naturally to be discovered by the outward signs with which they are invested, so ours ought to be discernible by the soul. That is, the believer ought to be manifest not by the gift only, but also by the new life. The believer ought to be the light and salt of the world... Yea, the believer ought to shine forth not only by what he hath received from God, but also by what he himself hath contributed; and should be discernible by everything, by his gait, by his look, by his garb, by his voice. And this I have said, not that display, but that the profit of beholders, may be the rule by which we frame ourselves" (Homily on Matt. 1:17).

A profession of faith is worthless unless it is accompanied by the fruits of the Spirit. A Christian's whole life should show that he is not of this world. As a rule, Holiness people are much more careful about this than non-Holiness people.

"Do thou show forth a life worthy of the love of Him who calls thee, and of thy citizenship in that world, and of the honor that is given thee. Crucified as thou art to the world, and having crucified it to thyself, show thyself with all strictness a citizen of the city of the heavens. And do not, because thy body is not translated unto heaven, suppose that thou hast anything to do with the earth; for thou hast thy Head abiding above. Yea with this very purpose the Lord, having first come here and having brought His angels, did then, taking thee with Him, depart thither; that even before thy going up to that place, thou mightest understand that it is possible for thee to inhabit earth as it were heaven.

"Let us then keep watch over that noble birth, which we received from the beginning; and let us every day seek more and more the palaces there, and account all that is here to be a shadow and a dream...

"Now then, having to partake of such blessings, do I see thee minding money, and clinging to the pomp which is here? And dost thou not esteem all that is seen to be more vile than beggars rags? And how wilt thou appear worthy of this honor? And what excuse wilt thou have to plead? or rather, what punishment wilt thou not have to suffer, who after so great a gift art running to thy former vomit? For no longer art thou punished merely as a man, but as a son of God that hath sinned; and the greatness of thy honor becomes a means of bringing a sorer punishment on thee...

"For if he [Adam] who had paradise for his portion, for one disobedience underwent such dreadful things after his honor; we, who have received Heaven, and are become joint heirs with the Only Begotten, what excuse shall we have, for running to the serpent after the dove? For it will be no longer, 'Dust thou art, and unto dust shalt thou return,' and thou 'tillest the ground,' and those former words, that will be said to us; but what is far more grievous than these, the 'outer darkness,' the bonds that may not be burst, the venomous worm, the 'gnashing of teeth;' and this with great reason. For he that is not made better even by so great a benefit, would justly suffer the most extreme, and a yet more grievous punishment" (Homily on Matt 3:13).

The more knowledge of God we have, the greater is our responsibility.

It is often possible to tell when somebody is from another country, by means of accent, dress, mannerisms, etc. If we are truly citizens of Heaven, that fact will show in our lives.

"For since the law was laboring at this, to make man righteous, but had not power, He came and brought in the way of righteousness by faith, and so established that which the law desired: and what the law could not by letters, this He accomplished by faith. On this account He saith, 'I am not come to destroy the law.'

"But if any one will inquire accurately, he will find also another, a third sense, in which this hath been done. Of what sort is it then? In the sense of that future code of laws, which He was about to deliver to them.

"For His sayings were no repeal of the former, but a drawing out, and filling up of them. Thus, 'not to kill,' is not annulled by the saying, Be not angry, but rather is filled up and put in greater security: and so of all the others...

" 'Whosoever therefore shall break one of these least commandments, and shall teach men so, he shall be called least in the kingdom of Heaven.'...

"For what cause then doth He call these commandments 'least,' though they were so great and high? Because He Himself was about to introduce the enactment of them; for as He humbled Himself, and speaks of Himself frequently with measure, so likewise of His own enactments, hereby again teaching us to be modest in everything. And besides, since there seemed to be some suspicion of novelty, He ordered His discourse for a while with reserve.

"But when thou hearest, 'least in the kingdom of Heaven,' surmise thou nothing but hell and torments. For He was used to mean by 'the kingdom,' not merely the enjoy-ment thereof, but also the time of the resurrection, and that awful coming. And how could it be reasonable, that while he who called his brother fool, and trangressed but one commandment, falls into hell; the breaker of them all, and instigator of others to the same, should be within the kingdom. This therefore is not what He means, but that such a one will be at that time least, that is, cast out, last. And he that is last will surely then fall into hell. For, being God, He foreknew the laxity of the many, He foreknew that some would think these sayings were merely hyperbolical, and would argue about the laws, and say, What, if any one call another a fool, is he punished? If one merely look on a woman, doth he become an adulterer? For this very cause He, destroying such insolence beforehand, hath set down the strongest denunciation against either sort, as well them who transgress, as them who lead on others so to do.

"Knowing then His threat as we do, let us neither ourselves transgress, nor discourage such as are disposed to keep these things" (Homily on Matt 5:17).

The Mosaic law is a mere trifle, so to speak, compared with the moral law. If we do not obey God in every point, to the best of our ability, we will most assuredly go to Hell.

Homilies on Romans

"What does 'Let us have peace [with God]' mean? Some say, 'Let us not be at variance, through a peevish obstinacy for bringing in the Law.' But to me he seems to be speaking now of our conversation. For after having said much on the subject of faith, he had set it before righteousness which is by works, to prevent any one from supposing what he said was a ground for listlessness, he says, 'let us have peace,' that is, let us sin no more, nor go back to our former estate. For this is making war with God. And 'how is it possible,' saith one, 'to sin no more?' How was the former thing possible? For if when liable for so many sins we were freed from all by Christ, much more shall we be able through Him to abide in the estate wherein we are. For it is not the same thing to receive peace when there had been none, and to keep it when it has been given, since to acquire surely is harder than to keep. Yet nevertheless the more difficult hath been made easy, and carried out into effect. That which is the easier thing then will be what we shall easily succeed in, if we cling to Him who hath wrought even the other for us. But here it is not the easiness only which he seems to me to hint at, but the reasonableness. For if He reconciled us when we were in open war with Him, it is reasonable that we should abide in a state of reconciliation, and give unto Him this reward for that He may not seem to have reconciled untoward and unfeeling creatures to the Father" (Homily on Romans 4:23).

The power of God is enough not only to cleanse our previous sins, but also to keep us from falling back into sin. Our opponents don't seem to understand this.

"Since then he showed the greatness of the grace by the greatness of the sins it healed, and owing to this it seemed in the eyes of the unthinking to be an encouragement to sin (for if the reason, they would say, why greater grace was shown, was because we had done great sins, let us not give over sinning, that grace may be more displayed still), now that they might not say this or suspect it, see how he turns the objection back again. First he does it by his deprecation. 'God forbid.'

"And this he is in the habit of doing at things confessed on all hands to be absurd. And then he lays down an irrefragable [irrefutable] argument. And what is it?

" 'How shall we,' he says, 'that are dead to sin, live any longer therein?'

"What does 'we are dead' mean? Does it mean that as for that, and as far as it goes, we have all received the sentence of death? or, that we became dead to it by believing any being enlightened. This is what one should rather say, since the sequel makes this clearly right. But what is becoming dead to it? The not obeying it in anything any more.

For this baptism effected once for all, it made us dead to it. But this must of our own earnestness thenceforth continually be maintained, so that, although sin issue countless commands to us, we may never again obey it, but abide unmovable as a dead man doth" (Homily on Romans 5:12).

This is something that opponents of the second work don't seem to understand. When we get saved, we turn our backs on sin. Turning back to sin is a choice.

"Here then he says there are two mortifyings, and two deaths, and that one is done by Christ in Baptism, and the other it is our duty to effect by earnestness afterwards. For that our former sins were buried, came of His gift. But the remaining dead to sin after baptism must be the work of our own earnestness, however much we find God here also giving us large help... As then in the case of the former, thy contribution was faith that they might be obliterated, so also in those subsequent to this, show thou forth the change in thine aims, that thou mayest not defile thyself again...

"If then sin hath no more dominion over us, why does he lay so great a charge upon them as he does in the words, 'Let not sin reign in your mortal body,' and, 'yield not ye your members as instruments of unrighteousness unto sin?' What does that here said mean then? He is sowing a kind of seed in this statement, which he means to develop afterwards, and to cultivate in a powerful argument. What then is this statement? It is this; that our body, before Christ's coming, was an easy prey to the assaults of sin. For after death a great swarm of passions entered also. And for this cause it was not light-some for running the race of virtue. For there was no Spirit present to assist, nor any baptism of power to mortify. But as some horse that answereth not the rein, it ran indeed, but made frequent slips, the Law meanwhile announcing what was to be done and what not, yet not conveying into those in the race anything over and above exhortation by means of words. But when Christ had come, the effort became afterwards more easy, and therefore we had a more distant goal set us, in that the assistance we had given us was greater... But this he says more clearly in the sequel. But at present he alludes here briefly to it, to show that unless we stoop down very low to it, sin will not get the better of us. For it is not the Law only that exhorteth us, but grace too which also remitted our former sins, and secures us against future ones...

"Let us then continue living this life; for many of those who seem to breathe and to walk about are in a more wretched plight than the dead... For what would be the advantage, pray, of a king dressed in a purple robe and possessed of arms, but without a single subject, and exposed to all that had a mind to attack and insult him? In like manner it will be no advantage to a Christian to have faith, and the gift of baptism, and yet be open to all the passions. In that way the disgrace will be greater, and the shame more. For as such an one having the diadem and purple is so far from gaining by this dress any honor to himself, that he even does disgrace to that by his own shame: so the believer also, who leadeth a corrupt life, is so far from becoming, as such, an object of respect, that he is only the more one of scorn... To prevent this from happening then, let us do away with this fountain of evil, and extinguish the furnace, and let us draw up the root of wickedness from beneath, since you will do no good by cutting the tree off from above, if the root remains below, and sends up fresh shoots of the same kind again" (Homily on Romans 6:5).

We in the Holiness movement today often use this analogy of tree roots being pulled out. It is interesting to see how old it is. I personally was not aware of that.

Chrysostom has a very different attitude than our opponents do. They say that sinning is inevitable; he says "unless we stoop down very low to it, sin will not get the better of us."

" 'For when ye were the servants of sin, ye were free from righteousness.'

"Now what he says is somewhat of this kind, When ye lived in wickedness, and impiety, and the worst of evils, the state of compliance ye lived in was such that ye did absolutely no good thing at all. For this is, 'ye were free from righteousness.' That is ye were not subject to it, but estranged from it wholly. For ye did not even so much as divide the manner of servitude between righteousness and sin, but gave yourselves wholly up to wickedness. Now, therefore, since ye have come over to righteousness, give yourselves wholly up to virtue, doing nothing at all of vice, that the measure you give may be at least equal...

"Neither is it a small point which he has gained by showing what an evil sin is, and unfolding the whole of its poison, and bringing it to view. For this is what he shows, by saying, 'that sin by the commandment might become exceeding sinful.' That is, that it may be made clear what an evil sin is, what a ruinous thing. And this is what was shown by the commandment. Hereby he also shows the preeminence of grace above the Law, the preeminence above, not the conflict with, the Law. For do not look to this fact, that those who received it were the worse for it; but consider the other, that the Law had not only no design of drawing wickedness out to greater lengths, but even seriously aimed at hewing down what already existed. But if it had no strength, give to it indeed a crown for its intention, but adore more highly the power of Christ, which abolished, cut away: and plucked up the very roots an evil so manifold and so hard to be overthrown" (Homily on Romans 6:19).

It is utterly astonishing to me that anybody would insist that we have to tolerate this pernicious thing in our lives, all life long. It is abundantly clear that Chrysostom believed in the possibility of a sinless life.

Chapter 5

The Darkness Descends: 400-1500

The year 400 marks the approximate point where the Church world began tipping towards false doctrines and wide-spread spiritual darkness. It could be argued that the Papacy began right around this time. There had been a few tentative moves in that direction decades previously, but now the idea of a supreme religious ruler began to take hold. The growth of the Catholic Church was not the only attack by Satan, but it grew to be the main one. For some time after this year, there was still a significant amount of light, but gradually it was extinguished until there were only a few bright lights for God over hundreds of years—and even those were almost invariably mixed with significant error.

* * * * *

Augustine (354-430)

He was born in the province of Numidia, in what is now Algeria. His education was largely in Carthage. He became Bishop of Hippo in 396. He produced a tremendous output of writings; far more than most influential authors. His output is so vast, and so varied, that most groups within Christendom have claimed him as a major influence. However, his influence has been a mixed blessing. He did much great work in combating various heresies; however, partly as a result of that, he went to the opposite extreme in some cases, and fell into error himself. He also, especially late in life, managed to read into the Bible things that are not there. These errors also influenced people, and not in a good way. Nevertheless, there is much good in his writings.

" 'For from the heart go out,' saith He, 'evil thoughts, murders, adulteries, fornications, thefts, false witness, blasphemies; these are what defile the man.' There is surely no one of those evils, which can be committed also by the members of the body, but that the evil thoughts go before and defile the man, although something hinder the sinful and wicked deeds of the body from following. For if, because power is not given, the hand is free from the murder of a man, is the heart of the murderer forsooth therefore clean from sin? Or if she be chaste, whom one unchaste wishes to commit adultery with, hath he on that account failed to commit adultery with her in his heart? Or if the harlot be not found in the brothel, doth he, who seeks her, on that account fail to commit fornication in his heart? Or if time and place be wanting to one who wishes to hurt his neighbor by a lie, hath he on that account failed already to speak false witness with his inner mouth? Or if any one fearing men, dare not utter aloud blasphemy with tongue of flesh, is he on this account guiltless of this crime, who saith in his heart, 'There is no God.' Thus all the other evil deeds of men, which no motion of the body performs, of which no sense of the body is conscious, have their own secret criminals, who are also polluted by consent alone in thought, that is, by evil words of the inner mouth. Into which he (the Psalmist) fearing lest his heart should fall aside, asks of the Lord that the door of Continence be set around the lips of this mouth, to contain the heart, that it fall not aside into evil words: but contain it, by not suffering thought to proceed to consent: for thus, according to the precept of the Apostle, sin reigneth not in our mortal body, nor do we yield our members as weapons of unrighteousness unto sin. From fulfilling which precept they are surely far removed, who on this account turn not their members to sin, because no power is allowed them; and if this be present, straightway by the motions of their members, as of weapons, they show, who reigneth in them within...

"And on this account that, which, the parts that beget being bridled by modesty, is most chiefly and properly to be called Continence, is violated by no transgression, if the higher Continence, concerning which we have been some time speaking, be preserved in the heart. For this reason the Lord, after He had said, 'For from the heart go forth evil thoughts,' then went on to add what it is that belongs to evil thoughts, 'murders, adulteries,' and the rest. He spake not of all; but, having named certain by way of instance, He taught that we are to understand others also. Of which there is no one that can take place, unless an evil thought have gone before, whereby that is prepared within which is done without, and going forth out of the mouth of the heart already defiles the man, although, through no power being granted, it be not done without by means of the members of the body. When therefore a door of Continence hath been set in the mouth of the heart, whence go out all that defile the man, if nothing such be permitted to go out thence, there followeth a purity, wherein now the conscience may rejoice; although there be not as yet that perfection, wherein Continence shall not strive with vice" (*On Continence*, secs. 4, 5).

Plain old self-control will go a long way in preventing us from falling into certain sins. This is something that many people seem to have forgotten. Many churches these days say little or nothing about self-control. We can't prevent thoughts from entering our minds, but we can control our reaction. A person must be pure in mind and heart, or he is not pure at all.

"This therefore is the business in hand, so long as this our mortal life under Grace lasts, that sin, that is the lust of sin, (for this he in this place calls by the name of sin,) reign not in this our mortal body. But it is then shown to reign, if obedience be yielded to its desires. There is therefore in us lust of sin, which must not be suffered to reign; there are its desires, which we must not obey, lest obeying it reign over us. Wherefore let not lust usurp our members, but let Continence claim them for herself; that they be weapons of righteousness unto God, that they be not weapons of unrighteousness unto sin; for thus sin shall not rule over us" (*On Continence*, sec. 8).

He shows us that anybody who commits sin is letting it reign over him. All too many people start off well, and then let sin conquer them once again.

The City of God

"Let this, therefore, in the first place, be laid down as an unassailable position, that the virtue which makes the life good has its throne in the soul, and thence rules the members of the body, which becomes holy in virtue of the holiness of the will" (Book 1, ch. 16).

If the inner life is holy, the outer life will be, too. We have the power of choice between purity and impurity.

"Our God is everywhere present, wholly everywhere; not confined to any place. He can be present unperceived, and be absent without moving; when He exposes us to adversities, it is either to prove our perfections or correct our imperfections; and in return for our patient endurance of the sufferings of time, He reserves for us an everlasting reward" (Book 1, ch. 29).

Even Augustine writes of perfection in the Christian life.

"We, however, seek for a mind which, trusting to true religion, does not adore the world as its god, but for the sake of God praises the world as a work of God, and, purified from mundane defilements, comes pure to God Himself who founded the world" (Book 7, ch. 26).

Every aspect of our life can and will be purified if we obey God completely.

"Thus a true sacrifice is every work which is done that we may be united to God in holy fellowship, and which has a reference to that supreme good and end in which alone we can be truly blessed. And therefore even the mercy we show to men, if it is not shown for God's sake, is not a sacrifice. For, though made or offered by man, sacrifice is a divine thing, as those who called it *sacrifice* meant to indicate. Thus man himself, consecrated in the name of God, and vowed to God, is a sacrifice in so far as he dies to the world that he may live to God. For this is a part of that mercy which each man shows to himself; as it is written, 'Have mercy on thy soul by pleasing God.' Our body, too, as a sacrifice when we chasten it by temperance, if we do so as we ought, for God's sake, that we may not yield our members instruments of unrighteousness unto sin, but instruments of righteousness unto God" (Book 10, ch. 6).

It's impossible for an unsanctified Christian to be completely dead to the world—the carnal nature has too much influence.

On the Holy Trinity

"First we have had to be persuaded how much God loved us, lest from despair we should not dare to look up to Him. And we needed to be shown also what manner of men we are whom He loved, lest being proud, as if of our own merits, we should recede the more from Him, and fail the more in our own strength. And hence He so dealt with us, that we might the rather profit by His strength, and that so in the weakness of humility the virtue of charity might be perfected... And knowing this, we shall not trust in ourselves; and this is to be made 'weak.' But He Himself makes us perfect, who says also to the Apostle Paul, 'My grace is sufficient for thee, for my strength is made perfect in weakness.' Man, then, was to be persuaded how much God loved us, and what manner of men we were whom He loved; the former, lest we should despair; the latter, lest we should be proud... Now that which is declared to us as already done, was shown also to the ancient righteous as about to be done; that through the same faith they themselves also might be humbled, and so made weak; and might be made weak, and so perfected" (Book 4, ch. 1).

God's love is perfect, and it can make us perfect. But in order to do so, it must fill us so completely that there is no longer any room for sin of any kind.

"Listen how greatly the Apostle John commends brotherly love: 'He that loveth his brother abideth in the light, and there is none occasion of stumbling in him.' It is manifest that he placed the perfection of righteousness in the love of our brother; for he certainly is perfect in whom 'there is no occasion of stumbling.' And yet he seems to have passed by the love of God in silence; which he never would have done, unless because he intends God to be understood in brotherly love itself. For in this same epistle, a little further on, he says most plainly thus: 'Beloved, let us love one another: for love is of God; and every one that loveth is born of God, and knoweth God. He that loveth not, knoweth not God; for God is love.' And this passage declares sufficiently and plainly, that this same brotherly love itself (for that is brotherly love by which we love each other) is set forth by so great authority, not only to be from God, but also to be God. When, therefore, we love our brother from love, we love our brother from God" (Book 8, ch. 8).

This is the reason why love fulfills the law. Furthermore, love is the foundation of Christian perfection.

"Perfection in this life, he [Paul] tells us, is nothing else than to forget those things which are behind, and to reach forth and press in purpose toward those things which are before. For he that seeks has the safest purpose, [who seeks] until that is taken hold of whither we are tending, and for which we are reaching forth" (Book 9, ch. 1).

If we do this whole-heartedly, it will fill our whole lives, and leave no room for sin.

The Enchiridion

"Moreover, when the mind has been imbued with the first elements of that faith which worketh by love, it endeavors by purity of life to attain unto sight, where the pure and perfect in heart know that unspeakable beauty, the full vision of which is supreme happiness" (ch. 5).

By this point in Augustine's life, he had fallen into serious error on some points. Nevertheless, he still recognized the relationship between purity and perfection. It is impossible to have perfection without having purity.

"I wrote three volumes shortly after my conversion, to remove out of my way the objections which lie, as it were, on the very threshold of faith. And assuredly it was necessary at the very outset to remove this utter despair of reaching truth, which seems to be strengthened by the arguments of these philosophers. Now in their eyes every error is regarded as a sin, and they think that error can only be avoided by entirely suspending belief. For they say that the man who assents to what is uncertain falls into error; and they strive by the most acute, but most audacious arguments, to show that, even though a man's opinion should by chance be true, yet that there is no certainty of its truth, owing to the impossibility of distinguishing truth from falsehood...

"But as to those matters in regard to which our belief or disbelief, and indeed their truth or supposed truth or falsity, are of no importance whatever, so far as attaining the kingdom of God is concerned: to make a mistake in such matters is not to be looked on as a sin, or at least as a very small and trifling sin. In short, a mistake in matters of this kind, whatever its nature and magnitude, does not relate to the way of approach to God, which is the faith of Christ that 'worketh by love.' For the 'mistake pleasing to parents' in the case of the twin children was no deviation from this way; nor did the Apostle Peter deviate from this way, when, thinking that he saw a vision, he so mistook one thing for another, that, till the angel who delivered him had departed from him, he did not distinguish the real objects among which he was moving from the visionary objects of a dream; nor did the patriarch Jacob deviate from this way, when he believed that his son, who was really alive, had been slain by a beast. In the case of these and other false impressions of the same kind, we are indeed deceived, but our faith in God remains secure. We go astray, but we do not leave the way that leads us to Him. But yet these errors, though they are not sinful, are to be reckoned among the evils of this life which is so far made subject to vanity, that we receive what is false as if it were true, reject what is true as if it were false, and cling to what is uncertain as if it were certain. And although they do not trench upon that true and certain faith through which we reach eternal blessedness, yet they have much to do with that misery in which we are now living" (chs. 20, 21).

For some reason, our opponents have great difficulty grasping the difference between human perfection and Christian perfection. Augustine, to his credit, did not have that problem.

"Now the daily prayer of the believer makes satisfaction for those daily sins of a momentary and trivial kind which are necessary incidents of this life. For he can say, 'Our Father which art in heaven,' seeing that to such a Father he is now born again of water and of the Spirit. And this prayer certainly takes away the very small sins of daily life" (ch. 71).

Here Augustine's errors begin to be apparent on these issues. Notwithstanding his realization that errors are not sins, he thinks that certain things are sins, when they are not. The next quote will illustrate this.

"Now, what sins are trivial and what heinous is not a matter to be decided by man's judgment, but by the judgment of God. For it is plain that the apostles themselves have given an indulgence in the case of certain sins: take, for example, what the Apostle Paul says to those who are married: 'Defraud ye not one the other, except it be with consent for a time, that ye may give yourselves to fasting and prayer: and come together again, that Satan tempt you not for your incontinency.' Now it is possible that it might not have been considered a sin to have intercourse with a spouse, not with a view to the procreation of children, which is the great blessing of marriage, but for the sake of carnal pleasure, and to save the incontinent from being led by their weakness into the deadly sin of fornication, or adultery, or another form of uncleanness which it is shameful even to name, and into which it is possible that they might be drawn by lust under the temptation of Satan. It is possible, I say, that this might not have been considered a sin, had the apostle not added: 'But I speak this by permission, and not of commandment.' Who, then, can deny that it is a sin, when confessedly it is only by apostolic authority that permission is granted to those who do it?" (ch. 78).

And here we see just how far he went astray. As hard as it is to believe, he views sex, even with a person's spouse, as a sin if it is done for pleasure, not for the purpose of procreation. This sort of mistake is one of the big reasons why people oppose the doctrine of a second work. I am not aware of any modern opponents who go quite so far off the deep end as Augustine did here, at least in this particular way, but they think that all sorts of things are sins, when they're actually mistakes or errors in judgment.

In later centuries, all sorts of people and organizations seized upon Augustine's writings as proof that their mistaken theology was actually correct. This is why I've included this quote: Augustine, although a Christian himself, marked in many ways the real beginning of the Church's descent into the spiritual dark ages. There were still people after him who held to correct and pure doctrine, but they became fewer as time went on.

Augustine was a decidedly mixed blessing to the Church. He did a vast amount of good, but later in life he fell into errors that had a lasting impact, because of his great influence.

Many people carelessly assume that the person for which any given idea or movement is named for was the originator of that thing. In many cases that's true, but it's far from a universal rule. John Calvin was neither the first nor the most influential Calvinist. Both distinctions belong to Augustine, for he was the one who came up with the idea of predestination, as well as some of the other characteristic ideas of Calvinism. Once his teaching became widely known, it caused a great deal of controversy; people pointed out that this idea contradicted not only the Bible, but also Augustine's earlier writings. Nevertheless, the damage was done. Calvin admitted that he relied heavily on Augustine's writings for his own ideas.

* * * * *

Sulpitius (or Sulpicius) Severus (363-420)

He was born in Aquitaine (present-day southwestern France). He was well-educated, and started his adult life as a lawyer. He was apparently ordained at some point. Most of his writings were historical in nature. Beyond these facts, we know almost nothing about his life.

"A certain young man from Asia, exceedingly wealthy, of distinguished family, and having a wife and little son, happening to have been a tribune in Egypt, and in frequent campaigns against the Blembi to have touched on some parts of the desert, and having also seen several tents of the saints, heard the word of salvation from the blessed John. And he did not then delay to show his contempt for an unprofitable military life with its vain honor. Bravely entering into the wilderness, he in a short time became distinguished as being perfect in every kind of virtue" (Dialogue 1, ch. 22).

This sort of testimony is what our opponents scoff at. They want to reject any evidence that says we can be perfect in virtue.

"But because you have desired from me in all my letters which I had sent to you precepts to nourish your life and faith, it has come to pass that, through the frequency of my writings to you, I have now exhausted language of that kind; and I can really write nothing new to you, so as to avoid what I have written before. And in truth, through the goodness of God, you do not now need to be exhorted, inasmuch as, perfecting your faith at the very beginning of your saintly life, you display a devoted love in Christ. One thing, however, I do press upon you, that you do not go back on things you have already passed away from, that you do not long again for things you have already scorned, and that, having put your hand to the plow, you do not look back again, retracing your steps; for, undoubtedly, by falling into this fault, your furrow will lose its straightness, and the cultivator will not receive his own proper reward. Moreover, he does not secure even a measure of the reward, if he has, in a measure, failed. For, as we must flee from sin to righteousness, so he who has entered on the practice of righteousness must beware lest he lay himself open to sin. For it is written that 'his righteousness shall not profit the righteous on the day on which he has gone astray.' For this, then, we must take our stand, for this we must labor, that we, who have escaped from sins, do not lose the prepared rewards" (Letter to his sister Claudia concerning the last judgment; ch. 2).

The second work of grace helps to establish and steady a person in his walk with God. This greatly increases the chances that he will remain faithful unto death.

"But you perhaps say here, 'Teach me, then, what righteousness is, so that knowing it, I may be able more easily to fully practice it.' Well, I shall briefly explain it to you, as I am able, and shall use the simplicity of common words, seeing that the subject of which we treat is such as ought by no means to be obscured by attempts at eloquent description, but should be opened up by the simplest forms of expression. For a matter which is necessary to all in common ought to be set forth in a common sort of speech. Righteousness, then, is nothing else than not to commit sin; and not to commit sin is just to keep the precepts of the law. Now, the observance of these precepts is maintained in a two-fold way—thus, that one do none of those things which are forbidden, and that he strive to fulfill the things which are commanded" (Letter to his sister Claudia concerning virginity; ch. 6).

Righteousness and sin are mutually exclusive. Righteousness, if maintained, leaves no room for falling back into sin.

"I believe that I have now set forth, briefly indeed, but, at the same time, fully, what is implied in a woman's purity of body: it remains that we should learn what it is to be pure also in spirit; i.e. that what it is unlawful for one to do in act, it is also unlawful for one even to imagine in thought. For she is holy, alike in body and in spirit, who sins neither in mind nor heart, knowing that God is one who examines also the heart; and, therefore, she takes every pains to possess a mind as well as a body free from sin. Such a person is aware that it is written, 'Keep thy heart with all diligence'; and again, 'God loveth holy hearts, and all the undefiled are acceptable to him'; and elsewhere, 'Blessed are those of a pure heart; for they shall see God.' I think that this last statement is made regarding those whom conscience accuses of the guilt of no sin; concerning whom I think that John also spoke in his Epistle when he said, 'If our heart condemn us not, then have we confidence towards God, and whatsoever we ask we shall receive from him.' I do not wish you to think that you have escaped the accusation of sin, although act does not follow desire, since it is written, 'Whosoever looketh on a woman to lust after her, hath already committed adultery with her in his heart.' And do not say, 'I had the thought, indeed, but I did not carry it out in act'; for it is unlawful even to desire that which it is unlawful to do" (Letter to his sister Claudia concerning virginity; ch. 11).

He follows a long line of writers in insisting that absolute purity (which is another name for complete freedom from sin) is possible in this life.

"O Virgin, maintain thy purpose which is destined for a great reward. Eminent with the Lord is the virtue of virginity and purity, if it be not disfigured by other kinds of lapses into sins and wickedness. Realize your state, realize your position, realize your purpose. You are called the bride of Christ; see that you commit no act which is unworthy of him to whom you profess to be betrothed. He will quickly write a bill of divorcement, if he perceive in you even one act of unfaithfulness. Accordingly, whosoever receives those gifts which, as an earnest, are bestowed in the case of human betrothals, immediately begins earnestly and diligently to enquire of domestics, intimates, and friends, what is the character of the young man, what he especially loves, what he receives, in what style he lives, what habits he practices, what luxuries he indulges in, and in what pursuits he finds his chief pleasure and delight. And when she has learned these things, she so conducts herself, in all respects, that her service, her cheerfulness, her diligence, and her whole mode of life, may be in harmony with the character of her betrothed. And do thou, who hast Christ as thy bridegroom, enquire from the domestics and intimates of that bridegroom of thine what is his character; yes, do thou zealously and skillfully enquire in what things he specially delights, what sort of arrangement he loves in thy dress, and what kind of adornment he desires. Let his most intimate associate Peter tell thee, who does not allow personal adorning even to married women, as he has written in his epistle, 'Let wives, in like manner, be subject to their own husbands, so that, if any believe not the word, they may, without the word, be won over by the conduct of their wives, contemplating their chaste behavior in the fear of God; and let theirs not be an outward adornment of the hair, or the putting on of gold, or elegance in the apparel which is adopted, but let there be the hidden man of the heart in the stainlessness of a peaceful and modest spirit, which is in the sight of God of great price.' Let another apostle also tell thee, the blessed Paul, who, writing to Timothy, gives his approval to the same things in regard to the conduct of believing women: 'Let wives in like manner adorn themselves with the ornament of a habit of modesty and sobriety, not with curled hair, or gold, or pearls, or costly array, but as becomes women that profess chastity, with good and upright behavior' " (Letter to his sister Claudia concerning virginity; ch. 12).

He is talking about spiritual virginity here—the possession and state of every Christian. But if we fall back into sin, that state of purity is lost. Notice also that our outer life should reflect that purity. There is no need for baubles and trinkets.

* * * * *

John Cassian (360-435)

He does not seem to be well-known in general Church circles. We don't know a great deal about his early life, not even for sure where he was born. We do know that he was well-educated, and became a monk fairly young. The work that he is best-known for is a collection of reports about his travels to various monasteries in Egypt. He reported on his conversations with several of the monks that he met. Much of his writing is not his own thoughts, but reflects what various monks said. Thus we have a cross-section of Christian thought from this period. Later in life, he became acquainted with a large number of other Christian leaders, and the Church world in general held him in very high esteem. This led to an interesting situation: he differed with Augustine on certain points, primarily regarding predestination and Divine grace, and the people in Augustine's camp tended to refer to him in a round-about fashion, being unwilling to directly criticize him by name.

Institutes of the Coenobia

"The fear of the Lord is our cross. As then one who is crucified no longer has the power of moving or turning his limbs in any direction as he pleases, so we also ought to affix our wishes and desires—not in accordance with what is pleasant and delightful to us now, but in accordance with the law of the Lord, where it constrains us. And as he who is fastened to the wood of the cross no longer considers things present, nor thinks about his likings, nor is perplexed by anxiety and care for the morrow, nor disturbed by any desire of possession, nor inflamed by any pride or strife or rivalry, grieves not at present injuries, remembers not past ones, and while he is still breathing in the body considers that he is dead to all earthly things, sending the thoughts of his heart on before to that place whither he doubts not that he is shortly to come: so we also, when crucified by the fear of the Lord ought to be dead indeed to all these things, i.e. not only to carnal vices but also to all earthly things, having the eye of our minds fixed there whither we hope at each moment that we are soon to pass. For in this way we can have all our desires and carnal affections mortified" (Book 4, ch. 35).

This is speaking of complete, utter abandonment of our own will, and utter submission to God's will. Beware, however—this is not irreversible. Just like Jesus could have come down from the physical cross, if He had so chosen, we too can reverse our decision and once again heed our own will.

"Coenobia" refers to monks that lived in monasteries, rather than hermit-type monks.

"Beware therefore lest at any time you take again any of those things which you renounced and forsook, and, contrary to the Lord's command, return from the field of evangelical work, and be found to have clothed yourself again in your coat which you had stripped off; neither sink back to the low and earthly lusts and desires of this world, and in defiance of Christ's word come down from the rod of perfection and dare to take up again any of those things which you have renounced and forsaken... For it is too bad that when you ought to be carried on from the rudiments and beginnings, and go forward to perfection, you should begin to fall back from these to worse things. For not he who begins these things, but he who endures in them to the end, shall be saved" (Book 4, ch. 36).

We have a solemn warning here against turning back to sin and to the things of the world.

"The possession of money must not only be avoided, but the desire for it must be utterly rooted out. For it is not enough not to possess it,—a thing which comes to many as a matter of necessity: but we ought, if by chance it is offered, not even to admit the *wish* to have it. The madness of anger should be controlled; the downcast look of dejection be overcome; vainglory should be despised, the disdainfulness of pride trampled under foot, and the shifting and wandering thoughts of the mind restrained by continual recollection of God. And the slippery wanderings of our heart should be brought back again to the contemplation of God as often as our crafty enemy, in his endeavour to lead away the mind a captive from this consideration, creeps into the innermost recesses of the heart" (Book 5, ch. 10).

We have here the analogy of rooting out sin. But that rooting out will ultimately be fruitless if we do not practice self-control.

"The deadly poison of anger has to be utterly rooted out from the inmost corners of our soul. For as long as this remains in our hearts, and blinds with its hurtful darkness the eye of the soul, we can neither acquire right judgment and discretion, nor gain the insight which springs from an honest gaze, or ripeness of counsel, nor can we be partakers of life, or retentive of righteousness, or even have the capacity for spiritual and true light... Nor can we become partakers of wisdom, even though we are considered wise by universal consent, for 'anger rests in the bosom of fools.' Nor can we even attain immortal life, although we are accounted prudent in the opinion of everybody, for 'anger destroys even the prudent.' Nor shall we be able with clear judgment of heart to secure the controlling power of righteousness, even though we are reckoned perfect and holy in the estimation of all men, for 'the wrath of man worketh not the righteousness of God.' Nor can we by any possibility acquire that esteem and honour which is so frequently seen even in worldlings, even though we are thought noble and honourable through the privileges of birth, because 'an angry man is dishonoured.' Nor again can we secure any ripeness of counsel, even though we appear to be weighty, and endowed with the utmost knowledge; because 'an angry man acts without counsel' " (Book 8, ch. 1).

John devotes separate chapters of the *Institutes* to each of the "Deadly Sins." I have decided to give several quotes from this chapter on anger, partly because I believe that many people do not fully realize how dangerous anger is. Not only is it deadly to the soul in and of itself, if left unchecked, but it is also the parent to many other sins.

Righteousness drives out sin, and sin drives out righteousness; and there is no salvation without righteousness being present in the heart.

"Wherefore if we wish to gain the substance of that divine reward of which it is said, 'Blessed are the pure in heart, for they shall see God,' we ought not only to banish it from our actions, but entirely to root it out from our inmost soul. For it will not be of any good to have checked anger in words, and not to have shown it in deeds, if God, from whom the secrets of the heart are not hid, sees that it remains in the secret recesses of our bosom. For the word of the gospel bids us destroy the roots of our faults rather than the fruits; for these, when the incitements are all removed, will certainly not put forth shoots any more; and so the mind will be able to continue in all patience and holiness, when this anger has been removed, not from the surface of acts and deeds, but from the very innermost thoughts" (Book 8, ch. 20).

Advocates of a sinning religion say that being sinless in any form, much less even in our thoughts, is altogether too high a standard. But the smallest unforgiven sin will keep us out of Heaven.

"But you should know that in this, which is found in many copies, 'Whosoever is angry with his brother without a cause, is in danger of the judgment,' the words 'without a cause' are superfluous, and were added by those who did not think that anger for just causes was to be banished: since certainly nobody, however unreasonably he is disturbed, would say that he was angry without a cause. Wherefore it appears to have been added by those who did not understand the drift of Scripture, which intended altogether to banish the incentive to anger, and to reserve no occasion whatever for indignation; lest while we were commanded to be angry with a cause, an opportunity for being angry without a cause might occur to us. For the end and aim of patience consists, not in being angry with a good reason, but in not being angry at all. Although I know that by some this very expression, 'without a cause,' is taken to mean that he is angry without a cause who when he is angered is not allowed to seek for vengeance. But it is better so to take it as we find it written in many modern copies and all the ancient ones" (Book 8, ch. 21).

This is a very interesting bit of history. If I ever knew that the phrase in question was not in the earliest manuscripts, I had forgotten it.

"Wherefore the athlete of Christ who strives lawfully ought thoroughly to root out the feeling of wrath. And it will be a sure remedy for this disease, if in the first place we make up our mind that we ought never to be angry at all, whether for good or bad reasons: as we know that we shall at once lose the light of discernment, and the security of good counsel, and our very uprightness, and the temperate character of righteousness, if the main light of our heart has been darkened by its shadows: next, that the purity of our soul will presently be clouded, and that it cannot possibly be made a temple for the Holy Ghost while the spirit of anger resides in us; lastly, that we should consider that we ought never to pray, nor pour out our prayer to God, while we are angry. And above all, having before our eyes the uncertain condition of mankind, we should realize daily that we are soon to depart from the body, and that our continence and chastity, our renunciation of all our possessions, our contempt of wealth, our efforts in fastings and vigils will not help us at all, if solely on account of anger and hatred eternal punishments are awarded to us by the judge of the world" (Book 8, ch. 22).

In my research for this book I read quite a bit from opponents of the second work. Most of them, if they mention self-control at all, do so only briefly and glancingly. This really is not very surprising: such a strong belief that there is no remedy for the carnal nature, and no remedy to prevent sinning (no matter how much it's bewailed), naturally leads to a fatalistic attitude. As such, what point is there in self-control? Indeed, to hear many of these people talk, one would think that they were still the servants of sin.

"Wherefore it is now time to produce, in the very words in which they hand it down, the opinion of the Fathers; viz., of those who have not painted the way of perfection and its character in high-sounding words, but rather, possessing it in deed and truth, and in the virtue of their spirit, have passed it on by their own experience and sure example. And so they say that no one can be altogether cleansed from carnal sins, unless he has realized that all his labours and efforts are insufficient for so great and perfect an end; and unless, taught, not by the system handed down to him, but by his feelings and virtues and his own experience, he recognizes that it can only be gained by the mercy and assistance of God. For in order to acquire such splendid and lofty prizes of purity and perfection, however great may be the efforts of fastings and vigils and readings and solitude and retirement applied to it, they will not be sufficient to secure it by the merits of the actual efforts and toil. For a man's own efforts and human exertions will never make up for the lack of the divine gift, unless it is granted by divine compassion in answer to his prayer" (Book 12, ch. 13).

In other words, perfection in the Christian life is not merely a theory; there were identifiable, specific people who possessed the blessing, and somebody who wanted to talk about perfection could name names and give real-life examples.

Conferences

"It arises that in the case of some who have despised the greatest possessions of this world, and not only large sums of gold and silver, but also large properties, we have seen them afterwards disturbed and excited over a knife, or pencil, or pin, or pen. Whereas if they kept their gaze steadily fixed out of a pure heart they would certainly never allow such a thing to happen for trifles, while in order that they might not suffer it in the case of great and precious riches they chose rather to renounce them altogether... And from this it clearly follows that perfection is not arrived at simply by self-denial, and the giving up of all our goods, and the casting away of honours, unless there is that charity, the details of which the Apostle describes, which consists in purity of heart alone. For 'not to be envious,' 'not to be puffed up, not to be angry, not to do any wrong, not to seek one's own, not to rejoice in iniquity, not to think evil' etc., what is all this except ever to offer to God a perfect and clean heart, and to keep it free from all disturbances?" (Conference 1, ch. 6).

Opponents of the second work often mention various godly people who bewailed the remnants of the carnal nature in their own hearts. It is clear that that disturbed the hearts of those godly people. But here he mentions a perfect heart that has no such disturbance. It is God's love and purity, filling and overflowing the heart to the exclusion of everything else, that produces Christian perfection.

"As the kingdom of the devil is gained by consenting to sin, so the kingdom of God is attained by the practice of virtue in purity of heart and spiritual knowledge. But where the kingdom of God is, there most certainly eternal life is enjoyed, and where the kingdom of the devil is, there without doubt is death and the grave. And the man who is in this condition, cannot praise the Lord, according to the saying of the prophet which tells us: 'The dead cannot praise Thee, O Lord; neither all they that go down into the grave (doubtless of sin).' 'But we,' says he, 'who live (not forsooth to sin nor to this world but to God) will bless the Lord, from this time forth for evermore: for in death no man remembereth God: but in the grave (of sin) who will confess to the Lord?' i.e., no one will. For no man even though he were to call himself a Christian a thousand times over, or a monk, confesses God when he is sinning: no man who allows those things which the Lord hates, remembereth God, nor calls himself with any truth the servant of Him, whose commands he scorns with obstinate rashness: in which death the blessed Apostle declares that the widow is involved, who gives herself to pleasure, saying 'a widow who giveth herself to pleasure is dead while she liveth.' There are then many who while still living in this body are dead, and lying in the grave cannot praise God; and on the contrary there are many who though they are dead in the body yet bless God in the spirit, and praise Him" (Conference 1, ch. 14).

Here again we see that sinning and living a Christian life are mutually exclusive.

The first two quotes that he gives within this larger quote are taken from Psalm 6:5;

Psalm 88:10-12; and Isaiah 38:18.

"This, I say, is the end of all perfection, that the mind purged from all carnal desires may daily be lifted towards spiritual things, until the whole life and all the thoughts of the heart become one continuous prayer" (Conference 10, ch. 7).

This is a very high standard indeed, and one that leaves no room for sin. Despite the strictness of the standard, it is clear that many people in the early Church regarded it as an achievable one.

"When then any one has acquired this love of goodness of which we have been speaking, and the imitation of God, then he will be endowed with the Lord's heart of compassion, and will pray also for his persecutors, saying in like manner: 'Father, forgive them, for they know not what they do.' But it is a clear sign of a soul that is not yet thoroughly purged from the dregs of sin, not to sorrow with a feeling of pity at the offences of others, but to keep to the rigid censure of the judge: for how will he be able to obtain perfection of heart, who is without that by which, as the Apostle has pointed out, the full requirements of the law can be fulfilled, saying: 'Bear one another's burdens and so fulfil the law of Christ,' and who has not that virtue of love, which 'is not grieved, is not puffed up, thinketh no evil,' which 'endureth all things, beareth all things' " (Conference 11, ch. 10).

Anybody who is full of God's love will also have God's compassion.

* * * * *

Leo the Great (390/400-461)

He was likely born in Tuscany, but we don't know when. He lived in tumultuous times, when the Western Roman Empire was crumbling. Leo has a mixed record; on the one hand, he vigorously combated ideas that were unquestionably heretical; on the other, he laid much of the groundwork for the full-blown institution of the Papacy. It could be argued that he was the first real Pope, although it seems that he genuinely tried to use his power and position to advance the cause of God. He became Bishop of Rome in 440. Even though there was still much correct doctrine during this period, the catholic Church was fast becoming the Catholic Church.

"How much of the divine love we feel for you, beloved, you will be able to estimate from this, that we are anxious to establish your beginnings on a surer basis, lest anything should seem lacking to the perfection of your love, since your meritorious acts of spiritual grace, as we have proved, are already in your favour" (Letter 9; to Dioscorus, Bishop of Alexandria).

Once again we return to the theme of perfection. Notice how he links perfection to a steady and stable Christian life.

"The forgiveness of a sin does not grant a licence to do wrong" (Letter 12; to all the bishops of Mauritania Caesariensis in Africa).

Many, perhaps most, people who oppose the doctrine of a second work think that they can sin more or less with impunity, except possibly for temporary punishment. Many of them would vehemently object to having it stated in such bald terms, but their actions belie their words. Leo disposes of that viewpoint in one short sentence.

"For the catholic, and especially the Lord's priest, must not only be entangled in no error, but also be corrupted by no covetousness; for, as says the Holy Scripture, 'Go not after thy lusts, and decline from thy desire.' Many enticements of this world, many vanities must be resisted, that the perfection of true self-discipline may be attained the first blemish of which is pride, the beginning of transgression and the origin of sin" (Letter 106; to Anatolius, Bishop of Constantinople).

What he quotes here is actually from one of the apocryphal books. However, we see here that perfection and complete purity go together.

"Although one must be diffident of merit, yet it is one's bounden duty to rejoice over the gift, since He who is the Imposer of the burden is Himself the Aider in its execution: and lest the weak recipient should fall beneath the greatness of the grace, He who conferred the dignity will also give the power... And by this His work what does the Lord suggest and commend to our hearts but that no one should presume upon his own righteousness nor distrust God's mercy which shines out more pre-eminently then, when the sinner is made holy and the downcast lifted up" (Sermon 2; Delivered on the anniversary of his Consecration).

Another mistake that our opponents make is overemphasizing imputed righteousness. It is true that God imputes righteousness to us, but that's only part of the story. God also imparts His righteousness to us, and, as Leo says, actually **makes** us holy.

In addition, whenever God gives us a command, He will see to it that there is some way for us to obey that command, whether it is by direct intervention or more indirect means.

"For this is the purpose of the Judge's might and of the Saviour's graciousness, that the unrighteous may forsake his ways and the sinner give up his wicked habits" (Sermon 9; Upon the Collections, #4).

This is something that our opponents don't seem to understand—they claim to get saved, but they go right on sinning.

"A man will not be puffed up with pride, nor crushed with despair, if he uses the gifts which God gave to His glory, and withholds his inclinations from those things, which he knows will harm him. For in abstaining from malicious envy, from luxurious and dissolute living, from the perturbations of anger, from the lust after vengeance, he will be made pure and holy by true fasting, and will be fed upon the pleasures of incorruptible delights, and so he will know how, by the spiritual use of his earthly riches, to transform them into heavenly treasures, not by hoarding up for himself what he has received, but by gaining a hundred-fold on what he gives" (Sermon 19; On the Fast of the Tenth Month, #8).

Here he compares fasting—abstaining from food—to abstaining from sin. In other words, we can choose to avoid certain things.

"They who have peace with God and are always saying to the Father with their whole hearts 'thy will be done' can be overcome in no battles, can be hurt by no assaults. For accusing ourselves in our confessions and refusing the spirit's consent to our fleshly lusts, we stir up against us the enmity of him who is the author of sin, but secure a peace with God that nothing can destroy, by accepting His gracious service, in order that we may not only surrender ourselves in obedience to our King but also be united to Him by our free-will. For if we are like-minded, if we wish what He wishes, and disapprove what He disapproves, He will finish all our wars for us, He Who gave the will, will also give the power: so that we may be fellow-workers in His works, and with the exultation of Faith may utter that prophetic song: 'the Lord is my light and my salvation: whom shall I fear? the Lord is the defender of my life: of whom shall I be afraid?' " (Sermon 26; On the Feast of the Nativity, #6).

Opponents of Holiness doctrine admit that sinning destroys fellowship with God: but if we don't sin, then nothing can destroy that peace and fellowship. Leo seems to regard it as self-evident that a close, pure walk with God will enable us to have consistent victory over temptation.

"As we approach then, dearly-beloved, the beginning of Lent, which is a time for the more careful serving of the Lord, because we are, as it were, entering on a kind of contest in good works, let us prepare our souls for fighting with temptations, and understand that the more zealous we are for our salvation, the more determined must be the assaults of our opponents. But 'stronger is He that is in us than He that is against us,' and through Him are we powerful in whose strength we rely: because it was for this that the Lord allowed Himself to be tempted by the tempter, that we might be taught by His example as well as fortified by His aid. For He conquered the adversary, as ye have heard, by quotations from the law, not by actual strength, that by this very thing He might do greater honour to man, and inflict a greater punishment on the adversary by conquering the enemy of the human race not now as God but as Man. He fought then, therefore, that we too might fight thereafter: He conquered that we too might likewise conquer... Let every Christian scrutinise himself, and search severely into his inmost heart: let him see that no discord cling there, no wrong desire be harboured. Let

chasteness drive incontinence far away; let the light of truth dispel the shades of deception; let the swellings of pride subside; let wrath yield to reason; let the darts of ill-treat-
ment be shattered, and the chidings of the tongue be bridled; let thoughts of revenge fall
through, and injuries be given over to oblivion. In fine, let 'every plant which the heavenly Father hath not planted be removed by the roots.' For then only are the seeds of
virtue well nourished in us, when every foreign germ is uprooted from the field of wheat.
If any one, therefore, has been fired by the desire for vengeance against another, so that
he has given him up to prison or bound him with chains, let him make haste to forgive
not only the innocent, but also one who seems worthy of punishment, that he may with
confidence make use of the clause in the Lord's prayer and say, 'Forgive us our debts,
as we also forgive our debtors.' Which petition the Lord marks with peculiar emphasis,
as if the efficacy of the whole rested on this condition, by saying, 'For if ye forgive men
their sins, your Father which is in heaven also will forgive you: but if ye forgive not men,
neither will your Father forgive you your sins.'... And he that, aided by God's grace,
shall strain every nerve after this perfection, will keep this holy fast faithfully; free from
the leaven of the old wickedness, in the unleavened bread of sincerity and truth, he will
reach the blessed Passover, and by newness of life will worthily rejoice in the mystery
of man's reformation through Christ our Lord Who with the Father and the Holy Spirit
lives and reigns for ever and ever. Amen" (Sermon 39; On Lent, #1).

Again we see the idea of uprooting sin.

Our opponents have a most peculiar habit of ignoring the fact that many promises
in the Bible are conditional. We must abandon sin if we wish to see those promises
fulfilled.

Even Jesus depended to some extent on our Heavenly Father's power; and yet many
Christians stumble along through life, stubbornly refusing to believe the extent of help
and power that is available to them.

* * * * *

Gregory the Great (540-604)

He was born into a wealthy Roman family. We don't know a great deal about his early life, but we do know that he was well-educated. His parents were apparently Christians. He became a monk in 574, and would have greatly preferred to remain a simple
monk for the rest of his life. However, he was chosen a few years later to serve as the
Pope's representative in Constantinople. He was unwillingly elected Pope in 590. As
Pope, Gregory became almost by default the secular ruler of Rome, simply because there
was no effective local government.

Despite the growing body of false doctrine, and other forms of error, Gregory
preached high standards, both on a personal level, and collectively for the Church in
general. John Calvin called him "the last good Pope." He was the first to use the phrase
"servant of the servants of God," and, unlike many later Popes, he actually meant it. Nor

did he make the sort of claim to absolute authority that later Popes would. "Gregory asserted Rome's right to judge on certain moral issues, but he made no claims of Roman primacy as the term later would be understood" (Encyclopedia Britannica).

The Book of Pastoral Rule

"That man, therefore, ought by all means to be drawn with cords to be an example of good living who already lives spiritually, dying to all passions of the flesh; who disregards worldly prosperity; who is afraid of no adversity; who desires only inward wealth; whose intention the body, in good accord with it, thwarts not at all by its frailness, nor the spirit greatly by its disdain: one who is not led to covet the things of others, but gives freely of his own; who through the bowels of compassion is quickly moved to pardon, yet is never bent down from the fortress of rectitude by pardoning more than is meet; who perpetrates no unlawful deeds, yet deplores those perpetrated by others as though they were his own; who out of affection of heart sympathizes with another's infirmity, and so rejoices in the good of his neighbour as though it were his own advantage; who so insinuates himself as an example to others in all he does that among them he has nothing, at any rate of his own past deeds, to blush for; who studies so to live that he may be able to water even dry hearts with the streams of doctrine" (Part 1, ch. 10).

He speaks at great length in this book regarding how pastors should live. The example of a consistently holy life is a powerful testimony as well as being a rebuke to sinners—especially religious sinners.

"The ruler should always be pure in thought, inasmuch as no impurity ought to pollute him who has undertaken the office of wiping away the stains of pollution in the hearts of others also; for the hand that would cleanse from dirt must needs be clean, lest, being itself sordid with clinging mire, it soil whatever it touches all the more. For on this account it is said through the prophet, 'Be ye clean that bear the vessels of the Lord.' For they bear the vessels of the Lord who undertake, on the surety of their own conversation, to conduct the souls of their neighbours to the eternal sanctuary. Let them therefore perceive within themselves how purified they ought to be who carry in the bosom of their own personal responsibility living vessels to the temple of eternity" (Part 2, ch. 2).

"Ruler" here means pastor. The pastor must set a very high example for his congregation, or he will fall under God's condemnation.

"Prelates ought to know that, if they ever perpetrate what is wrong, they are worthy of as many deaths as they transmit examples of perdition to their subjects. Wherefore it is necessary that they guard themselves so much the more cautiously from sin as by the bad things they do they die not alone, but are guilty of the souls of others, which by their bad example they have destroyed" (Part 3, ch. 4).

He becomes more explicit about the danger that faces a pastor who has become unworthy. All "dumb dogs" (Isaiah 56:10) will face a terrible judgment.

"Those who lament their transgressions and yet forsake them not are to be admonished to learn to consider anxiously that they cleanse themselves in vain by their weeping, if they wickedly defile themselves in their living, seeing that the end for which they wash themselves in tears is that, when clean, they may return to filth. For hence it is written, 'The dog is returned to his own vomit again, and the sow that was washed to her wallowing in the mire.' For the dog, when he vomits, certainly casts forth the food which weighed upon his stomach; but, when he returns to his vomit, he is again loaded with what he had been relieved from. And they who mourn their transgressions certainly cast forth by confession the wickedness with which they have been evilly satiated, and which oppressed the inmost parts of their soul; and yet, in recurring to it after confession, they take it in again. But the sow, by wallowing in the mire when washed, is made more filthy. And one who mourns past transgressions, yet forsakes them not, subjects himself to the penalty of more grievous sin, since he both despises the very pardon which he might have won by his weeping, and as it were rolls himself in miry water; because in withholding purity of life from his weeping he makes even his very tears filthy before the eyes of God... For he neglects being clean after washing, whosoever after tears keeps not innocency of life. And they therefore are washed, but are in no wise clean, who cease not to bewail the things they have committed, but commit again things to be bewailed...

"Those who bewail transgressions, yet forsake them not, are to be admonished to acknowledge themselves to be before the eyes of the strict judge like those who, when they come before the face of certain men, fawn upon them with great submission, but, when they depart, atrociously bring upon them all the enmity and hurt they can. For what is weeping for sin but exhibiting the humility of one's devotion to God? And what is doing wickedly after weeping but putting in practice arrogant enmity against Him to whom entreaty has been made? This James attests, who says, 'Whosoever will be a friend of this world becomes the enemy of God.' Those who lament their transgressions, yet forsake them not, are to be admonished to consider anxiously that, for the most part, bad men are unprofitably drawn by compunction to righteousness, even as, for the most part, good men are without harm tempted to sin. Here indeed is found a wonderful measure of inward disposition in accordance with the requirements of desert, in that the bad, while doing something good, but still without perfecting it, are proudly confident in the midst of the very evil which even to the full they perpetrate; while the good, when tempted of evil to which they in no wise consent, plant the steps of their heart towards righteousness through humility all the more surely from their tottering through infirmity" (Part 3, ch. 30).

This describes many of our opponents: "Those who bewail transgressions, yet forsake them not." Gregory certainly did not believe that the idea of a sinless life is a myth. I suspect that a lot of people who do believe it's a myth will be offended at his characterization of their lives, or else will feel that it doesn't apply to them. The truth can be hard to take sometimes.

"Those who in no wise complete the good things they have begun are to be admonished to consider with cautious circumspection how that, when they accomplish not their purposes, they tear up with them even the things that had been begun. For, if that which is seen to be a thing to be done advances not through assiduous application, even that which had been well done falls back. For the human soul in this world is, as it were, in the condition of a ship ascending against the stream of a river: it is never suffered to stay in one place, since it will float back to the nethermost parts unless it strive for the uppermost. If then the strong hand of the worker carry not on to perfection the good things begun, the very slackness in working fights against what has been wrought. For hence it is that it is said through Solomon, 'He that is feeble and slack in work is brother to him that wasteth his works.' For in truth he who does not strenuously execute the good things he has begun imitates in the slackness of his negligence the hand of the destroyer. Hence it is said by the Angel to the Church of Sardis, 'Be watchful, and strengthen the things which remain, that are ready to die; for I find not thy works complete before my God.' Thus, because the works had not been found complete before his God, he foretold that those which remained, even such as had been done, were about to die. For, if that which is dead in us be not kindled into life, that which is retained as though still alive is extinguished too. They are to be admonished that it might have been more tolerable for them not to have laid hold of the right way than, having laid hold of it, to turn their backs upon it" (Part 3, ch. 34).

He regards those who do not go on to perfection as being slack in works of righteousness. And it is, I believe, universally recognized by every true Christian that slackness in regards to Christian living is at a minimum very undesirable, if not downright dangerous.

"But since often, when preaching is abundantly poured forth in fitting ways, the mind of the speaker is elevated in itself by a hidden delight in self-display, great care is needed that he may gnaw himself with the laceration of fear, lest he who recalls the diseases of others to health by remedies should himself swell through neglect of his own health; lest in helping others he desert himself, lest in lifting up others he fall. For to some the greatness of their virtue has often been the occasion of their perdition; causing them, while inordinately secure in confidence of strength, to die unexpectedly through negligence. For virtue strives with vices; the mind flatters itself with a certain delight in it; and it comes to pass that the soul of a well-doer casts aside the fear of its circumspection, and rests secure in self-confidence; and to it, now torpid, the cunning seducer enumerates all things that it has done well, and exalts it in swelling thoughts as though superexcellent beyond all beside. Whence it is brought about, that before the eyes of the just judge the memory of virtue is a pitfall of the soul; because, in calling to mind what it has done well, while it lifts itself up in its own eyes, it falls before the author of humility" (Part 4).

Here we have a solemn warning against pride. Satan is very subtle. Someone who succumbs to the temptation to become proud of his work for God is in just as much danger before God as someone who falls into open sin.

* * * * *

John of Damascus (675-749)

He was born into a Christian family, but not a Christian nation. The Muslims had conquered Syria in the 630s. However, these Muslims were of a tolerant branch; John's father, although a Christian, held a high-ranking position in the Caliph's court. John at first followed in his father's footsteps. Somewhere around 730, he became a monk. He wrote several books and hymns. One of his books contains an early refutation of Islam. Much of his writing was a collection and summary of earlier writers; thus he gathered into one place much of the accumulated theology of the past centuries. He is considered the last of the Church Fathers.

"The remission of sins, therefore, is granted alike to all through baptism: but the grace of the Spirit is proportional to the faith and previous purification. Now, indeed, we receive the firstfruits of the Holy Spirit through baptism, and the second birth is for us the beginning and seal and security and illumination of another life.

"It behoves us, then, with all our strength to steadfastly keep ourselves pure from filthy works, that we may not, like the dog returning to his vomit, make ourselves again the slaves of sin. For faith apart from works is dead, and so likewise are works apart from faith. For the true faith is attested by works" (*An Exact Exposition of the Orthodox Faith*; Book 4, ch. 9).

As a point of clarification, just like the other Fathers, he notes elsewhere that baptism is only a symbol.

We see here that complete purity equals freedom from sin. And returning to sin equals becoming once again the slave of sin.

"Man, however, being endowed with reason and free will, received the power of continuous union with God through his own choice, if indeed he should abide in goodness, that is in obedience to his Maker. Since, however, he transgressed the command of his Creator and became liable to death and corruption, the Creator and Maker of our race, because of His bowels of compassion, took on our likeness, becoming man in all things but without sin, and was united to our nature. For since He bestowed on us His own image and His own spirit and we did not keep them safe, He took Himself a share in our poor and weak nature, in order that He might cleanse us and make us incorruptible, and establish us once more as partakers of His divinity.

118

"For it was fitting that not only the first-fruits of our nature should partake in the higher good but every man who wished it, and that a second birth should take place and that the nourishment should be new and suitable to the birth and thus the measure of perfection be attained. Through His birth, that is, His incarnation, and baptism and passion and resurrection, He delivered our nature from the sin of our first parent and death and corruption, and became the first-fruits of the resurrection, and made Himself the way and image and pattern, in order that we, too, following in His footsteps, may become by adoption what He is Himself by nature, sons and heirs of God and joint heirs with Him. He gave us therefore, as I said, a second birth in order that, just as we who are born of Adam are in his image and are the heirs of the curse and corruption, so also being born of Him we may be in His likeness and heirs of His incorruption and blessing and glory" (*An Exact Exposition of the Orthodox Faith*; Book 4, ch. 13).

Jesus was perfectly pure by nature, even though He was here on earth. We can become perfectly pure as well; the first step is to be adopted into God's family, and begin partaking of the Divine nature.

* * * * *

St. Francis of Assisi (c.1181-1226)

He was born into a wealthy family; his father was a very successful merchant. He spent his youth in pursuit of pleasure. After his conversion, that all changed—he followed Christ's example of poverty and humility, with great vigor. He founded the Franciscan Order of friars, and helped found an equivalent order for women. He died young, possibly as a result of years of extreme poverty and physical self-denial. By Francis' lifetime, the Catholic Church had accumulated centuries of false doctrine, and of course he was handicapped by that. However, he had such a burning desire to be like Jesus that he was able to rise above that, to a significant degree, and discover a large measure of Divine truth. Francis was one of God's shining lights during a time of great spiritual darkness.

"Harken my lords, my children, and my brethren; listen to my words. Incline the ears of your heart and obey the voice of the Son of God. Keep His commandments with your whole heart, and fulfil His counsels with a perfect mind. Praise Him, for He is good, and exalt Him in your works" (Letters of St. Francis, Letter 12).

Even in the midst of great darkness and error, there were still a few who realized the importance of perfection. Note, however, that perfection consists of the heart and not of the mind. Francis had the right idea, but the wrong details.

"Let us desire nothing, wish for nothing, and let nothing please or delight us but our Creator" (The First Rule of the Friars Minor, ch. 23).

This attitude is a prerequisite for sanctification.

" 'Blessed are the clean of heart, for they shall see God.' Those are truly clean of heart who despise the things of earth and aspire to those of heaven, and who never desist from adoring and contemplating the living God with a pure heart and mind" (Admonitions of St. Francis to his Brethren, #15).

This sort of attitude will almost automatically keep a person from a multitude of sins. We are more accustomed to reading "pure" of heart, rather than "clean." But the two are synonymous.

"Where charity and wisdom are, there is neither fear nor ignorance. Where patience and humility are, there is neither anger nor perturbation of mind. Where joyful poverty is found, there is neither cupidity nor avarice. Where there are quietness and meditation, there is neither solicitude nor dissipation. Where the fear of God guards the house, the enemy can find no entrance" (Admonitions of St. Francis to his Brethren, #21).

We see here how a close walk with God keeps us from sinning. Many Christians live just close enough to God to bewail the remnants of the carnal nature, but they don't live close enough to realize that there is a remedy.

"O all ye holy virtues, may the Lord, from Whom ye proceed, save you! There is absolutely no man in the world who can possess one of you unless he first die to himself" (Salutation of the Virtues).

Dying to self is something that must be done to reach a place where we desire absolutely nothing outside of God's will. We will never be sanctified without first dying to self.

"Whoever wishes to attain to perfect Poverty must renounce not only all worldly prudence, but also in some degree all literary aquirements, that so, stripped of all things, he may enter into the power of God, and, naked, offer himself into the arms of the Crucified. No one has perfectly renounced the world who reserves the most secret place in his heart for his self-love" (Monastic Conferences of St. Frances, Conference 5).

As long as there is any area of our lives that is not completely surrendered to God, it will be a barrier that will prevent us from getting as close to God as we should. And we cannot completely surrender to God as long as we are under the influence of carnality, regardless of how much that influence is deplored and bewailed.

"I own to you that I asked Our Lord that He would deign to make known to me when I am His servant, and when I am not. This most benign Lord, in His mercy, thus answered me: 'Thou mayest know thyself to be My true servant when thou thinkest holy thoughts, speakest holy words, and performest holy works' " (Monastic Conferences of St. Frances, Conference 13).

A person who matches this description will have no time or desire to commit sin. Nor is it likely that such a person will fall prey to temptation.

"The soul dead to herself, and entirely despoiled of selfish affections, humbly permits herself to be guided by the Holy Ghost, that He may work in her according to His good pleasure, as a perfect Master of the excellent doctrine which Christ has left written in the book of His humility, patience, and suffering, which is the sure road to Christian perfection. Hence this soul, which has been purified by God, desires most vehemently to be transformed into His sufferings; ... and that the more she is transformed into Christ Crucified, the more she is transformed into the Most High and Glorious God" (Monastic Conferences of St. Frances, Conference 24).

Our opponents agree on the one hand that we should be like Christ—and on the other hand, they claim that it's impossible. It is sad and tragic to see them so earnestly struggling to be holy, and yet at the same time they reject the best means of achieving their goal.

"I will sacrifice to the Lord that which has hindered my sacrifice" (Sayings of St. Francis).

If there is anything in our lives which prevents or hinders us from getting close to God, that thing should go.

"Take a dead body, and place it where thou wilt. It will not refuse to be moved; it will not complain of its position; it will not expostulate if it be abandoned. If it be placed in a elevated seat, it still looks down, not up; if it be clothed in purple, it appears paler. This is like a truly obedient man, who does not inquire why he is moved, does not care where he is placed, does not beg to be changed; being raised to dignities, he preserves his wonted humility, and the more he is honoured, the more unworthy does he consider himself to be" (Parables and Similitudes of St. Francis, Similitude 1).

This is a very useful analogy, but a word of caution is in order. Some people have taken it too far. They think that natural emotion is a sin or imperfection. We are still human, and we have natural human emotions. For example, we can be sad about the death of a loved one and yet at the same time be perfectly resigned to God's will.

* * * * *

Jan van Ruysbroeck (1293-1381)

He was born near Brussels. Ruysbroeck is not actually a last name, but rather was the name of Jan's village. His mother was very devout; he also had an uncle who was a priest, and apparently fervent for the things of God. Ruysbroeck was ordained as a priest in 1317. In 1343 he, his uncle, and a very good friend of his uncle's, all moved to a nearby forest, and started what grew into a religious community. There Ruysbroeck wrote several books. Late in life he said that he never wrote anything unless he felt moved upon by God. Several of his works were translated into Latin, and therefore had a much bigger following than they would have otherwise. His best-known book, *The Adornment of the Spiritual Marriage,* is essentially a sermon on Matt. 25:6b: "Behold, the bridegroom cometh; go ye out to meet him."

The Adornment of the Spiritual Marriage

"But although, even as God is common to all, the sun shines upon all trees, yet many a tree remains without fruits, and many a tree brings forth wild fruits of little use to men. And for this reason such trees are pruned, and shoots of fruitful trees are grafted into them, so that they may bear good fruits, savoury and useful to man.

"The light of Divine grace is a fruit-bearing shoot, coming forth from the living paradise of the eternal kingdom; and no deed can bring refreshment or profit to man if it be not born of this shoot. This shoot of Divine grace, which makes man pleasing to God, and through which he merits eternal life, is offered to all men. But it is not grafted into all, because some will not cut away the wild branches of their trees; that is, unbelief, and a perverse and disobedient will opposed to the commandments of God.

"But if this shoot of God's grace is to be grafted into our souls, there must be of necessity three things: the prevenient grace of God, the conversion of one's own free will, and the purification of conscience. The prevenient grace touches all men, God bestowing it upon all men. But not all men give on their part the conversion of the will and the purification of conscience; and that is why so many lack the grace of God, through which they should merit eternal life" (Book 1, ch. 1).

Here he is talking about salvation, but what he says applies in large part to sanctification. God offers His grace and power to thoroughly cleanse the heart from all carnality, but many people reject it because of unbelief. As a result, they go through life showing only a small fraction of the fruit that God would like them to produce.

Humility, that is lowliness or self-abasement, is an inward bowing down or prostrating of the heart and of the conscience before God's transcendent worth. Righteousness demands and orders this, and through charity a loving heart cannot leave it undone. When a lowly and loving man considers that God has served him so humbly, so lovingly, and so faithfully; and sees God so high, and so mighty, and so noble, and man so poor, and so little, and so low: then there springs up within the humble heart a great awe and a great veneration for God. For to pay homage to God by every outward and inward act, this is the first and dearest work of humility, the most savoury among those of charity, and most meet among those of righteousness. The loving and humble heart cannot pay homage enough, either to God or to His noble manhood, nor can it abase itself as much as it would. And that is why a humble man thinks that his worship of God and his lowly service are always falling short...

From this humility there springs obedience, for none can be inwardly obedient save the humble man.

Obedience means an unassuming, submissive, and pliable humour, and a will in readiness for all that is good. Obedience makes a man submit to the biddings, the forbiddings, and the will of God... To be obedient in will and deed adorns and enlarges and reveals the humility of a man.

From this obedience there springs the renunciation of one's own will and one's own opinion, for none can submit his own will in all things to the will of another, save the obedient man: though one may obey in outward things and yet remain self-willed.

The forsaking of one's own will causes a man to live without preference for either this or that, in doing or leaving undone, in those things which are strange and special in the saints, in their precepts and in their practice; but it makes him to live always according to the glory and the commandments of God, and the will of his prelates, and in peace with all men in his neighbourhood, so far as true prudence permits.

By renouncing self-will in doing, in leaving undone, and in suffering, the material and occasion of pride are wholly cast out, and humility is made perfect in the highest degree. And God becomes the Lord of the man's whole will; and the man's will is so united with the will of God that he can neither will nor desire in any other way...

From the renunciation of self-will springs patience; for none can be perfectly patient in all things save the man who has subjected his own will to the will of God, and also in all profitable and seemly things, to the will of all other men.

Patience is a peaceful endurance of all things that may befall a man either from God or from the creatures. Nothing can trouble the patient man; neither the loss of earthly goods, of friends and kinsmen, nor sickness, nor disgrace, nor life, nor death, nor purgatory, nor devil, nor hell. For he has abandoned himself in perfect charity to the will of God, and as he is not burdened by mortal sin, everything that God imposes on him, in time and in eternity, is light to him. By this patience a man is also adorned and armed against peevishness and sudden wrath, and impatience in suffering; which often stir a man from within and from without, and lay him open to many temptations.

From this patience there spring meekness and kindliness, for none can be meek in adversity save the patient man.

Meekness gives a man peace and rest in all things. For the meek man can bear provoking words and ways, uncivil looks and deeds, and every kind of injustice towards himself and his friends, and yet in all things remain in peace, for meekness is peaceful endurance...

Out of the same source wherein meekness takes its rise springs kindliness, for none can be kind save the meek man.

This kindness makes a man show a friendly face, and give a cordial response, and do compassionate deeds, to those who are quarrelsome, when he hopes that they will come to know themselves and mend their ways.

By gentleness and kindness, charity is kept quick and fruitful in man, for a heart full of kindness is like a lamp full of precious oil; for the oil of mercy enlightens the erring sinner with good example, and with words and works of comfort it anoints and heals those whose hearts are wounded or grieved or perplexed. And it is a fire and a light for those who dwell in the virtues, in the fire of charity; and neither jealousy nor envy can perturb it.

Out of kindliness springs compassion, which is a fellow-feeling with all men; for none can share the griefs of all, save him who is kind.

Compassion is an inward movement of the heart, stirred by pity for the bodily and ghostly [spiritual] griefs of all men. This compassion makes a man suffer with Christ in His passion; for he who is compassionate marks the wherefore of His pains and the way of His resignation; of His love, His wounds, His tenderness; of His grief and His nobleness; of the disgrace, the misery, and the shame He endured; of the way in which He was despised; of His crown; of the nails; of His mercifulness; of His destruction and dying in patience...

Compassion marks the errors and disorders of our fellow-creatures, how little they care for their God and their eternal blessedness, their ingratitude for all the good things which God has done for them, and the pains He suffered for their sake; how they are strangers to virtue, unskilled and unpractised in it, but skilful and cunning in every wickedness; how attentive they are to the loss and gain of earthly goods, how careless and reckless they are of God, of eternal things, and their eternal bliss. When he marks this, a good man is moved to compassion for the salvation of all men.

Such a man will also regard with pity the bodily needs of his neighbours, and the manifold sufferings of human nature; seeing men hungry, thirsty, cold, naked, sick, poor, and abject; the manifold oppressions of the poor, the grief caused by loss of kinsmen, friends, goods, honour, peace; all the countless sorrows which befall the nature of man...

From this compassion springs generosity; for none can be generous in a supernatural way, with faithfulness and goodwill towards all, save him who has a pitiful heart— though a man may often show generosity to a particular person without charity and without supernatural generosity.

Generosity is a liberal flowing forth of the heart which has been touched by charity and pity... And the generous man who sees the errors and disorders of others, and their unrighteousness, beseeches and prays God, with ardent faith, that He will let His Divine gifts flow forth, that He will show His generosity to all men, and they may know Him and turn to the Truth. The generous man also marks with compassion the bodily needs of all men, and he serves, and he gives, and he lends, and he consoles everyone, according to the needs of each, in so far as he is able, with prudent discretion.

Because of this generosity men are wont to practise the seven works of mercy; the rich do them by their alms and because of their riches, the poor by their good-will and by their hearty desire to do as the rich if they could. And thus the virtue of generosity is made perfect...

Out of this generosity there spring a supernatural zeal and diligence in all virtues and all that is seemly. And none can feel this zeal save him who overflows with generosity. It is an inward restless striving after every virtue, after the likeness of Christ and of all His saints. In this zeal a man longs to devote his heart and his senses, his soul and his body, and all that he is, and all that he has and all toward which he aspires, to the glory and praise of God.

This zeal makes a man grow in reason and prudence, and practise the virtues, both of soul and of body, in righteousness. Through this supernatural zeal all the powers of the soul are laid open to God, and are made ready for all virtues. And the conscience rejoices, and the grace of God is increased; the virtues are practised with joy and gladness, and the outward works are adorned...

From this zeal there spring temperance and sobriety, both inward and outward; for none can possess the right measure of sobriety save him who is greatly zealous and diligent to keep his soul and body in righteousness. Sobriety divides the higher powers from the animal powers; it saves a man from intemperance and from excess. Sobriety wishes neither to taste, nor to know, those things which are forbidden... Man should consider nature, and the Scriptures, and all creatures, and take from these that which profits him and nothing more. Such is sobriety of spirit.

A man should keep his senses in sobriety and should restrain the animal powers by means of the reason; so that the lusts of the flesh do not enter too far into the savouring of food and of drink; but he should eat and drink as the sick take their physic, because it is needful to support his strength, that he may serve God therewith. This is sobriety of body. He should also observe method and moderation in doing and in leaving undone, in words and in works, in silence and in speaking, in food and in drink, according to the custom of Holy Church, and after the example of the saints.

By inward and ghostly temperance and sobriety a man preserves firmness and constancy of faith, purity of intelligence, that tranquillity of reason necessary to the comprehension of truth, an impulse towards all virtues according to the will of God, peace of heart, and serenity of conscience. And herewith he possesses an enduring peace, in God and in himself...

From this temperance there springs purity both of soul and of body, for none can be perfectly pure in body and in soul save him who is temperate in body and in soul.

Purity of spirit is this: that a man should not cleave to any creature with desirous affection, but to God alone; for we should use all creatures, but enjoy only God. Purity of spirit makes a man cleave to God, above all understanding, and above all feelings, and above all the gifts which God may pour into his soul: for all that a creature receives in his understanding and in his feeling, purity will pass by, to rest in God...

Purity of heart is this: that a man, in every bodily temptation or natural inclination, of his own free will, and with an ever-renewed confidence and without hesitation, turns to God; with an ever-renewed faithfulness and with a firm will ever to remain with Him. For consenting to those sins or satisfactions, which the bodily nature seeks like a beast, is a departure from God.

Purity of body is this: that a man withdraws from, and bewares of, all unchaste deeds, in whatsoever manner they be, which his conscience teaches and declares to be unchaste, and contrary to the commandments, the honour, and the will of God...

Now you should know that purity of spirit keeps a man in the likeness of God, untroubled by any creature and inclined towards God, and united with Him.

Purity of body is likened to the whiteness of lilies and to the cleanness of the angels. In withstanding, it is likened to the redness of roses and to the nobleness of martyrs. If it is kept for the love and the glory of God, it is perfect. And so it is likened to the sunflower, for it is one of the highest ornaments of nature.

Purity of heart works a renewal and increase of the grace of God. By purity of heart all the virtues are prompted, practised and preserved. It guards and keeps the senses from without; it quells and restrains the animal lusts from within; it is an adornment of all inwardness. And it is the door of the heart; barred against all earthly things and all deceit, but opened to all heavenly things and to all truth. And of all such Christ says: Blessed are the pure in heart: for they shall see God; and in this vision consist our eternal joy, our reward and our entrance into bliss. Therefore men should be sober and temperate in all things, and beware of all intercourse and occasion whereby purity, whether of soul or of body, may be defiled (Book 1, chs. 12-22).

I don't believe that I can add anything to this. About all I can say is that this is a remarkable, highly-detailed portrait of the perfect Christian. There is a great contrast between this picture and how many Christians are living.

"Christ desires of us a special going out of ourselves, toward a life that shall accord with the way of His coming. And therefore He says in ghostly wise within our hearts at each coming: Go ye out in your lives and in your practices in the way in which My graces and My gifts shall urge you. For according to the manner and way in which the Spirit of God urges, and drives, and draws, and streams into us, and stirs us; in this way we must go out and progress in our inward practices, if we are to become perfect. But if we withstand the Spirit of God by a life that does not accord with it, we lose that inward urge, and then the virtues will depart from us" (Book 2, ch. 7).

Obedience to God is absolutely vital. It is a necessary ingredient for growing in grace, for reaching Christian perfection, or for getting to Heaven at all.

"Now all holiness and all blessedness lie in this: that the spirit is led upwards, through likeness and by means of grace or glory, to rest in the essential unity. For the grace of God is the way by which we must always go... And this is why the sinners and the damned spirits dwell in darkness; for they lack the grace of God, which should enlighten them, and lead them, and show them the way to the fruitive unity... But sin builds up a barrier, and gives rise to such darkness and such unlikeness between the powers and the essence in which God lives, that the spirit cannot be united with its proper essence; which would be its own and its eternal rest, did sin not impede it. For whosoever lives without sin, he lives in likeness unto God, and in grace, and God is his own. And so we have need of grace, which casts out sin, and prepares the way, and makes our whole life fruitful" (Book 2, ch. 60).

He follows a long list of people who regard a sinless life as a possibility here on earth. Entire sanctification removes the last of the sin-barrier between us and God, and that enables the possibility of a completely sinless life in every respect.

The Sparkling Stone

"Hear now three things which constitute a good man. The first, which a good man must have, is a clean conscience without reproach of mortal sin. And therefore whosoever wishes to become a good man must examine and prove himself with due discernment, from that time onward when he could first have committed sin. And from all these sins he must purge himself, according to the precept and the custom of Holy Church.

"The second thing which pertains to a good man is that he must in all things be obedient to God, and to Holy Church, and to his own proper convictions. And to each of these three he must be equally obedient: so shall he live without care and doubt, and shall ever abide without inward reproach in all his deeds.

"The third thing which behoves every good man is that in all his deeds he should have in mind, above all else, the glory of God. And if it happens that by reason of his business or the multiplicity of his works, he has not always God before his eyes, yet at least there should be established in him the intention and desire to live according to the dearest will of God.

"Behold, these three things, when they are possessed in this way, make a man good. And whosoever lacks any one of these three is neither good nor in the grace of God; but whenever a man resolves in his heart to fulfil these three points, how wicked soever he may have been before, in that very instant he becomes good, and is susceptible of God, and filled with the grace of God" (ch. 1).

We see here from the mention of "Holy Church" and "mortal sin" that he couldn't get rid of all the Catholic influence, but, nevertheless, he is spot-on regarding his main points.

Our opponents focus too much on our state as redeemed sinners—with great, heavy, and continual emphasis on the "sinner" part. They talk about how gracious and merciful God was in reaching down to offer salvation to us—and that's where many of them stop. They talk little or nothing regarding how salvation changes a person's life, and how that change manifests itself, or should manifest itself.

It's been said that the Catholics too often leave Jesus on the Cross, and hardly seem to talk about the Resurrection. Opponents of the second work leave us at the point of salvation, and too often don't talk about how that work changes us from wicked to righteous.

"The Divine Unity, of which every God-seeing spirit has entered into possession in love, eternally draws and invites the Divine Persons and all loving spirits into its self. And this inward drawing is felt by each lover, more or less, according to the measure of his love and the manner of his exercise. And whosoever yields himself to this indrawing, and keeps himself therein, cannot fall into mortal sin" (ch. 2).

This last statement may seem quite shocking to a lot of people, but it is entirely Biblical. All sin is "mortal." If it does seem shocking, it's because it is from a part of the Bible that a lot of people ignore, because it conflicts with their theology. See I John 3:9. I will talk more about this verse later.

"The grace of God works according to order in every man, after the measure and the way in which he is able to receive it. And thereby, through the universal working of the grace of God, every sinner, if he desires it, receives the discernment and strength which are needful, that he may leave sin and turn towards virtue. And, through that hidden cooperation of the grace of God, every good man can overcome all sins, and can resist all temptations, and can fulfil all virtues, and can persevere in the highest perfection, if he be in all things submissive to the grace of God" (ch. 5).

Our opponents don't seem to understand that God's power is not only capable of rescuing us from sin, but also capable of keeping us from sin afterward.

* * * * *

The Cloud of Unknowing (1350-1400)

The author of this book was likely a monk. It is clear that he was a deeply spiritual man. Beyond this, there is no good ground for even guessing his identity or anything else. It was most likely written somewhere about 1375. It was written in Middle English, so there are some unfamiliar words. However, anybody who is accustomed to the KJV probably won't have much trouble. Other readers might have more trouble; however, I have added notes as seemed necessary.

"Ghostly [spiritual] friend in God, thou shalt well understand that I find, in my boisterous [clumsy] beholding, four degrees and forms of Christian men's living: and they be these, Common, Special, Singular, and Perfect. Three of these may be begun and ended in this life; and the fourth may by grace be begun here, but it shall ever last without end in the bliss of Heaven" (ch. 1).

128

No matter the times or the circumstances, we keep running into the idea of Christian perfection.

"Lift up thine heart unto God with a meek stirring of love; and mean Himself, and none of His goods. And thereto, look the loath [be unwilling] to think on aught but Himself. So that nought work in thy wit, nor in thy will, but only Himself. And do that in thee is to forget all the creatures that ever God made and the works of them; so that thy thought nor thy desire be not directed nor stretched to any of them, neither in general nor in special, but let them be, and take no heed to them. This is the work of the soul that most pleaseth God" (ch. 3).

Everything else, no matter how important in an earthly sense, ought to be rated as nothing compared to God. Only God's grace can enable a person to have and keep this attitude; and this in turn produces and maintains Christian perfection.

"Weep thou never so much for sorrow of thy sins, or of the Passion of Christ, or have thou never so much mind of the joys of heaven, what may it do to thee? Surely much good, much help, much profit, and much grace will it get thee. But in comparison of this blind stirring of love, it is but a little that it doth, or may do, without this. This by itself is the best part of Mary without these other. They without it profit but little or nought. It destroyeth not only the ground and the root of sin as it may be here, but thereto it getteth virtues. For an [if] it be truly conceived, all virtues shall truly be, and perfectly conceived, and feelingly comprehended, in it, without any mingling of the intent. And have a man never so many virtues without it, all they be mingled with some crooked intent, for the which they be imperfect" (ch. 12).

Perfect love is the foundation for all other virtues, and it also serves as a shield against sin. It digs out and destroys even the deepest roots of sin in the heart.

"And feel sin a lump, thou wottest [know] never what, but none other thing than thyself. And cry then ghostly ever upon one: a 'Sin, sin, sin! Out, out, out!' This ghostly cry is better learned of God by the proof, than of any man by word. For it is best when it is in pure spirit, without special thought or any pronouncing of word; unless it be any seldom time, when for abundance of spirit it bursteth up into word, so that the body and the soul be both filled with sorrow and cumbering of sin.

"On the same manner shalt thou do with this little word 'God.' Fill thy spirit with the ghostly bemeaning of it without any special beholding to any of His works—whether they be good, better, or best of all—bodily or ghostly, or to any virtue that may be wrought in man's soul by any grace; not looking after whether it be meekness or charity, patience or abstinence, hope, faith, or soberness, chastity or wilful poverty. What recks [matters] this in contemplatives? For all virtues they find and feel in God; for in Him is all thing, both by cause and by being. For they think that an they had God they had all good, and therefore they covet nothing with special beholding, but only good God. Do thou on the same manner as far forth as thou mayest by grace: and mean God all, and all God, so that nought work in thy wit and in thy will, but only God.

"And because that ever the whiles thou livest in this wretched life, thee behoveth [need] always feel in some part this foul stinking lump of sin, as it were oned and congealed with the substance of thy being, therefore shalt thou changeably mean these two words—sin and God. With this general knowing, that an thou haddest God, then shouldest thou lack sin: and mightest thou lack sin, then shouldest thou have God" (ch. 40).

Good and evil are opposites. This is all the more reason to seek after the second work. There are a great many people who know theology, and yet don't comprehend the awfulness of sin.

"And therefore I pray thee, lean listily to this meek stirring of love in thine heart, and follow thereafter: for it will be thy guide in this life and bring thee to bliss in the tother. It is the substance of all good living, and without it no good work may be begun nor ended. It is nought else but a good and an according will unto God, and a manner of well-pleasedness and a gladness that thou feelest in thy will of all that He doth.

'Such a good will is the substance of all perfection. All sweetness and comforts, bodily or ghostly, be to this but as it were accidents, be they never so holy; and they do but hang on this good will. Accidents I call them, for they may be had and lacked without breaking asunder of it. I mean in this life, but it is not so in the bliss of heaven; for there shall they be oned with the substance without departing, as shall the body in the which they work with the soul. So that the substance of them here is but a good ghostly will. And surely I trow [believe] that he that feeleth the perfection of this will, as it may be had here, there may no sweetness nor no comfort fall to any man in this life, that he is not as fain and as glad to lack it at God's will, as to feel it and have it" (ch. 49).

Christian perfection entails surrendering our will to God. Once we have fully surrendered everything to God, then we are united to God in a fuller and purer way than was possible before.

* * * * *

Thomas a Kempis (c.1380-1471)

He was born in a village named Kempen, near Dusseldorf, Germany. As a boy, he became acquainted with a religious group called the Brethren of the Common Life. This group also had a strong influence on the Dutch scholar Erasmus, who was one of the leading lights of the early Renaissance, and a supporter (albeit somewhat indirectly) of the Reformation. Thomas was ordained a priest in 1413. For much of his life, he was involved in the work of copying the Bible, which for many centuries was done by hand. He wrote several books, although most people know only the *Imitation of Christ*. Other than the Bible itself, this book has often been considered the most influential book in all of Christian history.

The Imitation of Christ

"We must not trust every word of others or feeling within ourselves, but cautiously and patiently try the matter, whether it be of God. Unhappily we are so weak that we find it easier to believe and speak evil of others, rather than good. But they that are perfect, do not give ready heed to every news-bearer, for they know man's weakness that it is prone to evil and unstable in words" (Book 1, ch. 4).

And here we see Christian perfection once again! Notice that he speaks confidently of it as an attainable thing.

"Whensoever a man desireth aught above measure, immediately he becometh restless. The proud and the avaricious man are never at rest; while the poor and lowly of heart abide in the multitude of peace. The man who is not yet wholly dead to self, is soon tempted, and is overcome in small and trifling matters. It is hard for him who is weak in spirit, and still in part carnal and inclined to the pleasures of sense, to withdraw himself altogether from earthly desires. And therefore, when he withdraweth himself from these, he is often sad, and easily angered too if any oppose his will" (Book 1, ch. 6).

The presence of carnality in the heart makes it very difficult to keep right with God on a consistent basis.

"How came it to pass that many of the Saints were so perfect, so contemplative of Divine things? Because they steadfastly sought to mortify themselves from all worldly desires, and so were enabled to cling with their whole heart to God, and be free and at leisure for the thought of Him. We are too much occupied with our own affections, and too anxious about transitory things. Seldom, too, do we entirely conquer even a single fault, nor are we zealous for daily growth in grace. And so we remain lukewarm and unspiritual...

"If we would quit ourselves like men, and strive to stand firm in the battle, then should we see the Lord helping us from Heaven. For He Himself is alway ready to help those who strive and who trust in Him; yea, He provideth for us occasions of striving, to the end that we may win the victory. If we look upon our progress in religion as a progress only in outward observances and forms, our devoutness will soon come to an end. But let us lay the axe to the very root of our life, that, being cleansed from affections, we may possess our souls in peace" (Book 1, ch. 11).

When a person begins to pursue God whole-heartedly, to the point where he is willing to give up everything else, he is well on the road to Christian perfection.

Notice also how he talks about standing firm. God expects us to stand and fight temptation, not give in to it, and then (having given in to it) console ourselves that we live in a sin-stained, imperfect world, and therefore sinning is inevitable.

"He who only resisteth outwardly and pulleth not up by the root, shall profit little; nay, rather temptations will return to him the more quickly, and will be the more terrible" (Book 1, ch. 13).

The work of sanctification removes the root of sin from the heart. Until that is done, a person's Christian experience is very likely to be a weak, wavering one, no matter how much such a circumstance is bewailed.

"Rarely is any one found so spiritual as to be stripped of all selfish thoughts, for who shall find a man truly poor in spirit and free of all created things? 'His value is from afar, yea from the ends of the earth.' A man may give away all his goods, yet that is nothing; and if he do many deeds of penitence, yet that is a small thing; and though he understand all knowledge, yet that is afar off; and if he have great virtue and zealous devotion, yet much is lacking unto him, yea, one thing which is the most necessary to him of all. What is it then? That having given up all things besides, he give up himself and go forth from himself utterly, and retain nothing of self-love; and having done all things which he knoweth to be his duty to do, that he feel that he hath done nothing. Let him not reckon that much which might be much esteemed, but let him pronounce himself to be in truth an unprofitable servant, as the Truth Himself saith, When ye have done all things that are commanded you, say, we are unprofitable servants. Then may he be truly poor and naked in spirit, and be able to say with the Prophet, As for me, I am poor and needy. Nevertheless, no man is richer than he, no man stronger, no man freer. For he knoweth both how to give up himself and all things, and how to be lowly in his own eyes" (Book 2, ch. 11).

Again we have the theme of total surrender to God.

Opponents of the second work sometimes speak of carnality as having a humbling influence on a Christian. There MAY be a few cases where this is true, but in most cases it has the opposite effect. Pride is a very large part of carnality. For anybody who has a tendency to pride (which is almost everybody), carnality in the heart—even **if** bewailed—will tend to lead to pride, and thence to wilfulness.

"That seemeth a hard saying to many, *If any man will come after Me, let him deny himself and take up his Cross and follow Me.* But it will be much harder to hear that last sentence, *Depart from me, ye wicked, into eternal fire.* For they who now willingly hear the word of the Cross and follow it, shall not then fear the hearing of eternal damnation. This sign of the Cross shall be in heaven when the Lord cometh to Judgment. Then all servants of the Cross, who in life have conformed themselves to the Crucified, shall draw nigh unto Christ the Judge with great boldness...

"Behold everything dependeth upon the Cross, and everything lieth in dying; and there is none other way unto life and to true inward peace, except the way of the Holy

Cross and of daily mortification. Go where thou wilt, seek whatsoever thou wilt, and thou shalt find no higher way above nor safer way below, than the way of the Holy Cross...

"Know thou of a surety that thou oughtest to lead the life of a dying man. And the more a man dieth to himself, the more he beginneth to live towards God. None is fit for the understanding of heavenly things, unless he hath submitted himself to bearing adversities for Christ. Nothing more acceptable to God, nothing more healthful for thyself in this world, than to suffer willingly for Christ. And if it were thine to choose, thou oughtest rather to wish to suffer adversities for Christ, than to be refreshed with manifold consolations, for thou wouldest be more like Christ and more conformed to all saints. For our worthiness and growth in grace lieth not in many delights and consolations, but rather in bearing many troubles and adversities" (Book 2, ch. 12).

He speaks of being conformed to Christ. Jesus did not go around living as He pleased, or living a sinful life; He took great pains to keep a pure heart.

"O Lord my God, Thou art all my good, and who am I that I should dare to speak unto Thee? I am the very poorest of Thy servants, an abject worm, much poorer and more despicable than I know or dare to say. Nevertheless remember, O Lord, that I am nothing, I have nothing, and can do nothing. Thou only art good, just and holy; Thou canst do all things, art over all things, fillest all things, leaving empty only the sinner. Call to mind Thy tender mercies, and fill my heart with Thy grace, Thou who wilt not that Thy work should return to Thee void" (Book 3, ch. 3).

He returns here to the theme of humbleness. Very few people realize just how humble they need to be.

" 'My Son! even thus thou must stand if thou desirest to walk with Me. Thou must be ready alike for suffering or rejoicing. Thou must be poor and needy as willingly as full and rich.'

"Lord, I will willingly bear for Thee whatsoever Thou wilt have to come upon me. Without choice I will receive from Thy hand good and evil, sweet and bitter, joy and sadness, and will give Thee thanks for all things which shall happen unto me Keep me from all sin, and I will not fear death nor hell. Only cast me not away for ever, nor blot me out of the book of life. Then no tribulation which shall come upon me shall do me hurt" (Book 3, ch. 17).

God has ample power to protect us from sin, if we will let Him. But we must do our part, firstly by humbly submitting to whatever our Heavenly Father sees fit to send our way; and secondly by standing firm against temptation.

"Lord, this is the work of a perfect man, never to slacken his mind from attention to heavenly things, and among many cares to pass along as it were without care, not after the manner of one indifferent, but rather with the privilege of a free mind, cleaving to no creature with inordinate affection...

"O my God, sweetness unspeakable, turn into bitterness all my fleshly consolation, which draweth me away from the love of eternal things, and wickedly allureth toward itself by setting before me some present delight. Let not, O my God, let not flesh and blood prevail over me, let not the world and its short glory deceive me, let not the devil and his craftiness supplant me. Give me courage to resist, patience to endure, constancy to persevere. Grant, in place of all consolations of the world, the most sweet unction of Thy Spirit, and in place of carnal love, pour into me the love of Thy Name" (Book 3, ch. 26).

This is the attitude of Christian perfection. Many Christians may meet some of this description, and/or they may meet all of it for short periods of time; but to meet all of it all the time requires the eradication of carnality.

"Therefore it is not gaining or multiplying of this thing or that which advantageth thee, but rather the despising it and cutting it by the root out of thy heart; which thou must not only understand of money and riches, but of the desire after honour and vain praise, things which all pass away with the world" (Book 3, ch. 27).

Once again we see the idea of uprooting sin from the heart.

"My son, thou oughtest not to be turned aside, nor immediately cast down, because thou hast heard the way of the perfect. Rather oughtest thou to be provoked to higher aims, and at the least to long after the desire thereof" (Book 3, ch. 32).

One of the reasons given for opposing entire sanctification is that such a high standard discourages people. As we see here, that's the wrong reaction. It is very difficult to grow or improve in any way, in any thing, either secular or religious, without first being challenged.

" 'My Son, lose thyself and thou shalt find Me. Stand still without all choosing and all thought of self, and thou shalt ever be a gainer. For more grace shall be added to thee, as soon as thou resignest thyself, and so long as thou dost not turn back to take thyself again.'

" 'O Lord, how often shall I resign myself, and in what things shall I lose myself?'

" 'Always; every hour: in that which is little, and in that which is great. I make no exception, but will that thou be found naked in all things. Otherwise how canst thou be Mine and I thine, unless thou be inwardly and outwardly free from every will of thine own? The sooner thou doest this, the better shall it be with thee; and the more fully and sincerely, the more thou shalt please Me, and the more abundantly shalt thou be rewarded.

" 'Some resign themselves, but with certain reservations, for they do not fully trust in

God, therefore they think that they have some provision to make for themselves. Some again at first offer everything; but afterwards being pressed by temptation they return to their own devices, and thus make no progress in virtue. They will not attain to the true liberty of a pure heart, nor to the grace of My sweet companionship, unless they first entirely resign themselves and daily offer themselves up as a sacrifice; without this the union which bringeth forth fruit standeth not nor will stand.

" 'Many a time I have said unto thee, and now say again, Give thyself up, resign thyself, and thou shalt have great inward peace. Give all for all; demand nothing, ask nothing in return; stand simply and with no hesitation in Me, and thou shalt possess Me. Thou shalt have liberty of heart, and the darkness shall not overwhelm thee. For this strive thou, pray for it, long after it, that thou mayest be delivered from all possession of thyself, and nakedly follow Jesus who was made naked for thee; mayest die unto thyself and live eternally to Me. Then shall all vain fancies disappear, all evil disturbings, and superfluous cares. Then also shall immoderate fear depart from thee, and inordinate love shall die' " (Book 3, ch. 37).

Perfect surrender to God produces perfect peace. There is tremendous rest in knowing that we have turned everything over to God.

"My Son, in many things it behoveth thee to be ignorant, and to esteem thyself as one dead upon the earth, and as one to whom the whole world is crucified. Many things also thou must pass by with deaf ear, and must rather think upon those things which belong unto thy peace" (Book 3, ch. 44).

The image of crucifixion is another theme that keeps popping up. It is another way of talking about dying to self and to the world.

Chapter 6

The Darkness Lifts: 1500-1725

After the apostles and their immediate successors, the spiritual life of the Church began a long decline. Even when the books of the Canon were being written, heresies were already springing up. Things weren't too bad for a while. Persecution kept the church up to a high standard. But later on, there was a period of several hundred years in length during which spiritual darkness was very deep. The flame of Divine truth flickered, and seemingly almost went out, but God still had a few bright lights during that period.

And then the day began, once more, to dawn. John Wycliffe (c.1330-1384), Jan Hus (c.1369-1415), and Girolamo Savonarola (1452-1498) were the morning stars heralding the Reformation. But even after the Reformation brought daylight, much of Christendom was still in some degree of spiritual infancy. It took close to another two hundred years for the fields to be prepared for still more spiritual light. Only then—in a burst of light and activity that could almost be considered as a "second Reformation"—did the full bloom of Divine truth once again shine on the world, largely through the agency of the Wesley brothers and their close associates.

*****

Brother Lawrence (1610/14-1691)
His birth name was Nicolas Herman, and he was born into a peasant family. He changed his name when he became a Carmelite monk. He stayed in this monastery, in Paris, for the rest of his life. He was never a priest; he worked in the monastery's kitchen most of the time. Over the years, he gained a reputation as a godly man, and many

people sought his advice on spiritual matters. He was another of God's shining lights, who, although a Catholic, was able to overcome Catholic dogma sufficiently to live close to God.

The Practice of the Presence of God

"You so earnestly desire that I describe the method by which I arrived at that habitual sense of God's presence, which our merciful Lord has been pleased to grant me. I am complying with your request with my request that you show my letter to no one. If I knew that you would let it be seen, all the desire I have for your spiritual progress would not be enough to make me comply.

"The account I can give you is: Having found in many books different methods of going to God and divers practices of the spiritual life, I thought this would serve rather to puzzle me than facilitate what I sought after, which was nothing but how to become wholly God's. This made me resolve to give the all for the All. After having given myself wholly to God, to make all the satisfaction I could for my sins, I renounced, for the love of Him, everything that was not He, and I began to live as if there was none but He and I in the world" (First Letter).

Again we see that the theme of renouncing the world, and dying out to the world and to self, keeps cropping up. This must be done before a person can be sanctified. Unsanctified Christians sometimes talk about this, but it seems that they generally don't get very far.

"Sometimes I consider myself as a stone before a carver, whereof He is to make a statue. Presenting myself thus before God, I desire Him to make His perfect image in my soul and render me entirely like Himself" (Second Letter).

This necessarily entails living a sinless life.

"I am taking this opportunity to tell you about the sentiments of one of our society concerning the admirable effects and continual assistance he receives from the presence of God. May we both profit by them.

"For the past forty years his continual care has been to be always with God; and to do nothing, say nothing, and think nothing which may displease Him. He does this without any view or motive except pure love of Him and because God deserves infinitely more.

"He often points out our blindness and exclaims that those who content themselves with so little are to be pitied. God, says he, has infinite treasure to bestow, and we take so little through routine devotion which lasts but a moment. Blind as we are, we hinder God, and stop the current of His graces. But when He finds a soul penetrated with a lively faith, He pours into it His graces and favors plentifully. There they flow like a torrent, which, after being forcibly stopped against its ordinary course, when it has found a passage, spreads itself with impetuosity and abundance" (Fourth Letter).

Such a standard—to do, say, and think nothing that displeases God—automatically excludes sin from a person's life.

"I cannot imagine how religious persons can live satisfied without the practice of the presence of God. For my part I keep myself retired with Him in the depth and center of my soul as much as I can. While I am with Him I fear nothing; but the least turning from Him is insupportable. This practice does not tire the body. It is, however, proper to deprive it sometimes, nay often, of many little pleasures which are innocent and lawful. God will not permit a soul that desires to be devoted entirely to Him to take pleasures other than with Him. That is more than reasonable" (Sixth Letter).

And yet many church-goers today talk excitedly about almost everything else. Step into a modern church, and you will often hear conversations about fashion, sports, and other worldly activities—everything except the God that they claim to be there to worship.

"Let us often consider that our only business in this life is to please God, that perhaps all besides is but folly and vanity. You and I have lived over forty years in the monastic life. Have we employed them in loving and serving God, who by His mercy has called us to this state and for that very end? I am sometimes filled with shame and confusion when I reflect, on the one hand, upon the great favors which God has done and continues to do for me; and, on the other, upon the ill use I have made of them and my small advancement in the way of perfection" (Ninth Letter).

I wonder if our opponents are getting tired of all this talk about Christian perfection. Unfortunately for them, we're nowhere near done with it yet.

I have visited many different churches. Even many that are better than average tend to have a host of congregants who seem to have no clear conception of pleasing God. If they are Christians at all, they are often very shallow, un-informed ones.

* * * * *

George Fox (1624-1691)

The founder of the Quaker movement was born in central England, into a fairly well-off family; his father was a weaver. From an early age, he was deeply distressed by the sin and religious carelessness of many people who professed to be Christians. He was influenced by the Puritans and the early Baptists. In 1647, he began traveling around England, preaching as he went. The conditions he faced were in many ways nearly identical to those experienced by John Wesley and George Whitefield decades later: he was beaten and otherwise attacked numerous times. He was also jailed on several occasions. Late in life, he wrote his *Journal*, which (in edited form) is also known as his *Autobiography*.

"I went among the professors [of religion] at Duckingfield and Manchester, where I stayed awhile, and declared truth among them. There were some convinced who received the Lord's teaching, by which they were confirmed and stood in the truth. But the professors were in a rage, all pleading for sin and imperfection, and could not endure to hear talk of perfection, and of a holy and sinless life. But the Lord's power was over all, though they were chained under darkness and sin, which they pleaded for, and quenched the tender thing in them" (*Autobiography*, ch. 1).

George Fox developed his theology through Bible study, prayer, and meditation. For the most part, he had no one to teach him. And yet his view of Christian perfection, and Christian living, lines up beautifully with earlier writers.

"While I was here in prison diverse professors came to discourse with me. I had a sense, before they spoke, that they came to plead for sin and imperfection. I asked them whether they were believers and had faith. They said, 'Yes.' I asked them, 'In whom?' They said, 'In Christ.' I replied, 'If ye are true believers in Christ, you are passed from death to life; and if passed from death, then from sin that bringeth death; and if your faith be true, it will give you victory over sin and the devil, purify your hearts and consciences (for the true faith is held in a pure conscience), and bring you to please God, and give you access to Him again.'

"But they could not endure to hear of purity, and of victory over sin and the devil. They said they could not believe any could be free from sin on this side of the grave. I bade them give over babbling about the Scriptures, which were holy men's words, whilst they pleaded for unholiness" (*Autobiography*, ch 4).

Fox was bold and direct; he was well-suited for confronting sin wherever he found it. We see here that unbelief in God's power and in His Word has a long, sordid history.

* * * * *

Robert Barclay (1648-1690)

He was born in northeastern Scotland. He attended college in Paris. While in Paris, an uncle who was quite rich offered to make Robert his heir, if only Robert would become a Catholic—a condition which was refused. Robert returned to Scotland in 1666, and very shortly thereafter joined the new religious movement called Quakers. He became the first Quaker theologian, and wrote several books in defense of the movement. His most important book, *Apology for the True Christian Divinity*, was first published in 1676 (in Latin), and republished in English in 1678. He was jailed more than once for his faith.

"In whom this holy and pure birth is fully brought forth, the body of death and sin comes to be crucified and removed, and their hearts united and subjected unto the truth, so as not to obey any suggestion or temptation of the evil one, but to be free from actual sinning, and transgressing of the law of God, and in that respect perfect. Yet doth this perfection still admit of a growth; and there remaineth a possibility of sinning, where the mind doth not most diligently and watchfully attend unto the Lord" (*Theological Theses*, Eighth Proposition; Concerning Perfection).

As we have seen, Christian writers since the very beginning of the Church have written about Christian perfection. However, many of them did not really define it, at least not in the extant writings. Here we have the beginnings of the first major theological expression of the doctrine.

Apology for the True Christian Divinity
"That the *saints nor can nor ever will be free of sinning in this life,* is inconsistent with the wisdom of God, and with his glorious power and majesty, *who is of purer eyes than to behold iniquity;* who having purposed in himself to gather to him that should worship him, and be witnesses for him on earth, a *chosen people,* doth also no doubt sanctify and purify them. For God hath no delight in iniquity, but abhors transgression; and though he regard man in transgression so far as to pity him, and afford him means to come out of it; yet he loves him not, neither delights in him, as he is joined thereunto. Wherefore if man must be always joined to sin, their God would always be at a distance with him... But *God* is *light,* and *every sin is darkness* in a measure: What greater *stain* then can there be than this upon *God's wisdom,* as if he had been wanting to prepare a means whereby his children might perfectly serve and worship him, or had not provided a way whereby they might serve him in any thing, but that they must withal still serve the devil no less, yea, more than himself? For *he that sinneth is the servant of sin,* Rom. vi. 16 and every sin is an act of service and obedience to the devil. So then if the saints sin daily in *thought, word,* and *deed,* yea, if the very *service* they offer to God be sin, surely they serve the devil more than they do God: for besides that they give the devil many entire services... : and if their prayers and all their spiritual performances be sinful, the devil is as much served by them in these as God, and in most of them much more, since they confess that many of them are performed without the leadings and influence of God's Spirit. Now who would not account him a foolish master among men, who being able to do it, and also desirous it might be so, yet would not provide a way whereby his children and servants might serve him more entirely than his avowed enemy; or would not guard against their serving of him, but be so imprudent and unadvised in his contrivance, that whatever way his servants and children served him, they should no less, yea often much more, serve his enemy? What may we then think of that doctrine that would infer this folly upon the *Omnipotent* and *Only Wise God?*" (Proposition 8, sec. 3).

In other words, the claim that we can never be free from sin is to impugn the power and wisdom of God.

"We have elsewhere spoken of the *injustice* these men [Calvinists] ascribe to God, in making him to *damn the wicked, to whom* they allege *he never afforded any means of being good;* but this is yet an aggravation more irrational and inconsistent, to say, *that God will not afford to those, whom he hath chosen to be his own,* (whom they confess he loveth,) *the means to please him.* What can allow then from so strange a doctrine?

"This *imperfection* in the saints either proceeds from God or from themselves: If it proceeds from them, it must be because they are short in improving or making use of the power given them, whereby they are capable to obey; and so it is a thing possible to them, as indeed it is by the help of that power: but this our adversaries deny: they are then not to be blamed for their imperfection and continuing in sin, since it is not possible for them to do otherwise. If it be not of themselves, it must be of God... But these men confess we ought to seek of God power to redeem us from sin, and yet believe they are never to receive such a power; such prayers then cannot be in faith, but are all vain" (Proposition 8, sec. 4).

He touches on something that I have observed independently: the doctrine of those who oppose the second work is riddled with inconsistencies and illogic.

"This evil doctrine is *highly injurious to Jesus Christ, and greatly derogates from the power and virtue of his sacrifice, and renders his coming and ministry,* as to the great end of it, *ineffectual.* For Christ, as for other ends, so principally he appeared for the removing of sin, for the gathering a righteous generation, that might serve the Lord in purity of mind, and walk before him in fear, and to bring in everlasting righteousness, and that evangelical perfection which the law could not do. Hence he is said, Tit. ii. 14. to have given himself for us, that he might redeem us from all iniquity, and purify unto himself a peculiar people, zealous of good works. This is certainly spoken of the saints while upon earth; but, contrary thereunto, these men affirm, that *we are never redeemed from all iniquity,* and so make Christ's giving of himself for us void and ineffectual, and give the apostle *Paul* the lie plainly, by denying that *Christ purifieth to himself a peculiar people, zealous of good works.* How are they *zealous of good works,* who are ever committing evil ones? How are they a *purified people,* that are still in impurity, as they are that daily sin, unless sin be accounted no impurity?" (Proposition 8, sec. 5).

He continues on here in the same vein. Some of our opponents, evidently feeling that such Bible verses as Titus 2:14, as referenced in this quote, can't actually be ignored, adopt the expedient of shifting them in time. Yes, they agree, God wants to purify us— but not here, and not now; only in Heaven.

"This doctrine is *contrary to common reason and sense.* For the two opposite *principles,* whereof the one rules in the children of *darkness,* the other in the children of *light,* are *sin* and *righteousness;* and as they are respectively leavened and actuated by them, so they are accounted either as reprobated or justified, seeing it is *abomination in the sight of God, either to justify the wicked or condemn the just.* Now to say that men cannot be so leavened by the one as to be delivered from the other, is in plain words to affirm, that *sin* and *righteousness* are consistent; and that a man may be truly termed *righteous,* though he be daily *sinning* in every thing he doth; and then what difference betwixt *good* and *evil?* Is not this to fall into that great abomination of putting *light* for *darkness,* and calling *good evil,* and *evil good?"* (Proposition 8, sec. 7).

In my study for this book, I have become convinced that very few, possibly none, of our opponents have ever truly thought through the ramifications of their doctrine.

"If thou desirest to know this perfection and freedom from sin possible for thee, turn thy mind to the *light and spiritual law of Christ in the heart,* and suffer the reproofs thereof; bear the judgment and indignation of God upon the unrighteous part in thee as therein is revealed, which Christ hath made tolerable for thee, and so suffer *judgment in thee* to be *brought forth into victory,* and thus come to partake of the fellowship of *Christ's sufferings,* and be made *conformable unto his death,* that thou mayest feel thyself *crucified with him to the* world *by the power of his cross in thee;* so that that life that sometimes was alive in thee to this world, and the love and lusts thereof, may die, and a new life be raised, by which thou mayest live hence forward to God, and not to or for thyself...

"This perfection or freedom from sin is possible, because many have attained it, according to the express testimony of the scripture; some before the law, and some under the law, through witnessing and partaking of the benefit and effect of the gospel, and much more many under the gospel" (Proposition 8, sec. 8).

He follows many earlier writers in talking about being crucified with Christ. This concept is an integral part of Holiness doctrine. All forms of sin and carnality must be dealt with at some point. Why not get it over with as soon as possible?

"The *duty of man* towards God lieth chiefly in these two generals. 1. *In an holy conformity to the pure law and light of God, so as both to forsake the evil, and be found in the practice of those perpetual and moral precepts of righteousness and equity. And 2. In rendering that reverence, honour, and adoration to God, that he requires and demands of us;* which is comprehended under *worship"* (Proposition 11, sec. 1).

If we actually conform ourselves to God, there will be no sin in us.

* * * * *

Madame Guyon (1648-1717)

Jeanne Guyon was born in north-central France. She was forced into an arranged marriage at age 16, and was widowed at 28. After her husband died, she diligently sought after God, and found Him. After some time, she received the second work of grace. She was not content to remain quiet about her experience; the upshot was that the Catholic Church considered her a heretic. She was imprisoned for her faith in 1688 for seven months, and was imprisoned again in 1695 for more than seven years.

"Prayer is the key to perfection, and the sovereign good; it is the means of delivering us from every vice, and obtaining us every virtue; for the one great means of becoming perfect, is to walk in the presence of God" (*Method of Prayer*, ch. 1).

One of the requirements for the second work is to intensely desire to have the purity and holiness of God manifested in one's life.

"We must surrender our whole being to Christ Jesus, and cease to live any longer in ourselves, that He may become our life; 'that being dead, our life may be hid with Christ in God.' (Col. iii. 3.) 'Pass ye into me,' sayeth God, 'all ye who earnestly seek after me.' But how is it we pass into God? In no way but by leaving and forsaking ourselves, that we may be lost in Him; and this can be effected only by annihilation, which, being the true prayer of adoration, renders unto God alone, all 'blessing, honor, glory, and power, forever and ever' (Rev. v. 13.)" (*Method of Prayer*, ch. 20).

God should be everything to us, and we should be willing to give up everything else for Him. See Matt. 10:37-39.

* * * * *

Francois Fenelon (1651-1715)

He was born into a noble family, in southwestern France. Many of his ancestors had served the Catholic Church, and he wanted to do the same. He studied at a seminary in Paris, and was ordained as a priest in 1676. In 1688, he became acquainted with Madame Guyon, a friendship that was to be very consequential for them both. In 1689, Louis XIV appointed him tutor of the King's oldest grandson. In 1696, Fenelon became an archbishop. Shortly thereafter, he caused much controversy by his support of Madame Guyon. He wrote *Maxims of the Saints* in support of her position. The Pope condemned this book a few years later. Fenelon, who (like Madame Guyon) lived and died a loyal Catholic, submitted to the Pope's authority. Nevertheless, he remained a warrior for Divine truth, to the best of his knowledge and ability, filled with the love and gentleness of God.

Christian Counsel

"O! how few there are who pray! for how few are they who desire what is truly good! Crosses, external and internal humiliation, renouncement of our own wills, the death of self and the establishment of God's throne upon the ruins of self love, these are indeed good; not to desire these, is not to pray; to desire them seriously, soberly, constantly, and with reference to all the details of life, this is true prayer; not to desire them, and yet to suppose we pray, is an illusion like that of the wretched who dream themselves

143

happy...

"On the other hand, that heart in which the true love of God and true desire exist, never ceases to pray. Love, hid in the bottom of the soul, prays without ceasing, even when the mind is drawn another way. God continually beholds the desire which He has himself implanted in the soul, though it may at times be unconscious of its existence; his heart is touched by it; it ceaselessly attracts his mercies; it is that Spirit which, according to St. Paul, helpeth our infirmities and maketh intercession for us with groanings which cannot be uttered...

"We should greatly fear and be exceedingly cautious to avoid all things that have a tendency to make us lose this state of prayer. Thus we should decline those worldly occupations and associates which dissipate the mind, pleasures which excite the passions, and everything calculated to awaken the love of the world and those old inclinations that have caused us so much trouble" (ch. 4).

This would serve very nicely as a commentary on Eph. 6:18.

If we tried always to consciously pray, we would be utterly unfit for normal life; we would never get anything done. But we can have always the spirit of prayer.

"You desire, perhaps, to know more in detail in what this self-abandonment consists. I will endeavor to satisfy you.

"There is little difficulty in comprehending that we must reject criminal pleasures, unjust gains, and gross vanities, because the renouncement of these things consists in a contempt which repudiates them absolutely, and forbids our deriving any enjoyment from them; but it is not so easy to understand that we must abandon property honestly acquired, the pleasures of a modest and well-spent life, and the honors derivable from a good reputation, and a virtue which elevates us above the reach of envy.

"The reason why we do not understand that these things must be given up, is, that we are not required to discard them with dislike, but, on the contrary, to preserve them to be used according to the station in which the Divine Providence places us.

"We have need of the consolation of a mild and peaceful life, to console us under its troubles; in respect to honors, we must regard 'that which is convenient,' and we must keep the property we possess to supply our wants. How then are we to renounce these things at the very moment when we are occupied in the care of preserving them? We are, moderately and without inordinate emotion, to do what is in our power to retain them, in order to make a sober use of them, without desiring to enjoy them or placing our hearts upon them...

"Remember that we must not only renounce evil, but also good things; for Jesus has said, 'Whatsoever he be of you that forsaketh not all he hath, he cannot be my disciple" (Luke xiv. 33.)

"It follows, then, that the Christian must abandon everything that he has, however innocent; for, if he do not renounce it, it ceases to be innocent.

"He must abandon those things which it is his duty to guard with the greatest possible care, such as the good of his family, or his own reputation, for he must have his heart on none of these things; he must preserve them for a sober and moderate use; in short, he must be ready to give them all up whenever it is the will of Providence to deprive him of them...

"Having abandoned everything exterior, and which is not self, it remains to complete the sacrifice by renouncing everything interior, including self" (ch. 10).

We must also take care to ensure that our sacrifice and abandonment **remains** complete. Satan has very subtle ways of trying to get us to renege on our consecration. We must be on guard against temptation as long as we are on earth.

"Christian Perfection is not that rigorous, tedious, cramping thing that many imagine. It demands only an entire surrender of everything to God from the depths of the soul, and the moment this takes place, whatever is done for Him becomes easy. They who are God's without reserve, are in every state content; for they will only what He wills, and desire to do for Him whatever he desires them to do; they strip themselves of everything, and in this nakedness find all things restored an hundred fold. Peace of conscience, liberty of spirit, the sweet abandonment of themselves and theirs into the hand of God, the joy of perceiving the light always increasing in their hearts, and finally the freedom of their souls from the bondage of the fears and desires of this world, these things constitute that return of happiness which the true children of God receive an hundred fold in the midst of their crosses, while they remain faithful...

"What God requires of us, is a will which is no longer divided between Him and any creature; a simple, pliable state of will which desires what He desires, rejects nothing but what He rejects, and wills without reserve what He wills, and under no pretext wills what He does not. In this state of mind, all things are proper for us; our amusements, even, are acceptable in his sight.

"Blessed is he who thus gives himself to God! He is delivered from his passions, from the opinions of men, from their malice, from the tyranny of their maxims, from their cold and miserable raillery, from the misfortunes which the world attributes to chance, from the infidelity and fickleness of friends, from the artifices and snares of enemies, from the wretchedness and shortness of life, from the horrors of an ungodly death, from the cruel remorse that follows sinful pleasures, and finally from the everlasting condemnation of God!

"The true Christian is delivered from this innumerable multitude of evils, because, putting his will into the hands of God, he wills only what He wills, and thus finds comfort in the midst of all his suffering in the way of faith, and its attendant hope.

"What weakness it is, then, to be fearful of consecrating ourselves to God, and of getting too far into so desirable a state!

"Happy those who throw themselves, as it were, headlong, and with their eyes shut, into the arms of 'the Father of mercies, and the God of all comfort!' (2 Cor. i. 3.) Their whole desire then, is to know what is the will of God respecting them; and they fear nothing so much as not perceiving the whole of his requirements. So soon as they behold a new light in his law, they are transported with joy, like a miser at the finding of a treasure…

"What folly to fear to be too devoted to God! to fear to be happy! to fear to love the will of God in all things! to fear to have too much courage under inevitable crosses, too much consolation in the love of God, and too great a detachment from the passions which make us miserable! …

"Many are affrighted at these truths, and their fear arises from this: that while they know the exacting nature of religion, they are ignorant of its gifts, and of the spirit of love which renders everything easy. They are not aware that religion leads to the highest perfection, while bestowing peace through a principle of love that smooths every rough place" (ch. 23).

I would like to emphasize this sentence: "What weakness it is, then, to be fearful of consecrating ourselves to God, and of getting too far into so desirable a state!" Carnality is the reason and the essence of that weakness. It will do anything to save itself from death. Every Christian agrees—in theory—that consecration is a good thing. But many people seem to have only a weak, temporary version. Thus they go to the altar every Sunday, "reconsecrating" themselves to God, because it never seems to last.

Many people have twisted Titus 1:15a ("Unto the pure all things are pure"), and similar verses, into a pretext for lawlessness. The second paragraph of this quote, especially the last sentence, is the proper meaning of that verse.

"We have nothing but our wills only; all the rest belongs elsewhere. Disease removes life and health; riches make to themselves wings; intellectual talents depend upon the state of the body. The only thing that really belongs to us is our will, and it is of this, therefore, that God is especially jealous, for He gave it to us, not that we should retain it, but that we should return it to Him, whole as we received it, and without the slightest reservation.

"If the least desire remain, or the smallest hesitation, it is robbing God, contrary to the order of creation; for all things come from Him, and to Him they are all due" (ch. 26).

I have observed that many of our opponents have a sincere desire to have a close walk with God: but somehow they don't seem to fully realize that carnality is a barrier, or what to do about it. They have to work ten times harder to have that close walk than they would otherwise; and it will never be as close as it could be as long as they have carnality in their hearts.

Philipp Jakob Spener (1635-1705)

He was born in a town in what was then the Holy Roman Empire, but now is in the extreme eastern part of France. He was born into a Lutheran family. While in college, he became concerned with the state of Lutheranism, which had grown cold, rigid, and formal. He became a pastor in 1666, and began to put his ideas into practice. He published his first book, *Pia Desideria* ("Pious Desires"), in 1675. History has closely associated him with Pietism. This was something of a reform movement within Lutheranism; it focused on individual piety, separation from the world, and a vigorous inward life.

"Pietism was the most important development in Protestant spirituality. Its roots can be traced to Lutheran and Calvinist-Puritan concerns with the practice of piety in the late sixteenth and seventeenth centuries... In both its churchly and radical forms the influence of Pietism was great. Without it, it is difficult to understand the growth of 'evangelical' Christianity in Europe and America, and its adherents played central roles in the development of Protestant, hymnological, devotional, theological, and biblical studies" (*Pietists: Selected Writings*, Ed. Peter Erb).

I have taken a couple of people slightly out of chronological order, to more clearly show the lines of influence that existed.

"Holiness of life itself contributes much to conversion [of others], as Peter teaches (1 Pet. 3:1-2)" (*Pia Desideria*).

Just like Jesus was a living, breathing example to the apostles, and the apostles became examples to subsequent Christians, we should be examples of holy living to people around us.

"Surely, students of theology ought to lay this foundation, that during their early years of study they realize that they must die unto the world and live as individuals who are to become examples to the flock, and that this is not merely an ornament but a very necessary work" (*Pia Desideria*).

"Living a holy life" is simply another way of stating that a person shows abundant fruit of the Spirit. To state the obvious, a holy life is the opposite of a sinful life. If we are truly holy, that holiness will fill every nook and cranny of our lives, and thus leave no room for sin.

"The virtue of resignation: Partly a fruit of faith, partly a piece of the divine order to faith.

"1. It requires a denial of everything which a person can have in the world and on which his heart can hang. Note Matthew 10:37 and particularly Luke 14:26, 33.

"2. The denial of one's own will. This is true denial of one's self, without which we are not able to be the disciples of the Lord (Matt. 16:24). To this belongs the crucifying of the flesh (Gal. 5:24; Rom. 8:13) and the denial of the desire for one's own honor, value, pleasure, and freedom to which we are naturally inclined.

"3. Giving ourselves over to the divine will so that we desire nothing other than what will come to us will be pleasing to the Lord. This is as we pray in the third petition: Thy will be done. This virtue must be practiced at all times.

"4. The understanding that God will work in us what is pleasing to him without opposition, that is, that no place will be given in us to Satan and the world. We wish that we will be able to do nothing for ourselves, but that the Lord is to do with us as he pleases.

"5. Patient waiting that God will bring about his will in us, and that we will be satisfied that if that which we otherwise would desire does not come about, we will accept the circumstances without great sorrow. See the example of David in 2 Samuel 15:25-26.

"6. Where we discover and feel divine movement and stirring in us, that we follow it obediently and that we do that to which we are directed. At the same time to resign to God our understanding, will, affections, and members so that he may use them as he wishes... We must give ourselves to the Holy Spirit as an empty canvas on which he is to paint" ("Resignation"; from *Pietists: Selected Writings*).

No carnal Christian can do all this: the carnal nature is simply too strong. There are a great many people who think that they are consecrated to God, but they are only partly consecrated. He speaks here of total consecration. Anybody who meets this description is, at minimum, well on the road to entire sanctification.

* * * * *

August Hermann Francke (1663-1727)

He was born in northern Germany. He received a very good education, including a good knowledge of Hebrew and Greek. He was heavily influenced by Spener. He gave lectures promoting Pietism, which earned him the opposition of much of the Lutheran Church. In 1691, Frederick III, Elector of Brandenburg, invited him to teach at the new University of Halle. Franke also became the pastor in a near-by town. The two positions gave him latitude to spread his ideas. Franke was also supported by an influential member of the Prussian nobility. In 1698, he founded an orphanage; this act later had an influence on George Muller. He was instrumental in founding the Canstein Bible Institute. According to the 1911 Encyclopedia Britannica, this was the first modern Bible society; this organization remained active for about 300 years, and published 6 million Bibles during that time.

"Christ left us an image. This means a copy text, a *hupogrammon* and in fact the kind of copy text which one places beneath another piece of paper so that one can clearly see through it all the letters and marks and can learn to imitate these from the copy text just as they stand in the original" ("Following Christ"; from *Pietists: Selected Writings*).

Many Christians don't understand what Jesus' example really means. And they don't seem to understand how far short of it they are, or what to do about it. The second work of grace helps a great deal on all these points.

"If God wishes to perfect his gracious visitation in a person's soul, that person must then not be dissolute or otherwise weary or sleepy in his thoughts, but must be prepared to experience the workings of the Spirit of God in his soul... One must therefore enter into oneself through the spirit of propriety and thoughtfulness so that through this spirit he might be disentangled from Satan's bonds, turn once again into his own heart, acknowledge what is needed for his eternal salvation, and thus be watchful over his own heart and guard it with all industry so that the Lord might perfect his work in his heart and destroy Satan's work and kingdom in it" ("Pure and Unblemished Worship"; from *Pietists: Selected Writings*).

Satan has so blinded some people, that they refuse to let God work in their lives to the full extent of His power.

"I consider also the duties of self-denial and putting off of the world and its carnal pleasures, and, in short, from all the present things of sense and time, to be among those more important and necessary subjects which ministers should often preach on, oftener indeed than most of them do. These are subjects which our Savior Christ, when he was a preacher upon earth, very much insisted on in his sermons... And how needful are these subjects now. For alas! how many persons there are who can talk well about Christ and religion, who carry a fair appearance of virtue and godliness, and who perform many outward duties with reputation and honor, and yet not having learned to deny themselves; their love of the world not being sufficiently mortified, they are easily overcome in a day of trial, and sacrifice their religion and their souls to their worldly interest" ("A Letter to a Friend Concerning the Most Useful way of Preaching"; from *Pietists: Selected Writings*).

There are many Christians who seem to be satisfied with a shallow religious life. They miss out on a great many blessings because of that, and they sometimes find themselves in avoidable difficulties.

* * * * *

Johann Friedrich Starck (1680-1756)

He was born in northern Germany. He, too, came under the influence of Pietism. His influence was apparently primarily just during his lifetime; he wrote several hundred hymns, but they have fallen into obscurity. He also wrote several books. He was a pastor as well. I have found very little in English about his life.

"Pray to God at daybreak to keep thee throughout the day in his grace, that thou mayest not sin against him nor against thy neighbor... Surrender thyself unto God, so that throughout the day thou mayest stand in his love, speak of him, think of him, and not offend him wittingly or willingly, and then doubt not that the Lord will be graciously pleased to hear thy sighs and prayers, and give and grant unto thee throughout the day the things that shall be profitable to thy body and thy soul" (*Daily Handbook for Days of Joy and Sorrow*; Exhortation for Prayer on Sabbath Morning).

He is another of the multitude throughout Church history who speaks of the possibility of living a sinless life. He notes, too, that such a thing is possible only through God's power.

"God is love, and because he is love, he wills that all his children and believers should stand in true love. Love is the tie which rivets our hearts to God, but also to the hearts of our neighbor.

"1. A true believer prays to God that he will fill his heart with his holy love.

"2. He must not despise the means whereby the love of God can be commenced and increased in him, devout attention to and reflection on the Word of God, and the proper use of the Communion.

"3. If he stands in the love of God he must prove it by a holy Christian walk, becoming speech, and works well pleasing unto God.

"4. But he must be well on his guard, lest, like Demas, he come to love the world again; for who so loves the world, the love of the Father is not in him. Therefore, out of love to God, he must eschew the world, which would lead him away from God again.

"5. In such love he must remain till death.

"6. The love of God must increase constantly with increasing years; it is a shame to spend twenty, thirty, or forty years in the pleasures and follies of the world, forgetting the love of God" (*Daily Handbook for Days of Joy and Sorrow*; Exhortation on I John 4:16, 19).

Many church-goers are fond of saying that the inside of a person's life, not the outside, is what really matters. Starck mentions here how the inside and outside should agree.

Chapter 7

Full Flower of Light: 1725-Present (Part 1)

Now we come to the time where, at last, the theology of sanctification was finally given full form and flower. Most centuries before this had only a few writers to choose from; now, especially in the 1800s, we suffer from an embarrassment of riches. If I had included material from every writer that I wanted to, this section would be much longer than it is.

* * * * *

Nicolas Ludwig, Count von Zinzendorf (1700-1760); & the Moravians

He was born in Dresden, Germany, although his family was actually of Austrian descent. His father died when Zinzendorf was very young, and so he was largely raised by his grandmother, by all accounts a godly woman. His godfather was Philipp Jakob Spener. As a teenager, Zinzendorf studied at the school started by August Hermann Francke. He studied law at the University of Wittenberg. In 1722, he allowed a small group of religious refugees primarily from Moravia (now the eastern part of the Czech Republic) to form a small settlement on his estate in Berthelsdorf. The refugees named their new settlement Herrnhut.

Zinzendorf is a wonderful example of how one person's life can start a chain of influence that exists long after that person is dead. Spener had a strong influence on Francke; both of them and their ideas set the whole tenor of Zinzendorf's life—and Zinzendorf and his immediate followers had a huge impact on John Wesley. I am going to spend some time on Zinzendorf and the Moravians, because in a very large measure they set the stage for Wesley. Without them, it's entirely possible that Wesley never would

151

have been the man that he became; he was saved in a Moravian meeting. The Holiness movement owes Count Zinzendorf a tremendous debt of gratitude—both for his own work, and also for the influence that he and his followers had on John Wesley.

"Herrnhut, and its original old inhabitants must remain in a constant bond of love with all children of God belonging to the different religious persuasions—they must judge none, enter into no disputes with any, nor behave themselves unseemly toward any, but rather seek to maintain among themselves the pure evangelical doctrine, simplicity, and grace...

"Whoever does not daily prove it by his whole conversation, that it is his full determination to be delivered from sin, through the merits of Jesus, and to follow daily more after holiness, to grow in the likeness of his Lord, to be cleansed from all spiritual idolatry, vanity, and self-will, to walk as Jesus did, and to bear his reproach and shame: such a one is not a genuine brother...

"Everyone should be careful to comprehend the true foundation of the saving doctrine on which we are all agreed, so that we may be able to give an answer to all our adversaries in meekness, yet with wisdom and power, and all may mutually defend and support one another...

"For the sake of the weak, no light conversation is to be allowed concerning God and spiritual things, but such subjects ought always to be treated with the greatest reverence...

"The doctrine and example of Jesus and his apostles shall be the general and special rule of all our ministry and instruction...

"All who are influenced by the love of God must keep up a friendly and cordial fellowship with all who are like-minded, making in this respect no exceptions" ("Brotherly Union and Agreement at Herrnhut"; from *Pietists: Selected Writings*).

This is a remarkable document, and well worth reading in its entirety. It was drawn up by Zinzendorf. He understood the connection between God's love for us and His desire that we should be perfectly pure, perfectly humble, and perfectly loving towards one another.

Zinzendorf the Ecumenical Pioneer by A. J. Lewis
"A little before he married the Countess Erdmuth Dorothea von Reuss on 7 September 1722, Zinzendorf wrote to his grandmother: 'There will be some difficulties for I am but a poor match, and, I confess the Countess will have to content herself with a life of self-denial. She will have to cast all ideas of rank and quality to the winds, as I have done, for they are not things of divine institution but inventions of human vanity. If she wishes to aid me, she must give herself to what is the sole object of my life—namely, to win souls for Christ, and that in the midst of contempt and reproach' " (ch. 7).

Zinzendorf did not pay much attention to theology, but we see here that he had the spirit of Christ. Many people in the church pews would be better off if they followed his example in this.

"Tell them about the Lamb of God till you can tell them no more." "Let the people see what sort of men you are, and then they will be forced to ask 'Who makes such men as these?' " "If you take a penny more than you need, I will dismiss you from the service." "The missionary must seek nothing for himself; no seat of honour, no report of fame. Like the cab-horses in London, he must wear blinkers and be blind to every danger and to every snare and conceit. He must be content to suffer, to die and be forgotten" (ch. 5).

These are excerpts from Zinzendorf's instructions to various missionaries, and his attitudes towards missionary work. He knew that Christians should live as a people set apart from the world.

"Zinzendorf challenged the fashionable world and the fashionable Churchianity of his day not with neat theological theories but with the slaughtered Lamb of God who was truly Man... 'We must carry an *Image* of our Incarnate God in our hearts', said Zinzendorf, 'and whoever is too refined and philosophical for this, is an unconverted person and an alien from God's Household' " (ch. 4).

Many of our opponents are so fixated on the supposed inevitability of committing sin, that they (seemingly, at least) ignore this principle. They talk too much about the power of sin, and not enough about the power of God. If they would share Zinzendorf's attitude, instead of expending so much time and energy on "inevitable" sin, I believe that the world would be better off, and our opponents would, in many cases, be better examples of Christian living.

"As Herrnhut grew, so did the variety of its inhabitants. Refugees came from Moravia and Bohemia and from different parts of Germany, all eager to worship in freedom and to uphold those principles which Catholic persecution had failed to purge out of them. Beside the descendants of the ancient Unitas Fratrum ["Unity of Brethren"], there came exiles from Lutheran homes, Pietist, Reformed, Separatist, Anabaptist, Gichtelian and Roman Catholic—and their variety brought the almost inevitable discord. Indeed, the continued existence of Herrnhut hung by a very slender thread...

"On arrival at Herrnhut, the emigrants were subjected to the strictest examination, and only those who could prove that they had come purely for the gospel's sake were allowed to stay. Internal discord grew because it was not to be expected that men and women who had left everything for conscience' sake would lightly surrender their own individual and peculiar convictions" (ch. 3).

This was before Zinzendorf drew up the agreement of unity. Herrnhut was started in 1722, and had a promising beginning, and then things started going south. There were arguments, periods of backsliding, etc.—much like the disciples during Jesus' ministry. After a few years, it looked like things might fall apart.

But then things began to change for the better on May 12, 1727, the day of reconciliation, when Zinzendorf presented the agreement of unity. This set the stage for "the golden summer of 1727," as the Moravians call it.

"[In July and August] there was a contagious and a holy expectancy... On 5 August Zinzendorf and fourteen of the Brethren spent the whole night in religious conversation and prayer... Whilst conducting the afternoon service at Herrnhut on 10 August, Rothe [the pastor] was so overcome by the nearness of God that he sank down into the dust before him. The whole congregation followed the pattern of the pastor and they continued together until midnight, praising God and covenanting with one another, with many tears and earnest supplications, to dwell together in love and unity" (ch. 3).

When God visits in power, everybody in the congregation knows it. This was a remarkable visitation. But God had even greater things in store for them.

"The great day of 13 August dawned: the great day which was to manifest the Lord's blessing on the faith of the 'Hidden Seed' and on Zinzendorf's prodigious zeal and industry in his vineyard; the day which has always been regarded as the spiritual birthday of the Renewed Unitas Fratrum or Moravian Church.

"Early in the morning, Rothe gave an address at Herrnhut on the meaning of the Lord's Supper. Then as the people walked the mile to the church at Berthelsdorf, little groups of two or three were seen to converse closely together in mutual friendship and love. The experience of the preceding weeks, it was said, had humbled the exiles under the conviction of their individual sinfulness, need and helplessness, and taught them to think meanly of themselves and kindly of one another. All seemed to be awaiting an extraordinary visitation at the church. The service opened with the hymn 'Deliver me, O God, from all my bonds and fetters' and then Rothe pronounced a truly apostolic blessing and confirmed Anna and Catharine [two young girls of the community]. The whole congregation responded with a fervent *Amen*. They all knelt down and sang... And this was accompanied with such a powerful emotion that loud weeping almost drowned the singing. Several brethren prayed with great power and fervour. They prayed not only for themselves, but for their brethren still living under persecution... Zinzendorf made a penitential confession in the name of the congregation... An inner anointing flowed through every person and with inexpressible joy and love they all partook of one bread and one cup and were 'baptised into one spirit'. All were convinced that, partaking of the benefits of the Passion of the Lamb in real fellowship with one another, the Holy Spirit had come upon them in all his plenitude of grace. They had already been one *body* in a religious community with its own Statutes, but now from this day they were one *spirit*" (ch. 3).

This was quite possibly the largest outpouring of the Holy Ghost since the Day of Pentecost itself. And just like what happened to the apostles, the lives of the Moravians were changed by this day. They had more love, more purity, and more power for God's service than before.

I don't think that Zinzendorf and the Moravians ever fully understood the theology of what happened to them that day. But it's hard to argue with the results.

"All the members of this flock in general were touched in a singular manner by the efficacy of the Word of reconciliation through the Blood of Christ, and were so convinced and affected that their hearts were set on fire with new faith and love towards the Saviour, and likewise with burning love toward one another." "Then were we baptized by the Holy Spirit Himself to one love." "A day of the outpouring of the Holy Spirit upon the Congregation; its Pentecost" (ch. 3).

These are excerpts from the descriptions by people who were present on Aug. 13, 1727. It is no coincidence that the theme of love figures so prominently in these descriptions; for love is the height, the depth, the fullness, and the fulfillment of all Christian experience.

"On 27 August, twenty-four brethren and twenty-four sisters covenanted together to spend one hour each, day and night, in praying to God for his blessing on the Congregation and its witness. Encouraged by Zinzendorf, this covenant spread wider, and for over a hundred years the members of the Moravian Church all shared in the 'Hourly Intercession'. At home and abroad, on land and sea, this prayer-watch ascended unceasingly to the Lord. Thus all the Moravian ventures for the Lamb and for unity in him were begun and surrounded and ended in prayer" (ch. 3).

We see here some more of the results of that great day. Besides love and purity, prayer is one of the great sources of power for God's service.

"At the Cross [the Moravians] found a full assurance of faith which admits of no doubt or fear; a repose in the blood of Christ; a firm confidence in God, and a persuasion of his favour; serenity and tranquillity of mind; with deliverance from all outward and inward sin, not by frontal assault or the rigours of a planned asceticism but by abandoning themselves entirely to the leading of the Lamb" (ch. 4).

Zinzendorf and the Moravians never believed in perfection, at least as they defined it, in this life; but they believed in living a truly holy life. They did for a time fall into excesses, and theological errors, but they were able to recover from many of those. Before the recovery came, however, Zinzendorf and Wesley had major disagreements regarding some of these points. I speculate that much of this could have been avoided if Zinzendorf had been more interested in theology. Nevertheless, he did a tremendous work for God.

"[In Aug. 1732, Leonard Dober and Tobias Leupold] set out on foot for Copenhagen, bundles on their backs, thirty shillings in their pockets, and the invincible all-embracing love of Christ in their hearts. Thus the modern world-wide missionary movement was born.

" 'By 1760', said Dr. Gustav Warneck, the eminent historian of Protestant Missions, 'the Moravian Church had done more for the heathen than all the other Protestant Churches put together.' By 1740, sixty-eight Moravian missionaries had been sent out; and by the time of Zinzendorf's death in 1760, no less than 226 missionaries had gone to destinations ranging from the Arctic to the tropics...

"Zinzendorf's conception of the missionary, his message and strategy, was the first coherent contribution to the vast enterprise of Christian missions in the modern era... There was direct Moravian influence in the foundation of both the Basel and the Leipzig Missionary Societies. The Methodist missionary enterprise followed the Moravian path" (ch. 5).

Here we see some long-lasting results of God's power being poured out. The Moravian missionary endeavors also influenced William Carey, who many people mistakenly think is the father of modern missions.

"When Rosalie Nitschmann was once asked in Herrnhut if she was anxious about her husband away in America, she replied: 'No! He is the Saviour's servant. But we are very fond of one another' " (ch. 7).

This is the mark of somebody who is **fully** committed to God. True love to God casts out both fear and worry.

* * * * *

John Wesley (1703-1791)

Of all the people mentioned in this book, he is probably the most famous. Many people are familiar with the broad outline of his life. What some might not know is that he was ordained a priest in 1728, but was not saved until 1738. This sort of thing was all too common in England during that period; the life of the Church, and of religion in general, was at a very low ebb.

"The state of this country [England] in a religious and moral point of view in the middle of last century was so painfully unsatisfactory that it is difficult to convey any adequate idea of it... Christianity seemed to lie as one dead, insomuch that you might have said 'she is dead.'... Sermons everywhere were little better than miserable moral essays, utterly devoid of anything likely to awaken, convert, or save souls. Both [Anglicans and Dissenters] seemed at last agreed on one point, and that was to let the devil alone, and to do nothing for hearts and souls... The celebrated lawyer, Blackstone, had the curiosity, early in the reign of George III, to go from church to church and hear every clergyman of note in London. He says... that it would have been impossible for him to discover, from what he heard, whether the preacher were a follower of Confucius, of Mahomet, or of Christ!

"What were the parochial clergy of those days? The vast majority of them were sunk in worldliness, and neither knew nor cared anything about their profession. They neither did good themselves, nor liked any one else to do it for them. They hunted, they shot, they farmed, they swore, they drank, they gambled. They seemed determined to know everything except Jesus Christ and him crucified.

"So extreme was the ignorance [of the general population], that a Methodist minister in Somersetshire was charged before the magistrates with swearing, because in preaching he quoted the text, 'He that believeth not shall be damned!' " (J. C. Ryle; *Christian Leaders of the 18th Century*).

John Wesley (in common with many of the great preachers and reformers) did not intend to start a new denomination. His goal was to reform the group that he was in. He lived and died a priest in the Church of England.

In 2002, the BBC did a TV series called "100 Greatest Britons." About 30,000 people submitted nominations of who they thought were the greatest British people throughout history. More than two hundred years after Wesley's death, modern Great Britain—unchurched, no-longer-Christian Great Britain—still ranked him as #50.

A Plain Account of Christian Perfection
"Q. What is Christian perfection?

"A. The loving God with all our heart, mind, soul and strength. This implies that no wrong temper, none contrary to love, remains in the soul; and that all the thoughts, words and actions are governed by pure love.

"Q. Do you affirm that this perfection excludes all infirmities, ignorance and mistake?

"A. I continually affirm quite the contrary, and always have done so.

"Q. But how can every thought, word and work be governed by pure love, and the man be subject at the same time to ignorance and mistake?

"A. I see no contradiction here. A man may be filled with pure love, and still be liable to mistake. Indeed, I do not expect to be freed from actual mistake till this mortal puts on immortality. I believe this to be a natural consequence of the soul's dwelling in flesh and blood. For we cannot now think at all but by the mediation of these bodily organs, which have suffered equally with the rest of our frame. And hence we cannot avoid sometimes thinking wrong till this corruptible shall have put on incorruption."

Far from being unscriptural, as our critics claim, Wesley follows James, John, Paul, Peter, and Jesus in declaring love to be the embodiment of all Christian life and experience. In addition, notice how careful he is to draw a clear distinction between Christian perfection and human perfection.

"Pure love reigning alone in the heart and life—this is the whole of Christian perfection.

"Q. When may a person judge himself to have attained this?

"A. When, after having been fully convinced of inbred sin by a far deeper and clearer conviction than that which he experienced before justification, and after having experienced a gradual mortification of it, he experiences a total death to sin and an entire renewal in the love and image of God, so as to 'rejoice evermore,' to 'pray without ceasing,' and 'in everything to give thanks.' Not that 'to feel all love and no sin' is a sufficient proof. Several have experienced this for a time before their souls were fully renewed. None, therefore, ought to believe that the work is done till there is added the testimony of the Spirit, witnessing his entire sanctification as clearly as his justification."

A vessel may be mostly full of something, and still have room for another type of item. But when it is full and overflowing, there is no room for anything else. When a person's heart is **completely** filled with Divine love, there is no room left for any type of sin.

I should note that not everybody really experiences the gradual mortification that Wesley talks about here. There is always a process leading up to the experience of sanctification, but for some people, that process goes quite quickly.

"Q. Is this death to sin and renewal in love gradual or instantaneous?

"A. A man may be dying for some time, yet he does not, properly speaking, die till the instant the soul is separated from the body; and in that instant he lives the life of eternity. In like manner he may be dying to sin for some time, yet he is not dead to sin until sin is separated from his soul; and in that instant he lives the full life of love."

Some people have tried to claim that Wesley taught a gradual process of sanctification. Such an idea is a gross misinterpretation and misunderstanding of his writings. The preliminary part leading up to the work may be gradual, but the work itself is instantaneous.

"One commends me. Here is a temptation to pride; but instantly my soul is humbled before God, and I feel no pride, of which I am as sure as that pride is not humility.

"A man strikes me. Here is a temptation to anger. But my heart overflows with love, and I feel no anger at all; of which I am as sure as that love and anger are not the same.

"A woman solicits me. Here is a temptation to lust. But in the instant I shrink back, and I feel no desire or lust at all; of which I am as sure as that my hand is cold or hot.

"Thus it is, if I am tempted by a present object; and it is just the same if, when it is absent, the devil recalls a commendation, an injury, or a woman, to my mind. In the instant the soul repels the temptation and remains filled with pure love.

"And the difference is still plainer when I compare my present state with my past, wherein I felt temptation and corruption too."

This is something that can be fully understood only by experiencing it. No amount of theoretical understanding can do it justice. Carnality in the heart makes itself felt, and the absence of carnality likewise makes itself felt. Our critics are very loath to believe this; I don't know why. Their position is analogous to saying that somebody with severe pain would not notice any difference when the pain is cured.

JOHN AND CHARLES WESLEYS' GENERAL RULES

I. There is one only condition previously required of those who desire admission into these Societies, *a desire to flee from the wrath to come, and be saved from their sins*: But, whenever this is really fixed in the soul, it will be shown by its fruits. It is therefore expected of all who continue therein, that they continue to evidence their desire of salvation,

First, By doing no harm, by avoiding evil in every kind; especially that which is most generally practised. Such as

The taking the name of God in vain:

The profaning the day of the Lord, either by doing ordinary work thereon, or buying or selling:

Drunkenness, *buying or selling spirituous liquors; or drinking them,* unless in cases of extreme necessity:

Fighting, quarrelling, brawling; brother *going to law* with brother; returning evil for evil, or railing for railing: The *using many words* in buying or selling:

The *buying or selling uncustomed goods* [smuggled items]:

The *giving or taking things on usury*: i. e. unlawful interest:

Uncharitable or unprofitable conversation; particularly speaking evil of magistrates, or of ministers:

Doing to others as we would not they should do unto us:

Doing what we know is not for the glory of God:

As, The *putting on of gold or costly apparel*:

The *taking such diversions* as cannot be used in the name of the Lord Jesus:

The *singing* those *songs*, or *reading* those *books*, which do not tend to the knowledge or love of God:

Softness, and needless self-indulgence.

Laying up treasure upon earth:

Borrowing without a probability of paying; or taking up goods without a probability of paying for them.

II. It is expected of all who continue in these Societies, that they continue to evidence their desire of salvation,

Secondly, by doing good, by being in every kind merciful after their power, as they have opportunity, doing good of every possible sort, and, as far as is possible to all men:

To their bodies, of the ability which God giveth, by giving food to the hungry, by clothing the naked, by visiting or helping them that are sick or in prison.

To their souls, by instructing, reproving, or exhorting all we have any intercourse with; trampling under foot that enthusiastic doctrine of devils, that "We are not to do good unless *our hearts be free to it.*"

By doing good especially to them that are of the household of faith, or groaning so to be; employing them preferable to others, buying one of another, helping each other in business, and so much the more, because the world will love its own and them *only.*

By all possible *diligence and frugality*, that the Gospel be not blamed.

By running with patience the race that is set before them, *denying themselves, and taking up their cross daily*; submitting to bear the reproach of Christ; to be as the filth and offscouring of the world; and looking, that men should *"say all manner of evil of them falsely, for the Lord's sake."*

III. It is expected of all who desire to continue in these Societies, that they continue to evidence their desire of salvation.

Thirdly, By attending on all the ordinances of God:—such are,

The public worship of God: The ministry of the word, either read or expounded:

The Supper of the Lord; family and private prayer: searching the Scriptures; and fasting or abstinence.

These are the general rules of our Societies, all which we are taught of God to observe, even in his written word, the only rule, and the sufficient rule both of our faith and practice. And all these, we know his Spirit writes on every truly awakened heart. If there be any among us who observe them not, who habitually break any of them, let it be made known unto them who watch over that soul, as they that must give an account. We will admonish him of the error of his ways, we will bear with him for a season. But then, if he repent not, he hath no more place among us. We have delivered our own souls.

JOHN WESLEY,

CHARLES WESLEY.

London, May 1, 1743.

(As given in the 1830 *Discipline* of the Methodist Protestant Church.)

The reader may remember in the first chapter that I mentioned the practical, everyday application of Holiness theology. This is a detailed example of that. To recap the three heads of the foregoing rules: avoiding all evil; doing as much good of all sorts as we can; and diligently attending to the "means of grace"; i.e., the practices by which God speaks to us and increases our faith and love, and by which we speak with God.

The Wesleys give examples under each heading. Anybody who follows these rules will automatically set themselves apart from the world—and even our opponents admit that "sanctification" means being set apart—although in our opponents' case, that setting apart generally seems to be considered a nice theory that is more or less ignored in actual practice. These Rules put that into daily practice. It is a very high standard; but there is Scriptural support for every single point.

"Let us next take an illustration of the manner in which [Wesley] used to advise his preachers individually. To one who was in danger of becoming a noisy, clamorous preacher, he writes:—

" 'Scream no more at peril of your soul. God now warns you by me, whom he has set over you. Speak as earnestly as you can, but do not scream. Speak with all your heart, but with a moderate voice. It was said of our Lord, "He shall not *cry*." The word means properly, he shall not *scream*. Herein be a follower of me, as I am of Christ. I often speak loud, often vehemently; but I never scream; I never strain myself; I dare not; I know it would be a sin against God and my own soul' " (J. C. Ryle; *Christian Leaders of the 18th Century*).

This is an example of how much care Wesley took to avoid sin, not only in his own life, but also in the lives of the people around him. Some preachers these days make a great point of being independent from any organization. In many ways that's good, but in some ways it's bad, because there is nobody outside the congregation to correct mistakes or sins that either the preacher or the congregation might fall into. We should never be so independent as to be above correction.

* * * * *

John Fletcher (1729-1785)

He was born in Switzerland, into a family of Huguenot descent. As a young man, he wanted to be a soldier, and tried more than once to become one, but God foiled his plans every time. After this, he visited England, and heard about the Methodists. He became a tutor to the sons of a wealthy Englishman. While there, he was rebuked for his sins by one of the servants of the household. This incident eventually led to his conversion.

He was ordained in 1757. He eventually became Methodism's first major theologian. John Wesley planned for him to be Wesley's successor as leader of the Methodists, but Fletcher died first.

He was widely renowned for his humility and all-around Christ-like spirit. Even many of his theological opponents never had one bad thing to say about his character. In my opinion, it is quite possible that he was the holiest man to walk the earth since the days of the apostles.

Letters of John Fletcher, Ed. Edward Cook

"If I did not write to you before Mrs. Wesley had asked me, it was not that I wanted a remembrancer within, but rather an encourager without. There is generally such a sense of my own unworthiness upon my heart that I sometimes dare hardly open my mouth before a child of God; and I think it an unspeakable honor to stand before one who has recovered something of the image of God, or sincerely seeks after it. Is it possible that such a sinful worm as I should have the privilege to converse with one whose soul is sprinkled with the blood of my Lord? The thought amazes me, confounds me, and fills my eyes with tears of humble joy" (letter to John Wesley, May 26, 1757).

Several of his letters have passages like this. Many people readily agree that they have nothing good in and of themselves, and yet they would never dream of using language such as this.

"Remember that you are brought from darkness to light to show forth the praises of Him Who calleth you; and that your feet are set at liberty for you to run with patience the race of prayer and praise, self-denial and obedience, which the Lord hath set before you.

"If you would go on comfortably and steadily for the time to come, beg of the Lord to give you grace to observe the following advice:

"1. Live above earthly and creature comforts.

"2. Beware of flatness and lukewarmness as this, if not carried immediately to the Lord, ends often in darkness and deadness.

"3. Value divine comforts above all things, and prize Christ above all comforts; that, if they should fail, you may still glory in the God of your salvation.

"4. Let that which torments others make your happiness—I mean self-denial and renouncing your own will.

"5. Be ready to yield with joy to every conviction of the Spirit of God.

"6. Be faithful to present grace and aspire after a continual growth.

"7. Live the present moment to God, and avoid perplexing yourself about your past or future experience.

"By giving up yourself to Christ as you are, and being willing to receive Him now, as He is, leaving all the rest to Him, you will cut up a thousand temptations by the roots!" (to Miss Hatton, Jan. 28, 1763).

He talks here about the importance of being fully committed to God—not just in theory, but in reality. Doing this will quite often rob temptation of its power; or, at least, make resisting significantly easier.

"You ask from me some directions to get a *mortified* spirit. To get this, get recollection. Recollection is a dwelling within ourselves—being abstracted from the creature and turned towards God It is both outward and inward.

"Outward recollection consists in silence from all idle and superfluous words, and a wise disentanglement from the world, keeping to our own business, observing and following the order of God for ourselves, and shutting the ear against all curious and unprofitable matters.

"Inward recollection consists in shutting the door of the senses, a deep attention to the presence of God, and a continual care of entertaining holy thoughts for fear of spiritual idleness. Through the power of the Spirit, let this recollection be steady even in the midst of hurrying business. Let it be calm and peaceable. Let it be lasting. 'Watch and pray, lest ye enter into temptation.'

"To maintain this recollection, beware of engaging too deeply—beyond what is necessary—in outward things. Beware of suffering your affections to be entangled by worldly vanities, your imagination to amuse itself with unprofitable objects, and of indulging yourself in the commission of what are called 'small faults' " (to Miss Hatton, March 5, 1764).

Again we see the theme of separation from the world, this time in a slightly different form. There is often more than one way of expressing an idea.

If we take care to commune with God, even when busy with necessary things, that by itself will go a long way towards keeping us from sin.

"Consider the temptation that most easily besets you, whether it be hurry, vanity, lightness, or want of recollection to do what you do as unto God. Ponder the consequences of those sins, see your weakness to resist them, and endeavor to obtain a more feeling sense of your helplessness. When you have this, you will naturally watch unto prayer and look to Christ for strength from moment to moment" (to Miss Hatton, Sep. 3, 1764).

I have come across a few people who seemed to feel that weakness in resisting temptation is so common that it's a valid excuse for succumbing to it. Not so! Such a realization *should* drive us to seek help from God. If it doesn't, we have failed in our duty.

"I am confounded when I receive a letter from you. Present and eternal contempt from Christ and all His members is what I deserve. A sentence of death is my due, but, instead of it, I am favored with lines of love. God write a thousand, for them, upon your own heart! and help you to read, with still more triumphant and humbler demonstrations of gratitude, redeeming love, so deeply engraven upon the palms of our Savior's hands, and to assist many thousands more to spell out the mysterious words!" (to George Whitefield, May 18, 1767).

Here is another example of his humility. I have observed in my own experience that deeply godly men are deeply humble men.

"You and I have nothing to do but to die to all that is of sinful nature and to pray for the power of an endless life. God make us faithful to our convictions and keep us from the snares of outward things. You are in danger from music, children, poetry; and I from speculation, controversy, sloth, etc., etc. Let us watch against the deceitfulness of self and sin in all their appearances" (to Charles Wesley, Jan. 1775).

Satan is perfectly capable of turning something useful or important into a snare. If he can't get someone to fall into open sin, he will often try to get such a person to place something good or useful above God.

"The sum of all I have preached to you is contained in the following four propositions: First, heartily repent of your sins, original and actual. Secondly, believe the Gospel of Christ in sincerity and truth. Thirdly, in the power which true faith gives (for all things commanded are possible to him that believeth), run with humble confidence the way of God's commandments before God and men. Fourthly, by continuing to take up your cross and by continuing to receive the pure milk of God's Word, grow in grace and in the knowledge of Jesus Christ. So shall you grow in peace and joy all the days of your life; and when rolling years shall be lost in eternity, you will for ever grow in bliss and heavenly glory...

"Should God bid me stay on earth a little longer to serve you in the Gospel of His Son; should He renew my strength (for no word is impossible with Him) to do among you the work of a pastor, I hope I shall, by God's grace, prove a more humble, zealous, and diligent minister than I have hitherto been. Some of you have supposed that I made more ado about eternity and your precious souls than they were worth, but how great was your mistake! Alas! It is my grief and shame that I have not been, both in public and private, a thousand times more earnest and importunate with you about your spiritual concerns" (to the parishioners of Madeley, Dec. 28, 1776).

No matter how holy and Christ-like a person is, there is always room for improvement. Some people have misunderstood the doctrine of Christian perfection as meaning otherwise.

"I humbly thank you for the honor and consolation of your two kind letters. Your vouchsafing to remember a poor, unprofitable worm is to me a sure token that my heavenly Father earnestly remembers me still. He is God—therefore I am not consumed. He is a merciful, all-gracious God—therefore I am blessed with sympathizing friends and gracious helpers on all sides...

"I thank God that I am a little stronger than when I came hither. I kiss the rod, lean on the staff, and wait the end. I yesterday saw a physician who told me my case is not yet an absolutely lost case. But the prospect of languishing two or three years longer, a burden to every body, an help to none, would be very painful, if the will of God and the covenant of life in Christ Jesus did not sanctify all circumstances and dispel every gloom" (to Vincent Perronet, Sep. 6, 1777).

Here we see a perfect submission to God's will. Reader, could you say this along with Fletcher? If not, you are nowhere near the Christian that you can be, and should be.

"1. Do I feel any pride? or am I a partaker of the meek and lowly mind that was in Jesus? Am I dead to all desire of praise? If any despise me, do I like them the worse for it? Or if they love and approve me, do I love them more on that account? Am I willing to be accounted useless and of no consequence—glad to be made of no reputation?...

"2. Does God bear witness in my heart that it is purified—that in all things I please Him?

"3. Is the life I live, 'by the faith of the Son of God,' so that Christ dwelleth in me? Is Christ the life of all my affections and designs, as my soul is the life of my body? Is my eye single, and my soul full of light—all eye within and without—always watchful?

"4. Have I always the presence of God? Does no cloud come between God and the eye of my faith? Can I rejoice evermore, pray without ceasing, and in every thing give thanks?

"5. Am I saved from the fear of man? Do I speak plainly to all, neither fearing their frowns nor seeking their favors? Have I no shame of religion; and am I always ready to confess Christ, to suffer with His people, and to die for His sake?

"6. Do I deny myself at all times, and take up my cross as the Spirit of God leads me? Do I embrace the cross of every sort, being willing to give up my ease and convenience to oblige others? Or do I expect them to conform to my hours, ways, and customs? Does the cross sit light upon me, and am I willing to suffer all the will of God? Can I trample on pleasure and pain?...

"7. Are my bodily senses and outward things all sanctified to me? Do I not seek my own things, to please myself? Do I seek grace more for God than myself, preferring the glory of God to all in earth or Heaven—the Giver to the gift?

"8. Am I poor in Spirit? Do I take pleasure in infirmities, in necessities, in distresses, in reproaches; so that out of weakness, want, and danger, I may cast myself on the Lord?...

"9. Do I not lean to my own understanding? Am I ready to give up the point, when contradicted—unless conscience forbid—and am I easy to be persuaded? Do I esteem every one better than myself? Am I as willing to be a cipher as to be useful, and does my zeal burn bright notwithstanding this willingness to be nothing?

"10. Have I no false wisdom, goodness, strength; as if the grace I feel were my own? Do I never take that glory to myself which belongs to Christ? ... Do I find joy in being thus nothing, empty, undeserving, giving all the glory to Christ? Or do I wish that grace made me something, instead of God all?

"11. Have I meekness? Does it bear rule over all my tempers, affections, and desires; so that my hopes, fears, joy, zeal, love, and hatred are duly balanced? Do I feel no disturbance from others, and do I desire to give none? If any offend me, do I still love them and make it an occasion to pray for them? If condemned by the world, do I entreat? If condemned by the godly, am I one in whose mouth there is no reproof—replying only as conscience and not as impatient nature dictates? If in the wrong, do I confess it? If in the right, do I submit (being content) to do well and suffer for it?" ("The Test of a New Creature; Or, Heads of Examination for Adult Christians").

Some people may think that the standard he gives here is altogether too high, despite the fact that he is practically taking words right from the mouth of Paul, and some of the other apostles. If you can say with Thomas Chisholm, "I have one deep, supreme desire, / That I may be like Jesus," then you have taken at least one step towards meeting this standard. But an unsanctified person can't fully meet it—carnality gets in the way.

"Dying to pleasure, even the most innocent, we shall live to God. Of pleasures there are four sorts: (1) Sensual pleasures—of the eye, ear, taste, smell, ease, indulgence, etc. (2) Pleasures of the heart—attachments, entanglements, creature love, unmortified friendships. (3) Pleasures of the mind—curious books, deep researches, speculations, hankerings after news, wit, fine language. (4) Pleasures of the imagination—schemes, fancies, suppositions.

"God requires that we should deny ourselves in all these respects because (1) God will have the heart, which He cannot have if pleasure hath it; and God is a jealous God. (2) There is no solid union with God until, in a Christian sense, we are dead to creature comforts. Pleasure is the Gordian knot. (3) God is purity; hankering after pleasures is the cause of almost all our sins—the bait of temptation. (4) God calls us to show our faith and love by a spirit of sacrifice. Pleasure is Isaac. (5) Denying ourselves, hating our life, dying daily, crucifying the flesh, putting off the old man, are Gospel precepts— so is cutting off the right hand, plucking out the right eye, and forsaking all to follow Christ. (6) God makes no exceptions. All the offending members must be cut off; every leak must be stopped, or the corrupting pleasure spared gets more ascendant. (7) Pleasures render the soul incapable of the operations of the Spirit, and obstruct divine consolations.

"Earthly pleasures are of a corrupting nature... Indulgence enervates and renders us incapable of suffering from God, men, devils, or self. It stands continually in the way of our doing, as well as suffering, the will of God. It is much easier, therefore, to fly from pleasure than to remain within due bounds in its enjoyment. The greatest saints find nothing so difficult, nothing makes them tremble so, as the use of pleasure; for it requires the strictest watchfulness and the most vigorous attention. He must walk steadily who can walk safely on the brink of a precipice" ("On Pleasure").

This is something that causes problems for many Christians. I have observed people who I had reason to believe were Christians, but they gave undue precedence to pleasure. Partly as a result of this, they had terribly shallow spiritual lives. Among non-Holiness churches, even ones that are better than average, a disturbing amount of the service is sometimes given over to announcements of pleasure—sports and other worldly activities. I have heard some non-Holiness preachers talk from the pulpit about sports when they should have been talking about God. And some churches seem to think that it's more important to feed the body than to feed the soul, based on the activities and physical space given over to the kitchen. It's nearly unheard of for a Holiness church to have a kitchen or a dining hall on the premises.

Christian Leaders of the 18th Century by J. C. Ryle
"If I preach the gospel ten years here, and see no fruit of my labours, in either case

I promise to bless God, if I can only say from my heart, 'I am nothing, I have nothing, I can do nothing' " (from a letter to Lady Huntingdon on Jan. 6, 1761).

Fletcher was a living embodiment of Charles Wesley's hymn:

"Now let me gain perfection's height!
  Now let me into nothing fall,
Be less than nothing in my sight,
  And feel that Christ is all in all!"

"The best account of Fletcher's proceedings as Principal of Trevecca is to be found in the writings of one of the undermasters... He says:—'... Mr. Fletcher visited us frequently, and was received as an angel of God. It is not possible for me to describe the veneration in which we all held him. Like Elijah in the school of the prophets, he was revered, he was loved, he was almost adored; and that not only by every student, but by every member of the family. And indeed he was worthy. Prayer, praise, love, and zeal, all-ardent, elevated above what we would think attainable in this state of frailty, was the element in which he continually lived. And as to others, his one employment was to call, entreat, and urge them to ascend with him to the glorious source of being and blessedness... Being convinced that to be filled with the Holy Ghost was a better qualification for the ministry of the gospel than any classical learning, after speaking awhile in the school-room he used often to say, "As many of you as are athirst for the fulness of the Spirit, follow me into my room." ' "

Trevecca College was started as a school to train preachers. Many of the people connected with it were Calvinists; yet Fletcher, an Arminian through and through, was chosen as the first Principal. He resigned after a few years, primarily because of acrimonious debate over theology, but also because it was extremely difficult to run the school and preach too.

"It is recorded that many English people used to go to hear him [Fletcher] preach in French to the French congregations in London, though they could not understand a word that he said. 'We go,' they used to say, 'to look at him, for heaven seems to beam from his countenance.' "

Inner holiness has a way of making itself noticed.

"Mr. Fletcher was a luminary. A luminary, did I say? He was a sun. I have known all the great men for these fifty years, but I have known none like him. I was intimately acquainted with him, and was under the same roof with him once for six weeks, during which I never heard him say a single word which was not proper to be spoken, and which had not a tendency to minister grace to the hearers."

This was the testimony of Henry Venn (1724-1797); a Calvinist.

Let's stop and consider what this means. It's usually pretty easy to be on one's best behavior for a day or two. But as the days and weeks go by, we inevitably let down our guard. We relax and just "be ourselves"—the good, the bad, the ugly all on display at some point. But for six weeks, John Fletcher showed that he had no bad or ugly side. How many could go for even two weeks without showing some flash of anger or irritability? I daresay that a few placid people could do that. But it seems to me that a six-week stretch goes beyond the bounds of human nature. I think that only a deep, continual flow of God's grace could do that.

"I heard Mr. Fletcher preach upon the same subject [of a second work]... He also dwelt largely on these words, 'Where sin abounded, grace did much more abound.' He asked, 'How did sin abound? Had it not overpowered your whole soul? Were not all your passions, tempers, propensities, inordinate and evil? Did not pride, anger, self-will, and unbelief, all reign over you? And, when the Spirit of God strove with you, did you not repel all His convictions, and put Him far from you? Well, my brethren, ye were then the servants of sin, and were free from righteousness; but, now, being made free from sin, ye became servants to God; and holiness shall overspread your whole soul, so that all your tempers and passions shall be henceforth regulated and governed by Him who now sitteth upon the throne of your heart, making all things new. As you once resisted the Holy Spirit, so now ye shall have power to resist all the subtle frauds or fierce attacks of Satan.'

"Mr. Fletcher then, with lifted hands, cried, 'Who will thus be saved? Who will believe the report? You are only in an improper sense called believers who reject this. Who is a believer? One who believes a few things which God has spoken? Nay, but one who believes all that ever proceeded out of His mouth. Here then is the word of the Lord: *As sin abounded, grace shall much more abound! As no good* thing was in you by nature, so now *no evil* thing shall remain. Do you believe this? Or are you a *half* believer only? Come! Jesus is offered to thee as a *perfect Saviour*. Take Him, and He will make thee a *perfect saint*. O ye *half* believers, will you still plead for the murderers of your Lord? Which of these will you hide as a serpent in your bosom? Shall it be anger, pride, self-will, or *accursed unbelief*? O be no longer befooled! Bring these enemies to thy Lord, and let Him slay them" (J. Gilchrist Lawson; *Deeper Experiences of Famous Christians*).

This is from a letter written by Hester Ann Rogers. People who don't believe in a second work of grace make all sorts of excuses for why they shouldn't take God at His word.

Fletcher on Christian Perfection

"Resolve to be perfect in yourselves, but not of yourselves. The Antinomians boast that they are perfect only in their heavenly Representative. Christ was filled with perfect humility and love: they are perfect in His person: they need not a perfection of humble love in themselves. To avoid their error, be perfect in yourselves, and not in another.

Let your perfection of humility and love be inherent; let it dwell in you. Let it fill your own heart, and influence your own life: so shall you avoid the delusion of the virgins, who give you to understand, that the oil of their perfection is all contained in the sacred vessel which formerly hung on the cross, and therefore their salvation is finished; they have oil enough in that rich vessel; manna enough and to spare in that golden pot. Christ's heart was perfect and therefore theirs may safely remain imperfect; yea, full of indwelling sin, till death, the messenger of the bridegroom, come to cleanse them, and fill them with perfect love at the midnight cry! Delusive hope? Can anything be more absurd, than for a sapless, dry branch to fancy that it has sap and moisture enough in the vine which it cumbers? Or for an impenitent adulterer to boast, that in the Lord he has chastity and righteousness? Where did Christ ever say, Have salt in another? Does He not say, 'Take heed that ye be not deceived: have salt in yourselves?' Mark 9:50. Does He not impute the destruction of stony-ground hearers to their 'not having root in themselves?' Matt. 13:21. If it was the patient man's comfort, that the root of the matter was found in him, is it not deplorable to hear modern believers say, without any explanatory cause, that they have nothing but sin in themselves? But is it enough to have the root in ourselves? Must we not also have the fruit, yea, 'be filled with the fruits of righteousness?' Phil. 1:11. Is it not St. Peter's doctrine, where he says, 'If these things be in you, and abound, ye shall neither be barren nor unfruitful in the knowledge of Christ?' 2 Pet. 1:8. And is it not that David, where he prays, 'Create in me a clean heart,' etc.? Away then with all Antinomian refinements; and if, with St. Paul, you will have salvation and rejoicing in yourselves, and not in another, make sure of holiness and perfection in yourselves, and not in another.

"But, while you endeavor to avoid the snare of Antinomians, do not run into that of the Pharisees, who will have their perfection of themselves; and therefore, by their own unevangelical efforts, self-concerted willings, and self-prescribed runnings, endeavor to 'raise sparks of their own kindling,' and to warm themselves by their own painted fires and fruitless agitations. Feel your impotence. Own that 'no man has quickened' and perfected 'his own soul.' Be contented to invite, receive, and welcome the light of life; but never attempt to form or to engross it. It is your duty to wait for the morning light, and to rejoice when it visits you; but if you grew so self-conceited as to say, 'I will create a sun, Let there be light;' or if, when the light visits your eyes you said, 'I will bear a stock of light; I will so fill my eyes with light today, that tomorrow I shall almost be able to do my work without the sun, or at least without a constant dependence upon its beams;' would ye not betray a species of self-denying idolatry and Satanical pride? If our Lord Himself, as Son of man, would not have one grain of human goodness of Himself; if He said, 'Why callest thou me good? There is none good' (self-good, or good of himself) 'but God;' who can wonder enough at those proud Christians, who claim some self-originated goodness; boasting of what they have received as if they had not received it; or using what they have received without an humble sense of their constant dependence upon their heavenly Benefactor? To avoid this horrid delusion of the Pharisees, learn to see, to feel and to acknowledge that of the Father, through the Son, and by the Holy Ghost, are all your Urim and Thummim, your lights and perfections" (sec. 2, sub-section 6).

He starts out with a crucial distinction. We cannot create perfection, or attain it on our own. Our perfection comes **from** God, **into** our hearts, where it becomes our possession—one that is simultaneously renewed day by day, but is also permanant, unless we do something to lose it.

Antinomian ("against law"; the word was coined by Martin Luther) has been used by many different people in several ways, but generally means those who believe that a Christian has no obligation and/or no ability to keep the moral law or to live a holy life.

" 'Where the' loving 'Spirit of the Lord is, there is liberty.' Keep, therefore, at the utmost distance from the shackles of a narrow, prejudiced, bigoted spirit. The moment ye confine your love to the people who think just as you do, and your regard to the preachers who exactly suit your taste, you fall from perfection and turn bigots... Let your benevolence shine upon all; let your charity send its cherishing beams towards all, in proper degrees. So shall ye be perfect as your heavenly Father, who makes His sun to shine upon all, although He sends the brightest and warmest beams of His favor upon 'the household of faith,' and reserves His richest bounties for those who lay out their five talents to the best advantage" (sec. 3, sub-section 9).

There are two extremes we need to avoid. One is compromising on essential points for the sake of unity; the other is thinking that every Christian must agree with us on everything. A person who does not have the spirit of love for all of God's children is not a Christian.

* * * * *

Adam Clarke (1760/2-1832)

He was born in Northern Ireland. He became acquainted with the Methodists in his teens, and shortly thereafter was saved. When he was about 20, he felt called to preach. Shortly after he arrived at school, to study for the ministry, he found a gold coin in the garden. He asked around, but nobody knew who it belonged to; therefore he used it to buy books and supplies. He always felt in later years that the finding of that coin was an act of Providence.

He was an active preacher for many years, and wrote various books and articles. But by far and away his most lasting claim to fame was his massive *Commentary on the Bible*, which took him more than forty years of labor. It consisted of six volumes, each one approximately 1,000 pages. It is very likely the most comprehensive commentary ever written by a single person—and Clarke did it while active as a preacher.

He was also a first-rate scholar. He learned the Biblical languages, as well as several others. For a time, he was an adviser to the project of translating the Bible into Arabic.

His *Commentary* is by turns expository, scholarly, and devotional.

Clarke's Commentary

"Be just such as the *holy* God would have thee to be, as the *almighty* God can make thee and live as the *all-sufficient* God shall support thee; for he alone who makes the soul holy can preserve it in holiness. Our blessed Lord appears to have had these words pointedly in view, Matt. v. 48: *Ye* SHALL BE *perfect, as your Father who is in heaven is perfect.* But what does this imply? Why, to be saved from all the power, the guilt, and the contamination of sin. This is only the *negative* part of salvation, but it has also a *positive* part; to be made *perfect*—to be perfect as our Father who is in heaven is perfect, to be filled with the fulness of God, to have Christ dwelling continually in the heart by faith, and to be rooted and grounded in love. This is the state *in* which man was created, for he was made in the image and likeness of God. This is the state *from* which man fell, for he broke the command of God. And this is the state *into* which every human soul must be raised, who would dwell with God in glory; for Christ was incarnated and died to put away sin by the sacrifice of himself. What a glorious privilege! And who can doubt the possibility of its attainment, who believes in the omnipotent love of God, the infinite merit of the blood of atonement, and the all-pervading and all-purifying energy of the Holy Ghost? How many miserable souls employ that time to dispute and cavil against the possibility of being saved *from* their sins, which they should devote to praying and believing that they might be saved out of the hands of their enemies!" (on Gen. 17:1).

Our opponents don't seem to understand that God made possible a perfect deliverance from sin; not only the guilt, but also the contamination.

"On this verse we may observe that the second clause, as it is here translated, renders the *supposition* in the first clause entirely nugatory; for if there be *no man that sinneth not*, it is useless to say, IF *they sin*; but this contradiction is taken away by reference to the original, which should be translated IF *they shall sin against thee*, or *should they sin against thee*; *for there is no man that* MAY *not sin*; i.e., there is no man *impeccable*, none *infallible*, none that is not *liable* to transgress. This is the true meaning of the phrase in various parts of the Bible, and so our translators have understood the original: for even in the thirty-first verse of this chapter they have translated [the Hebrew] IF *a man* TRESPASS; which certainly implies he *might* or *might not* do it; and in this way they have translated the same word, IF a *soul* SIN, in Lev. v. 1; vi. 2; 1 Sam. ii. 25; 2 Chron. vi. 22, and in several other places...

"This text has been a wonderful strong hold for all who believe that there is no redemption from sin in this life, that no man can live without committing sin, and that we cannot be entirely freed from it till we die. 1. The text speaks no such doctrine: it only speaks of the possibility of every man sinning, and this must be true of a state of *probation.* 2. There is not another text in the Divine records that is more to the purpose than this. 3. The doctrine is flatly in opposition to the design of the Gospel; for Jesus came to save his people from their sins, and to destroy the works of the devil. 4. It is a dangerous and destructive doctrine, and should be blotted out of every Christian's creed. There are too many who are seeking to excuse their crimes by all means in their power; and we need not embody their excuses in a creed, to complete their deception, by stating that their sins are *unavoidable*" (on I Kings 8:46).

For some inexplicable reason, many opponents have great difficulty understanding the import of conditional statements. They seem to feel that "if" implies certainty, rather than possibility.

"He that hath *clean hands*] He whose conscience is irreproachable; whose heart is without deceit and uninfluenced by unholy passions" (on Psalm 24:4).

A few chapters ago, I quoted a passage from Clement of Rome, in which he talks about lifting up undefiled hands to God. This is another way of saying that a person's life is morally blameless.

"*They also do no iniquity*] They avoid all idolatry, injustice, and wrong; and they walk in God's ways, not in those ways to which an evil heart might entice them, nor those in which the thoughtless and the profligate tread.

"*Thy precepts diligently*] 'superlatively, to the uttermost.' God has never given a commandment, the observance of which he knew to be *impossible*. And to whatsoever he has commanded he requires *obedience*; and *his grace is sufficient for us*. We must not trifle with God.

"*Unto all thy commandments*] God requires *universal obedience*, and all things are possible to him whom Christ strengthens; and all things are possible to him that believes. *Allow* that *any* of God's commandments *may* be transgressed, and we shall soon have the whole decalogue set aside" (on Psalm 119:3, 4, 6).

There is a very great deal in the Bible about avoiding sin, and doing what is right. Most opponents of the second work openly admit that their lives are far below this standard; yet they reject the most effective way of walking closer to God, and raising the moral tenor of their lives.

"Satan shall have neither a *being in*, nor *power over*, the hearts of sincere believers in Christ" (on Zech. 13:2).

Our opponents sometimes claim that Satan no longer has power over their lives. But they contradict themselves when they say that it's impossible to live without sin.

"The law was a *spirit of death*, by which those who were under it were bound down, because of their sin, to condemnation and death. The Gospel proclaims Jesus the

Saviour; and what the *law* bound unto death, IT looses unto life eternal. And thus the apostle says, whether of *himself* or the man whom he is still personating, *the law of the Spirit of life in Christ Jesus hath made me free from the law of sin and death*. Most people allow that St. Paul is here speaking of his *own state*; and this state is so totally different from that described in the preceding chapter, that it is absolutely impossible that they should have been the state of the same being, at *one* and the *same time*. No creature could possibly be *carnal, sold under sin, brought into captivity to the law of sin and death*; and at the same time be *made free from* that *law of sin and death, by the law of the Spirit of life in Christ Jesus!* Until the most palpable absurdities and contradictions can be reconciled, these two opposite states can never exist in the same person at the same time" (on Romans 8:2).

There is a fundamental contradiction between saying on the one hand that Jesus has freed us from a life of sin, and saying on the other hand that sinning is inevitable.

"Sin not, and avoid even the *appearance* of it. Do not drive your morality so near the bounds of evil as to lead even weak persons to believe that ye actually touch, taste, or handle it. Let not the *form* of it appear with or among you, much less the *substance*. Ye are called to holiness; *be ye holy, for God is holy*.

"That same God who is the author of peace, the giver of peace; and who has sent, for the redemption of the world, the *Prince of peace*; may that very God *sanctify you wholly*; leave no more evil *in* your hearts than his precepts tolerate evil in your conduct... May he sanctify you to the end and to the uttermost, that, *as sin hath reigned unto death, even so may grace reign through righteousness unto eternal life, by Jesus Christ our Lord*" (on I Thess. 5:22, 23).

God's plan, will, and desire is that we should lead truly **holy** lives, without any taint of sin.

* * * * *

J. A. Wood (1828-1905)

John Allen Wood was born about 60 miles north of New York City, into a religious but not Christian family. He relates in his *Autobiography* that he was the first person to be saved in his immediate family. He became a Methodist preacher, and was instrumental in reviving the practice of camp meetings in the Holiness movement. He wrote several books. He was well-known in his day; but there is surprisingly little information about his life readily available, outside of his own writings.

Perfect Love

"The lowest type of a Christian sinneth not, and is not condemned. The *minimum* of salvation is salvation from *sinning*. The *maximum* is salvation from *pollution*—the inclination to sin" (sec. 2).

Sin brings condemnation—see John 3:18; Romans 5:18; and I Tim. 3:6. Someone under condemnation does not have eternal life—see John 5:24.

"What is entire sanctification or Christian perfection?

"Negatively, it is that state of grace which excludes all sin from the heart. *Positively,* it is the possession of pure love to God... In the grace of justification, sins, as *acts* of transgression, are *pardoned.* In the grace of sanctification, sin, as a malady, is *removed,* so that the heart is pure. In the nature of the case, the eradication of sin in principle from the human heart completes the Christian character. When guilt is forgiven in justification, and all pollution is removed in entire sanctification, so that grace possesses the heart and nothing contrary to grace, then the moral condition is reached to which the Scriptures give the name of perfection, or entire sanctification" (sec. 6).

Our opponents often claim that "perfection" should properly be understood as "completeness." This objection does not carry as much weight as they think. In many cases, it is a distinction without a difference. But notice that he says that sanctification **completes** a Christian's character.

"Much of the prejudice and opposition to this doctrine comes from remaining depravity in unsanctified believers. Indwelling sin is an antagonism to holiness, and, in so far as any Christian has *inbred sin,* he has *within him* opposition to holiness. Many, most, do not yield to it, but resist it, pray against it, and keep it under; others, we are sorry to know, both in the ministry and laity, yield to their depravity, and stand in opposition to God's work" (sec. 6).

There are good, well-meaning Christians who oppose this doctrine out of a sincere belief that God's children must remain contaminated with sin all their lives. They may object to it being stated so bluntly, but that is an accurate summary, whether they like it or not. And, ironically, this is a form of perfection on their part—being perfectly mistaken.

"Does Christian Perfection exclude growth in grace?

"By no means. The pure in heart grow *faster* than any others. We believe in no state of grace excluding *progression,* either in this world or in heaven, but expect to grow with increasing rapidity forever. It is the same with the soul wholly sanctified as with the merely regenerate: it must progress in order to retain the favor of God and the grace possessed. Here many of both classes have fallen" (sec. 6).

Many people, both pro- and anti-Holiness doctrine, have made the mistake of thinking of perfection as an ending. It is merely an **intermediate** goal; nothing more.

"A vast majority of church-members appear to think, between regeneration and entire sanctification must be a lifetime of growth in grace. This is a serious mistake, and we fear has overthrown millions. It is unscriptural to teach growth as a substitute for cleansing. Entire sanctification is the divine preparation of heart for the growth or development of all the fruit and graces of the Holy Spirit" (sec. 6).

There generally is a period of growing in grace between salvation and sanctification, but there doesn't have to be. Indeed, a small handful of people have gotten both saved and sanctified in the same church service. My grandmother witnessed one such case.

"Why is it that many who desire holiness, and read, and pray, and resolve, and weep, and struggle, yet make but little progress?

"It is mainly because they refuse to comply with the conditions on which the blessing is suspended. One man sees that if he would be holy he must adopt a new system of benevolence. Another sees, as he approaches the clear light of perfect love, a probable call to the ministry, should he go forward. Another sees a large class of duties, hitherto neglected, which must be performed. A sister sees, if holiness is obtained and retained, she will have to conform to the simplicity of the gospel of Christ, and undergo a material change in her equipage and costume. Many cease to seek holiness when the knife of excision is put to the heart to amputate its idols" (sec. 8).

When a person seeks holiness, God gives him new light. Some people refuse to walk in that light, and perish.

"Did Mr. Wesley profess Christian perfection?

"He did. Any minister who speaks of entire sanctification as Mr. Wesley did, is regarded as a professor of holiness. He says:

" 'You have over and over denied instantaneous sanctification to me; but *I have known* and taught it above these twenty years.' — Vol. iv. p. 140.

" 'Many years since, I saw that without holiness no man shall see the Lord. I began by following after it and inciting all with whom I had any intercourse to do the same. Ten years after, God gave me a clearer view than I had before of the way how to attain it, namely, by faith in the Son of God. And immediately *I declared* to all, *"We are saved from sin, we are made holy by faith."* This *I testified in private*, in *public*, in *print*, and God confirmed it by *a thousand witnesses*.' — Vol. vii. p. 38.

"This was written in 1771. In 1744, nearly thirty years before, he writes:

" 'In the evening, while I was reading prayers at Snowsfield, I found such light and strength as I never remember to have had before. I saw every thought as well as action or word, just as it was rising in my heart, and whether it was right before God, or tainted with pride or selfishness.

" 'I waked the next morning, by the grace of God, in the same spirit; and about eight, being with two or three that believed in Jesus, I felt such an awe, and tender sense of the presence of God, as *greatly confirmed me therein;* so that God was before me all the day long. I sought and found Him in every place; and could truly say, when I lay down at night, "*now I have lived a day.*" ' — Vol. iii. p. 324.

"Those who say Mr. Wesley did not profess perfect love, do so because he does not, as they claim, state it in his Journals. We admit Mr. Wesley seldom recorded his *personal religious experience* in his Journals, and yet we have as much regarding his experience of sanctification as of justification. The most he says about his justification was that at Aldersgate, when he felt 'his heart strangely warmed.' This is often quoted respecting his justification, while the foregoing is both as *clear*, and as *definite* respecting his sanctification. There is just as much propriety, in the light of his Journals, in asserting that he did not profess justification, as that he did not profess entire sanctification" (sec. 10).

Even without what John Wesley says in his Journals, is it logical to claim that he would preach the doctrine so long and so consistently without having experienced it for himself?

"Will you reply to the following objections to entire holiness?
" 'If all sin were expelled from the heart, the Christian warfare would cease.'

"When the heart is pure, Satan is not chained in hell, and a pure heart may have war with outside enemies, both *offensive* and *defensive*. After all sin is expelled from the heart, we shall have a warfare to KEEP it out. It is a mistake to suppose that the Christian warfare is confined to *inward, bosom foes*. The world is our enemy...

" 'This doctrine leads to pride.'

"That cannot be, as *perfect humility* is an *essential* part of it. When it can be shown that health leads to sickness, strength to weakness, light to darkness, wealth to poverty, or virtue to vice, then, in the nature of things, this objection may be true. No Christian (other circumstances being equal) has so clear and correct views of original and acquired depravity, of actual sin, of his dependence on Christ, and of his *numberless weaknesses* and *infirmities* as he who is made perfect in love...

" 'It sets aside repentance.'

"No, indeed! Perfect Christians have a deeper abhorrence of sin, more pungent conviction of their former depravity and guilt before God, and greater holy shame and grief over their present defects, than any other class of Christians. They have shortcomings, but not such as the unholy are guilty of,—they do not neglect any known duty, or do anything which they believe will be displeasing to God; but short-sightedness, infirmities of body, and defective knowledge, all involve *involuntary* failures, entirely consistent with pure intentions and perfect love to God. Purity of heart involves a *tender conscience, spiritual poverty,* and *perfect repentance*" (sec. 19).

I have read objections like this from several sources. Such objections show a fundamental misunderstanding of what sanctification is, and what it does in a person's life.

Will you relate your experience of regeneration, and of entire sanctification?
It pleased the Lord to call me in early life to seek pardon and converting grace. At

ten years of age I first tasted the joys of a Saviour's love. I remember as early as then to have realized a sweet satisfaction and delight in prayer and effort to obey God...

[After early trials] I maintained a steady purpose to obey God, received many spiritual refreshings from the presence of the Lord, and suffered but few doubts in regard to my justification and membership in the family of God.

During this period I was often convicted of remaining corruption of heart and of my need of purity. I desired to be a decided Christian and a useful member of the church; but was often conscious of deep-rooted inward evils and tendencies in my heart un-friendly to godliness. My bosom-foes troubled me more than all my foes from with-out. They struggled for the ascendency. They marred my peace. They obscured my spiritual vision. They were the instruments of severe temptation. They interrupted my communion with God. They crippled my efforts to do good. They invariably sided with Satan. They occupied a place in my heart which I knew should be possessed by the Holy Spirit. They were the greatest obstacles to my growth in grace, and rendered my service to God but partial.

I was often more strongly convicted of my need of inward purity than I ever had been of my need of pardon. God showed me the importance and the necessity of holi-ness as clear as a sunbeam. I seldom studied the Bible without conviction of my fault in not coming up to the Scripture standard of salvation...

Being so often convicted of my need of perfect love, and failing to obtain it, I, after a while, like many others, became somewhat skeptical in regard to the Wesleyan doc-trine of entire sanctification, as a *distinct* work, subsequent to regeneration. I held no clear or definite ideas in regard to the blessing of perfect love, but thought of it, and taught it, as only a deeper work of grace, or a little more religion. I taught, as many now do, a gradual growth into holiness, and threw the whole matter into indefinite-ness and vague generalities. I expected to grow into holiness somehow, somewhere, and at some time, but knew not how, nor where, nor when. I urged believers to seek a deeper work of grace, and to get more religion, but seldom said to them, "Be ye *holy*," "This is the will of God, even your *sanctification*," or, seek "*perfect love*."

I became somewhat prejudiced against the Bible terms "sanctification," "holiness," and "perfection," and disliked very much to hear persons use them in speaking of their experience; and opposed the profession of holiness as a blessing distinct from regeneration. I became prejudiced against the special advocates of holiness; and at camp-meetings and in other places discouraged and opposed direct efforts for its promotion. If a pious brother exhorted the preachers to seek sanctification, or the members to put away worldliness, tobacco and gaudy attire, and seek holiness, I was distressed in spirit, and disposed to find fault...

In May, 1858, I was appointed to Court Street Church, Binghamton, and went there much prejudiced against the professors of holiness in that church; and they were, doubtless, prejudiced against me, as they had cause to believe I would oppose them.

I soon found in my pastoral visitations, that where those persons lived who professed the blessing of holiness, there I felt the most of divine influence and power, and realized a liberty in prayer, and an access to God in those families, which I did not elsewhere...

Through the entire summer of 1858 I was seeking holiness, but kept the matter to myself...

The Binghamton district camp-meeting commenced that year the 1st day of September, and about eighty of the members of my charge attended it with me. During six days of the meeting, the sanctification of my soul was before my mind constantly, and yet I neither urged others to seek it, nor intimated to any one my convictions and struggles on the subject...

On the last day of the meeting, a few minutes before preaching, a faithful member of the church came to me weeping, and said, "Brother Wood, there is no use in trying to dodge this question. You know your duty. If you will lead the way, and define your position as a seeker of entire sanctification, you will find that many of the members of your charge have a mind to do the same." The Lord had so humbled my heart that I was willing to do any thing to obtain relief. After a few moments' reflection I replied, "Immediately after preaching I will appoint a meeting in our tent on the subject of holiness, and will ask the prayers of the church for my own soul."

Glory be to God! the Rubicon was passed. The moment of decision was the moment of triumph. In an instant I felt a giving away in my heart, so sensible and powerful, that it appeared physical rather than spiritual; a moment after I felt an indescribable sweetness permeating my entire being. It was a sweetness as real and as sensible to my soul as ever the sweetest honey to my taste. I immediately walked up into the stand. Just as the preacher gave out his text,—Eccl. xii. 13, "Let us hear the conclusion of the whole matter," &c.,—the baptism of fire and power came upon me.

For me to describe what I then realized is utterly impossible. It was such as I need not attempt to describe to those who have felt and tasted it, and such as I can not describe to the comprehension of those whose hearts have never realized it. I was conscious that Jesus had me in his arms, and that the Heaven of heavens was streaming through and through my soul in such beams of light and overwhelming love and glory, as can never be uttered. *The half can never be told!*

It was like marching through the gates of the city to the bosom of Jesus, and taking a full draught from the river of life.

Halleluiah! Glory! glory! I have cause to shout over the work of that precious hour.

It was a memorable era in the history of my probation, a glorious epoch in my religious experience—*never,* NEVER to be forgotten. Jesus there and then—all glory to his blessed name!—sweetly, completely, and most powerfully sanctified my soul and body to himself. He *melted, cleansed, filled,* and *thrilled* my feeble, unworthy soul with holy, sin-consuming power...

There was a divine fragrance and sweetness imparted to my soul when the Saviour cleansed and filled it with pure love, that has ever remained with me, and I trust it ever will. I make a record of this to the glory of God. Glory, honor, and eternal praise be to his blessed name, forever and ever! His own arm hath brought salvation to my feeble, helpless soul. And I do love the Lord my God with all my heart, soul, and strength. Yet I am nothing, and Jesus is my all. Sweet portion! Oh, the blessedness of this inward, spiritual kingdom! Oh, the depths of solid peace my soul has felt! ...

In the purified soul, the flow of love is *deeper* and *steadier* than ever before. It breathes an atmosphere of purity, and is conscious that its entire inner being has been cleansed, and harmonized by Christ himself...

Some of the precious results of the cleansing power of Jesus in my soul have been:—

1. A sacred nearness to God my Saviour. The distance between God and my soul has appeared annihilated, and the glory and presence of divinity have often appeared like a flood of sunlight, surrounding, penetrating, and pervading my whole being. Glory be to God that even the most unworthy may be "brought nigh by the blood of Christ."

2. A sense of indescribable sweetness in Christ. The fact that he is "the rose of Sharon;" "the lily of the valley;" "the brightness of his [the Father's] glory," and "altogether lovely," has at times so penetrated my soul as to thrill and fill it with ecstatic rapture...

5. A triumph over temptation more complete and habitual. When Satan comes he finds the sympathies and affinities of my soul strongly against him; hence he receives no favorable response. Before, I often found elements in my heart siding with the tempter, and felt that all was not right within. There appeared to be an aching void, or a place in my soul which grace had never reached; but since Jesus sent the refining fire through and through my poor heart, I have been sweetly assured that grace has permeated every faculty and fibre of my being, and scattered light, love, and saving power through every part. Oh, the beauty, the loveliness, the sweetness of heart-purity!

6. A great increase in spiritual power. This I have realized in my closet devotions, in my pastoral duties, and especially in the ministrations of the blessed truth. Blessed be the Lord, I have learned by experience that men may receive the Holy Ghost in *measure* limited only by their *capacity to receive,* and feeble *ability* to *endure.* God could easily bless men beyond the power of the body to endure and live, if he were disposed to take them to heaven in that way.

This increase of power has delivered me from all slavish fear of man, or of future evil. It has given me such love to the Saviour and to his glorious gospel as to make all my duties sweet and delightful. Truly, "Her ways are ways of pleasantness, and all her paths are peace."

7. A clear and distinct witness of purity through the blood of Jesus. The testimony of the Holy Spirit, and of my own spirit, to the entire sanctification of my soul, has been more clear and convincing than any I ever had of my regeneration...

Dear reader, I wish I could tell you how clear and sweet the light of purity has shown through the very depths of my soul, the complete satisfaction I have realized since I obtained this pearl of great price! But it can never be told! Its fullness, its richness, and its sweetness can never be expressed. You can know it only by experience, and this is your solemn duty and most exalted privilege. Will you not seek it? Will you not begin now? A holy life is the happiest life, the easiest life, and the safest life you can live. Be persuaded to settle the matter at once, and begin now to seek for purity, and never yield the struggle until you obtain the glorious victory (sec. 24).

One thing that stood out to me was that he began questioning the doctrine after trying, and failing, several times to obtain the blessing. He says in one of the portions I omitted that he wasn't willing to do what God required of him. But notice how he says at the crisis point, "the Lord had so humbled my heart that I was willing to do any thing to obtain relief."

Many people have tried and failed to obtain the blessing, and have decided because of their failure that there is a mismatch between theory and reality regarding the doctrine. Unlike Wood, many of those don't recover from that. Some critics of the doctrine have observed this, and come to the same erroneous conclusion. They criticize the doctrine for creating what they view as unrealistic and unattainable expectations. However, whenever somebody fails to get sanctified, it is **always** because of some issue on their part—either they're not paying enough attention to the leading of the Lord, or else they're not willing to do something that the Lord is requiring of them.

I would like to draw special attention to two of the results he discovered—greater ease in resisting temptation; and more spiritual power, especially in preaching. Many people have had the same results, including our next witness.

Chapter 8

Full Flower of Light: 1725-Present
(Part 2)

A. B. Earle (1812-1895)

He was born in a small town in New York, about 150 miles north of New York City. He got saved when he was 16, and started preaching two years later, and was ordained three years after that. He held one pastorate, but after that he served as a Baptist evangelist for fifty-eight years. It is estimated that he traveled 370,000 miles in his lifetime. He also wrote several books. His preaching was described by a witness as not being eloquent. But he had something more important than eloquence: the power of God rested on him. At some point, he became aware of the doctrine of entire sanctification; and after much questioning and searching, he gained the experience.

The Rest of Faith

"I will next answer the anxious inquiry that comes from so many struggling, longing, Christian hearts: —

" 'How can I reach this state of rest in Jesus?'

"The very first thing to be settled in your own mind is this: 'Do I fully believe Christ has made provision for me to abide, without interruption, in the fulness of his love?' If one doubt remains in your mind about this, you will not obtain it, however anxious or earnest you are in your efforts.

"As it is attained by faith, it is necessary for you to believe it attainable. Think of the absurdity of praying and searching for a thing you doubt can be obtained. Would not such an effort be solemn mockery? 'What things soever ye desire when ye pray, believe that ye receive them, and ye shall have them.'

"Let this point be fully settled. Take time, if necessary. Search the Scriptures for light. Pray in faith. If your unbelief is in your way, turn all your batteries on that; ask those you think are walking with Christ to help you. Continue these efforts until all doubt is gone on the subject, until you become entirely satisfied that Christ has made ample provision for you to abide in his love without condemnation.

"When this is clear to your own mind, then come to the Saviour just as you would if you could see him with your natural eyes. Come at once, by a childlike, simple faith, believing just what he has said…

"Do not stop to inquire of Jesus how he can give rest to one so sinful and unworthy as you are,—to one who has made so many vows and resolutions to be faithful, and failed. Leave all that to him: let him take his own time and way to fulfil his promise. It is enough for you that he has said, 'I will give you rest.' Expect him to do as he has said" (ch. 4).

He did not grow up in the Methodist tradition, so he describes sanctification somewhat differently than most Holiness people do. I want to make certain that there is no room for misunderstanding, however: he is most definitely describing the same thing. Notice how he says in the third paragraph, "without interruption." This is another way of saying "without sinning." Even our opponents admit that sinning breaks fellowship with God.

About ten years ago, I began to feel an inexpressible hungering and longing for the fulness of Christ's love. I had often had seasons of great joy and peace in Christ, and in his service. I had seen many precious souls brought into the fold of Christ. I fully believe I then belonged to Christ, that my name was in his family record.

I loved the work of the ministry, but had long felt an inward unrest, a void in my soul that was not filled. Seasons of great joy would be followed by seasons of darkness and doubt. If I had peace, I feared it would not continue; and it did not.

Many anxious Christians came to me, complaining of the same thing. How could I help them on that point, when I did not know how to get right myself? I took them to the seventh chapter of Romans, and there left them, saying, "O wretched man that I am! who shall deliver me from the body of this death?" I was there myself, and supposed I must live and die there.

In this state I was exposed to severe temptations and attacks of the enemy. I made strong and repeated resolutions that I would be faithful, but could not keep them. Then I sought and found forgiveness again, and was happy, and said, "Oh that I could always enjoy such peace!" But it was soon disturbed by some word, or act, or heart-wandering.

Thus I lived on for many years: now happy in my Christian experience, and now unhappy; sometimes doubting and fearing, and sometimes resting. God gave me success in winning souls, and granted me many hours of sweet communion with my Saviour, for which I am truly grateful; still I was unsatisfied,—I wanted an *uninterrupted* rest and peace.

I often read those precious words, uttered by our Saviour, "If ye abide in me, and my words abide in you, ye shall ask what ye will, and it shall be done unto you." I longed and prayed to be there, but knew not the way. Oh that some one had then taught me the way of rest in Jesus!

I frequently met Christians who claimed sinless perfection: many of them were, indeed, a better type of Christians than ordinary professors; but they did not seem perfect to me. The rest in Jesus, for which I longed, was still unfound.

At last I felt that the question for me to settle was this,—Can an imperfect Christian sweetly and constantly rest in a perfect Saviour, without condemnation?

This I revolved in my mind for a long time. I read, as far as I could, the experiences of those who seemed to live nearest to Christ. I searched the Scriptures for light, and asked such as I believed had power with God to pray with and for me, that I might be led aright on this great question. At length I became satisfied that Christ had made provision for me and all his children to abide in the fulness of his love without one moment's interruption.

Having settled this, I said: I need this; I long for it; I cannot truly represent religion without it, and Christ is dishonored by me every day I live without it.

I therefore deliberately resolved, by the help of my Redeemer, to obtain it at any sacrifice; little realizing how unlike Christ I then was, or how much would be needed to bring me there...

I think I then came nearer to Christ. But as clearer light began to shine into my heart, I saw more of its vileness.

I find in my journal [of Dec. 22, 1859] the following: —

"The last three weeks have been weeks of great searching of heart. I never had my heart so searched before. I detect pride, envy, self-will, a great deal of unbelief, my love to the Saviour to be very weak. Yet I have consecrated all to Christ, and cannot withdraw it from the altar. Oh, can a worm so vile be like Christ? I know it is possible; and if I am ever to be like him, why not now, while I am where I can do good in leading others to him?" ...

At times my joy and peace were almost unbounded. Sometimes I felt that I grasped the prize so earnestly sought, but was shown some hidden sin in my heart which greatly humbled and distressed me. How fully I realized the words of J. B. Taylor, who said, while seeking this blessing, "Notwithstanding my profession that I had crucified the world, the flesh, and the devil, I have had keener sorrows for indwelling sin than I ever experienced before conversion." ...

My faith was very deficient and weak: to believe the promises fully was not easy. I believed the theory of religion; but to have my heart grasp the reality, without wavering, was more difficult. Yet I found my faith growing stronger, until at last I came to believe just what God has said in his word. I found first the blade of faith, then the ear, and then the full corn in the ear. No rest could be obtained until I could believe just what God had said, and trust him fully.

I felt that I must have in my heart something I did not then possess. Before I could be filled with the fulness of Christ's love I must be emptied of self. Oh, the longing of my heart for what I then believed, and now believe, to be sweet and constant rest in Jesus! I believed I should receive it, and thought it was near.

I soon found it easier to resist temptation. I began to trust Christ and his promises more fully.

With this mingling of faith, desire, and expectation, I commenced a meeting on Cape Cod. After re-dedicating myself, in company with others, anew to God, I was in my room alone, pleading for the fulness of Christ's love, when all at once a sweet, heavenly peace filled all the vacuum in my soul, leaving no longing, no unrest, no dissatisfied feeling in my bosom. I felt, I knew, that I was accepted fully of Jesus. A calm, simple, childlike trust took possession of my whole being...

Then, for the first time in my life, I had that rest which is more than peace. I had felt peace before, but feared I should not retain it; now I had peace without fear, which really became rest.

That night I retired to sleep without one fear,—much like a tired babe resting in its mothe's arms. I believed Jesus had received me, and would keep me. I had no fear of losing that happy state: the fear which had so disturbed my rest was taken away. I seemed in a new world: my burden was gone, my cup was full, and Jesus was present with me. I felt not only that I was forgiven and cleansed, but that Jesus would hereafter keep me; that I should not have to help him keep me, as I had been vainly trying to do, but could trust it all to him; that now I had two hands instead of one to work with.

I was a Christian before. I loved Christ, and his people, and his cause; yet did not, could not, trust myself without fear in his hands. But now I seemed all at once to lose a great burden of care and anxiety...

The Bible seemed like a new book. I had, as it were, read with a veil before my eyes. All through the week I labored on without fear of losing the long-sought, and now so highly-prized blessing. I believed, in the hour of temptation, Christ would keep me, and I should not lose that happy state.

This change occurred about five o'clock on the evening of the second day of November, 1863; and although I never felt so weak and small, yet Jesus has been my all since then. There has not been one hour of conscious doubt or darkness since that time. A heaven of peace and rest fills my soul. Day and night the Saviour seems by me. Preaching is a luxury,—it is a glorious work. In prayer Christ does not seem far away, but near and with me. The Bible still appears like a new book. All Christians are dearer to me than ever before...

My success in leading souls to Jesus has been much greater than before. My joy in telling the world of Christ and his goodness constantly increases...

Temptation is presented, but the power of it is broken. I seem to have a present Saviour in every time of need; so that for several years I have done the trusting and Jesus the keeping; it is much easier now to resist temptation than it was before.

I feared the crosses would be much heavier if I was nearer Jesus; but they are much lighter now; so that I can sum it all up in a few words, and call it, not perfection, not a sinless state, but *rest*—the rest of faith,—a calm, sweet resting all with Christ. This state of heart is reached only by faith, and retained only by faith; not by helping Christ take care of us, but by trusting him to do it all (ch. 6).

This is a marvelous testimony. He went from knowing little or nothing about sanctification to being convinced that he needed it, and therefore he sought and found it. Notice how he says, "I searched the Scriptures for light, and asked such as I believed had power with God to pray with and for me, that I might be led aright on this great question." And the result—"at length I became satisfied that Christ had made provision for me and all his children to abide in the fulness of his love without one moment's interruption." And notice the results of sanctification once he received it—greater power for God's work; a closer walk with God; and less trouble with temptation.

The doctrine of a second work is often thought of as a specifically Methodist/Wesleyan thing. But as I said in the first chapter, it cuts across denominational lines. Here we see a Baptist receiving the blessing.

"Does any one ask how an imperfect Christian can rest in a perfect Saviour, and feel no condemnation?

"For many years I stumbled at this point. I could not then find, and cannot now, the doctrine of sinless perfection, in this life, in the word of God. And yet I find imperfect and erring Christians sweetly abiding in Christ's love, walking with him, without condemnation...

"After a long search and much prayer, I found that the secret of rest in Christ was not in our perfect soundness, nor in our entire obedience; but in our entire surrender of all to Christ, with an unwavering, unquestioning trust; and his meeting all the demands of the law in such a way that the soul realizes no condemnation. He 'is the end of the law for righteousness to every one that believeth;' that is, meets all the demands of the law, fulfils all its requirements for us, on the simple condition that we fully believe in him, and confide all to him; no merit in us, no righteousness, no equivalent rendered by us; Jesus does it all, redeems, keeps, and sanctifies" (ch. 7).

I don't think that he ever fully understood the theology of the second work—entire surrender IS entire obedience, because a heart that is fully surrendered to God will automatically want whatever God wants. He stumbled over some of the terminology, but it is clear that he both experienced and preached Christian perfection, but using other ways to describe it.

Reader, if you, too, stumble over terminology, if you believe that any type of perfection is impossible in this life, then seek the blessing in some other way. Like Earle, you might think of it as complete rest in God, rather than sinless perfection. If so, then seek it that way—but seek the blessing of heart-holiness, and don't give up until you find it.

* * * * *

John Hartley (19ᵗʰ century)

This is a man who has sunk into total obscurity: I can find virtually nothing about his life. He was a Methodist preacher. He was probably the first governor of the Wesleyan College in Handsworth (now part of Birmingham, England). He served in that post for eleven years, during much if not all of the 1880s.

Chapters on Holiness: Expository and Practical

"It is assumed that the reader knows by experience how 'the kingdom of God is... peace and joy in the Holy Ghost.' Set up in your heart, it has brought you real happiness. It has given a holy calm to your spirit, a strangely sweet and solemn joy, a hope elevating and glorious. But why are these at all marred or interrupted? Why have you not a settled tranquillity? Why is not your 'peace as a river,' ever flowing and full? Why do you not always abound in hope? Why cannot you 'rejoice evermore'?

"It is because religion has not undisputed and constant sway. You fail sometimes in the discharge of duty; and then, instead of having as your rejoicing the testimony of a good conscience, you are mortified with yourself and troubled. Unhallowed feelings and propensities, which though subdued are not extirpated, stir within, and thus the atmosphere of your soul is disturbed and darkened. There cannot but be dissatisfaction when the consecration to God is not entire and constant. Where He is not our supreme joy, our portion, our all, but we pine inordinately after creature happiness, then is there unrest. We make idols, and we find them clay. What we would enjoy apart from God is either emptied of its power to gladden, or embittered, or taken from us.

"But when the tumult of sinful desires is stilled; when we are purged from the filth of self and pride; when sin, inward sin as well as outward, is abolished; when no one disputes the throne of the heart with its rightful, blessed Lord; when, by the power of an indwelling Redeemer, we do always the things that please God: our happiness is pure, constant, deep. We find untroubled repose in God. The mind that is stayed on Him as its strength, its salvation, its centre, its rest, has *perfect peace*" (ch. 1).

This is a good summary of the difference between the unsanctified and the sanctified believer.

"We are *channels* through which Divine grace is conveyed to men's souls. How sad when the channel is choked by remaining corruption, by pride, by low and sinister aims, by selfishness and earthliness, and by other hidden evils! Were all these taken away, then a full tide of heavenly life might pour along, and carry blessing to many around" (ch. 1).

It is deeply sad, and tragic, that so many Christians have been fooled into thinking that they must put up with being choked channels all their lives.

When somebody who names the name of Christ says or does something that would be more fitting for an unbeliever, it shames and disparages God's name, grace, power, and holiness in the eyes of the world.

If the reader truly loves God, but still has carnality in his heart, this point alone should be a powerful incentive to seek entire sanctification, so that you no longer disgrace the Lord you love and serve.

"Mr. Wesley often declared that 'where Christian perfection is not strongly and explicitly preached, there is seldom any remarkable blessing from God' " (ch. 2).

I have found this to be true in my experience. Non-Holiness churches, even though they may have a good preacher, even though their doctrine may be largely correct, even though they may gladly sing the old hymns, still are missing something. They just don't seem to have the same degree of Divine presence and power that I have observed in Holiness churches.

"They form their own idea of what an entirely sanctified Christian should be, no little of the angelic mingling therewith, and because they cannot meet with any who are the exact counterpart of that idea, the Scripture-teaching itself is impugned. No allowance is made for human infirmity, for mistakes of judgment, for information that is but partial or even erroneous, for faults of manner, for peculiar physical or mental temperament. Hence it is not perceived that there may be superficial blemishes while yet the 'heart is sound' in God's 'statutes' " (ch. 6).

He is talking here about opponents of the doctrine, and how they mix up the different types of perfection. This mistake (among others) leads them to reject the doctrine.

"There is *a goodly company of thoughtful and well instructed Christians* who can testify that in the hour when they made an entire surrender of themselves, and trusted Jesus for full salvation, in that self-same hour the last fetter of sin was knocked off from the soul, and they rejoiced in the perfect liberty of the sons of God. It was upon finding such everywhere in his societies, that Mr. Wesley was first led to inquire into the truth on this matter, and to search 'the Scriptures daily, whether these things were so,' until he came to the deliberate conviction that such a salvation might at once be wrought in any believing heart. Since his day, how many have blessedly entered into the same experience! May we refer here to the explicit statement of Dr. Mahan? 'Sanctification,' he says, 'like pardon, I have found in experience to be an *instantaneous* work. Propensities which, from childhood up, and not less during the first years of my Christian life than during my impenitency, had had absolute control when strongly excited, in a moment lost utterly and for ever their power, being superseded by a new and right spirit of an opposite character. If I am conscious of anything, I am conscious of being, by the cross of Christ, crucified to the world, and the world to me. Nor was this crucifixion a long and painful process. When a penitent, self-renouncing, fully consecrated, and trustful soul has put itself into the hands of Christ for pardon, or for cleansing, a short work will the Lord make; and an equally short one in each case' " (ch. 6).

Our critics base much of their opposition on the fact that many godly people have never found a complete deliverance from carnality. But for every anecdote they produce, we can produce one showing that such a deliverance is possible.

I am reminded of an inspirational saying. It takes various forms, but it goes something like this: "Those who say 'it can't be done' are usually interrupted by somebody doing it." But when it comes to fully purifying the heart, some people steadfastly believe that it's just not possible, and they ignore or explain away all evidence to the contrary.

"Willingness to be made whole is essentially necessary to our having a perfect cure.

"There lies at the bottom of many of our hearts—so deep and subtle, as perhaps hitherto to have eluded our notice—a half dread of being sanctified wholly, a shrinking from it. We start back from the sacrifices which may be required. We are not prepared to give up our idols; to surrender our whole selves, and the control of everything in our lot and life, to the Lord; to go without the camp, bearing the reproach of Christ; to follow the Lord fully; and honestly to say,

'No cross, no sufferings I decline,

Only let all my heart be Thine.'

We fear the confession we may have to make, and the consequent singularity; the care and circumspection, the tension of thought and effort, needful to keep ourselves unspotted from the world. We do not wish to part with a certain license and apathy into which our religion at times degenerates" (ch. 7).

Sanctification makes many aspects of the Christian life easier; others it makes harder (in a certain sense). Untold numbers of people have found, after sanctification, that they could no longer do certain things they used to do, and keep a clear conscience. This is the result of more light. God narrows the boundaries of acceptable behavior. Note, however, that most of the difficulty of keeping within the narrower boundaries is greatly exaggerated by the perspective of the unsanctified state. There is sometimes some difficulty, however. Just like any Christian has struggles that an unawakened sinner never has, the sanctified man sometimes has battles that the unsanctified man generally doesn't have.

"Then too, even when entirely sanctified, we shall be conscious of *the defective degree* (in one sense) *of our religion*. Who that loves the glorious and blessed Redeemer can love enough? Who honours Him with the rapt, adoring, reverent homage which is His due? Whose heart kindles and bounds as it ought to do at the mention of His ineffably precious name? Whose soul springs forth towards Him as His transcendent worth and dying love should make it do? Who that knows Him can help exclaiming—

'Weak is the effort of my heart,

And cold my warmest thought'?

"And the purer our love is, the more we feel as if it were anything but so ardent, absorbing, and lofty as it should be. All genuine affection, when placed on a worthy object, engenders such fear" (ch. 8).

Holiness is not the be-all, end-all of the Christian experience. As stated earlier, there is always room for growth in grace.

"And when at length, as the result of deeper thought, fuller scrutiny, and clearer light, a course is seen to be unworthy of a follower of the Lamb, we must at once renounce it, or peace with God and purity of heart cannot for one hour be retained. Even when entirely sanctified, we are bound still honestly and prayerfully to inquire whether all in us, all thoughts, purposes, words, actions, are according to God's will. They who have, in infinite love, been brought into the way of holiness, must still, with the clearer spiritual vision, quickened sensibilities, and godly jealously which they have received, *take heed* thereto according to God's word" (ch. 10).

History and experience both show that when God reveals more of Himself, He raises the standards that He expects of His followers. The Sermon on the Mount is a prime example. Jesus tightened up the Old Testament standards considerably on several points. The same is true on an individual level.

He also talks here about making sure that everything accords with God's will. On numerous occasions, I have sent up a quick little prayer, asking God if I am still *fully* within His will in every little detail. I feel that it is only prudent for a person to double-check that he is avoiding all danger. In the event that I am starting to veer off the straight line, I do not want to wait until God warns me to find that out; I want to find out sooner.

* * * * *

A. B. Simpson (1843-1919)

Albert Benjamin Simpson was born in Prince Edward Island, into a family of Scottish, Calvinistic background. He got saved at 15, and at 21 he became a Presbyterian preacher. At some point in the mid-to-late-1870s, he became aware of Holiness doctrine, and got sanctified. Two more turning points came in 1881: he experienced a Divine healing in his own life; and he left the Presbyterian Church in order to have more freedom to preach to the un-churched masses. During the next several years, he started various groups and magazines, which culminated in 1897 in the founding of The Christian and Missionary Alliance. He preached what he called the "Fourfold Gospel"—Jesus as Savior, Sanctifier, Healer, and Coming King. He did so because he felt that certain aspects of God, such as His ability to heal people, were being neglected, and thus many churches were preaching an unbalanced Gospel. He also wrote dozens of books and hymns, including the beloved missionary hymn, "The Regions Beyond."

The Holy Spirit, or Power From on High; Volume 1

"This is the work of the Holy Spirit, to put to death the life of self and sin. We cannot do it, He alone can. We may try to crucify ourselves and mutilate ourselves with a thousand blows; but every time we will succeed in just missing a vital part, and the old 'I' will come through the process, all alive still. Only the flaming sword can smite to death the self-centered, self-destroying life of the natural man...

"Even the very best things become a curse to us so long as we hold them with our natural hands and hearts and self-centered spirits. That sweet and innocent child whom God has taught you to love, can be only an idol until he ceases to be your child, and becomes God's child, and the death stroke passes upon your love, and you learn in the resurrection life to hold him for God, and love him not as a selfish pleasure but as a sacred trust...

"Even your Christian influence, your reputation as a worker for God, and your standing among your brethren, may be to you an idol that must die, before you can be free to live for Him alone.

"If you have ever noticed the type on a printed page, you must have seen that the little 'i' has always a dot over it, and that this dot elevates above the other letters in the line.

"Now, each of us is a little 'i'; and over every one of us there is a little dot of self-importance, self-will, self-interest, self-confidence, self-complacency, or something to which we cling and for which we contend, which just as surely reveals self-life as if it were a mountain of real importance.

"This 'i' is a rival of Jesus Christ, an enemy of the Holy Ghost, and of our peace and life. Therefore, God has decreed its death, and the Holy Spirit, with His flaming sword, is waiting to destroy it, that we may be able to enter through the gates and come to the Tree of Life.

"How can this be accomplished?

"We must ourselves consent to it. We must recognize the true character of our self-life and the real quality of the evil thing. We must consent to its destruction, and we ourselves must take it as Abraham did Isaac, and lay it at the feet of God in willing sacrifice. This is a hard work for the natural heart; but the moment the will has been yielded and the choice has been made, that death is past; the agony is over, and we are astonished to find that the death is accomplished" (ch. 3).

An unsanctified believer generally does not realize just what is standing between him and perfect communion with God, until God turns His searchlight upon the heart. Moreover, we must ask for this to be done, and we must be walking in all the light that we possess.

"It is a very serious thing to want the Holy Ghost simply to give us power to work for God. It is much more important that we should receive the Holy Spirit for personal character and personal holiness...

"It is very remarkable how fully God can possess a human soul. We read of demoniac possession through which the entire being of a man becomes so controlled by evil spirits that they are able to add tenfold intensity and force to his life. Why may not a man be just as much God-possessed as he can be Satan-possessed, so that every faculty and power of his being shall be filled with the power of the Holy Ghost, and his energy and capability shall be redoubled?" (ch. 11).

Absolute purity should be the main goal. It is astonishing how so many Christians seem to think that God can't do as much for His followers as Satan can do for his. Although I daresay that very few have thought about the matter in such terms.

"Alas, beloved, many of us have fortunes in our Bibles without knowing it, or without using our infinite resources. The Holy Spirit is given to us to be used for every sort of need; and yet, with all the power of heaven at our call, many of us are going about in starvation, simply because we do not know our treasure, and do not use our redemption rights. 'Know ye not,' the apostle asks us, 'that your body is the temple of the Holy Ghost?' If we but use the power that is given within our breast, behind the name of Jesus and the promises of God, we would fail no more, we would fear no more, we would no more be a reflection upon our Savior and a dishonor to His name, as well as a discouragement to the world, but we would rise up into victory, and cry, 'Thanks be to God, who always causeth us to triumph, in Christ' " (ch. 14).

In some unfathomable way, a large number of Christians have been tricked into thinking that a large part of the Bible is not applicable to us today, but only for after we reach Heaven. In reality, the verses that talk about power to overcome, and absolute purity, are for us today.

"He does not give us the Holy Ghost that we should receive a clean heart merely, and then spend our lives complacently looking at it and telling people about it, but that we should go forth in the power of His Spirit and His indwelling life, to conquer this world for Him. We, too, have a great foe to face and a great trust to fulfill. We are sent to conquer the world, the flesh, and the devil, and to give the Gospel to the whole inhabited earth" (ch. 15).

This quote and the one from ch. 11 should be read together. This is the other side of things. We should want the purity more, but the power comes with it. God expects us to use the gifts that He gives us. Unfortunately, some Holiness people have failed in their duty on this point.

"The second thing we learn about this river [in Ezekiel 47] is that it flows from a sanctuary. What is a sanctuary? It is a sacred, separated, holy, and divine place. First, it must be separated from sinful and common uses. Secondly, it must be dedicated to God and belong exclusively to Him. Thirdly, it must be occupied by God and be filled with Him as its Possessor, its Guest, and the Object of its worship.

"In this sense the truly consecrated believer is God's sanctuary when he separates himself from all evil unto God, dedicates himself to be the property of the Most Holy, and receives the Holy Ghost to dwell in him, and to represent the Trinity as the occupant and owner of his heart and life. This is the sanctuary. This is holiness. This is the true Christian life, and from such a soul as this the river will always flow.

"But you cannot be a blessing to others beyond your personal experience. You cannot give what you have not got. You cannot bring pure water out of an unclean fountain. Why are we not greater blessings? Because our hearts are not sanctuaries. We try to do a little for God and then find the whole hindered by a thousand forbidden uses; and God will have no partnership with evil, and will accept no service which is mixed or compromised" (ch. 22).

Untold numbers of people have tried to cling to the world, or to some pet sin, while at the same time trying to please God. It can't be done. Many others, while not actually clinging to any sin, fail to go all the way with God. As a result, they end up fighting a life-long battle with inbred carnality that could have been avoided.

The Holy Spirit, or Power From on High; Volume 2

"Peter and the other disciples were born of the Spirit before the day of Pentecost; but Jesus promised them that they should be baptized with the Holy Ghost at the appointed time, and when that day was fully come there was added to their true Christian life the divine personality, the infinite presence and all-sufficiency of God, the indwelling Holy Ghost, who had lived and wrought in Jesus Christ.

"Beloved, have we entered into this experience? Have we received the Holy Ghost since we believed, or have we allowed our theological traditions and our preconceived ideas to shut us out from our inheritance of blessing and of power? Let us do so no longer. Let us, with the Master, step down to Jordan, enter with Him into death, rise with Him in resurrection life into the baptism of the Holy Ghost, and then to go forth in the fulness of His power and liberty, even as He.

"Oh, if the Son of God did not presume to begin His public work until He had received this power from on high, what presumption it is that we should attempt in our own strength to fulfill the ministry committed to us and be witnesses unto Him!" (ch. 1).

Opposition to the idea of a second work is nothing new. Whether on this subject or on another, there has never been a shortage of people who try to explain away the clear meaning of Scripture.

"The change produced by the baptism of the Holy Ghost upon the first disciples was more remarkable in their own lives than even in their service and testimony...

"The spirit of unselfish love, that led to the entire consecration of all their means to the service of Christ and the help of one another, was an example that could not fail to impress the skeptical and selfish world. The 'great grace' that was upon them all was more wonderful than 'the great power' with which they bore witness to the death and resurrection of Jesus Christ. The heroic fortitude with which they endured unparalleled sufferings, 'rejoicing that they were counted worthy to suffer shame for the name of Jesus,' was an exhibition of power that no man can gainsay, and carried a weight of conviction that nothing can counterpoise.

"This is the power which the church needs today to convince an unbelieving world; the power that will make us, not inspired apostles, but 'living epistles, known and read of all men.' Nothing is so strong as the influence of a consistent, supernatural, and holy character. Many a skeptic, whom all the books in the universe would never have convinced, has been converted by the sweet example of his Christian wife.

"Many a missionary among the heathen has found that the failure of his temper and spirit has done more in a moment to counteract all his teaching than years could undo. 'He that keepeth his spirit is greater than he that taketh a city.' And the power that can surpass the angry word, and stand in sweetness in the hour of provocation in the humble kitchen and laundry, has often become an object lesson to the proud and cultured mistress, until her heart has hungered for the blessing which has made her lowly servant's life a ministry of power, and her humble heart a heaven of love" (ch. 8).

It is very often the case that the world knows how Christians (or people who call themselves Christians) ought to behave. And they judge us—and judge the power of God—by whether we live up to those standards. One of the reasons why Voltaire became an atheist was because of the corruption in the Catholic Church.

"Just as the law of life lifts us above the law of gravitation, and the power of my will can raise my hand in spite of that physical law which makes dead matter fall to the ground, so the Holy Ghost, bringing Christ as a living presence into my heart and life, establishes a new law of feeling, thinking, choosing, and acting, and this new law lifts me above the power of sin and makes it natural for me to be holy, obedient, and Christ-like" (ch. 10).

The work of sanctification is in some respects almost as much of a change in a person's life as the work of salvation is. Sanctification brings a degree of victory over sin that is nearly unheard of in the unsanctified believer's life.

"The word, sanctify, has three specific meanings; namely, to separate from, dedicate to, and fill with.

"First, we must lay off, and separate from, the old life of self and sin. There are some things we cannot consecrate to God, but we must lay them down. The old sin-offering could not be laid on the altar—it was unclean, because the sin of the people had been transferred to it; it must be carried outside the camp and there burned with fire in the place of judgment. And so we cannot consecrate our sin and our sinfulness to God. We must renounce it; we must lay it off; we must die to it; we must be separated from it.

"Then, secondly, comes the dedication to God. This is the place for consecration. This is the place for the burnt-offering. That was laid on the altar and accepted as a sweet-smelling savor. And so when we have separated from our sinful self, we offer our new life in Christ to God in entire dedication, and He accepts it as a sweet savor. But even then it is nothing but a consecrated will, a mere possibility, an empty vessel, clean, but empty still, and the very power to make the consecration worth anything to God, must come from God Himself. He has the vessel, but He must fill it and keep it full. And so this is the third meaning of sanctification. It is the filling of the Holy Ghost, who takes our consecrated will, our clean and empty vessel and all the possibilities of our new and yielded life, and so unites them to Jesus, and fills them with the very life of Jesus, that we just live out the life of Christ from day to day, and we shed forth the fullness which the Holy Ghost supplies within...

"Now this is the sanctification of the Spirit. It is His peculiar province thus to sanctify the souls that have been justified through the grace and the blood of Christ.

"First, He shows the soul its need of sanctification, its inherent and hopeless sinfulness, and its utter inability to bring a clean thing out of an unclean, or live a holy life, with an unholy heart. Next, He shows us God's provision for our sanctification in the free gift of Christ, the efficacy of His atonement for the death of our old self, the power of His blood, and the willingness of the Holy Spirit to undertake this work, to cleanse our heart, and to dwell within it. Then He leads us to the next step—a glad and full surrender and committal of our soul to Him for this blessed work, an unreserved separation from all evil, and an equally unreserved dedication of our all to God, and to His perfect will.

"Then He accepts us, and makes real the transaction into which we have entered; by full surrender and appropriating faith, He puts to death our old life of self and sin and He enters and dwells within our consecrated heart, uniting us to Jesus, filling us with His own all-sufficient grace and presence, and leading us henceforth moment by moment, in constant dependence upon His glorious grace.

"In one sense, this work is instantaneous; it has a definite beginning and moment in which we count it all eternally settled. In another sense, it is progressive, as He leads us on from step to step, from strength to strength, from grace to grace, from glory to glory, even as by the Spirit of the Lord.

"As each new revelation of light comes, He calls for new obedience and new advances; yet while we walk in the light, we are fully accepted according to the light we have, and counted holy and well-pleasing in His sight" (ch. 18).

Virtually all non-Holiness people talk about sanctification only in the sense of being set apart. They miss out on the best part of the meaning—being made holy in heart and in every aspect of life. I have heard several Christians talk about their struggles with sin, and how sometimes they did serious damage to their witness for God by succumbing to temptation. And as I listened, my heart bled for them—for they did not know how to have consistent victory over sin.

* * * * *

Samuel Logan Brengle (1860-1936)

He was born in Indiana. His father was wounded in the Civil War, and died a few months later. His mother was of Methodist background. She remarried a few years later. Brengle was saved when he was 12 or 13—sources differ. After graduating from college, he became a Methodist preacher. Not too long afterward, he felt led to join the Salvation Army. General Booth made him start at the bottom—polishing the boots of his fellow cadets. After proving himself to Booth's satisfaction, he was allowed to start preaching again. He stayed with the Salvation Army for the rest of his life, and became the first American to reach the rank of Commissioner (the second-highest rank). He wrote several books, and became one of the best-loved Holiness theologians.

Heart Talks on Holiness

"Holiness is not necessarily a state in which there is perpetual rapturous joy... Joy is the normal state of a holy man, but it may be mingled with sorrow and grief and perplexities and heaviness on account of manifold temptations. The low water mark, however, in the experience of a holy person is one of perfect peace—the high water mark is up in the third heaven somewhere...

"Holiness is not a state of freedom from infirmities. It does not produce a perfect head, but rather a perfect heart! ...

"Holiness is not a state of freedom from affliction. The saints of all ages have been chosen 'in the furnace of affliction' (Isa. xlviii. 10). Job and Jeremiah and Daniel and Paul and the mighty army of martyrs have, and shall always, come up through great tribulations. It is not God's purpose to take us to heaven on flowery beds of ease, clothe us in purple and fine linen, and keep a sugar plum in our mouths all the time. That would not develop strength of character, nor cultivate simplicity and purity of heart... Other things being equal, the holy man is less liable to afflictions than the sinner. He does not run into the same excesses that the sinner does; he is free from the pride, the temper, the jealousies, the vaulting ambitions, and selfishness, that plunge so many sinners into terrible affliction and ruin; and yet he must not presume that he will get through the world without heavy trials, sore temptations and afflictions...

"Holiness is not a state in which there is no further development. When the heart is purified it develops more rapidly than ever before.

"Holiness is not a state from which we cannot fall... It is an unscriptural and dan-

195

gerous doctrine that there is any state of grace in this world from which we cannot fall. Probation does not end the moment we believe on Jesus, but rather the moment we quit the body. It is only those who endure to the end who shall be saved. While here, we are in the enemy's country, and must watch and pray and daily examine ourselves, and keep ourselves in the love of God, lest we fall from His grace and make shipwreck of our faith" (ch. 2).

Some people on both sides of the fence have an exaggerated notion of what sanctification is and what it does. Brengle gives a good summary of what it doesn't do.

"Many are familiar with the Word of God, but they have not an appropriating faith. They read the exceeding great and precious promises, but it never occurs to them that on the fulfillment of the conditions they can have and will have the things promised... Instead of crying to God to bring their experience up to the standard of the Bible, they explain the Bible down to the level of their experience, and so never receive the glorious revelation of Jesus to their hearts and the fullness of grace therein promised...

"Now holiness makes one good all the time; not only in conduct, but also in character; not only in outward act, but also in inward thought and wish and feeling, and those who are content with anything below this, will miss the blessing" (ch. 4).

If only more people would take God at His word, the Church would accomplish much more than it does. But instead, many people make up reasons why large parts of the Bible don't apply to them.

"To keep it [a clean heart], there must be continued joyful and perfect consecration. We have put all on the altar to get it. We must leave all on the altar to keep it... And this consecration must keep pace with increasing light... There must be steadfast, childlike faith. It took faith unmixed with doubt to grasp the blessing. Unbelief was banished. Doubts were put away. The assurance of God's love in Jesus was heartily believed. His ability and willingness to save to the uttermost was fully accepted, and His word simply trusted when the blessing was received; and, of course, this same faith must be maintained in order to keep it. God cannot require less of the sanctified man to keep the blessing than He did of the unsanctified man to get it... We must constantly live in the spirit of self-denial. By yielding to fleshly desires, to selfish ambitions, to the spirit of the world, we may lose the labor of years in an instant. The hard hand of the old enemy is ever stretched forth to snatch from us our treasure. We must watch and pray, and keep low at Jesus' feet in profoundest humility, if we would keep it" (ch. 6).

Many sanctified people have testified that they have been tempted to doubt God, or to withdraw a small portion of their consecration. This temptation is sometimes presented in a very subtle form.

"Many souls draw back and fail. They flinch at the final test of faith. Just when all is on the altar and there is not one thing more to do but to stand still and see God come, 'an evil heart of unbelief' draws back, or Satan comes suggesting something more to do. And the soul, dropping its eyes from the bending heavens, gets into the endless treadmill of endeavor to either help itself or to get somebody to help it, and so misses the prize and never finds God, or rather never gives God a chance to show forth His saving power, and make His presence known.

"While Faith stands waiting and trembling, taunted by mocking devils and all manner of suggestions to doubt, it is hard not to flinch; but flinching will prove as fatal to the revelation of Jesus to your soul as a movement will prove to your picture when before the photographer's camera. Be still in your heart and trust, look and wait, and Jesus will surely come. There may be ceaseless outward activity; but this inward soul-quiet and watchfulness and faith are absolutely necessary to the revelation of the Lord...

"A ministerial friend of mine lost the blessing of full salvation. I found him in this state and dealt faithfully with him. He went to his church that night, and told his people his condition, and called them around the altar with him; but he failed to get the blessing. A wise friend of mine, who happened to be present, explained his failure by saying: 'He didn't stay on his knees long enough. He was in too big a hurry. He didn't give God time to deal with him.' The fact was, he flinched when the time to steadily watch and wait and trust came" (ch. 20).

A great many churches today promote a terribly shallow walk with God by giving "altar calls" that last (at most) five minutes. Sometimes it's possible to get everything straightened out with God in that length of time, but in many cases it takes longer, sometimes much longer.

"Entire consecration is not entire sanctification. You are commanded to 'present your bodies a living sacrifice, holy, acceptable unto God' (Rom. xii. 1). This is entire consecration; but it is also said, 'For with the heart man believeth unto righteousness; and with the mouth confession is made unto salvation' (Rom. x. 10). So then, there must be entire consecration, unwavering faith, and a frank, artless confession of both to Jesus. This is man's part, and, when these simple conditions are met and steadfastly maintained, against all contrary feelings, God will suddenly come into His Holy temple, filling the soul with His presence, purity, and power. This twofold work by man and God constitutes the one experience of entire sanctification. When this experience is yours, at your very earliest opportunity confess it before men" (ch. 21).

Some people have tended to get confused about this. It is true that some people are led by a shorter, easier route than others; but it is important to realize that consecration and sanctification are separate things.

Unsanctified people, until God starts dealing with them, generally have no conception of how far short they typically are of entire consecration.

"I am under as much obligation now to be holy, to be empowered by the Spirit, and to be about my Lord's business, as I shall be in Heaven. And, bless God, this is not only an obligation, but an inspiration!" (ch. 22).

Many people of all walks of life, both religious and non-religious, have fallen for the lie that it doesn't matter how they live; they think that they can live however they please, and God will still let them into Heaven regardless.

* * * * *

E. E. Shelhamer (1869-1947)

Elmer Ellsworth Shelhamer was born in western Pennsylvania. He was saved at 16, and a few years later became a Free Methodist preacher. He largely labored in the South, especially Georgia and Florida, but he also preached in several foreign countries. For a time he was associated with God's Bible School in Cincinnati. He often signed himself, "Yours for a clean, rather than a big, work."

Sermons that Search the Soul

"Brother, you ought to be so well saved that God can let come what will and in every instance the adversary is put to shame. You should come out of every trial in a better shape than you went in. Only those who are sanctified through and through can do this. You ought to seek heart purity in self-defence, if nothing more. You are not safe a moment while carrying around with you an explosive that may blow you up any minute" (sermon 10).

Many unsanctified people openly admit, that, far too often, it is the cause of God that is put to shame by their failures, while Satan gets the upper hand. Many times the failure is just when somebody around them would be helped the most by a display of Divine grace or love. The work of sanctification is a tremendous help in living a Christ-like life.

"Get rid of sin, or it will get rid of you.

"Friends, we are repeating history. Do you realize that while you are sitting here enjoying life, multitudes have gone and are forgotten, who at one time had as bright, or brighter prospects than any of you? They had better clothes, a better education, a larger circle of friends; they were more tactful, more winsome in their ways—in short, their possibilities far surpassed ours. But where are they? On the dump heaps of Satan— worn out, rusty, broken, twisted, disfigured, and hardly recognizable. Why? Because like King Saul, they spared Agag—a type of the carnal mind.

"Saul was a fine, modest, all-round fellow, standing head and 'shoulders higher than any of the people.' A splendid beginning, had he only kept humble. God planned that his kingdom should be 'established upon Israel forever.' But instead, he died before his time, in despair and a suicide. Yes, carnality has dethroned Kings, crushed empires, annihilated nations, filled insane asylums, disrupted churches, disgraced ministers, and caused hell to be enlarged. Carnality is the most dangerous and ruinous thing outside of the pit. It is as old as the fall, hence is called, 'The old man'—the only begotten child of the devil" (sermon 12).

I cannot understand how anybody who realizes even a portion of the truth about carnality would insist that the best we can expect in life is to tolerate it, instead of having it removed.

"I heard a mighty man of God tell his experience—how he had preached and professed holiness for twenty-five years without it. But when the Holy Ghost revealed to him his depravity—'The depths of pride, self will and hell,' (as Wesley taught) he cried out 'Let me die! Let me die!' He said he was three days confessing and deploring carnality, when suddenly the refining fire of God purified him through and through. When I heard this, immediately I said, this is the Bible route—the *death* route" (sermon 13).

The cry of "Let me (i.e., the old man) die!" used to be far more common than it is today. The lack of this is a contributor to the increasing worldliness of many segments of the Church.

"While seeking salvation these thoughts came, 'If I lose my religion I will have to come back to the altar and go through this same process again.' After three days seeking God's smile I was wonderfully converted. The tree of sin was cut down in my life. For three months I was singing and shouting, day and night, and you couldn't have preached to me a second work of grace. I believe souls ought to get so soundly converted that they do not feel the need of Holiness for several months. They feel that the bottom of heaven has dropped out into their souls—that they are saved, sanctified, and almost glorified.

"But, I also remember one sultry day when I was shoeing a big lazy horse, and the sweat was pouring off. I was working hard to get in at least five nails before I let his foot down so the shoe would not get out of place. He fell asleep on my back and I said, 'Stand up here!' I was not the least provoked. I had to speak positively to make the horse mind. In a moment he was bearing down again and I was hammering nails for all that was in it. He did this several times, when he was annoyed by a fly, and switching this way and that, finally hit me in the eyes. The sensation was as though a handful of red pepper had been thrown into my face.

" 'O, but that hurts!' I grabbed his bit and said, 'You need an old fashioned kicking,' and was about to give it to him when suddenly the blessed Holy Ghost arrested me and said, 'That's the way you used to do.' Then I dropped the bit and can see myself now going over into the corner and crawling behind an old barrel, where I knelt in prayer. 'O, Jesus, help me! I almost gave that horse an awful kicking!' A volcano of anger boiled up inside so that I felt like eating that horse without salt. 'What is this thing in me? I thought I was saved. Like lightning that thing boiled up. Jesus have mercy!' After prayer he gave me the sweet kiss of reconciliation, but told me that I ought to get rid of that awful thing. *Now*, I was ready to listen to the preaching of holiness as a second work of grace. I was ready to read anything on the subject.

"Finally, the Holy Ghost—the great stump puller—fastened onto the sin of my heart and extricated carnality. Since then I have not been troubled with the roots of bitterness. Jesus came, not only to cut the tree down, but to take the root out" (sermon 16).

It is a tragedy in the Church that so many get saved, and then stop short of God's full blessing. Even though carnality troubles them, they don't turn to God and get it handled. Either they try to handle it on their own (and fail), or else they try to grow out of it, or else they just give up.

* * * * *

Peter Wiseman (20ᵗʰ century)

I can find virtually nothing about his life, which is surprising for somebody who lived so recently. He lived in Ottawa, Ontario, and was connected with Ansley College there. He wrote a few books. One of them, *Scriptural Sanctification,* was published in 1951.

Scriptural Sanctification

"While failure is a possibility even in sanctification, it is not at all so probable and so common as it is with those without this experience; for sanctification is a glorious inward protection on this line. Purity within is a mighty protection against impurity without and all round us. 'Preserved,' said Paul" (sec. 1).

In this quote and the next one, he is commenting on Heb. 12:14-17. The vast majority of unsanctified Christians bemoan their frequent failures and backslidings. If the average unsanctified Christian falls so often, isn't that perhaps a sign that he needs more help from God? Sanctification is the best way to get that help.

"Esau was not a fornicator or profane person in the sense that we know such today; but he was guilty of spiritual fornication and spiritual profanity, as unsanctified people often are. He lightly valued his birthright. Did Paul not speak of 'covetousness, which is idolatry'? (Col. 3:5). Sanctification is the cure and the protection. 'Kneeling in utter self-abandonment,' said Miss Frances E. Willard, 'I consecrated myself anew to God. But I felt humiliated to find that the simple bits of jewelry I wore, gold buttons, rings and pin, all of them plain in their style, came up to me as the separating causes between my spirit and my Saviour. All this seemed so unworthy of that sacred hour that I thought at first it was mere temptation. But the sense of it remained so strong that I unconditionally yielded my pretty little jewels, and great peace came to my soul. All my friends knew and noticed the change.' There is no protection comparable to inward purity" (sec. 1).

As long as we retain inward purity, we cannot be defiled. No outward event or circumstance can harm us. Heb. 12:15 talks about roots of sin. It is extremely difficult to live as we should unless those roots are gone.

"Consecration is comprehensive. It is not a partial thing. It means all. It comprehensively includes the gift of the person with all his possessions, now and forevermore.

"Consecration involves a readiness to do what God requires, to give self and all one's possessions as a living sacrifice (Romans 12), to be or not to be, to go or stay, anything or nothing, if God will only deliver from this 'heart foe' within. Any conscious withholding from God or any desire or ambition to do or be other than His will is sin within, self-will, 'enmity against God.' The believer hates all ungodliness within and without. This hating and abhorring of it comes from the grace of repentance, and because of it there will arise the possibility of sanctifying faith; a faith not only that God has made provision for full deliverance, or that He is able to deliver, or that He has promised to deliver, but a faith that appropriates the promise of God for present deliverance, the faith that says, 'He does it now,' and it is done that very moment" (sec. 2).

Faith is the most important thing required for sanctification. Without it, there is no point in asking for deliverance from sin. Many people talk about how they hate and deplore their carnality, but that's as far as they get. They don't have faith that God can remove it, so they never get beyond the talking stage.

"Methodism's greatest historian, Dr. Abel Stevens, says of the early Methodist preachers that every one of them at his ordination either professed the experience of perfect love or to be groaning after it. 'Perhaps,' said he, 'no single fact so well accounts for their success.' Yes, a pure heart is a passionate heart!" (sec. 5).

God's full purity brings power into a believer's life in a new and stronger way than ever before.

* * * * *

Esther Lacy (1894-1982)
She was born not very far north of Lincoln, Nebraska. She lived in Colorado most of her adult life.

I have decided to close this history section with the testimony of a humble, obscure servant of God. She has no claim to fame. Most people would have no idea that she ever existed. Only a tiny handful of people, relatively speaking, have read her biography. For several years, she attended the same church that I later attended. I never met her, but I know several people who knew her.

Light After Darkness by Dawn L. West
We had moved from our homestead fifty miles away to Bellvue, Colorado, in the spring of 1929 to put our children in high school. In that community was a little, holiness church. In fact we drove right past it when we were moving into Bellvue.

There was the name printed in large, bold letters over the door—PILGRIM HOLINESS CHURCH. We all saw it. Holiness—that was a new word to us. People in the neighborhood were careful to warn us concerning that church. They told us many scary stories of what went on within the four walls. "Of course, they are good people," they would always say, "but..." They called them "Holy Rollers." "A false doctrine"—that is what it all meant to us. Consequently, we each took warning and vowed together that *never* would we have anything to do with that church.

I declare unto you, though, if these weren't the very people we would be thrown into contact with, one way or the other; and much to my dismay, I was drawn to them... I always had such strange feelings when any of them were around. It was a hungry, dissatisfied feeling within me... One of the neighbor women told me, "Those holiness folk say you should never go any place you know you couldn't take Jesus with you."

Looking back over those first few years in Bellvue, I can see how God was preparing me to go to the little, despised church that we drove right past on our way to and from the large, modern church in Fort Collins nine miles away. God was getting "a hook in my jaw," but I didn't know it then... I felt such a hunger in my soul for something more. After church, I would say to my family, "I am just as hungry as I was before I went." I was getting so sick of all the pomp and show in that church. My husband was too, but what to do we did not know. It never occurred to us to go somewhere else to church, and above all we were *not* going to the holiness church. Had we not been warned that they taught a false doctrine?

I was a starved soul. I was thirty-eight years of age when it seemed that my soul had reached its climax of continually reaching out for something that it could not find. The Lord began dealing with my heart in a drastic manner. He moved in mysterious ways to put conviction upon me.

One particular Sunday, the teacher of my Sunday school class asked two different women to pray. Each one whispered something in her ear, after which she said, "Mrs. Lacy, will you pray?" I do not know how or what I prayed, but, no doubt, it was as dry as shucks. I do remember thinking that if they took off some of that excess jewelry, maybe they could pray; one woman had several strands of pearls around her neck.

As we sat in the balcony for the preaching service that morning, looking down on that large choir, I was not interested as I usually was, nor did I enter into the singing. I never heard anything the preacher said, for God had spoken to me. He knew my thoughts afar off. This is what He said, and I knew it was God:

"Suppose you three women were walking on the street together; would anyone guess that you could pray and that they couldn't? You do not have pearls around your neck; you do not have bracelets on your wrist, but how about your bobbed hair?"

I had told my family that I would not wear long hair again if I were the last woman on earth to wear short hair, for no longer did I have eczema on the back of my head as I had had when I wore long, heavy hair... [Her family] went on to remind me of all that I had vowed about not ever having long hair again. My answer was that God had spoken, and I told them about it. God was getting me ready to go with the holiness people, but that was the farthest thing from my mind right then.

Throughout all that spring and summer [of 1932] as I would be out in the brooder house putting the baby turkeys to bed for the night, I could hear the holiness church bell ring out on the night air: "You *ought* to be *there*; you *ought* to be *there*; you *ought* to be *there*," it would say over and over. *No*, I reasoned with myself, *I **hadn't** ought to be there.* I would put my fingers in my ears so as to shut out the sound, for I knew I was *not* going to a false-doctrine church.

[That August, most of her children starting going to the holiness church and quickly got saved.] I was "snowed clear under." ... God had moved on [her children's] young hearts. I was now ready to go to the holiness church. I remembered what the bell had said to me; there was no mistake about what that bell had said as it rang out over the night air a mile away. Now I was ready to go with the children. When Sunday came, we all went, and never did we go back to the formal church again. We knew we had found our church home. How different it was from that big, crowded church with a large choir and a hired leader who stood up before them and beat time with a stick.

Here in the little church, the preacher sang the special. Before he sang, he held up his hand and asked God's blessing on the song. He acknowledged his helplessness unless God undertook. In my heart I said, "Oh, God, I want what that man has." No longer was I bothered by all those scary stories we had heard: how these people knelt down when they prayed, how folks in the congregation led in prayer (in our old, formal church only the minister ever prayed), and how sometimes it sounded as if everybody prayed out loud all at the same time!

The next one at the altar was their mother, telling the Lord she wanted what the children had. He took me at my word, but I did not pray through so quickly as they did. I had more things to see and to make right, but I obeyed in detail, making confessions and restitutions. Step by step, He led me... These are some of the other things that God dealt with me about in conviction: taking sight-seeing drives on Sunday; Sunday picnic dinners, also big Sunday company dinners at home; ... wearing beads and jewelry, including my wedding ring. Many of these things involved my relationships with others—relatives and friends who had been in the habit of "stopping by" for a visit and a big feed on Sunday... Some folk were very upset when I told them plainly that I could no longer desecrate the Lord's Day in that way.

I have often wished that I knew the date when God gave me the witness that I was a born-again soul. It was in the spring of 1933, and it was at Herbert Mitchell's home during a cottage prayer meeting. In my heart, I saw that picture of Jesus walking on the waves, and Peter beginning to sink as he got his eyes on the waves instead of on Jesus. I kept my eyes on Jesus. I didn't seem to know what else was going on in that prayer meeting. But oh! what a load was lifted from my heart that day as God dealt with my soul. I was so sick in body that some of the women got uneasy about me. One of them called to me, and I remember I was disappointed, for I was out there so near God. But what a change had come in this old world as we faced those foothills coming home. The sky was never so blue, the trees so green. Everything was praising God! Now I knew why the children were so happy. As I look back now, that was the day that I was really justified in God's sight. It was a new creation that rode home that evening. But I didn't understand right then what had really taken place. I did not shout; I never made one bit of commotion, but what a peace!

After I was saved, it was glorious; it was victory all the time. But one day, I was so disappointed when I felt a stir in my heart that I thought was gone. I felt the check of the Spirit that enough had been said; I listened and didn't say another word, but I wanted to, oh, so much. Since we had been attending the holiness church, often James 1:8 had been quoted: "A double minded man is unstable in all his ways." I saw that was so true. I felt so ashamed and sorry, and I cried mightily to God for forgiveness. How sweet was God's presence; how tenderly He led me step by step. This old nature had to be crucified.

My husband had gone on a business trip the latter part of the week to be away for several days. Early Monday morning, as I awakened, God asked me if He might have my husband. I went about the task of preparing breakfast and the children's school lunches with an aching heart... I cried, I begged, I tried to tell God how much I loved my husband, how much the boys needed their father's counsel. I brought everything reasonable I could think of to God to spare my husband. But He never paid one bit of attention to my cries. At times, I would be about ready to tell Him that He could have him. Then the thought of seeing my husband lying in the casket cold in death swept over me. I would cry out, "I can't give him up; I can't." What suffering, for I did want God, but I also saw that I must come to His terms.

At 3:00 p.m., I completely let go, and said, "Yes, Lord, yes, You may have him." The burden lifted; it was all in God's hands now.

[She goes on to describe how she died out to various other things that she held dear.] I mourned after the Holy Ghost, mourned for a clean heart. When I was asked to return thanks at the table, I would ask for the Holy Ghost to come... On the morning of February 9, 1934, I awakened with a great expectancy. We had been in a revival for several weeks. This was to be a fasting and prayer day at Miss Maud Mitchell's home... We were the first ones there; I was so afraid lest I lose that grip on God that I felt that I went right to my knees. I did not want to converse with anyone, for I was in a realm that I had never been in before. I did not know what else was going on around me.

As that struggling was going on in my heart (it was a terrific struggle), I felt that something did not want to yield. I felt a drawback, and it frightened me. Again, between groans, I cried, "Hold me to the line, Lord; hold me to the line." ... All at once, I saw Jesus coming toward me in the distance. I began saying, "Jesus, Jesus." Closer and closer He came until He entered with His cleansing power... Wave after wave came with such power I couldn't seem to give vent to it. My hair had not grown out very far yet. I tried to keep it inside of a hairnet with lots of hairpins and bobby pins, but they flew in all directions. The room was not a large one, but I marched those women around and around and shouted and shouted. I quieted down a bit and sang a chorus of a song that I had heard a Sunday school worker sing when I was just a girl:

"He makes me clean, He makes me clean,
Mine eyes Thy holiness have seen.
Just now I feel the cleansing flame,
He makes me clean in Jesus' Name."

As we women were coming home that evening toward those same mountains as we did a few months before, the trees that had then looked so green now were clapping their hands; they really were! For days, I could not come down to earth. There were some songs that I hadn't liked to sing when we first began going with the holiness group. Now I sang them over and over as I marched through the house:

"Have you been to Jesus for the cleansing power?
Are you washed in the blood of the Lamb?"
and
"Have thy affections been nailed to the cross?
Is thy heart right with God?"

That was February 9, 1934, and it is even more wonderful now. I can say I have not slept outside of Canaan one night since that time. Glory to His name! The same fire that fell that day still burns in my heart. (Assorted excerpts from Esther Lacy's testimony.)

Many obstacles were thrown in her path. Holiness people have often faced more opposition from worldly churches and denominations than from non-religous people. But when someone has a hunger for Divine things, God will find a way to lead that person through all obstacles, as Sister Lacy's story shows.

One thing that stands out is the difference she felt when she got sanctified compared to when she got saved: she felt much more joy and much more of God's power when she got sanctified. That is common: many others have testified the same.

* * * * *

This concludes the history section. I believe that all readers of this book, regardless of their theology, will agree that I have proved that talk of Christian perfection and sinless living did not begin with John Wesley, but rather has been a staple of the Church since the very earliest days. I daresay that many readers have been greatly astonished to learn this. We will now turn our attention to the more common misunderstandings about the doctrine, and the common forms of opposition to it.

Opposition to the Doctrine, and Other Errors

Chapter 9

Misunderstandings and Opposition (Part 1)

Many people, both Holiness and non-Holiness, have at least one misunderstanding about the doctrine. This tends to do quite a bit of damage, in more ways than one.

Many of the people who oppose Holiness doctrine, and the very idea of a second work of grace, do so because they have one or more misunderstandings about the doctrine. I have divided these into five general types of misunderstandings, although there is often a fair bit of overlap between some of the categories.

1. Based on history. The Pentecostal movement grew out of the Holiness movement. But they are very different in theology. A shared background is just about the only thing they have in common. Some writers who are neither Holiness nor Pentecostal do not understand this, and tend to lump the two together.

2. Based on shared terminology. Many Christians of various stripes use words like "sanctification," but they use those words to mean very different things. A group that falls into both the first and second category is the Keswick movement. It, too, is a offshoot of the Holiness movement. It, too, teaches a second work of grace. But whereas Holiness teaches the complete and perfect eradication of the sin nature, the original form of Keswickianism teaches the complete and perfect suppression of the sin nature. This is a beautiful example of how a deviation that appears to be small can lead to a very different outcome. Again, some writers who are not Holiness have thought that Holiness and Keswickianism are the same thing.

3. Based on human frailty and mistakes. Some Holiness writers (being human, and therefore prone to mistakes and imperfect judgment), have accidentally over-emphasized some aspect of Holiness doctrine to the detriment of other aspects. This,

of course, is a phenomenon that is by no means confined to the religious realm. It is often possible to make a statement that is perfectly true when applied to a certain aspect of an issue, but is not entirely true, or at least not complete, when looking at the overall picture. This phenomenon has caused confusion and misunderstandings within Holiness circles, as well as without.

Another type of this category is that non-Holiness people sometimes don't have the background knowledge and vocabulary to understand what Holiness people are saying, and thereby misunderstand the intent of the speaker or writer. The writings of John Wesley in particular are especially prone to being misunderstood, partly because it took several years to fully develop the doctrine of Holiness into a definite set of principles. The earlier writings of Wesley could be viewed, in a sense, as Wesley musing out loud during that process. As he gained a fuller understanding of the Scriptures, he corrected his views on a few points.

Another thing that occasionally plays a part in this is the changing nature of language. Anybody who reads any kind of old book needs to be aware that certain words have changed their meanings.

4. Based on imperfect examples. Some people have looked at prominent Christians of previous years—Christians, who although very godly, did not know of the second work, or did not understand it—and concluded that since those people still had the carnal nature (we know they did, because they bewailed it loudly), therefore it is impossible to be rid of it while here on earth. Even though it is often quite helpful and desirable to look to other Christians, we must be careful not to rely on human examples too heavily. We must look to the perfect God as our ultimate example, rather than imperfect people.

Another form of this is based on the lives of biblical saints.

5. Based on well-meaning but mistaken interpretations of certain Bible passages. I will deal with this category in much greater detail later on. Suffice it to say here that some people genuinely feel that they have solid scriptural grounds for opposing the doctrine of entire sanctification. These people, by and large, have failed to apply the principles for reconciling seemingly-contradictory passages.

* * * * *

But I don't want to simply give my opinion of what Holiness opponents say. Let us hear their views in their own words.

"That believers are exhorted to 'perfect holiness in the fear of God'—to 'go on to perfection'—to 'be perfect,' no careful reader of his Bible will ever think of denying (2 Cor. 7:1; Heb. 6:1; 2 Cor. 13:11). But I have yet to learn that there is a single passage in Scripture which teaches that a literal perfection, a complete and entire freedom from sin, in thought, or word, or deed, is attainable, or ever has been attained, by any child of Adam in this world. A comparative perfection, a perfection in knowledge, an all-round consistency in every relation of life, a thorough soundness in every point of doctrine—this may be seen occasionally in some of God's believing people. But as to an *absolute literal perfection*, the most eminent saints of God in every age have always been the very last to lay claim to it! On the contrary, they have always had the deepest sense of their own utter unworthiness and imperfection. The more spiritual light they have enjoyed, the more they have seen their own countless defects and shortcomings. The more grace they have had, the more they have been 'clothed with humility' (1 Pet. 5:5).

"What saint can be named in God's Word, of whose life many details are recorded, who was literally and absolutely perfect? Which of them all, when writing about himself, ever talks of feeling free of imperfection? On the contrary, men like David, and St. Paul, and St. John, declare in the strongest language that they feel in their own hearts weakness and sin. The holiest men of modern times have always been remarkable for deep humility. Have we ever seen holier men than the martyred John Bradford, or Hooker, or Usher, or Baxter, or Rutherford, or McCheyne? Yet no one can read the writings and letters of these men without seeing that they felt themselves 'debtors to mercy and grace' every day, and the very last thing they ever laid claim to was perfection!" (J. C. Ryle; *Holiness: Its Nature, Hindrances, Difficulties, and Roots;* Introduction).

People such as Ryle (and all of our opponents) make the mistake of paying too much attention to fallible man, and too little attention to infallible God. In addition, he also mixes up the different kinds of perfection—love vs. knowledge, etc. He talks about perfection of knowledge, while we talk about perfection of love. He also probably conflates weakness and sin. There are two different types of weakness: one urges us to give in to temptation, but the other is purely human.

Furthermore, it is entirely possible, even probable, for somebody who has received the second blessing to feel themselves "debtors to mercy and grace"; we have even more than other Christians to be thankful for.

"Frequently you will see things in their spirit and demeanor which are not at all to be commended. One day we are told they disputed among themselves who should be greatest (Mark 9:34). Another day they considered not his miracles, and their hearts were hardened (Mark 6:52). Once two of them wished to call down fire from heaven upon a village, because it did not receive them (Luke 9:54). In the garden of Gethsemane the three best of them slept when they should have watched and prayed. In the hour of his betrayal they all forsook him and fled, and worst of all, Peter, the most forward of the twelve, denied his Master three times with an oath" (Ryle; ch. 12).

He is talking about the twelve disciples here; but notice that all the examples he gives are from **before** Pentecost. This distinction is crucially important.

"We may clearly perceive that it is they who are truly sanctified and holy, who are the most deeply sensible of the root of corruption which still remains within them, and which is ever springing up and producing that which defiles them; and therefore do they greatly bewail their pollutions, as that which is most dishonouring to God and most disturbing to their own peace; and earnestly do they endeavour after the mortification of it. A remarkable corroboration is found in the fact that the most godly and holy have been the very ones who most strongly affirmed their sinfulness and most loudly bewailed the same. It was one whom God himself declared to be a 'perfect (sincere) and an upright man, one that feareth God, and escheweth evil' (Job 1:8) who declared 'Behold, I am vile' (40:4)" (A. W. Pink; *The Doctrine of Sanctification*; ch. 5).

One thing that I find very interesting here is how he seems to be equating perfection with sincerity. This must be his own idea for the verse in question. At any rate, I could not find any other basis for this: no commentator that I can find suggests that the verse should be translated this way. I suppose that sincerity could be described as perfection of belief; but it's raw belief, unfiltered by facts or evidence. Mere sincerity of belief is no evidence that the belief in question is actually correct.

This quote is also an excellent example of the very strange and warped view that our opponents have of what God's grace actually does for a person. It also shows the fundamental illogic and contradictions inherent in their doctrine. Most people agree that (if nothing else) sanctification is a "setting apart." But how can we be set apart *from* sin if we still have sin *within* us? And how can we be "truly holy" if we still have *unholiness, corruption, and defilement* within us?

Pink says some good things in this book. I believe that he was a genuine Christian. It's clear from other places in the book that he grasped a large portion of the truth. But his testimony and reputation are woefully tarnished by his vehement opposition to the second work of grace.

As we have seen, our opponents point to the stories of the biblical saints as supporting evidence of their position. Even very godly men like Noah, Abraham, Moses, David, etc. sinned at least once.

They say that this means that sinless perfection is impossible. Nothing of the sort. Take bowling as an analogy. A perfect score is 300 points. Many bowlers will never achieve that feat. Even professionals have a hard time achieving it. So let's say that you see a dozen bowlers, all of whom you know to be very, very good at the game, try to get a perfect score; but none of them do. Does that mean that the thirteenth person has no chance? No. We KNOW that a perfect score is achievable—because it HAS been done.

It does no good to point to various saints as evidence that sinless perfection is impossible. Firstly, we know that it is possible because God has commanded it. Secondly, we know it is possible because people who do not lie have said that they have achieved it. Thirdly, the fact that a man such as David or Noah falls from that state once or twice during a multi-decade walk with God inherently means that during the vast majority of that time he DID have a perfect walk.

"The LORD rewarded me according to my righteousness: according to the cleanness of my hands hath he recompensed me. For I have kept the ways of the LORD, and have not wickedly departed from my God. For all his judgments were before me: and as for his statutes, I did not depart from them. I was also upright before him, and have kept myself from mine iniquity. Therefore the LORD hath recompensed me according to my righteousness; according to my cleanness in his eye sight" (II Sam. 22:21-25).

Note that this was *before* David's sin with Bathsheba (22:1). Opponents of the second work would say that David was either boasting or lying here. It seems odd that God would allow the pages of His Word to be stained with a boast or a lie from one of its writers; but I guess that's what happened.

Or is it? I hope that nobody seriously believes such a nonsensical thing. In reality, this is proof that we can remain without sin.

In actuality, the above claim from our opponents about the biblical saints is not quite correct. The biography of Enoch is extremely short, but there is no record that he ever lost his relationship with God. And as we know, God does not shy away from revealing when His followers fall into sin. Joseph has much more space devoted to his story, but there is no indication that he ever fell, either. In the New Testament, we have Stephen, Philip, and—in their lives after Pentecost—John, James the brother of John, and James the brother of Jesus. There are probably some others as well, but I did not take the time to check.

While thinking about some of this, and reading some things that have been written about the biblical saints, I had a realization about the attitude of our opponents. I'm not sure if any of them realize that they have this attitude, or would be able to articulate it. It seems to me that they regard sinless perfection as a type of **quantity**; something that can be counted. Remember, they base much of their opposition on the fact that no biblical saint (as far as they have been aware of) is recorded as having lived an absolutely sinless life all life-long. (Although some of the more prominent ones sinned only once.) So a person gets saved; even if he lives a truly sinless, blameless, holy life for a long time—day 1, day 2, day 3... day 2000, etc.—we come to day 5000, and he backslides. Our opponents say that this proves he was deluded in thinking that he had sinless perfection, and that sinless perfection is unattainable. This is why I feel that they regard it as a quantity. They evidently feel that a person must retain it "**all** the days" in order for it to actually be sinless perfection.

This is a ridiculous argument. If a man is successful in business, and becomes a millionaire, but then loses everything in a reversal, that does not mean that he never was a millionaire. At the risk of creating a tautology, he was a millionaire WHILE he was a millionaire.

Sinless perfection is a **quality**; an attribute. It is a quality that can be both gotten and lost. The unsanctified Christian has somewhat of a tendency to sin because of the remaining carnal nature, and must fight against that tendency in order to live a victorious life. Sanctification removes that, and replaces it with a tendency to NOT sin. But patterns can be broken in either direction. It is possible, although very difficult, for an unsanctified Christian to consistently live above sin. And it is possible for a sanctified Christian to fall into sin. And once or if he does, then (by definition) he loses sinless perfection.

Many people also point to the testimony of famous Christians like Richard Baxter, etc. Everybody who knows anything at all about such people would agree that they were godly men who labored long and hard for God. And yet they mourned the presence of carnality within them. Indeed, the more mature in their Christian walk they became, the more they felt that carnality.

Based partly on examples such as this, opponents of the second work think that it's impossible to have the carnal nature removed from the heart. But incredible things happen all the time. People have done unbelievable things: tightrope walking, for example; Charles Blondin was famous for his seemingly-impossible feats. Others have done great feats of strength or endurance. And those are merely human feats; perhaps literally one in a million, but still merely human. Why are our opponents so ready to believe incredible things of humanity, and yet so loath to believe incredible things of God?

They believe people, but the wrong ones. They believe those who say that it's impossible to live without sin, and not those who say that it is possible. But even in the secular realm, history shows that predictions of impossibilities are usually wrong. Many great scientific and technical advances have been preceded by learned men who confidently proclaimed that such a thing was impossible—and yet it happened. Such predictions were based on human experience and human knowledge. On January 13, 1920, the *New York Times* published a piece ridiculing Robert Goddard and his claims that rockets might one day reach the moon. They failed to understand that there are truths that are greater than human experience. Our opponents make the same mistake in the religious realm.

We who claim the possibility of a sinless life do not do so on the strength of human experience, but on the strength of God's infallible Word. God tells us that living a sinless life is possible, and this Word would remain true even if nobody on earth ever actually lived a sinless life. The fact that some people have indeed done so is simply corroboration that it is possible. Not proof—no human experience or knowledge can ever prove the Bible to be true. No inferior level can prove a superior one. The best it can do is provide corroborating evidence. But when people claim to have received the second work of grace, along with its attendant benefits, the Bible proves that such a claim is both possible and plausible.

Regarding the example set before us by Christians of the past: yes, they have much to teach us. But we should always hold their writings and teachings up to the illumination of the Bible. In many, perhaps most, cases, we will find that there was at least one thing that they got wrong, or one area where they placed either too much emphasis or not enough. We should be willing and able to take benefit from what we can, while at the same time rejecting whatever they got wrong. We should not take comfort from the fact that many prominent, godly Christians somehow failed to see that God could have removed the remains of the carnal nature from their hearts; and we most assuredly should not use their failure as an excuse. Customs and examples should be examined in the light of Scripture.

Until I started researching this book, I had no idea of the number of people who have somehow gotten the idea that sanctification is supposedly some sort of magical, mystical thing that keeps a person from sinning.

Here is an example from a pamphlet called "The Backslider," by Dr. John Rice, a Baptist preacher. He writes, "Holiness people sometimes claim that the carnal nature has been eradicated in them, that the fire of God has burned it all out. Yet, strangely enough, they too backslide.

"At Des Moines, Iowa a sad-faced man attended my services who told me he had been a Holiness preacher but was at the time living in the grossest sin and did not even now claim to be a Christian. The facts belied his doctrine. The carnal nature had not been taken away."

For starters, there's a possibility that Dr. Rice apparently never even considered—that the former preacher he met was telling the exact truth. It is, of course, possible that he had never been sanctified. But even if the man had been sanctified, that's no guarantee of anything. Dr. Rice doesn't come right out and say it, but it is clear that he fundamentally misunderstood the doctrine of holiness. He seems to think that if carnality was removed, a Christian would automatically never sin. But that's not how sanctification works.

I know that many others have had this same misunderstanding, so I wish to be very clear, very definite, and very explicit on this point. If the reader is somebody who opposes the doctrine of Holiness, take this from your reading, even if you take nothing else.

Sanctification does not take away a person's free will. Nor does it prevent temptation. We are tempted just as much after sanctification as before. But once the remnant of sin is removed, we are much more closely conformed to the image, grace, and holiness of Christ, and thus it is easier to resist temptation. Nor does it transform people into angels. (Although some non-Holiness people seemingly expect angelic perfection from us.) Adam and Eve were perfect in every respect—mind, spirit, soul, and body. Yet they *chose* to commit sin. I repeat—they deliberately chose to commit sin, even after being explicitly warned. Despite all that God had done for them, Eve willingly listened to the Serpent, and Adam willingly listened to Eve. Moses sinned (Num. 20:7-12). Aaron sinned (Num. 12; Exodus 32). There is no such thing on this earth as being so holy that it becomes impossible to fall. It is entirely possible to fall into sin after being sanctified (II Peter 3:17). No Holiness preacher, and no Holiness theologian, has EVER claimed otherwise.

* * * * *

Some objections to the doctrine are based on terminology: especially terms like "full salvation," which is sometimes used to describe sanctification. Some non-Holiness people have misunderstood this, and viewed the term as being a slight on the work of salvation; which leads them to reject the doctrine.

Holiness people sometimes use the term "full salvation" in reference to the second work; because once a person receives this work, he is saved not only from the stain of conscious sin, but also from the stain of the carnal nature. Unfortunately, Pentecostal people also sometimes use that term, which is another source of confusion. What they mean by it is something very different than what we mean by it.

Salvation saves us from the guilt of sin; sanctification saves us from the contamination of sin.

One of the biggest misunderstandings that non-Holiness people have about the doctrine has to do with the phrase "Christian perfection." They think it means something very different from what it actually does mean. Once I realized how wide-spread this misunderstanding is, I briefly decided to quit using the phrase, because it is such an error-prone subject. However, that decision did not last long, for a little Bible study made me realize that it is a valid term. It is really quite astonishing how many times the Bible speaks of Christians being perfect. Indeed, in several places, God commands us in no uncertain terms to be perfect.

However, we are still left with this perplexing error that so many people make. Quite frankly, I am at a loss to explain it. Somehow, some way, many opponents of Holiness doctrine manage to get the idea that we teach that a sanctified person doesn't make mistakes. Alternately, some have seized on the synonymous phrase that some Holiness people have used, "sinless perfection"—and then these opponents define any mistake or human weakness as a "sin," and then they point and laugh, and say, "Ah Ha! Your doctrine doesn't do what you claim it does!"

Now some of this opposition is malicious—but even many of the well-meaning opponents get tripped up on this point. The only possible explanation that I have been able to figure out is that somehow or another, when Holiness people say "**Christian** perfection," others somehow hear that as "**human** perfection."

No Holiness church, school, preacher, or theologian has ever claimed that the experience of sanctification prevents a person from making human mistakes and errors.

Nor will we necessarily be perfect in our theology. Nor does it change our *human* disposition. The experience of sanctification does not change an excitable person into a placid one, or vice versa. There are some aspects of life in which we will not be perfect until we enter Heaven. All of God's creation was tainted by the Fall, including the human body and mind. But we can, and should, be perfect in our walk before God. It is very likely impossible—or at the very least, extremely difficult—to completely fulfill God's command to "be perfect" without the experience of sanctification.

* * * * *

I have read several writers, and interacted with various people, who opposed the doctrine of entire sanctification. They claim that being completely cleansed in this life from the remnant of sin is impossible, but I find their explanations of why it is impossible to be unsatisfactory. (That is, for the relative few who actually try to explain.) Astonishingly, a large number of opponents never even try to explain why they think it's impossible.

Nowhere have I found anybody who claims that God is not powerful enough to do such a work. Nor do they claim that God is pleased when Christians fall into sin.

As far as I can tell, there are only four possibilities.

(1) God does not have the power to remove the remnant of sin from a person's heart.

I am confident that every true Christian will dismiss this possibility as being unscriptural.

(2) God has the power to perfectly cleanse the heart, but for some reason, it is His will that Christians should lead an unstable, sin-prone life, constantly falling into sin and out of God's favor.

I believe that every true Christian will also dismiss this possibility as being unscriptural, for there are numerous Bible verses that command us to be holy. Indeed, even many opponents of Holiness as a second work of grace recognize this.

(3) God has the power to perfectly cleanse the heart, but for some reason, it is His will that Christians should face a constant, life-long struggle against their sin nature, with the expectation that they will consistently be victorious over it.

For the sake of the argument, I am willing to concede that this MAY be the case. There are certainly several Bible passages that compare the Christian life to warfare and strife. However, if this option is the correct one, it is obvious that only a miniscule percentage of Christians live up to God's expectations, for the overwhelming majority of Christians who fight a daily struggle against their sin nature are only sometimes, rather than consistently, successful. While I concede this option as a theoretical possibility, I do not find it to be a likely one, for it makes a successful, consistent walk with God far harder than it probably needs to be.

(4) God has both the power and the desire to perfectly cleanse the heart. It is His will that every one of His children should lead a stable, holy, sinless life here on earth, with

215

perfect, complete victory over sin.

I believe that this option is the correct one. There are a very great many Bible verses that speak about living a holy life, unspotted by sin, and separate from the unholy things, attitudes, and practices of the world. The idea that God's people should be a righteous people runs throughout the Bible like a golden thread.

And yet—astonishing but true—a great many Christians ACT as if they don't believe that God is omnipotent. I am positive that if you asked them, they would unhesitatingly affirm their belief in conventional doctrine about God's power. Indeed, they would probably be either upset or astonished that anybody would accuse them of any other belief. **But they don't act like it**. I know some good, honest, well-meaning Christians, and I have read writings from several others, who bewail their sin nature. They wish that they did not have it. They struggle against it on a daily basis. They do everything they can to keep it subdued. But that is ALL they do. As far as I can tell, they go for years and years without even entertaining the possibility that the supposedly all-powerful God that they worship has the power to remove that sin nature! They do everything possible to fight against the old man—**EXCEPT** ask God to remove it!!!!

Pay attention to the prophet Isaiah—"Wherefore, when I came, was there no man? when I called, was there none to answer? Is my hand shortened at all, that it cannot redeem? or have I no power to deliver? behold, at my rebuke I dry up the sea, I make the rivers a wilderness: their fish stinketh, because there is no water, and dieth for thirst" (Isaiah 50:2). "Behold, the Lord's hand is not shortened, that it cannot save; neither his ear heavy, that it cannot hear" (Isaiah 59:1). And Moses—"And the Lord said unto Moses, Is the Lord's hand waxed short? thou shalt see now whether my word shall come to pass unto thee or not" (Num. 11:23).

There are many well-meaning, godly Christians who have been tricked by Satan into thinking that carnality cannot be removed in this life. He tells them, "Yes, the Lord's hand is waxed short." He whispers, "Even Divine power cannot help you in your current plight." And far too many Christians believe him.

In all my research, I found only one person who made what I consider to be a serious attempt to answer the question of why having carnality removed supposedly never happens.

"Perhaps the reader is inclined to ask, But *why* does God suffer the sinful nature to remain in the Christian: he could easily remove it. Beware, my friend, of calling into question God's infinite wisdom: he knows what is best, and his thoughts and ways are often the opposite of ours (Isa. 55:8). But let me ask, *Which* magnifies God's *power* the more: to preserve in this wicked world one who still has within him a corrupt nature, or one that has been made as sinless as the holy angels? Can there be any doubt as to the answer! But why does not God *subdue* my lusts: Would it not be more for his glory if he did? Again, we say, Beware of measuring God with *your* mind. He knows which is most for his glory. But answer this question: If your lusts were greatly subdued and you sinned far less than you do, would you appreciate and adore his *grace* as you now do?" (Pink; ch. 10).

His idea that God's power would be magnified by preserving somebody who still has carnality within him is a very pretty theory, but it is one that is contradicted by reality. Because such people, **by their own admission**, are NOT preserved; on the contrary, they are constantly falling into sin.

We are commanded to remember what God has done for us. So to answer Pink's last question: No; but not in the way that he was undoubtedly thinking of. The reason the answer is "no" is because we would appreciate and adore God *even more* than before. The greater the deliverance, the greater the thankfulness.

"And thou shalt remember that thou wast a bondman in the land of Egypt, and the LORD thy God redeemed thee: therefore I command thee this thing to day" (Deut. 15:15).

"Seek the LORD and his strength, seek his face continually. Remember his marvellous works that he hath done, his wonders, and the judgments of his mouth" (I Chron. 16:11, 12).

"I will remember the works of the LORD: surely I will remember thy wonders of old. I will meditate also of all thy work, and talk of thy doings. Thy way, O God, is in the sanctuary: who is so great a God as our God? Thou art the God that doest wonders: thou hast declared thy strength among the people" (Psalm 77:11-14).

"Bless the LORD, O my soul: and all that is within me, bless his holy name. Bless the LORD, O my soul, and forget not all his benefits: who forgiveth all thine iniquities; who healeth all thy diseases" (Psalm 103:1-3).

"Hearken to me, ye that follow after righteousness, ye that seek the LORD: look unto the rock whence ye are hewn, and to the hole of the pit whence ye are digged" (Isaiah 51:1).

"And Jesus answering said unto him, Simon, I have somewhat to say unto thee. And he saith, Master, say on. There was a certain creditor which had two debtors: the one owed five hundred pence, and the other fifty. And when they had nothing to pay, he frankly forgave them both. Tell me therefore, which of them will love him most? Simon answered and said, I suppose that he, to whom he forgave most. And he said unto him, Thou hast rightly judged. And he turned to the woman, and said unto Simon, Seest thou this woman? I entered into thine house, thou gavest me no water for my feet: but she hath washed my feet with tears, and wiped them with the hairs of her head. Thou gavest me no kiss: but this woman since the time I came in hath not ceased to kiss my feet. My head with oil thou didst not anoint: but this woman hath anointed my feet with ointment. Wherefore I say unto thee, Her sins, which are many, are forgiven; for she loved much: but to whom little is forgiven, the same loveth little" (Luke 7:40-47).

We see that Pink contradicts Jesus. God has done more for the sanctified man than for the unsanctified man; therefore the sanctified man loves Him more. **A lasting** deliverance from sin magnifies God's power more, and we are more thankful for it, than a deliverance from sin that is so weak that it has to be repeated over and over.

"What shall we say then? Shall we continue in sin, that grace may abound? God forbid. How shall we, that are dead to sin, live any longer therein?" (Romans 6:1, 2).

Pink also contradicts Paul. Pink thinks it is a good thing to continue in sin, that grace may "abound" (so-called). This is Antinomianism. The **only** way that grace can abound is when a person actually repents of his sin—and apologizers for a sin-filled life very seldom get around to repenting.

"But if our unrighteousness commend the righteousness of God, what shall we say? Is God unrighteous who taketh vengeance? (I speak as a man) God forbid: for then how shall God judge the world? For if the truth of God hath more abounded through my lie unto his glory; why yet am I also judged as a sinner? And not rather, (as we be slanderously reported, and as some affirm that we say,) Let us do evil, that good may come? whose damnation is just" (Romans 3:5-8).

* * * * *

Some people have argued against a second work of grace on the grounds that God does a perfect work in us, and for us, when we get saved. True, the work of regeneration is perfect—as far as it goes. But in some respects, the work of regeneration does not go all the way. Now, before the reader starts jumping up and down, and calling me a heretic, let me explain. It is manifestly obvious that if we got every possible thing in regeneration, then there would be no need, and no opportunity, for the command to "grow in grace" (II Peter 3:18). The work of regeneration is perfect and complete in the sense that nothing else is required to get us into Heaven. But every Christian should be aware that God wants to give us measures of grace, faith, etc. that we simply are not prepared to receive when we first get saved.

Everybody recognizes (whether they consciously realize it or not) that the work of regeneration is in one sense incomplete. After all, that's the precise point that people make when they bewail the remnants of the carnal nature within them. This is the reason for having a second work of grace. We must become alive towards God before we are ABLE to seek a closer, holier walk with God. An unsaved person doesn't have enough faith to ask for the complete eradication of the carnal nature—he has his hands full just asking for forgiveness of his conscious sins. But once we become alive unto God, THEN we have both the means and opportunity to ask for further help and grace beyond "merely" getting saved. Once this point is reached, then we can handle asking God to eradicate the carnal nature.

God often does His work in stages. Creation is a good example. God didn't actually need to take six days to do everything. He had the power to do it faster.

Another way of stating the same general type of objection is "when we get saved, we're as saved as we're ever going to be"; or, "we get everything at salvation."

This is absolutely true in a technical sense. We are either saved or not saved; there is no in-between. However, there are degrees both of goodness and wickedness. This is beautifully illustrated by verses in successive chapters of Ephesians. "And grieve not the holy Spirit of God, whereby ye are sealed unto the day of redemption" (Eph. 4:30). "And be not drunk with wine, wherein is excess; but be filled with the Spirit" (Eph. 5:18).

Paul had just told them that they were already **sealed** with the Spirit; and then he exhorts them to be **filled** with the Spirit. A seal is something that is typically placed on the outside of an object, and is often a mark of ownership; whereas "filling" refers to a purely inward change. All Christians are sealed with the Spirit; but, as we have just seen, not all Christians are filled with the Spirit.

Holiness doctrine does not teach that it's possible to be "more saved," although we do sometimes use terms that might create that impression among people who don't fully understand the doctrine. Rather, Holiness doctrine deals with the closeness of our walk with God. The purer our hearts are, the easier it is to walk more closely with a pure God. This is actually quite similar in some respects to growing in grace; but whereas "growing" is a process, sanctification is an instantaneous work. A Christian who has spent several years constantly growing in grace has a closer walk with God than he did when he first got saved, and thus the quality of his spiritual life is better. The same is true after a person is sanctified.

I was thinking one morning about the opposition to the work of sanctification, and I realized something very interesting. It is very common to oppose this doctrine on the grounds mentioned above—and yet, somehow, none of these people oppose the idea of growing in grace on the grounds that "we get everything at salvation."

To all people who oppose the idea of a second work on these grounds, I would implore you—at least be consistent, and oppose the idea of growing in grace on those same grounds.

If, however, you now realize that we in fact do **not** get everything at salvation, except in a narrow, technical sense; if you admit that there is room after salvation for growing in grace; then be consistent in that direction, and admit that there at least might be room for other types of spiritual improvement as well, such as a second work of grace.

* * * * *

Many opponents of sanctification seem to have a semi-Gnostic view of the physical body. The Gnostics were a grouping of heretical sects in early Christian times who believed that physical matter is inherently sinful. As a result, they believed that Jesus could not have had a physical body. Many of our opponents seem to have a touch (or more) of the same general attitude. As far as I can tell, this attitude seems to be the real, underlying reason why they believe that having carnality removed is impossible. That's why they interpret certain Bible verses the way they do. Perhaps they don't actually mean it this way; I cannot read minds. But after a while, it tends to come across as merely an excuse to avoid doing what God wants us to do.

Why do I say this? Because I remember that God deals with us where we are, both literally and figuratively. Somehow I just can't imagine that our circumstances here on earth have escaped God's notice. The Bible was written to sinful, fallible, error-prone mankind. And yet—AND YET—we have all these explicit commands to be holy and perfect.

This says to me that there is a way to fulfill these commands while we are still in our physical bodies.

"Yet let it be pointed out that, though the whole of the Christian's person is renewed by the Spirit, and all the faculties of his soul are renovated, nevertheless, there is no operation of grace upon his old nature, so that its evil is expelled: the 'flesh' or principle of indwelling sin is neither eradicated nor purified nor made good. Our 'old man' (which must be distinguished from the soul and its faculties) is 'corrupt according to the deceitful lusts', and remains so till the end of our earthly pilgrimage, ever striving against the 'spirit' or principle of holiness or 'new man'. As the soul at the very first moment of its union with the body (in the womb) becomes sinful, so it is not until the moment of its dissolution from the body that the soul becomes inherently sinless" (Pink; ch. 9).

He contradicts himself quite badly here—first the soul is separate from the old man, AND the soul has been renovated, but yet the soul is still sinful. This is an excellent example of how far astray a person can be led by opposition to the second work of grace. We see here a fascinating exercise in illogic. How can "all" the soul be renovated if it's still inherently sinful until the point of death? Just what is this renovation, and what does it actually accomplish? And how can the soul, especially one of an infant, be sinful at all if it is separate from the old man?

Notice how he seems to view the physical body as a source of sin that contaminates the soul.

"So deeply planted are the roots of human corruption, that even after we are born again, renewed, 'washed, sanctified, justified,' and made living members of Christ, these roots remain alive in the bottom of our hearts, and, like the leprosy in the walls of the house, we never get rid of them until the earthly house of this tabernacle is dissolved. Sin, no doubt, in the believer's heart, has no longer *dominion*. It is checked, controlled, mortified, and crucified by the expulsive power of the new principle of grace. The life of a believer is a life of victory and not of failure. But the very struggles which go on within his bosom, the fight that he finds it needful to fight daily, the watchful jealousy which he is obliged to exercise over his inner man, the contest between the flesh and the spirit, the inward 'groanings' which no one knows but he who has experienced them—all, all testify to the same great truth, all show the enormous power and vitality of sin" (Ryle; ch. 1).

"Checked, controlled, mortified, and crucified"—the last of these is not like the others. Crucifixion has to do with killing. The other three deal with managing something that is still alive. If something is crucified, it doesn't need to be managed, because it is dead.

The Bible rebuts Ryle's views.

"Moreover the law entered, that the offence might abound. But where sin abounded, grace did much more abound: that as sin hath reigned unto death, even so might grace reign through righteousness unto eternal life by Jesus Christ our Lord" (Romans 5:20, 21).

Leaving sin in the heart doesn't match this description. Leaving sin in the heart, in any form or degree, would mean that grace abounds to a **lesser degree** than sin did.

"And God is able to make all grace abound toward you; that ye, always having all sufficiency in all things, may abound to every good work" (II Cor. 9:8).

Notice this: "EVERY good work." Is carnality a good work? Or does it hinder good works?

"In whom we have redemption through his blood, the forgiveness of sins, according to the riches of his grace; wherein he hath abounded toward us in all wisdom and prudence" (Eph. 1:7, 8).

Removal of the carnal nature makes many aspects of Christian living easier, and improves the quality of a person's walk with God. It is therefore an inherent part of God's wisdom and prudence to make such a removal possible.

"That he would grant you, according to the riches of his glory, to be strengthened with might by his Spirit in the inner man; that Christ may dwell in your hearts by faith; that ye, being rooted and grounded in love, may be able to comprehend with all saints what is the breadth, and length, and depth, and height; and to know the love of Christ, which passeth knowledge, that ye might be filled with all the fulness of God. Now unto him that is able to do exceeding abundantly above all that we ask or think, according to the power that worketh in us, unto him be glory in the church by Christ Jesus throughout all ages, world without end. Amen" (Eph. 3:16-21).

"And this I pray, that your love may abound yet more and more in knowledge and in all judgment; that ye may approve things that are excellent; that ye may be sincere and without offence till the day of Christ; being filled with the fruits of righteousness, which are by Jesus Christ, unto the glory and praise of God" (Phil. 1:9-11).

Is having sin in the heart "excellent"? Does the presence of sin cause us to be "without offence"? Is sin a fruit of righteousness?

"For what thanks can we render to God again for you, for all the joy wherewith we joy for your sakes before our God; night and day praying exceedingly that we might see your face, and might perfect that which is lacking in your faith? And the Lord make you to increase and abound in love one toward another, and toward all men, even as we do toward you: to the end he may stablish your hearts unblameable in holiness before God, even our Father, at the coming of our Lord Jesus Christ with all his saints. Furthermore then we beseech you, brethren, and exhort you by the Lord Jesus, that as ye have received of us how ye ought to walk and to please God, so ye would abound more and more. For God hath not called us unto uncleanness, but unto holiness" (I Thess. 3:9, 10, 12, 13, 4:1, 7).

When there is still a remnant of sin in the heart, is that uncleanness, or holiness?

"He [the Christian] must fight *the flesh*. Even after conversion he carries within him a nature prone to evil, and a heart weak and unstable as water. That heart will never be free from imperfection in this world, and it is a miserable delusion to expect it" (Ryle; ch. 4).

"In thee, O LORD, do I put my trust: let me never be put to confusion. Deliver me in thy righteousness, and cause me to escape: incline thine ear unto me, and save me. Be thou my strong habitation, whereunto I may continually resort: thou hast given commandment to save me; for thou art my rock and my fortress" (Psalm 71:1-3).

Does this sound like weakness or instability? God will infuse us with His strength and stability if we ask.

"And I say also unto thee, That thou art Peter, and upon this rock I will build my church; and the gates of hell shall not prevail against it" (Matt. 16:18).

"Now therefore ye are no more strangers and foreigners, but fellowcitizens with the saints, and of the household of God; and are built upon the foundation of the apostles and prophets, Jesus Christ himself being the chief corner stone; in whom all the building fitly framed together groweth unto an holy temple in the Lord: in whom ye also are builded together for an habitation of God through the Spirit" (Eph. 2:19-22).

If something is "fitly framed together" it is solid: not weak or wavering, not unsteady or unstable. This phrase calls to mind the idea of tongue and groove woodwork. Such construction is stable; something made in such a way is very useful and dependable.

"For no man ever yet hated his own flesh; but nourisheth and cherisheth it, even as the Lord the church: for we are members of his body, of his flesh, and of his bones" (Eph. 5:29, 30).

In the context of this discussion, this is a tremendously solemn, even an appalling, statement. What it means is that if you still have carnality in your heart; if you are saved but not sanctified; you are, in a certain sense, introducing weakness, instability, evil, and death into the very flesh and bones of Christ.

"We are yet in the body. The devil is not dead. We are not yet like the angels. Heaven has not yet begun. The leprosy is not out of the walls of the house, however much we may scrape them, and never will be till the house is taken down. Our bodies are indeed the temple of the Holy Ghost, but not a perfect temple until they are raised or changed. Grace is indeed a treasure, but a treasure in earthen vessels. It is possible for a man to forsake all for Christ's sake, and yet to be overtaken occasionally with doubts and fears" (Ryle; ch. 12).

He mixes up the different kinds of perfection. Physical perfection is totally different from spiritual perfection.

As we have seen, opponents insist that we cannot be either perfect or without sin while in this physical body. Ryle uses the symbolism of leprosy, which is often used as a symbol of sin.

But leprosy, both literal and symbolic, can be healed by Divine power. Indeed, such healing is an unmistakable sign of Divine power. "And it came to pass, when the king of Israel had read the letter, that he rent his clothes, and said, Am I God, to kill and to make alive, that this man doth send unto me to recover a man of his leprosy? wherefore consider, I pray you, and see how he seeketh a quarrel against me" (II Kings 5:7).

Divine power provides a cure—there is no record in the Bible of leprosy being cured any other way. Jesus used that as one of the proofs that He was the Messiah, to John the Baptist. "Now when John had heard in the prison the works of Christ, he sent two of his disciples, and said unto him, Art thou he that should come, or do we look for another? Jesus answered and said unto them, Go and shew John again those things which ye do hear and see: the blind receive their sight, and the lame walk, the lepers are cleansed, and the deaf hear, the dead are raised up, and the poor have the gospel preached to them" (Matt. 11:2-5).

The Mosaic law gave a procedure to confirm that a leper had been healed, and to ceremonially cleanse the person (see Lev. 14). But in all of Old Testament times, there were only two people who were ever healed of leprosy. And they were both special cases.

Miriam, in Num. 12, was healed. But her leprosy was an explicit punishment from God, and He laid out a specific procedure for her to follow. The other person was Naaman. And he, being a Gentile, had no reason or obligation to follow the Mosaic law.

"And many lepers were in Israel in the time of Eliseus [Elisha] the prophet; and none of them was cleansed, saving Naaman the Syrian" (Luke 4:27). Luke is quoting Jesus in this passage. I assume that Jesus was in a position to know whereof He spoke.

In short, the procedure outlined by Moses sat, unneeded and unused, until Jesus came on the scene and starting healing lepers.

Now, stop and consider. Were the lepers that Jesus healed only partly or imperfectly healed? Was there a remnant of leprosy left in their bodies? Of course not. And yet—strange as it seems—many people insist that we must be content with a partial, imperfect healing from sin! Just as Jesus perfectly healed lepers while He was here on earth, in precisely the same way He can perfectly, completely heal the soul from sin, including removing the remains of the carnal nature.

* * * * *

Another type of misunderstanding is when people confuse the Holiness movement with the Pentecostal movement. This is compounded by the fact that some Holiness writers in the 1800s used "Pentecostal" to refer to the second work of grace (because, after all, the first recorded instance was on the Day of Pentecost). This usage was dropped once the Pentecostal movement began.

Pentecostals believe that speaking in tongues is part and parcel of receiving the Holy Ghost. Not so. The two things are entirely separate—they have absolutely no inherent connection whatsoever.

Jesus was baptized with the Holy Ghost right after being baptized with water. (Not that He needed to be purified; this was an example for us.) This incident is one of the few that is mentioned in all four Gospels. However, there is no mention—not even a hint—that Jesus spoke in tongues. On the contrary, the only voice heard on that occasion was the voice of God the Father directly from Heaven.

Acts 4:8 mentions that the reason that Peter was so bold in preaching before the Sanhedrin was because he previously had been filled with the Holy Ghost. Notably, however, there is no mention of him speaking in tongues on that occasion. Neither is there any record in Acts 8 of the Samaritans speaking in tongues when they received the Holy Ghost. In addition, there is not even a hint that Paul spoke in tongues when he received the Holy Ghost.

There are two occasions, besides the Day of Pentecost itself, when the baptism of the Holy Ghost was accompanied by the gift of tongues; Acts 10:46, and 19:6. However, in 19:6, they not only spoke in tongues, but they also prophesied, as well.

All this shows that speaking in tongues is not integral to the baptism of the Holy Ghost, but merely an occasional incidental. As a matter of fact, I have never heard of anybody in modern times who spoke in tongues when they got sanctified. I do not wish to claim that it has never happened, but it is certainly exceedingly rare. Pentecostals, by contrast, regard tongues as the end-all, be-all gift, and an infallible sign of the Holy Ghost; they seem (at least in practice) to exalt it above all the other spiritual gifts, even though Paul ranked it as the least important.

In short, the gift of tongues is not a reliable indicator of the second work.

So to be clear: the second work of grace has nothing to do with speaking in tongues. The Tongues movement is based on one of the biggest misunderstandings in recorded history. What the 120 did on the Day of Pentecost—which, by the way, was speaking in foreign languages, not some nonsensical gibberish—was a gift that God saw fit to give because of the specific circumstances. The supernatural ability to speak in another language is completely unrelated to the baptism of the Holy Ghost.

There is a misunderstanding that is found on both sides of the fence, although more so on our opponents' side.

It is the idea that perfection renders a man incapable of advancement, and also incapable of being taught/rebuked.

Not so: Christian perfection includes humility. Thus such a man is actually more likely to accept teaching/correction, instead of rejecting it because of pride or self-will.

"The meek also shall increase their joy in the LORD, and the poor among men shall rejoice in the Holy One of Israel" (Isaiah 29:19).

If you are not meek, it is inherently impossible to be sanctified. And sanctification increases a person's joy in the Lord.

"Come unto me, all ye that labour and are heavy laden, and I will give you rest. Take my yoke upon you, and learn of me; for I am meek and lowly in heart: and ye shall find rest unto your souls" (Matt. 11:28, 29).

In this passage Jesus rebuts the idea of our opponents that a claim of perfection or humility is automatically boasting. Jesus never boasted about anything: He would have lost His state of sinlessness. When somebody who is in possession of Christian perfection makes a statement about being humble, it is a simple statement of fact. Anything else would be a violation of Jesus' example.

Many of our opponents also have the idea that being forced to live with unwanted sin in a person's life produces humility. But Jesus was not humble because He had unwanted sin. He was humble because He was pure.

"But he giveth more grace. Wherefore he saith, God resisteth the proud, but giveth grace unto the humble. Submit yourselves therefore to God. Resist the devil, and he will flee from you. Draw nigh to God, and he will draw nigh to you. Cleanse your hands, ye sinners; and purify your hearts, ye double minded. Be afflicted, and mourn, and weep: let your laughter be turned to mourning, and your joy to heaviness. Humble yourselves in the sight of the Lord, and he shall lift you up" (James 4:6-10).

Our opponents seem to view any claim of perfection, humility, or sinlessness as boasting. But a simple statement of fact is not boasting. If a person wins first place at a prestigious competition of some kind, making a statement about it is not boasting. He could certainly **use** it **as** a boast; but the statement in and of itself is not a boast. In our case, since pride is a sin, a statement about perfection or sinlessness cannot be used as a boast without automatically destroying the condition in question.

I daresay that some opponents will try to use the previous sentence as a weapon against us; but the fact is, we have a choice in such a case. A statement about perfection or sinlessness cannot automatically be a boast; such a state of affairs would be a violation of free will.

Nor does Christian perfection preclude advancement or improvement. There are stages in a Christian's life: there are various milestones that can be achieved; but at no time this side of Heaven does there come a point where a Christian is incapable of learning more or drawing closer to God.

Many of our opponents claim that the word "perfect" as found in the KJV should more properly be translated "complete." I freely admit that there is an element of "completeness" in perfection. But there is a certain definite sense in which Christian perfection is *less than* completeness. If this statement puzzles or baffles the reader, it is a sign that you almost certainly have not yet learned how to distinguish between Christian perfection and human perfection. A perfect Christian will ALWAYS have room for growing in grace.

Even though this section is largely about our opponents and what they believe, I would like to address a few issues within the Holiness movement that lead to misunderstandings. There is a misunderstanding about sanctification that is mainly confined to the ranks of the Holiness movement.

Some people have gotten the idea that there is only one specific way to get sanctified. One of the biggest mistakes that people make when they are seeking sanctification is thinking that "because Sister Smith did steps X, Y, and Z, that I must do those same steps in order to get sanctified." Numerous people have needlessly delayed themselves from getting the blessing because of this misapprehension. Dictating to God how He must act never works. It is true that Sister Smith may have needed to do X, Y, and Z; but God led Brother Jones over steps P and Q, instead.

In these days, it seems that sanctification is an individual thing. The "laying on of hands" is not necessary to receive the blessing, even though the Bible says that the Apostles laid their hands on those who received it in those times. We should not be slaves to tradition; just because the apostles are recorded as doing a certain thing does not automatically mean that we have to.

Another misunderstanding on both sides has to do with the concept of "carnal Christians." The term comes from Paul.

"And I, brethren, could not speak unto you as unto spiritual, but as unto carnal, even as unto babes in Christ. I have fed you with milk, and not with meat: for hitherto ye were not able to bear it, neither yet now are ye able. For ye are yet carnal: for whereas there is among you envying, and strife, and divisions, are ye not carnal, and walk as men?" (I Cor. 3:1-3).

Many people on both sides misunderstand this passage, although in different ways, and for different reasons. I have heard Holiness people say, "There's no such thing as a carnal Christian"; meaning that if a person is still carnal, he's not even saved. But Paul is very clear that the people he is addressing are Christians; he calls them "brethren."

In reality, a carnal Christian is no more and no less than somebody who is saved but not sanctified.

On the other hand, many non-Holiness people oppose the phrase partly, at least, because they don't understand the context. They say, "There are only two classes of people: the saved and the unsaved. There is no scriptural warrant for dividing the world into three classes of people."

Actually, there is. This passage by itself is sufficient grounds for that. Paul very clearly divides the Church into two classes: babes in Christ, and full-grown Christians. That gives us three total classes. In addition, James 4:8 does the same general type of thing. For further evidence, refer back a few pages to where I quote and contrast Eph. 4:30 and 5:18. Unsanctified Christians are sealed with the Spirit, but not filled. Sanctified Christians are both sealed *and* filled.

But there's more.

The people who originally divided the Bible into chapters and verses did a great work. But in a few places, they unwittingly did the Church a disservice. In our Western way of thinking, with the customs that have grown up surrounding books, we have become trained to think that a new chapter often means a new subject. We treat a chapter break as a natural stopping point. But in some places in the Bible, including this one, the chapter divisions break up a paragraph or a subject between two chapters. This hinders comprehension, because we very seldom think to consider an adjoining chapter when we think about a particular passage.

Here is the FULL passage.

"Now we have received, not the spirit of the world, but the spirit which is of God; that we might know the things that are freely given to us of God. Which things also we speak, not in the words which man's wisdom teacheth, but which the Holy Ghost teacheth; comparing spiritual things with spiritual. But the natural man receiveth not the things of the Spirit of God: for they are foolishness unto him: neither can he know them, because they are spiritually discerned. But he that is spiritual judgeth all things, yet he himself is judged of no man. For who hath known the mind of the Lord, that he may instruct him? but we have the mind of Christ. And I, brethren, could not speak unto you as unto spiritual, but as unto carnal, even as unto babes in Christ. I have fed you with milk, and not with meat: for hitherto ye were not able to bear it, neither yet now are ye able. For ye are yet carnal: for whereas there is among you envying, and strife, and divisions, are ye not carnal, and walk as men?" (I Cor. 2:12-3:3).

In order of spiritual progression, from worst to best, we have the natural man (the unsaved), the carnal Christian, and finally the spiritual man. But Paul doesn't introduce them in that order, which may possibly have contributed to some of the confusion. He talks about the natural man first, then the spiritual man, and then informs the Corinthians that he could not talk to them as spiritual men, but only as carnal Christians. He does not call them natural, and he does not call them spiritual, but rather carnal.

So yes, there IS a solid scriptural basis for dividing people into three classes.

In the first part of this passage (verses 12-14), we see two great truths. Firstly, the great gulf between the things of humanity and the things of God. Secondly, that anybody who depends too heavily on human wisdom or human reasoning, or anything else in the natural world, will inevitably fail to understand the things of God.

There is a lesson in this passage for the opponents of the second work, if only they would be willing to see it. They rely far too heavily on human reasoning and experience. They are encouraged in this mistake by the remains of the natural man. Carnality, even in a Christian, can hinder the understanding of spiritual things. Thus they declare that the very idea of a second work of grace, or of Christian perfection, is "foolishness." This passage is very clear that trying to understand God by human means is a useless endeavor, but opponents of this doctrine persist in this course regardless. Even though some of these opponents are genuine Christians, Satan has managed to blind them to the higher things of God, to the point where they insist that God is bound and limited by human experience!

Of course, they don't state the proposition in such bald terms—Satan is much too subtle in his deceptions for that. Instead, he gets them to look around at other Christians, ones who never found the second work, and gets them to declare that a second work of grace is foolishness, impossible, unscriptural, or some such thing.

And why do they declare such things? Why, on the basis of **human experience**: no more and no less. They look at the human condition FIRST, and then build their theology to suit. This, and this alone, is why they have such extreme difficulty reconciling the Scriptures on this point.

By contrast, Holiness people look at the Bible first. We see the standard that it demands, and we see the procedure it outlines for bringing our lives up to that standard.

As I researched, and read what various opponents of this doctrine had to say, I noticed something interesting: a disproportionate number of them were Calvinists, or at least had Calvinistic leanings. I am not entirely sure why this would be. However, I do have some educated speculation on the matter. Calvinistic theology, including but not limited to the doctrine of predestination, has a tendency to produce a fatalistic attitude. Not all who believe these things fall victim to this, but it seems that a large percentage do, at least to some degree. After all, if you have no say and no choice over your eternal destination, then it truly does not matter what you do; you cannot change your fate. Thus, it doesn't matter (at least in the long run) how many sins a Christian commits. This is illustrated by one of the founding documents of Calvinistic teaching.

"Q. 149. *Is any man able perfectly to keep the commandments of God?*

"A. No man is able, either of himself, or by any grace received in this life, perfectly to keep the commandments of God; but doth daily break them in thought, word, and deed" (Westminster Larger Catechism of 1647).

Sometimes I wonder just what these people think that salvation actually does for a person; they don't seem to think that it produces noticeable results or any real change in a person's life. If we sin every day in thought, word, and deed before salvation, and sin every day in thought, word, and deed after salvation, then what, exactly, is the difference?

Chapter 10

Misunderstandings and Opposition (Part 2)

All opponents of Holiness doctrine have two main arguments to show why they think that a second work of grace does not exist. As we have seen, they point to many famous Christians who felt and bewailed the presence of indwelling sin all their lives, but never made any progress towards getting rid of it, and thus our opponents conclude that it's impossible to get rid of. The second line of argument is from the Bible. They use certain Bible passages to argue one or more of the following: (A) that we get everything at the moment of salvation (i.e., that a second work of grace does not exist); (B) that "perfection" does not mean sinless perfection, but rather means completeness and/or maturity; (C) that it is impossible to live without sinning; or (D) that the carnal nature is never eradicated from the human heart.

"Were the carnal nature gone from the Christian, he would be quite unfitted for such duties as the confessing of sins (1 John 1:9), loathing himself for them (Job 40:4), praying earnestly for the pardon of them (Matt. 6:12), sorrowing over them with godly sorrow (2 Cor. 7:10), accepting the chastisement of them (Heb. 12:5-11), vindicating God for the same (Ps. 119:75), and offering him the sacrifice of a broken and a contrite heart (Ps. 51:17)" (Pink; ch. 6).

Like many other opponents, he seems to think that removal of the carnal nature would automatically prevent a person from sinning. Notice what he says, that such a person would be "unfitted for such duties as the confessing of sins." As bizarre as it sounds, he says that like it would be a bad thing!

Some of the Bible verses he mentions I will deal with separately, a little later. But there are a couple that I would like to mention now.

"For godly sorrow worketh repentance to salvation not to be repented of: but the sorrow of the world worketh death" (II Cor. 7:10).

This is a simple statement that repentance and confession come before cleansing—but once cleansed, the work is done. There are no more sins that need to be confessed (unless we choose to sin again). Contrary to Pink, that's actually a desirable thing.

"The sacrifices of God are a broken spirit: a broken and a contrite heart, O God, thou wilt not despise" (Psalm 51:17).

Pink somehow seems to think that the absence of carnality would somehow prevent a person from having "a broken and a contrite heart." He is not the only person who has gone off the rails in this fashion. As I mentioned earlier, some opponents think that humility is produced by the fact of having unwanted sin. But sin produces more sin. It is carnality that produces a proud, hard heart. Sin cannot produce anti-sin. A repentant sinner has a broken and contrite heart *in spite of* carnality.

We still feel regret and/or shame over forgiven sins. God has forgotten them, but we have not. During part of my childhood years, there was a man in my church who had been a soldier during WWII. He was certainly a Christian when I knew him; but the memory of his past sins still haunted him. Many times I heard him lament that he had the blood of his fellow man on his hands.

Furthermore, since nobody is humanly perfect, there is always the possibility that we have unknowingly offended God. While an action that is not known to be a sin cannot be held against us, if God gives us greater measures of spiritual light, and we are then able to see some behavior or thing in a new light based on that, we should at once go to God in prayer, and ask forgiveness for our inadvertent failure. This sort of asking forgiveness is not quite the same as asking forgiveness for actual sin. A convicted criminal and somebody who accidentally breaks a glass figurine may both say "I'm sorry," but there is a different shade of meaning in each case.

The same is true of carnality, when a person is seeking sanctification. We repent of the root of sin in a sense—not in the same sense that we repented of our conscious sins, for this is a different type of sin: we are not responsible for its presence. Nevertheless, we know that its presence grieves God, and therefore we are sorry for its existence.

* * * * *

The story of Job is a popular argument for our opponents. They make much of the fact that God Himself called Job a perfect man, and yet Job did not call himself perfect; rather, he called himself vile. They also make much of the fact that toward the end of the story God rebuked him, and then Job repented.

"And the LORD said unto Satan, Hast thou considered my servant Job, that there is none like him in the earth, a perfect and an upright man, one that feareth God, and escheweth evil?" (Job 1:8).

"If I justify myself, mine own mouth shall condemn me: if I say, I am perfect, it shall also prove me perverse" (Job 9:20).

"Then Job answered the LORD, and said, behold, I am vile; what shall I answer thee? I will lay mine hand upon my mouth" (Job 40:3, 4).

"Wherefore I abhor myself, and repent in dust and ashes" (Job 42:6).

Opponents of the second work seem to take almost a sort of glee in pointing out how Job described himself. In 9:20 above, they take this to mean that any claim of perfection is sinful boasting.

But they ignore the context and circumstances. It seems to me that they try to impose normal standards of conduct on a very abnormal situation. Job said things that he probably would not have said at any other time. Remember, he was going through an almost unimaginable trial. A little hyperbole, not to mention depression, might well be expected (see 9:21, 22).

In 40:4, the Hebrew word translated "vile" is Strong's #7043. It has several possible meanings, including "small, abate, bring into contempt, slight, accursed"; other verses with the same word translated as "vile" are Deut. 25:3 and II Sam. 6:22. Remember, "vile" has both a moral meaning and a rhetorical meaning. And since God had just been speaking to Job about power and ability, it seems quite likely that Job used "vile" in a rhetorical way, not in a moral sense.

At any rate, Job was perfect when the story begins, and his actions prove it.

"Then Job arose, and rent his mantle, and shaved his head, and fell down upon the ground, and worshipped, and said, Naked came I out of my mother's womb, and naked shall I return thither: the LORD gave, and the LORD hath taken away; blessed be the name of the LORD. In all this Job sinned not, nor charged God foolishly" (Job 1:20-22). There is nothing here that would change his standing before God, because he "sinned not."

Even after all this, he was still perfect before God—after "not sinning." "And the LORD said unto Satan, Hast thou considered my servant Job, that there is none like him in the earth, a perfect and an upright man, one that feareth God, and escheweth evil? and still he holdeth fast his integrity, although thou movedst me against him, to destroy him without cause" (Job 2:3). Notice that perfection is linked to fearing God, and avoiding evil.

"Then said his wife unto him, Dost thou still retain thine integrity? curse God, and die" (Job 2:9). Of course Job did no such thing. "If any man offend not in word, the same is a perfect man, and able also to bridle the whole body" (James 3:2b). Job met this description.

I have noticed that many of our opponents seem dangerously cavalier about God's pronouncements concerning Job. They seem to more or less wave them away: "Job admitted that he wasn't perfect, and that's all that really matters." They apparently think that Job's assessment of himself is somehow more reliable than God's assessment.

Alternately, other opponents use this as evidence that whenever the Bible talks about perfection, it doesn't actually mean Christian/sinless perfection.

But if people are going to set such store by what Job said, here is another verse. This shows the importance of reconciling Scripture with Scripture. "I know it is so of a truth: but how should man be just with God?" (9:2).

This verse makes it sound like salvation itself is impossible. Oddly, however, our opponents don't seem as interested in it, or similar ones.

Later on, we are notified that Job may have lost perfection. "Then was kindled the wrath of Elihu the son of Barachel the Buzite, of the kindred of Ram: against Job was his wrath kindled, because he justified himself rather than God" (32:2).

It's difficult to say for sure, but it could be that Job was too eager to clear himself of an unjust charge, instead of letting God fight his battles for him.

On the other hand, it's possible that he may have simply been rash; i.e., he made a mistake, but not a sin. "Who is he that hideth counsel without knowledge? therefore have I uttered that I understood not; things too wonderful for me, which I knew not" (42:3).

One thing that is worthy of note is that in chapters 38-41, virtually every single question that God asks Job has to do with knowledge or power: NOT uprightness or righteousness. This is further evidence that perfection of heart is not the same as perfection in any other way.

But why did Job say in 42:6 that he repented? Surely this proves that he had sinned.

Not necessarily, however. The Hebrew word translated "repent" is Strong's #5162; it is often used in the sense of changing one's mind, rather than in a moral sense. The same word is used in the following verses.

"And it came to pass, when Pharaoh had let the people go, that God led them not through the way of the land of the Philistines, although that was near; for God said, Lest peradventure the people repent when they see war, and they return to Egypt" (Exodus 13:17).

"The LORD hath sworn, and will not repent, Thou art a priest for ever after the order of Melchizedek" (Psalm 110:4).

"Who can tell if God will turn and repent, and turn away from his fierce anger, that we perish not?" (Jonah 3:9).

I hate to burst our opponents' bubble, but the mere use of "repent" does not automatically mean that Job had sinned. But even if he did sin, all it shows is that perfection can be lost.

* * * * *

The following verses are often used as evidence that we get everything there is to get at the moment of salvation.

"Be it known unto you therefore, men and brethren, that through this man is preached unto you the forgiveness of sins: and by him all that believe are justified from all things, from which ye could not be justified by the law of Moses" (Acts 13:38, 39).

Our opponents use the phrase "justified from all things" to support their claim. But they misunderstand the verse.

As the end of verse 39 shows, Paul does nothing more here than contrast Law and Grace. We know that the Law is very limited in what it can do; not so with Grace. He talks here about what the work of salvation does for a person. He says nothing at all about what happens in a person's life **after** the moment of salvation. Even if Paul had explicitly written elsewhere that there were **five** different works of grace after salvation, and he named and described each one, and told how to get them—you would never know it from this passage.

"Therefore being justified by faith, we have peace with God through our Lord Jesus Christ" (Romans 5:1).

Words matter. Sometimes small words matter a great deal. Certainly, every Christian has peace "with" God; but that's not necessarily the same thing as having peace "in" God. When somebody is bewailing the sinful tendencies of the carnal nature inside him, I would not describe that as resting peaceably in God. But once carnality is totally removed, it makes a big difference. The sanctified man has a degree of inner peace that the unsanctified man simply does not possess.

"And this is the record, that God hath given to us eternal life, and this life is in his Son. He that hath the Son hath life; and he that hath not the Son of God hath not life" (I John 5:11, 12).

This passage simply restates the principle found elsewhere that faith and obedience to God bring spiritual life, whereas unbelief and disobedience to God bring spiritual death. In this particular place, John says nothing about any other aspect of our standing before God. There is nothing here about the **quality** of a person's spiritual life. To claim that this passage means that we get everything at salvation is like saying that a very sick person and a very healthy person are identical in every respect simply because they're both alive. It's like a doctor saying to a sick person, "You're alive, so you don't need to do anything."

* * * * *

These next verses are often used to "prove" the impossibility of going without sinning.

"If they sin against thee, (for there is no man that sinneth not,) and thou be angry with them, and deliver them to the enemy, so that they carry them away captives unto the land of the enemy, far or near" (I Kings 8:46).

I would strongly like to draw the reader's attention to the opening statement: "if"; "**if** they sin." This is a conditional statement; it is not describing a certainty.

But for the sake of the argument, let us ignore that part. We know that God is angry with sinners because of their sins. A few examples, besides this verse, are Deut. 9:7; II Chron. 29:6-8; Ezra 5:12; Romans 1:18; and Rev. 6:15-17. (And incidentally—God is not angry *at* sinners; He loves them. But He is angry *with* them. There's a difference.) Therefore, if we truly cannot avoid sinning, it necessarily follows that God is angry with us **all the time**. Reader, does that sound scriptural to you? It doesn't to me. And yet that is the only logical conclusion.

"God judgeth the righteous, and God is angry with the wicked every day. If he turn not, he will whet his sword; he hath bent his bow, and made it ready" (Psalm 7:11, 12).

Notice the beginning of verse 12: "if" the wicked turn not. The way that a lot of our opponents read the Bible, they would have to ignore that conditional part, and take this as a definite statement that the wicked would not repent—that is, if they wanted to be consistent with their reading of I Kings 8:46. I guess this verse must mean that nobody ever gets saved.

See how far astray we can go by ignoring key words?

"For there is not a just man upon earth, that doeth good, and sinneth not" (Eccl. 7:20).

God is consistent from beginning to end. Remember, the whole point of creating mankind was to have intelligent beings who could **choose** to worship Him. To set up conditions where even Christians cannot help sinning would be a violation of free will.

It is certainly true that "all have sinned": but we can now be free from sin. Of course, some people have different ideas.

"Note, [1.] It is the character of just men that they *do good*; for the tree is known by its fruits. [2.] The best men, and those that do most good, yet cannot say that they are perfectly free from sin; even those that are sanctified are not sinless. None that live on this side heaven live without sin... [3.] We sin even in our doing good; there is something defective, nay, something offensive, in our best performances. That which, for the substance of it, is good, and pleasing to God, is not so well done as it should be, and omissions in duty are sins, as well as omissions of duty" (Matthew Henry).

Notice how he confuses sin with human imperfections and frailties. If we do our duty to the best of our knowledge and ability, any omission or lack is a purely human shortcoming, not a moral one.

There is another issue, as well. He properly observes that "the tree is known by its fruits." But if righteous people truly cannot avoid sinning, then the unavoidable conclusion is that sin is a fruit of righteousness!

If you don't believe me, pay careful attention to the words of our Lord: "Even so every good tree bringeth forth good fruit; but a corrupt tree bringeth forth evil fruit. A good tree cannot bring forth evil fruit, neither can a corrupt tree bring forth good fruit" (Matt. 7:17, 18). In other words: if a Christian, being a good tree, brings forth sin, then sin MUST be a good fruit. Jesus did not allow for any exceptions in His statement. Either sin is a good fruit; or else a Christian who sins becomes a corrupt tree, and will therefore fall under the doom pronounced in Isaiah 5:1-6; Jer. 11:16, 17; Matt. 3:10; etc.

"How shall we, that are dead to sin, live any longer therein? Knowing this, that our old man is crucified with him, that the body of sin might be destroyed, that henceforth we should not serve sin. For he that is dead is freed from sin" (Romans 6:2b, 6, 7).

If you are dead to sin, then you are inherently freed from its power, and thus there is no excuse for committing sin. This is the theme of all of chapter 6.

"We know that whosoever is born of God sinneth not; but he that is begotten of God keepeth himself, and that wicked one toucheth him not" (I John 5:18).

John explicitly tells us two things: (A), that Satan and sin have no power over a believer; and (B), that Christians DO NOT sin.

Readers who believe in a sinning religion are going to have to either change their views, or else find some way of pretending that this verse doesn't mean what it says. I, on the other hand, am comparing Scripture with Scripture, and reconciling them; an exercise that our opponents apparently know very little about.

One issue that is perhaps worthy of note is that Jesus' blood was not yet shed when Ecclesiastes was written; Paul describes how the Law shows sin, but can't do anything else. It just **may** have been impossible back then to live without sin, but it certainly is possible now. I do not know whether this is the correct answer for reconciling this point; as a matter of fact, I rather doubt that it is. But the issue is worthy of consideration.

Another issue that should be taken into account is that this verse and I John 1:8 are the ONLY ones in the entire Bible that (appear to) declare in such strong, definite terms, without any qualifiers, that sinning is inevitable. On the other hand (as we shall see in the next section), there are a vast number of verses that **command** us to be holy, pure, without sin, etc. Add to that verses like this one, which flatly declare that sinning is utterly foreign to the Christian life. Our opponents would have us believe that Eccl. 7:20 and I John 1:8 outweigh all those others.

"Look to yourselves, that we lose not those things which we have wrought, but that we receive a full reward. Whosoever transgresseth, and abideth not in the doctrine of Christ, hath not God. He that abideth in the doctrine of Christ, he hath both the Father and the Son" (II John 8, 9).

"Who can understand his errors? cleanse thou me from secret faults" (Psalm 19:12).

Our opponents set great store by this verse. They almost gleefully claim that this verse means that everybody has secret faults.

However, this verse does not automatically mean that there are any faults. We need God's help and light to search our hearts; and, **if** we have hidden problems, to bring them to our attention. What opponents of Holiness doctrine never stop to consider here is this: what happens after the faults are cleansed? Doesn't God do a thorough job of cleansing, so that the faults don't come back? Or is it an issue of slowness? Is God so slow at the work of cleansing that it's always a life-long process?

"Who can say, I have made my heart clean, I am pure from my sin?" (Prov. 20:9).

This is a very popular verse among our opponents, and for the life of me, I cannot understand why. It has nothing to do with the subject in any way. They somehow confuse God's part and man's part. They evidently think that since we can't purify our own hearts, it is therefore impossible for any agency or power to purify the heart. We do not and cannot purify our own hearts: that is God's part of the equation.

"This question is not only a challenge to any man in the world to prove himself sinless, whatever he pretends, but a lamentation of the corruption of mankind, even that which remains in the best. Alas! *Who can say*, 'I am sinless?' " (Matthew Henry).

This is a good example of how twisted and tangled up people often get when they oppose the idea of a second work of grace. Notice that he asks an entirely different question than this verse asks while commenting on this verse! "I have made my heart clean" does NOT equal "I am sinless"! I repeat, very clearly and very emphatically, *that it is GOD who cleanses the heart.* Once God does the work, yes, we can say "I am sinless"—but it is 100% God's work, not ours.

Having said all this, however, I would like to emphasize that on virtually all other points, Matthew Henry was an excellent commentator. Use of his work should not be discouraged simply because he was so far off base on this issue.

The way that our opponents view and use this verse, it would make just as much sense to use this verse to argue that salvation itself is impossible. I am including another verse that sounds the same way.

"And enter not into judgment with thy servant: for in thy sight shall no man living be justified" (Psalm 143:2).

This is a verse that sounds like salvation itself is impossible. How can we be saved if it's impossible to be justified in God's sight? And yet nobody tries to argue that we can never be saved. So why do they argue that we can never be fully purified from the sin nature? It's the same power of God either way.

"For a just man falleth seven times, and riseth up again: but the wicked shall fall into mischief" (Prov. 24:16).

This verse shows persistence. If a Christian falls into sin but repents, he will still, in the end, reach Heaven. What this verse doesn't say is that he **has** to fall.

Now some people may object, and say that inevitability of falling is strongly implied. Perhaps so. Let's say that it is. In that case, this verse means one of two things: either (A), every Christian sins precisely seven times over the course of his life; no more and no less; or (B), forgiveness is available the first seven times a Christian sins, but not after that.

In my opinion, both of these are absurd, illogical, and unscriptural—which leaves only the original interpretation of persistence.

This is not, however, the only valid interpretation. In many cases, the interpretation that our opponents give to many of these passages is of more recent vintage than they would like to believe. Here is an example.

"[The number seven] is often put for all numbers together, as, 'A just man falleth seven times, and riseth up again,'—that is, let him fall never so often, he will not perish (and this was meant to be understood not of sins, but of afflictions conducing to lowliness). Again, 'Seven times a day will I praise Thee,' which elsewhere is expressed thus, 'I will bless the Lord *at all times.*' And many such instances are found in the divine authorities, in which the number seven is, as I said, commonly used to express the whole, or the completeness of anything" (Augustine; *The City of God*; Book 11, ch. 31).

I like how he just casually throws that out, and then goes on with his main point. It shows that the early Church did not imbue this verse with the meaning and importance that a lot of people do today. He evidently understood this verse as referring to trials that we go through; if we keep a right spirit, God will bring us through them with no harm done.

"The heart is deceitful above all things, and desperately wicked: who can know it?" (Jer. 17:9).

"Alas, they neither enter into *God's* estimate of Christ's blood, nor will they accept the fact that 'the heart is deceitful above all things, and *desperately* wicked' (Jer. 17:9). They neither realize that God has 'made Christ to be sanctification unto them' nor that 'the carnal mind is enmity against God' (Rom. 8:7)" (Pink; ch. 8).

Here he is talking about Holiness people. He shows how badly he misunderstands. **Of course** we realize all that—why else would we strive so strongly for the eradication of the carnal nature?

Opponents of Holiness doctrine claim that we can't know our hearts, and can't trust what we think we know. But we can. The answer is found in the very next verse: "I the LORD search the heart, I try the reins, even to give every man according to his ways, and according to the fruit of his doings" (verse 10).

This is the witness of God to the state of a person's heart, regardless of what that state is. When people talk about the deceitfulness of the heart, or of the impossibility of having the carnal nature eradicated, and/or of living a sinless life, they talk like they don't trust God to know a person's heart either.

There are other verses that talk about the witness of God.

"And thou, Solomon my son, know thou the God of thy father, and serve him with a perfect heart and with a willing mind: for the LORD searcheth all hearts, and understandeth all the imaginations of the thoughts: if thou seek him, he will be found of thee; but if thou forsake him, he will cast thee off for ever" (I Chron. 28:9).

Notice this: "with a perfect heart and with a willing mind": here is yet more evidence that Christian perfection is not the same as human perfection.

"Search me, O God, and know my heart: try me, and know my thoughts: and see if there be any wicked way in me, and lead me in the way everlasting" (Psalm 139:23, 24).

Pay attention to the language: "see IF there be any wicked way in me."

"Let us therefore, as many as be perfect, be thus minded: and if in any thing ye be otherwise minded, God shall reveal even this unto you" (Phil. 3:15).

The Bible outlines a clear sequence of events: God searches the heart and mind; God communicates His findings—either good or bad—to the person in question; and then the person decides what to do with that information. In short, we CAN know the state of our heart.

Besides—if it were otherwise, how would anybody ever know that they needed to get saved?

* * * * *

The next verses are often used as evidence of the continued presence of carnality, and the impossibility of removing it; and/or God's work of purification is not finished until death.

"Let not sin therefore reign in your mortal body, that ye should obey it in the lusts thereof" (Romans 6:12).

They seem to think that the existence of this verse means that carnality can never be eradicated. They apparently see only two possible options: either sin is reigning in a person's life, or else it is still present but subdued. There is no hint in this verse that those are the only two options, but somehow that is all that they see.

Paul links "reigning" with "obeying." If you obey sin, it is therefore necessarily reigning in your life. If sin is still present but truly subdued, you are obeying this verse. But once or if sin flares up again, you are no longer obeying this verse. It's much safer, not to mention more efficient, to get it altogether removed.

"The believer, no longer being under the full power of sin nor completely at enmity against God, does not resist the Spirit's operation as he once did, but has a genuine disposition to join with him against sin in himself; saying, Lord, correct, chasten me, do with me as thou wilt, only subdue my iniquities and conform me more and more unto thy image" (Pink; ch. 10).

Is partial enmity against God REALLY the best we can hope for? SERIOUSLY???

"For the flesh lusteth against the Spirit, and the Spirit against the flesh: and these are contrary the one to the other: so that ye cannot do the things that ye would" (Gal. 5:17).

They view this as describing a constant warfare between the new man and the old man. Our opponents get terribly tangled up when dealing with this overall passage (verses 16-25). In the book *Five Views on Sanctification* (Ed. Stanley Gundry), the Calvinist contributor to the book, Anthony Hoekema, has many good things to say, but he is terribly confused about the issue of sin. He contradicts himself horribly: "believers... are without the yeast of sin but yet must get rid of the old yeast (I Cor. 5:7)."

Umm—what!?

Verse 16 rebuts their view: "This I say then, Walk in the Spirit, and ye shall not fulfil the lust of the flesh."

Verse 17 is the **reason** for walking in the Spirit; so that we **don't** fall prey to the lust of the flesh. "Shall NOT fulfill": this says that even an unsanctified Christian will have victory over sin IF (and that's a big "if") he consistently walks in the Spirit—although the battle against temptation will likely be very difficult. Once the heart is completely purified, we can walk in the Spirit in a closer, holier, and more consistent way.

"And they that are Christ's have crucified the flesh with the affections and lusts. If we live in the Spirit, let us also walk in the Spirit" (verses 24, 25).

If you have actually "crucified the flesh," then—by definition—it is dead; and therefore it cannot possibly manage to overpower you. Our opponents apparently believe that Christians practice a spiritual form of necromancy on a daily basis.

Or maybe they think that Satan does it—I'm not sure where they think that this dead thing's power comes from. All I know for sure is that they claim that the flesh has been crucified and yet still has power and great vitality.

"Knowing this, that our old man is crucified with him, that the body of sin might be destroyed, that henceforth we should not serve sin. For he that is dead is freed from sin" (Romans 6:6, 7).

"Being confident of this very thing, that he which hath begun a good work in you will perform it until the day of Jesus Christ" (Phil. 1:6).

Some people latch onto the words "hath begun": they think this "good work" is incomplete, and will remain so until death. In reality, this verse talks about the keeping power of God: "will perform." It also means that salvation is just the beginning of the journey—a journey that won't finish until we reach Heaven. Our opponents have a very strange view of God—they think that He deliberately and unnecessarily keeps His work incomplete.

"Not as though I had already attained, either were already perfect: but I follow after, if that I may apprehend that for which also I am apprehended of Christ Jesus" (Phil. 3:12).

People gleefully point to this verse, and say, "Look! Even the great Apostle Paul didn't claim to be perfect!" But they take it out of context.

Here is the context. "That I may know him, and the power of his resurrection, and the fellowship of his sufferings, being made conformable unto his death; if by any means

I might attain unto the resurrection of the dead. Not as though I had already attained, either were already perfect: but I follow after, if that I may apprehend that for which also I am apprehended of Christ Jesus" (Phil. 3:10-12).

Verse 11 mentions the resurrection. Paul says at the beginning of verse 12 that he has not attained to that yet. In other words, he is still alive; he has not died and been resurrected. Now, remember, there are many different types of perfection. In verse 12, what he is saying is that since he has not yet attained the resurrection, he therefore has not yet attained the perfection of a glorified body. This verse has nothing to do with carnality in any way.

"Who shall change our vile body, that it may be fashioned like unto his glorious body, according to the working whereby he is able even to subdue all things unto himself" (Phil. 3:21).

Our opponents think that this verse refers to carnality remaining in Paul's heart (and in that of all Christians). But again, they take it out of context.

"For our conversation is in heaven; from whence also we look for the Saviour, the Lord Jesus Christ: who shall change our vile body, that it may be fashioned like unto his glorious body, according to the working whereby he is able even to subdue all things unto himself" (Phil. 3:20, 21).

Once again, he is talking about the resurrection and glorified bodies. The Greek word translated "vile" is Strong's #5014; it means basically the same as the Hebrew word mentioned in the section about Job. Even though the physical creation retains a large part of God's touch, it is indeed "vile" compared to the ineffable glories of the heavenly body that we will someday receive.

"Beloved, now are we the sons of God, and it doth not yet appear what we shall be: but we know that, when he shall appear, we shall be like him; for we shall see him as he is" (I John 3:2).

Again, they think that this refers to carnality. Once again, however, it's talking about Heaven. Contrast "we shall see him as he is" to "through a glass, darkly" (I Cor. 13:12).

* * * * *

These verses are typically used to show that we need continual/daily cleansing from sin.

"And forgive us our debts, as we forgive our debtors" (Matt. 6:12).

Many non-Holiness people think that we must pray this daily. If we have sins that need to be confessed every single day, then it's impossible to be sinless. But they misunderstand what this verse means.

Verse 9 says that this prayer is simply a pattern for us to follow. There is no need to use these actual words. Verse 11 mentions our daily bread. This is partly literal, but more importantly, it shows a dependence on God; not worry or anxiousness about our needs. This is what I mean by a pattern; it is vastly more important for us to have the attitude shown by this prayer than it is to pray the literal words.

What this particular verse does is link our attitude toward our fellow man with God's attitude toward us. Matt. 18:23-35 tells us that we must forgive sins against us before God will forgive our sins against Him. If we wish God to show mercy, we must show mercy. It is this attitude that we must have every day. This verse does not mean that we sin every day.

"For which cause we faint not; but though our outward man perish, yet the inward man is renewed day by day" (II Cor. 4:16).

Our opponents take that ending phrase "day by day" to mean that we need daily cleansing from sin; a continual process. They totally misunderstand the verse.

The ancient Israelites in the wilderness received a fresh supply of manna every day. Our inward man needs spiritual manna every bit as much as the physical body needs physical food. This is the meaning of this verse. It has nothing to do with the forgiveness of sin.

"That ye put off concerning the former conversation the old man, which is corrupt according to the deceitful lusts; and be renewed in the spirit of your mind; and that ye put on the new man, which after God is created in righteousness and true holiness" (Eph. 4:22-24).

There is a definite process shown in this passage: "put off"; "be renewed"; "put on." This is like changing clothes. But in this case, it is intended to be a one-time, **permanent** change. This is encapsulated in verse 28: "Let him that stole steal no more: but rather let him labour, working with his hands the thing which is good, that he may have to give to him that needeth."

According to the attitude of our opponents, this generic thief that Paul is talking about would try to earn an honest living, but somehow or another would invariably find himself stealing things; and not just once in a while, but continually.

Having said that, this spiritual "change of clothes" can be repeated if necessary; but the whole point is that it shouldn't be necessary.

"And have put on the new man, which is renewed in knowledge after the image of him that created him" (Col. 3:10).

This is another verse that many people misunderstand to mean a daily/continual cleansing from sin. They tend to link it to II Cor. 4:16. These verses actually refer to daily communication with God; devotions, prayer, etc.

"And ye have forgotten the exhortation which speaketh unto you as unto children,

My son, despise not thou the chastening of the Lord, nor faint when thou art rebuked of him: for whom the Lord loveth he chasteneth, and scourgeth every son whom he receiveth. If ye endure chastening, God dealeth with you as with sons; for what son is he whom the father chasteneth not? But if ye be without chastisement, whereof all are partakers, then are ye bastards, and not sons. Furthermore we have had fathers of our flesh which corrected us, and we gave them reverence: shall we not much rather be in subjection unto the Father of spirits, and live? For they verily for a few days chastened us after their own pleasure; but he for our profit, that we might be partakers of his holiness. Now no chastening for the present seemeth to be joyous, but grievous: nevertheless afterward it yieldeth the peaceable fruit of righteousness unto them which are exercised thereby" (Heb. 12:5-11).

A surprising number of people take this to mean that a state of sinlessness is impossible on this earth. I have noticed that many opponents of Holiness doctrine have a truly remarkable ability to read between the lines: so much so, in fact, that they read into the text things that aren't even there. Somehow, they take this passage to mean that we need daily punishment for sin.

But this passage doesn't say that. There is nothing in here to indicate that either sin or punishment must be daily or even frequently. God punishes us only when punishment is actually needed. Verse 11 mentions the fruit of righteousness. Sometimes a gardener will prune a tree to encourage more fruit production. But he doesn't keep continually pruning and pruning. He gives the tree periods of rest.

Furthermore, verse 9 mentions correction. Our opponents conflate punishment and correction. It is certainly true that they can be the same, but not always. When a student gets dates wrong on a history test, and the teacher corrects him, is that punishment? It might be painful and unpleasant, but it isn't punishment. In much the same way, God corrects us and leads us into ways of behavior that more accurately reflect His ways. Sometimes He does this before an issue gets to the point where it becomes sin.

"If we confess our sins, he is faithful and just to forgive us our sins, and to cleanse us from all unrighteousness" (I John 1:9).

They use the first part of this verse as evidence that we need daily or at least frequent confession. This is another example of reading into the text something that is not there. They also, for some strange reason, apparently seem to think that this verse applies ONLY to believers. At any rate, I have never heard or read any of them mention unbelievers when talking about this verse. Of all Holiness opponents that I have read who mention this verse, they unanimously mention it only in the context of Christians who have sinned and need to confess their sins.

But they misunderstand it. This verse is not saying that we **do** have unconfessed sins; but rather **if** we do, then we need to confess them. Furthermore, our opponents totally ignore the meaning of the last part of this verse. This is something I will expound on a little later.

* * * * *

"If we say that we have no sin, we deceive ourselves, and the truth is not in us" (I John 1:8).

This verse is probably the second-most frequently quoted verse to "prove" that a sinless life is impossible.

A careless reader, or one who does not know how to reconcile Scripture passages, would take this verse to mean that sinning is inevitable.

"Those who claim to have received the 'second blessing' and be 'entirely sanctified' in themselves, have never seen their hearts in the light of God. Those who boast of their sinless perfection are deceived by Satan, and 'the truth is not in them' (1 John 1:8)" (Pink; ch. 11).

Other opponents say much the same thing, although usually in slightly less vehement language.

Of course we have seen our hearts as God sees them! That is **precisely** the reason for seeking the second work! It's actually our opponents that much of Pink's description applies to. If they had EVER seen their carnality-infested hearts through God's eyes, they would not rest until that awful thing was removed from them.

This quote is more evidence of how Pink fundamentally misunderstood Holiness people. There is nothing to boast about in sanctification. We are sanctified in and through God's grace and power. Our part of the equation is to want what God wants, and to obey Him in faith. God does everything else. God dwells within us, and burns up the carnal nature, and thereby we partake of His presence, purity, and power that He graciously gives to us as our possession. But without His gifts, we are morally bankrupt. All the glory, and all the credit, belong to God.

Opponents of Holiness doctrine are VERY insistent on using this verse. They take it, stand it up until it seems to be a mile thick and ten miles tall, and firmly believe that it is an insurmountable, impenetrable obstacle. They claim, with great vigor and vehemence, that this verse nullifies any possible claim to a state of sinlessness. But there is a problem with their interpretation; they take it out of context. Verses 7 and 9 absolutely contradict their interpretation. Their view is a fundamental contradiction— how can we still inherently have sin if the Blood cleanses from ALL sin?

There is an old saying: "A text taken out of context is a pretext." And that is what many people have done with this verse. They take it out of context, and use it as a pretext for sinning.

But let us take the other side of the coin for a moment, and assume that their interpretation is indeed correct. In such a case, how is our state after salvation any different than our state before salvation? What does salvation actually **do**? If God is somehow unable to give us enough grace to resist temptation (for we must necessarily give in to temptation in order for there to be an act of sin), then what good is such a God?

In actuality, John did the same thing here that Jesus did in Mark 2:17. "And it came to pass, that, as Jesus sat at meat in his house, many publicans and sinners sat also together with Jesus and his disciples: for there were many, and they followed him. And when the scribes and Pharisees saw him eat with publicans and sinners, they said unto his disciples, How is it that he eateth and drinketh with publicans and sinners? When Jesus heard it, he saith unto them, They that are whole have no need of the physician, but they that are sick: I came not to call the righteous, but sinners to repentance" (Mark 2:15-17).

Why would Jesus say that? After all, we know beyond the shadow of any doubt that nobody can be righteous by their own efforts. What Jesus was talking about was people who incorrectly consider themselves to be righteous in and of themselves. Such people do not feel the need of a Savior. He was talking to the scribes and Pharisees in this verse. John is doing the same thing here. He just got done talking, in verse 7, about the cleansing power of the Blood. But he anticipates an objection from people who consider themselves "good." So in verse 8, he pauses for a moment, and addresses those who consider themselves to already be righteous, before the Blood is applied. He alternates back and forth between the two points for a little while. Let's look at the whole passage.

"This then is the message which we have heard of him, and declare unto you, that God is light, and in him is no darkness at all. If we say that we have fellowship with him, and walk in darkness, we lie, and do not the truth: but if we walk in the light, as he is in the light, we have fellowship one with another, and the blood of Jesus Christ his Son cleanseth us from all sin. If we say that we have no sin, we deceive ourselves, and the truth is not in us. If we confess our sins, he is faithful and just to forgive us our sins, and to cleanse us from all unrighteousness. If we say that we have not sinned, we make him a liar, and his word is not in us. My little children, these things write I unto you, that ye sin not. And if any man sin, we have an advocate with the Father, Jesus Christ the righteous" (I John 1:5-2:1).

I would like to spend some time on verse 1:7b: "the blood of Jesus Christ his Son cleanseth us from all sin."

What does that little word "all" mean? People who don't believe in the doctrine of Holiness interpret it one way, and people who do believe in the doctrine of Holiness interpret it in another way. Now, yes, it's true that being saved is the only thing that is necessary to get us to Heaven. But as every Christian knows, we still have remnants of the sin nature within us after being saved. So what does "all" really mean? Does it mean simply "all conscious sin that we need to repent of"? Does it mean "just barely enough to get us to Heaven"? Or does all really and truly mean "ALL"? When the Bible says "all sin," does that mean "conscious acts and omissions, but nothing else"? Or does it mean "ALL sin, including the remnants of the sin nature that remain after salvation"?

I know which interpretation I agree with. The reader must decide for himself which one is more consistent with a literal interpretation of the Bible.

But remember, as you ponder—if you hired somebody to clean your house, and they told you that they would clean **all** the dirt:

Would you feel that they were honest, or that they had fulfilled the bargain, if they left **part** of the dirt behind?

The Bible is absolutely true and trustworthy in every detail of doctrine. If we do not claim the promises that it contains, that is OUR fault.

And then, to pound the point home, in verse 9 John says "all unrighteousness." No matter how you characterize carnality, it is covered by the combination of verses 7 and 9. Jesus came to bring a complete deliverance from all forms of unholiness.

Many people have no problem taking God at His word elsewhere. "And the Spirit and the bride say, Come. And let him that heareth say, Come. And let him that is athirst come. And whosoever will, let him take the water of life freely" (Rev. 22:17).

This verse is notable for being the very last appeal to sinners before the Bible closes. It is very broad, and we take it literally. "Whosoever will"—sermons have been preached, and hymns have been written about the wide-reaching spread of this verse.

And yet—when this same breath of Divine inspiration told John to write, in verses 7 and 9, "all sin," and "all unrighteousness"—suddenly we're NOT supposed to take it literally?

I humbly suggest that opponents of Holiness doctrine have great problems with consistency.

I would also like to direct the reader's attention to verse 2:1.

"If"—for such a small word, it carries a tremendous weight of meaning. It is often used to introduce a conditional statement. In some cases, it lets us know that what follows may—not will, but may—happen. In other cases, it lets us know that a certain thing will happen only in the event that something else happens first. "If any man sin." Christians are not supposed to sin. Once we get saved, sinning again is NOT inevitable. "That ye sin not."

Now some readers are probably taking a look at their own experience right about now, and thinking "Yeah, right." I would like to ask you a very simple question. When we yield to temptation, whose fault is it—ours, or God's?

If it is God's fault, then yes—sinning is inevitable. But if it is our fault, then it logically follows that we could have used our power of choice to make the right decision. If we feel that the temptation overwhelmed us, then it is still our fault for not asking God to give us more of His power and presence.

"The blood of Jesus is a most precious thing; unfortunately, most only understand its excellence from the standpoint of the forgiveness of sins and being kept from hell in the future. They see the blood as something of value in the past and in the future, but have not considered its present worth. Any ignorance of the daily work of the blood in defeating all the enemies that man has is one of Satan's prized accomplishments, for the blood released in our life moment by moment means secured victory over every temptation, lying emotion, fear, frustration, and any other enemy" (Michael Wells; *Sidetracked in the Wilderness*).

As we shall see in the theology section, the Bible speaks at great length about living a pure life.

"The next day John seeth Jesus coming unto him, and saith, Behold the Lamb of God, which taketh away the sin of the world" (John 1:29).

If sin is **left** in the heart and life, then just how, exactly, is it taken **away**? I really wish that our opponents would explain this.

"Therefore if any man be in Christ, he is a new creature: old things are passed away; behold, all things are become new. And all things are of God, who hath reconciled us to himself by Jesus Christ, and hath given to us the ministry of reconciliation" (II Cor. 5:17, 18).

Another thing I wish our opponents would explain is just how, exactly, "all" things have become NEW, if the OLD man is still present in the heart. Or perhaps Paul was just careless; perhaps he didn't actually mean what he wrote. Is the old nature really part of the "all things" that "are of God"?

If opponents of entire sanctification really believe that I John 1:8 teaches a sinning religion, then they have no business accepting I John as part of the Bible. For their interpretation flatly contradicts I John 3:3-9.

"And every man that hath this hope in him purifieth himself, even as he is pure. Whosoever committeth sin transgresseth also the law: for sin is the transgression of the law. And ye know that he was manifested to take away our sins; and in him is no sin. Whosoever abideth in him sinneth not: whosoever sinneth hath not seen him, neither known him. Little children, let no man deceive you: he that doeth righteousness is righteous, even as he is righteous. He that committeth sin is of the devil; for the devil sinneth from the beginning. For this purpose the Son of God was manifested, that he might destroy the works of the devil. Whosoever is born of God doth not commit sin; for his seed remaineth in him: and he cannot sin, because he is born of God" (I John 3:3-9).

Notice in verse 3 that we are supposed to be as pure as God is. In verse 5, notice once again that Jesus came to **take away** our sins. None of this leaves any room for sin in the heart or life in any way, shape, form, or degree whatsoever!

Some people try to rebut verse 6 ("whosoever abideth in him sinneth not"). As mentioned at the end of the last chapter, Calvinists are incredibly insistent that it is impossible to live without sin; that everybody sins in thought, word, and deed, every day.

Many people, when discussing this verse, say that the Greek word translated "sinneth" refers to a habitual practice. Some have suggested that this verse could be more accurately translated into modern English something like "No man making a profession of faith goes on habitually sinning."

But, if anything, this makes their position even more untenable!

What, pray tell, is a habit, or a habitual practice? Isn't something that is done every day the very definition of a habit? If sinning every day is not habitually sinning, then words have no meaning!

Some people try to get around the apparent contradiction between verses 6 and 9 on the one hand, and 1:8 on the other, by discovering two classes of sin: sins of weakness, and sins of willfulness—i. e., sinning because temptation overwhelms you in a moment of weakness, versus deliberately setting out to sin.

I have to give these people points for ingenuity; but it's an ingenuity born out of (depending on the person) either (A), desperation at seemingly not being able to measure up to what they know is God's standard; or (B), a flat-out stubborn refusal to accept the fact that God means what He says about living a pure life.

In either case, they say that verses 6 and 9 refer only to sins of willfulness, not sins of weakness. What they're really saying by this is that "as long as I mean well, God will politely overlook any sins that I happen to commit." But sin is still sin, regardless of how or why it is born; and any breaking of God's law will be punished unless repented of.

I have come across various people who try to get around verses 6 and 9, but especially 9, by claiming that it is just the new nature that cannot sin. Note: strictly speaking, (in a very technical sense), they are correct. But this concept must be handled extremely carefully, lest it lead to undesirable outcomes. If it is used to defend, excuse, or ignore—in any degree or in any sense—either sin or the carnal nature, then it tends towards Antinomianism. This is, in general terms, the heresy that we are not responsible for our actions, and/or that we will not face any long-term consequences for our actions, because we're saved. Proponents of this theory tend to call it "Christian liberty," when really it is carnal and unholy liberty of the worst sort.

"Antinomians argue for a holiness in Christ which produces no radical change for the better in the Christian. This is another deceit of the devil, for a deceit it certainly is for anyone to imagine that the *only* holiness he has is in Christ. There is no such thing in reality as a perfect and inalienable standing in Christ which is divorced from heart-purity and a personal walk in righteousness. What a flesh-pleasing dogma is it, that one act of faith in the Lord Jesus secures eternal immunity from condemnation and provides a lifelong licence to wallow in sin. *My reader, a faith which does not transform character and reform conduct is worthless.* Saving faith is only proved to be genuine by bearing the blossoms of experimental godliness and the fruits of personal piety" (Pink; ch. 6).

Pink was on the right track here, but he failed to go all the way. As noted in the previous chapter, he had Antinomian tendencies himself. He recognizes that the change wrought by salvation is good—yet he denies the change wrought by sanctification.

I had a hard time formulating my thoughts on this particular issue of the new nature, and how it relates to verse 9. Even now as I write this, my thinking on this is not yet entirely clear; I'm attempting to imagine the thoughts of our opponents. This is difficult, partly because it seems to me that they haven't really thought this through either.

On the one hand, it seems that these people view the old and new natures as being inextricably linked. They insist on calling all Christians "sinners"; they claim that all Christians sin, and can't avoid doing so; and they claim that even though we can't lose salvation, having unconfessed sin in our lives cuts us off from fellowship with God.

On the other hand, it seems that they view the two natures as totally separate. For it to be impossible to lose salvation (or indeed to ever gain it in the first place), it seems to me that the new nature would have to BE "us"; our identity; in the most deeply intimate and innermost way possible. Before we got saved, the old nature was our identity, who we were; that is precisely why we needed saving in the first place. The new nature takes over that role.

But this presents a conundrum. If (A), the new nature is indeed "us"; and (B), it cannot sin, then where does that inevitable sin come from? The only thing left is that sinning is the work of the old nature. But that's not "us" any more; so how can it cut us off from fellowship with God? After all, the old nature never had fellowship with God to begin with. You can't lose what you never had. It's like the new nature is getting blamed (and punished) for something that it didn't have anything to do with. It also seems to me that this is simply the old saw "The Devil made me do it"; albeit dressed up in slightly more adult terms. A lot of people try to use some variation of that excuse; but if it ever works in "real life," it simply means that the offender gets locked up in a mental hospital, instead of being locked up in prison.

But the Bible contains many examples of people bearing responsibility for their own sin. See Joshua 7 (Achan was executed for his sin); Psalm 51 (David took personal responsibility for his sin); Matt. 18:15-17 (excommunications); Acts 16:30 ("What must I do to be saved?"); even Romans 7:24, according to our opponents' interpretation ("I"; "me").

The idea that the new nature can't sin and/or that we are not responsible for sin just doesn't work. The only reason that people come up with this idea about the new nature is because they're trying to reconcile verse 9 with the supposed inevitability of sinning. But attempting to square the circle in this manner quickly leads one into an illogical morass of unscriptural suppositions.

There is more evidence that Christians do not sin. The idea of sinning being inevitable is totally incorrect, and it is contradicted by the Bible, in almost any place that one cares to look.

"Forasmuch then as Christ hath suffered for us in the flesh, arm yourselves likewise with the same mind: for he that hath suffered in the flesh hath ceased from sin; that he no longer should live the rest of his time in the flesh to the lusts of men, but to the will of God" (I Peter 4:1, 2).

"But these, as natural brute beasts, made to be taken and destroyed, speak evil of the things that they understand not; and shall utterly perish in their own corruption; and shall receive the reward of unrighteousness, as they that count it pleasure to riot in the day time. Spots they are and blemishes, sporting themselves with their own deceivings while they feast with you; having eyes full of adultery, and that cannot cease from sin; beguiling unstable souls: an heart they have exercised with covetous practices; cursed children" (II Peter 2:12-14).

Pay attention to what Peter is saying here. It should be abundantly obvious that each passage describes a different class of people. If you have "ceased from sin," you are obviously no longer doing it. Notice that Peter confidently speaks of this as an established fact. Unlike Christians, who have "ceased from sin," this second passage describes people who "CANNOT cease from sin."

Sinners live a sin-*filled* life; Christians are supposed to live a completely, 100% sin-*free* life. In other words, by comparing Scripture with Scripture, we find that I John 1:8 cannot possibly mean what so many people have mistakenly thought it means. If you are not living a life of complete victory over sin 24/7/365, then you are not living up to God's standard.

Opponents of the second work plant their flag on I John 1:8 as if it were a wall a mile thick and ten miles tall. They feel that nobody can get through, over, or around this wall to reach a state of sinlessness here on earth. They seem to view this verse much like the walls of Jericho.

And in one sense, they are right. We cannot break down that wall on our own. But even the walls of Jericho cannot stand against the combined assault of faith and obedience. God can move where we cannot. He reaches down His hand to anybody who stands on the promises of verses 7 and 9, and pulverizes that wall to dust, thus letting us enter into the Promised Land of perfect love, peace, and sinlessness.

There are several verses in the Bible that talk about being cleansed from sin, but as far as I have found, verses 7 and 9 are the only ones in the Bible that so clearly, explicitly state "all": **all** sin; **all** unrighteousness. Perhaps John was led to write so clearly because God saw that verse 8 would be so badly misinterpreted.

The Bible declares in several places that God is a Father to those who serve Him. The Bible also declares that we must become as children if we wish to enter Heaven.

So, with child-like simplicity (Matt. 18:3; Mark 10:15), what does the word "all" really mean? Opponents of Holiness doctrine seem to have a very limited, restricted view of this word. To those of you who are opponents of the second work of grace, let me pose a question. When God says His blood cleanses from ALL sin, and ALL unrighteousness, just what, exactly, is so wrong and so horrible about taking our Heavenly Father at His word?

* * * * *

In many respects, Romans 7:14-25 is both the capstone and the cornerstone of opposition to Holiness doctrine. If somebody is going to mention just one passage as "proof" that entire sanctification does not exist, it will most likely be this passage.

"For we know that the law is spiritual: but I am carnal, sold under sin. For that which I do I allow not: for what I would, that do I not; but what I hate, that do I. If then I do that which I would not, I consent unto the law that it is good. Now then it is no more I that do it, but sin that dwelleth in me. For I know that in me (that is, in my flesh,) dwelleth no good thing: for to will is present with me; but how to perform that which is good I find not. For the good that I would I do not: but the evil which I would not, that I do. Now if I do that I would not, it is no more I that do it, but sin that dwelleth in me. I find then a law, that, when I would do good, evil is present with me. For I delight in the law of God after the inward man: but I see another law in my members, warring against the law of my mind, and bringing me into captivity to the law of sin which is in my members. O wretched man that I am! who shall deliver me from the body of this death? I thank God through Jesus Christ our Lord. So then with the mind I myself serve the law of God; but with the flesh the law of sin" (Romans 7:14-25).

Many opponents (although not all) believe that Paul was describing his own personal, current struggles with sin and with inbred carnality.

It is easy to see how a superficial reading of chapter 7 would support this opinion. However, despite the first-person, present-tense language, Paul was emphatically not describing his current spiritual state. He was saved on the way to Damascus, and sanctified when Ananias visited him, as described in Acts 9:17.

There is a rhetorical device that goes by several different names; the one that I prefer is "historic present." It is used to increase interest while relating a story of something that happened in the past. There are several examples of this in the Bible. Here is one: this story was long in the past when John was actually writing his Gospel. Notice how he switches tenses in mid-flow. "Simon Peter saith unto them, I go a fishing. They say unto him, We also go with thee. They went forth, and entered into a ship immediately; and that night they caught nothing" (John 21:3).

In other words, just because a description of something is written in the present tense, doesn't automatically mean that the writer is describing something that is currently going on at the time of writing.

"I admit fully that the point has been a disputed one for eighteen centuries, in fact ever since the days of St. Paul. I admit fully that eminent Christians like John and Charles Wesley, and Fletcher, a hundred years ago, to say nothing of some able writers of our own time, maintain firmly that St. Paul was not describing his own present experience when he wrote this seventh chapter. I admit fully that many cannot see what I and many others do see: viz., that Paul says nothing in this chapter which does not precisely tally with the recorded experience of the most eminent saints in every age, and that he does say several things which no unregenerate man or weak believer would ever think of saying, and cannot say. So, at any rate, it appears to me" (Ryle; Introduction).

I have given several examples in the history section where people gave first-hand accounts that did *not* tally with Ryle's interpretation of this passage; so Ryle is wrong on that point. Actually, as far as I have been able to determine from what I have read of the early writers, Ryle's view is more recent than he believed. At any rate, John Chrysostom did not agree with Ryle.

This is what John Chrysostom says about this passage.

After having said that great evils had taken place, and that sin, taking occasion by the commandment, had grown stronger, and the opposite of what the Law mainly aimed at had been the result, and after having thrown the hearer into a great deal of perplexity, he goes on next to give the rationale of these events, after first clearing the Law of any ill suspicion. For lest—upon hearing that it was through the commandment that sin took that occasion, and that it was when it came that sin revived, and through it deceived and killed—any one should suppose the Law to be the source of these evils, he first sets forth its defence with considerable advantage, not clearing it from accusation only, but encircling it also with the utmost praise... Whence then, was sin produced, if the teacher was so admirable? It was from the listlessness of its disciples. Wherefore he went on to say, "but I am carnal;" giving us a sketch now of man, as comporting himself in the Law, and before the Law...

"For that which I do, I know not."

What does the "I know not" mean?—I am ignorant. And when could this ever happen? For nobody ever sinned in ignorance. Seest thou, that if we do not receive his words with the proper caution, and keep looking to the object of the Apostle, countless incongruities will follow? For if they sinned through ignorance, then they did not deserve to be punished. As then he said above, "for without the Law sin is dead," not meaning that they did not know they were sinning, but that they knew indeed, but not so distinctly; wherefore they were punished, but not so severely: and again; "I should not have known lust;" not meaning an entire ignorance of it, but referring to the most distinct knowledge of it; and said, that it also "wrought in me all manner of concupiscence," not meaning to say that the commandment made the concupiscence, but that sin through the commandment introduces an intense degree of concupiscence; so here it is not absolute ignorance that he means by saying, "For what I do, I know not;" since how then would he have pleasure in the law of God in his inner man? What then is this, "I know not?" I get dizzy, he means, I feel carried away, I find a violence done to me, I get tripped up without knowing how. Just as we often say, Such an one came and carried me away with him, without my knowing how; when it is not ignorance we mean as an excuse, but to show a sort of deceit, and circumvention, and plot. "For what I would, that I do not: but what I hate, that I do." How then canst thou be said not to know what thou art doing? For if thou willest the good, and hatest the evil, this requires a perfect knowledge. Whence it appears that he says, "that I would not," not as denying free will, or as adducing any constrained necessity. For if it was not willingly, but by compulsion, that we sinned, then the punishments that took place before would not be justifiable. But as in saying "I know not," it was not ignorance he set before us, but what we have said; so in adding the "that I would not," it is no necessity he signifies, but the disapproval he felt of what was done...

Do you see, how he acquits the essence of the soul, as well as the essence of the flesh, from accusation, and removes it entirely to sinful actions? For if the soul willeth not the evil, it is cleared: and if he does not work it himself, the body too is set free, and the whole may be charged upon the evil moral choice. Now the essence of the soul and body and of that choice are not the same, for the two first are God's works, and the other is a motion from ourselves towards whatever we please to direct it. For willing is indeed natural, and is from God: but willing on this wise is our own, and from our own mind.

"I find then a law, that when I would do good, evil is present with me."

What he says is not very clear. What then is it that is said? I praise the law, he says, in my conscience, and I find it pleads on my side so far as I am desirous of doing what is right, and that it invigorates this wish. For as I feel a pleasure in it, so does it yield praise to my decision. Do you see how he shows, that the knowledge of what is good and what is not such is an original and fundamental part of our nature, and that the Law of Moses praises it, and getteth praise from it? For above he did not say so much as I get taught by the Law, but "I consent to the Law;" nor further on that I get instructed by it, but "I delight in" it. Now what is "I delight?" It is, I agree with it as right, as it does with me when wishing to do what is good. And so the willing what is good and the not willing what is evil was made a fundamental part of us from the first. But the Law, when it came, was made at once a stronger accuser in what was bad, and a greater praiser in what was good. Do you observe that in every place he bears witness to its having a kind of intensitiveness and additional advantage, yet nothing further? For though it praises and I delight in it, and wish what is good the "evil is" still "present with me," and the agency of it has not been abolished...

"For I delight," he says, "in the law of God after the inward man."

He means, for I knew even before this what was good, but when I find it set down in writing, I praise it...

"O wretched man that I am! who shall deliver me from the body of this death?"

Do you notice what a great thraldom that of vice is, in that it overcomes even a mind that delighted in the Law? For no one can rejoin, he means, that I hate the Law and abhor it, and so sin overcomes me. For "I delight in it, and consent to it," and flee for refuge to it, yet still it had not the power of saving one who had fled to it. But Christ saved even one that fled from Him. See what a vast advantage grace has! Yet the Apostle has not stated it thus; but with a sigh only, and a great lamentation, as if devoid of any to help him, he points out by his perplexity the might of Christ, and says, "O wretched man that I am! who shall deliver me from the body of this death?" The Law has not been able: conscience has proved unequal to it, though it praised what was good, and did not praise it only, but even fought against the contrary of it. For by the very words "warreth against" he shows that he was marshalled against it for his part. From what quarter then is one to hope for salvation?

"I thank God through Jesus Christ our Lord."

Observe how he shows the necessity of having grace present with us, and that the well-doings herein belong alike to the Father and the Son. For if it is the Father Whom he thanketh, still the Son is the cause of this thanksgiving. But when you hear him say, "Who shall deliver me from the body of this death?" do not suppose him to be accusing the flesh. For he does not say "body of sin," but "body of death:" that is, the mortal body—that which hath been overcome by death, not that which gendered death. And this is no proof of the evil of the flesh, but of the marring it has undergone... Why then, it may be said, the thraldom of sin being so great before the times of grace, were men punished for sinning? Because they had such commands given them as might even under sin's dominion be accomplished. For he did not draw them to the highest kind of conversation, but allowed them to enjoy wealth, and did not forbid having several wives, and to gratify anger in a just cause, and to make use of luxury within bounds. And so great was this condescension, that the written Law even required less than the law of nature... And besides this there are also many other ordinances of the Law, that one might see those who were before its day fully performing, being instructed by the law of nature. They therefore who lived under the old dispensation had no hardship done them by so moderate a system of laws being imposed upon them. But if they were not, on these terms, able to get the upper hand, the charge is against their own listlessness. Wherefore Paul gives thanks, because Christ, without any rigorousness about these things, not only demanded no account of this moderate amount, but even made us able to have a greater race set before us. And therefore he says, "I thank my God through Jesus Christ." And letting the salvation which all agreed about pass, he goes from the points he had already made good, to another further point, in which he states that it was not our former sins only that we were freed from, but we were also made invincible for the future. For "there is," he says, "now no condemnation to them which are in Christ Jesus, who walk not after the flesh." Yet he did not say it before he had first recalled to mind our former condition again in the words, "So then with the mind I myself serve the law of God, but with the flesh the law of sin."

"There is therefore no condemnation to them which are in Christ Jesus."

Then as the fact that many fall into sin even after baptism presented a difficulty, he consequently hastened to meet it, and says not merely "to them that are in Christ Jesus," but adds, "who walk not after the flesh;" so showing that all afterward comes of our listlessness. For now we have the power of walking not after the flesh, but then it was a difficult task. Then he gives another proof of it by the sequel, in the words,

"For the law of the Spirit of life hath made me free."

It is the Spirit he is here calling the law of the Spirit. For as he calls sin the law of sin, so he here calls the Spirit the law of the Spirit. And yet he named that of Moses as such, where he says, "For we know that the Law is spiritual." What then is the difference? A great and unbounded one. For that was spiritual, but this is a law of the Spirit. Now what is the distinction between this and that? The other was merely given by the Spirit, but this even furnisheth those that receive it with the Spirit in large measure. Wherefore also he called it the law of life in contradistinction to that of sin, not that of Moses. For when he says, It freed me from the law of sin and death, it is not the law of Moses that he is here speaking of, since in no case does he style it the law of sin: for how could [it be] one that he had called "just and holy" so often, and destructive of sin too? but it is that which warreth against the law of the mind. For this grievous war did the grace of the Spirit put a stop to, by slaying sin, and making the contest light to us and crowning us at the outstart, and then drawing us to the struggle with abundant help...

"That the righteousness of the Law might be fulfilled in us, who walk not after the flesh."

What meaneth this word, righteousness? Why, the end, the scope, the well-doing. For what was its design, and what did it enjoin? To be without sin. This then is made good to us now through Christ. And the making a stand against it, and the getting the better of it, came from Him. But it is for us to enjoy the victory. Then shall we never sin henceforth? We never shall unless we have become exceedingly relaxed and supine. And this is why he added, "to them that walk not after the flesh." For lest, after hearing that Christ hath delivered thee from the war of sin, and that the requisition of the Law is fulfilled in thee, by sin having been "condemned in the flesh," thou shouldest break up all thy defences; therefore, in that place also, after saying, "there is therefore no condemnation," he added, "to them that walk not after the flesh;" and here also, "that the requisition of the Law might be fulfilled in us," he proceeds with the very same thing; or rather, not with it only, but even with a much stronger thing. For after saying, "that the righteousness of the Law might be fulfilled in us that walk not after the flesh," he proceeds, "but after the Spirit."

So showing, that it is not only binding upon us to keep ourselves from evil deeds, but also to be adorned with good. For to give thee the crown is His; but it is thine to hold it fast when given. For the righteousness of the Law, that one should not become liable to its curse, Christ has accomplished for thee. Be not a traitor then to so great a gift, but keep guarding this goodly treasure. For in this passage he shows that the Font will not suffice to save us, unless, after coming from it, we display a life worthy of the Gift. And so he again advocates the Law in saying what he does. For when we have once become obedient to Christ, we must use all ways and plans so that its righteousness, which Christ fulfilled, may abide in us, and not come to naught...

It is vice then he means by carnal mindedness, and by spiritual mindedness the grace given, and the working of it discernible in the right determination of mind, not discussing in any part of this passage, a substance and an entity, but virtue and vice. For that which thou hadst no power to do under the Law, now, he means, thou wilt be able to do, to go on uprightly, and with no intervening fall, if thou layest hold of the Spirit's aid. For it is not enough not to walk after the flesh, but we must also go after the Spirit, since turning away from what is evil will not secure our salvation, but we must also do what is good. And this will come about, if we give our souls up to the Spirit, and persuade our flesh to get acquainted with its proper position, for in this way we shall make it also spiritual; as also if we be listless we shall make our soul carnal (Homily 13, on Romans 7:14).

To summarize this long quote, John Chrysostom views Paul in Romans 7:14-25 as describing somebody in Old Testament times who wants to obey the Law but has trouble doing so. And then in chapter 8 he views Paul as showing how Grace is so much superior to the Law. This interpretation has the advantage of making Paul's overall position consistent, as we will see shortly.

I like what he says near the end: "Then shall we never sin henceforth? We never shall unless we have become exceedingly relaxed and supine." It is clear that he viewed the Christian life as one of complete, consistent victory over sin.

Many of our opponents take Romans 7:14-25 out of context. This passage cannot be properly understood without looking at the entirety of chapters 6, 7, and 8. In chapter 6, the thought of being dead to sin is written three different times (verses 2, 6, 11), and the thought of being free from sin is mentioned seven times (verses 7, 12, 14, 17, 18, 20, 22). The theme of the whole chapter is that a Christian is dead to sin, and by that very fact thereby freed from its power and dominion. Chapter 7 starts out by telling us that Grace has made us dead to the Law. This is actually a continuation of the thought in chapter 6, because sin has its power through the Law (7:7-10). And chapter 8 starts out by telling us that anybody who is dead to sin and to the Law is also freed from the condemnation of the Law.

Only in the second work is the old man completely gone. Then, and only then, are we truly dead to the world and to sin, for there is nothing in us that responds eagerly or joyfully to temptation.

Romans is not an autobiography; it is not a description of Paul's personal life at the time of writing. The Church might have been better served down through the centuries to call the book of Romans "St. Paul's Manual of Christian Theology."

"It is difficult to conceive how the opinion could have crept into the Church, or prevailed there, that 'the apostle speaks here of his *regenerate state*; and that what was, in such a state, true of himself, must be true of all others in the same state.' This opinion has, most pitifully and most shamefully, not only lowered the standard of Christianity, but destroyed its influence and disgraced its character" (Adam Clarke on Romans 7:14).

Paul takes pains to assure his readers and hearers that his doctrine is in agreement with the other apostles. (See Acts 15:1-4, 22-27; I Cor. 15:11; Gal. 1:18 & 2:1, 2—I quoted some of these in chapter 2.) So if this passage does refer to the inevitability of sin, why is this found in only two of the New Testament writers, Paul and John? (And John mentions it only briefly.) Why don't the other writers refer to the carnal nature in the same terms? There is absolutely nothing of the sort in Peter, either in his writings or in his sermons that Luke records in Acts. James doesn't mention this either, nor does the unknown writer of Hebrews. The various writers were aware of what other people were writing (Luke 1:1; II Peter 3:15). It is also clear, from Acts and from the various apostolic salutations, that there were many travelers between the various churches. If the Church had not been in one accord on doctrinal matters, it would have been readily apparent.

Anybody who tries to use Romans 7:14-25 as a model of the Christian life is making null and void the concept of fulfilling the law through love.

People who love God keep His commandments.

"He that hath my commandments, and keepeth them, he it is that loveth me: and he that loveth me shall be loved of my Father, and I will love him, and will manifest myself to him. Judas saith unto him, not Iscariot, Lord, how is it that thou wilt manifest thyself unto us, and not unto the world? Jesus answered and said unto him, If a man love me, he will keep my words: and my Father will love him, and we will come unto him, and make our abode with him. He that loveth me not keepeth not my sayings: and the word which ye hear is not mine, but the Father's which sent me" (John 14:21-24).

If you do not always obey God's commands to avoid sin, you do not love God as much as you think you do. Love is the fulfilling of the law.

"Jesus said unto him, Thou shalt love the Lord thy God with all thy heart, and with all thy soul, and with all thy mind. This is the first and great commandment. And the second is like unto it, Thou shalt love thy neighbour as thyself. On these two commandments hang all the law and the prophets" (Matt. 22:37-40).

The only way to love God, and thereby fulfill the righteousness of the law, is by walking in the Spirit.

"That the righteousness of the law might be fulfilled in us, who walk not after the flesh, but after the Spirit" (Romans 8:4).

And that in turn frees us from all condemnation.

"There is therefore now no condemnation to them which are in Christ Jesus, who walk not after the flesh, but after the Spirit. For the law of the Spirit of life in Christ Jesus hath made me free from the law of sin and death" (Romans 8:1, 2).

If you feel that sin sometimes overwhelms you; if you feel that you truly cannot avoid sinning at times, regardless of how much you struggle against it—you may indeed be walking in all the light you have had up to this point, but I earnestly and lovingly assure you that you are not walking as close to God as you can be, should be, and need to be.

Now let us go to the detailed view, and deconstruct this passage verse by verse.

Verse 14 (sold under sin):

This phrase made me curious. I got to wondering where else the concept might be found.

"And Ahab said to Elijah, Hast thou found me, O mine enemy? And he answered, I have found thee: because thou hast sold thyself to work evil in the sight of the LORD" (I Kings 21:20).

"And they caused their sons and their daughters to pass through the fire, and used divination and enchantments, and sold themselves to do evil in the sight of the LORD, to provoke him to anger" (II Kings 17:17).

"Thus saith the LORD, Where is the bill of your mother's divorcement, whom I have put away? or which of my creditors is it to whom I have sold you? Behold, for your iniquities have ye sold yourselves, and for your transgressions is your mother put away" (Isaiah 50:1).

This is not a good place to be. If you're "sold under sin" you need to make changes, pronto. Only slaves and bondservants are sold. "Stand fast therefore in the liberty wherewith Christ hath made us free, and be not entangled again with the yoke of bondage" (Gal. 5:1).

The same people who claim that Paul was "sold under sin" also claim that he was no longer under the dominion of sin. But this is a complete contradiction. If you are once again sold under sin, then you have relinquished the liberty of Christ. You can be the slave of sin, or you can be the love-slave of Jesus—but you cannot be both.

Verses 15, 16, 19 (double minded & conflicted):

"No man can serve two masters: for either he will hate the one, and love the other; or else he will hold to the one, and despise the other. Ye cannot serve God and mammon" (Matt. 6:24).

"Jesus answered them, Verily, verily, I say unto you, Whosoever committeth sin is the servant of sin" (John 8:34).

"Know ye not, that to whom ye yield yourselves servants to obey, his servants ye are to whom ye obey; whether of sin unto death, or of obedience unto righteousness?" (Romans 6:16).

"While they promise them liberty, they themselves are the servants of corruption: for of whom a man is overcome, of the same is he brought in bondage" (II Peter 2:19).

Verse 18 (in me dwelleth no good thing):

"For God is my witness, whom I serve with my spirit in the gospel of his Son, that without ceasing I make mention of you always in my prayers" (Romans 1:9).

"Being filled with all unrighteousness, fornication, wickedness, covetousness, maliciousness; full of envy, murder, debate, deceit, malignity; whisperers, backbiters, haters of God, despiteful, proud, boasters, inventors of evil things, disobedient to parents, without understanding, covenantbreakers, without natural affection, implacable, unmerciful: who knowing the judgment of God, that they which commit such things are worthy of death, not only do the same, but have pleasure in them that do them. Therefore thou art inexcusable, O man, whosoever thou art that judgest: for wherein thou judgest another, thou condemnest thyself; for thou that judgest doest the same things. But we are sure that the judgment of God is according to truth against them which commit such things. And thinkest thou this, O man, that judgest them which do such things, and doest the same, that thou shalt escape the judgment of God?" (Romans 1:29-2:3).

If Paul was sinning, he would be under that same judgment that he himself wrote about.

"But even after that we had suffered before, and were shamefully entreated, as ye know, at Philippi, we were bold in our God to speak unto you the gospel of God with much contention. For our exhortation was not of deceit, nor of uncleanness, nor in guile: but as we were allowed of God to be put in trust with the gospel, even so we speak; not as pleasing men, but God, which trieth our hearts. Ye are witnesses, and God also, how holily and justly and unblameably we behaved ourselves among you that believe" (I Thess. 2:2-4, 10).

"I thank God, whom I serve from my forefathers with pure conscience" (II Tim. 1:3a).

"I have fought a good fight, I have finished my course, I have kept the faith: henceforth there is laid up for me a crown of righteousness, which the Lord, the righteous judge, shall give me at that day: and not to me only, but unto all them also that love his appearing" (II Tim. 4:7, 8).

If Paul were speaking of himself in verse 18, then his prayers, his possession of eternal life, etc. would be included in that "no good thing." In addition, he would not have been able to do all those things that he tells Timothy he did do.

Verses 17, 20 (sin that dwelleth in me):

"Ye are of your father the devil, and the lusts of your father ye will do. He was a murderer from the beginning, and abode not in the truth, because there is no truth in him. When he speaketh a lie, he speaketh of his own: for he is a liar, and the father of it" (John 8:44).

"He that saith, I know him, and keepeth not his commandments, is a liar, and the truth is not in him" (I John 2:4).

"Whosoever abideth in him sinneth not: whosoever sinneth hath not seen him, neither known him. Little children, let no man deceive you: he that doeth righteousness is righteous, even as he is righteous. He that committeth sin is of the devil; for the devil sinneth from the beginning. For this purpose the Son of God was manifested, that he might destroy the works of the devil. Whosoever is born of God doth not commit sin; for his seed remaineth in him: and he cannot sin, because he is born of God" (I John 3:6-9).

"For whatsoever is born of God overcometh the world: and this is the victory that overcometh the world, even our faith" (I John 5:4).

If Paul were speaking of himself, then these verses tell us that he would not be a Christian at all.

Verse 21 (evil is present in me):

"Having therefore these promises, dearly beloved, let us cleanse ourselves from all filthiness of the flesh and spirit, perfecting holiness in the fear of God. Receive us; we have wronged no man, we have corrupted no man, we have defrauded no man" (II Cor. 7:1, 2).

Is this the record of a man who has evil within him?

"For, brethren, ye have been called unto liberty; only use not liberty for an occasion to the flesh, but by love serve one another. This I say then, Walk in the Spirit, and ye shall not fulfil the lust of the flesh" (Gal. 5:13, 16).

Verse 23 (I see another law in my members):

"Neither yield ye your members as instruments of unrighteousness unto sin: but yield yourselves unto God, as those that are alive from the dead, and your members as instruments of righteousness unto God. I speak after the manner of men because of the infirmity of your flesh: for as ye have yielded your members servants to uncleanness and to iniquity unto iniquity; even so now yield your members servants to righteousness unto holiness" (Romans 6:13, 19).

"So then they that are in the flesh cannot please God. Therefore, brethren, we are debtors, not to the flesh, to live after the flesh. For if ye live after the flesh, ye shall die: but if ye through the Spirit do mortify the deeds of the body, ye shall live" (Romans 8:8, 12, 13).

"But fornication, and all uncleanness, or covetousness, let it not be once named among you, as becometh saints" (Eph. 5:3).

"Mortify therefore your members which are upon the earth; fornication, uncleanness, inordinate affection, evil concupiscence, and covetousness, which is idolatry" (Col. 3:5).

If Paul were speaking of himself in this passage, he would have been ignoring the commands and principles that he told others to follow.

Verse 24 (O wretched man that I am):

"Now thanks be unto God, which always causeth us to triumph in Christ, and maketh manifest the savour of his knowledge by us in every place" (II Cor. 2:14).

"But we have this treasure in earthen vessels, that the excellency of the power may be of God, and not of us. We are troubled on every side, yet not distressed; we are perplexed, but not in despair; persecuted, but not forsaken; cast down, but not destroyed; always bearing about in the body the dying of the Lord Jesus, that the life also of Jesus might be made manifest in our body" (II Cor. 4:7-10).

Are these the statements of a wretched man?

Verse 25 (with the flesh the law of sin):

"Even as I have seen, they that plow iniquity, and sow wickedness, reap the same" (Job 4:8).

"There is therefore now no condemnation to them which are in Christ Jesus, who walk not after the flesh, but after the Spirit" (Romans 8:1).

"Be not deceived; God is not mocked: for whatsoever a man soweth, that shall he also reap. For he that soweth to his flesh shall of the flesh reap corruption; but he that soweth to the Spirit shall of the Spirit reap life everlasting" (Gal. 6:7, 8).

Is there anything in Paul's life to suggest that he reaped the harvest of a lifetime of sin? On the contrary; everything that we know suggests the opposite. Therefore he could not have been talking in this verse about his own life.

Having gone through this passage in detail, I see four possible conclusions.

1. Despite centuries of protestations to the contrary, the Bible really does contradict itself.

2. Paul was a good man, a well-intentioned man, but not a true apostle.

3. Romans 7:14-25 is not a genuine part of the Canon, but was inserted later, and therefore should be ignored.

4. This passage means something other than what a lot of non-Holiness people think it means.

The choosing of the correct answer will be left as an exercise to the reader.

* * * * *

Despite the strong opposition that many people have towards Holiness doctrine, some of them still manage to grasp a large portion of the truth. It is both fascinating and deeply ironic that our opponents can say things like the following.

"That one of the great ends of the death of Christ was the moral purification of his people is clear from many scriptures. 'He died for all, that they which live should not henceforth live unto themselves, but unto him which died for them, and rose again' (2 Cor. 5:15); 'Who gave himself for us, that he might redeem us from all iniquity, and purify unto himself a peculiar people, zealous of good works' (Titus 2:14); 'How much more shall the blood of Christ, who through the eternal Spirit offered himself without spot to God, purge your conscience from dead works to serve the living God' (Heb. 9:14); 'Who his own self bare our sins in his own body on the tree, that we, being dead to sins, should live unto righteousness' (1 Pet. 2:24). From these passages it is abundantly plain that the purpose of the Saviour in all that he did and suffered, was not only to deliver his people from the *penal* consequences of their sins, but also to cleanse them from the *pollution* of sin, to free them from its enslaving power, to rectify their moral nature" (Pink; ch. 6).

How can we be without the stain and pollution of sin, and yet still have sin and carnality? He tries to have it both ways.

"He who supposes that Jesus Christ only lived and died and rose again in order to provide justification and forgiveness of sins for his people, has yet much to learn. Whether he knows it or not, he is dishonoring our blessed Lord, and making him only a half Savior" (Ryle; ch. 2).

I am absolutely confident that Ryle is in Heaven today. And yet he unknowingly described himself here.

I will include more quotes from Ryle later. Both of these men describe very well, although in different ways, the purpose of entire sanctification, and what the second work of grace is and does, even while at the same time opposing the formal doctrine of Holiness!

Next we will turn to the Bible, and discover how the doctrine is thoroughly grounded in the Scriptures.

Theology

Chapter 11

Foundation

Throughout this whole theology section, I quote quite liberally from the Old Testament. Every New Testament doctrine can be found in some form in the Old Testament. In addition, the Old Testament comprises the majority of God's written Word. The way that some Christians tend to ignore it is illogical and ludicrous.

So now we turn to the Bible to explain the doctrine of entire sanctification. There is a truly staggering number of verses that support the doctrine. Instead of diving into the main part right away, however, it is necessary to lay some background. Most of this background information will be familiar to most Christians; however, I am including it for the purposes of building a solid foundation.

God is holy, righteous, and pure.

"Who is like unto thee, O LORD, among the gods? who is like thee, glorious in holiness, fearful in praises, doing wonders?" (Exodus 15:11).

"For the righteous LORD loveth righteousness; his countenance doth behold the upright" (Psalm 11:7).

"The LORD is righteous in all his ways, and holy in all his works" (Psalm 145:17).

"For thus saith the high and lofty One that inhabiteth eternity, whose name is Holy; I dwell in the high and holy place, with him also that is of a contrite and humble spirit, to revive the spirit of the humble, and to revive the heart of the contrite ones" (Isaiah 57:15).

"And grieve not the holy Spirit of God, whereby ye are sealed unto the day of redemption" (Eph. 4:30).

"And ye know that he was manifested to take away our sins; and in him is no sin" (I John 3:5).

We are none of those things, in and of ourselves.

"The LORD looked down from heaven upon the children of men, to see if there were any that did understand, and seek God. They are all gone aside, they are all together become filthy: there is none that doeth good, no, not one" (Psalm 14:2, 3).

"But we are all as an unclean thing, and all our righteousnesses are as filthy rags; and we all do fade as a leaf; and our iniquities, like the wind, have taken us away" (Isaiah 64:6).

"As it is written, There is none righteous, no, not one: there is none that understandeth, there is none that seeketh after God. They are all gone out of the way, they are together become unprofitable; there is none that doeth good, no, not one" (Romans 3:10-12).

But there must be a change somehow, for God expects us, and indeed commands us, to be holy, righteous, and pure.

"O worship the LORD in the beauty of holiness: fear before him, all the earth" (Psalm 96:9).

"Blessed are the undefiled in the way, who walk in the law of the LORD" (Psalm 119:1).

"Blessed are the pure in heart: for they shall see God" (Matt. 5:8).

"Blessed be the God and Father of our Lord Jesus Christ, who hath blessed us with all spiritual blessings in heavenly places in Christ: according as he hath chosen us in him before the foundation of the world, that we should be holy and without blame before him in love" (Eph. 1:3, 4).

"For God hath not called us unto uncleanness, but unto holiness" (I Thess. 4:7).

"Now the end of the commandment is charity out of a pure heart, and of a good conscience, and of faith unfeigned" (I Tim. 1:5).

"I will therefore that men pray every where, lifting up holy hands, without wrath and doubting" (I Tim. 2:8).

"I give thee charge in the sight of God, who quickeneth all things, and before Christ Jesus, who before Pontius Pilate witnessed a good confession; that thou keep this commandment without spot, unrebukable, until the appearing of our Lord Jesus Christ" (I Tim. 6:13, 14).

"For the grace of God that bringeth salvation hath appeared to all men, teaching us that, denying ungodliness and worldly lusts, we should live soberly, righteously, and godly, in this present world; looking for that blessed hope, and the glorious appearing of the great God and our Saviour Jesus Christ; who gave himself for us, that he might redeem us from all iniquity, and purify unto himself a peculiar people, zealous of good works" (Titus 2:11-14).

"Pure religion and undefiled before God and the Father is this, To visit the fatherless and widows in their affliction, and to keep himself unspotted from the world" (James 1:27).

"Seeing ye have purified your souls in obeying the truth through the Spirit unto unfeigned love of the brethren, see that ye love one another with a pure heart fervently" (I Peter 1:22).

"But ye are a chosen generation, a royal priesthood, an holy nation, a peculiar people; that ye should shew forth the praises of him who hath called you out of darkness into his marvellous light" (I Peter 2:9).

"This second epistle, beloved, I now write unto you; in both which I stir up your pure minds by way of remembrance: wherefore, beloved, seeing that ye look for such things, be diligent that ye may be found of him in peace, without spot, and blameless" (II Peter 3:1, 14).

God wants and commands us to be holy **because** He is holy.

"For I am the LORD your God: ye shall therefore sanctify yourselves, and ye shall be holy; for I am holy" (Lev. 11:44a).

"And the LORD spake unto Moses, saying, speak unto all the congregation of the children of Israel, and say unto them, Ye shall be holy: for I the LORD your God am holy" (Lev. 19:1, 2).

"But as he which hath called you is holy, so be ye holy in all manner of conversation; because it is written, Be ye holy; for I am holy" (I Peter 1:15, 16).

"For even hereunto were ye called: because Christ also suffered for us, leaving us an example, that ye should follow his steps: who did no sin, neither was guile found in his mouth: who, when he was reviled, reviled not again; when he suffered, he threatened not; but committed himself to him that judgeth righteously: who his own self bare our sins in his own body on the tree, that we, being dead to sins, should live unto righteousness: by whose stripes ye were healed" (I Peter 2:21-24).

Furthermore, we must be holy to have fellowship with God.

"Can two walk together, except they be agreed?" (Amos 3:3).

"And what concord hath Christ with Belial? And what agreement hath the temple of God with idols? for ye are the temple of the living God; as God hath said, I will dwell in them, and walk in them; and I will be their God, and they shall be my people" (II Cor. 6:15a, 16).

"If we say that we have fellowship with him, and walk in darkness, we lie, and do not the truth" (I John 1:6).

Salvation takes care of much of this directly, and it starts us out on the path of and towards holiness of heart and life. Unfortunately, many churches teach a very watered-down version of salvation; one that is unlikely to do anybody much long-term good, and may even do harm. In reality, there are several steps involved, although some of them may run concurrently, at least to a degree.

1. One must recognize that there is only one way to Heaven.

"I, even I, am the LORD; and beside me there is no saviour" (Isaiah 43:11).

2. One must have a firm, genuine, heart-felt belief in God and His word.

"He that believeth on him is not condemned: but he that believeth not is condemned already, because he hath not believed in the name of the only begotten Son of God" (John 3:18).

"Jesus said unto her, I am the resurrection, and the life: he that believeth in me, though he were dead, yet shall he live: and whosoever liveth and believeth in me shall never die. Believest thou this? She saith unto him, Yea, Lord: I believe that thou art the Christ, the Son of God, which should come into the world" (John 11:25-27).

"I will therefore put you in remembrance, though ye once knew this, how that the Lord, having saved the people out of the land of Egypt, afterward destroyed them that believed not" (Jude 5).

3. Such belief, although necessary, is not sufficient.

"Thou believest that there is one God; thou doest well: the devils also believe, and tremble" (James 2:19).

4a. God wants people to repent of their sins.

"The Lord is not slack concerning his promise, as some men count slackness; but is longsuffering to us-ward, not willing that any should perish, but that all should come to repentance" (II Peter 3:9).

4b. What is repentance? Godly sorrow for sin.

"Now I rejoice, not that ye were made sorry, but that ye sorrowed to repentance: for ye were made sorry after a godly manner, that ye might receive damage by us in nothing. For godly sorrow worketh repentance to salvation not to be repented of: but the sorrow of the world worketh death" (II Cor. 7:9, 10).

4c. This produces a turning away from sin.

"Therefore say unto the house of Israel, Thus saith the Lord GOD; Repent, and turn yourselves from your idols; and turn away your faces from all your abominations" (Ezek. 14:6).

4d. God requires repentance and confession of sins in order for a person to be forgiven. This part is where many churches fail people. The modern "accepting Christ" is so weak and so pathetic. It reduces salvation to a purely human judgment call and system of values.

Many churches do this: "Do you accept Jesus as your Savior?"

Person: "Yes."

Church: "Then you're now a Christian."

And they say little, or in many cases, nothing, about actually repenting.

By contrast, the Divine plan of salvation requires much more than that of a person. Repentance is one difference.

"Then went out to him Jerusalem, and all Judaea, and all the region round about Jordan, and were baptized of him in Jordan, confessing their sins. But when he saw many of the Pharisees and Sadducees come to his baptism, he said unto them, O generation of vipers, who hath warned you to flee from the wrath to come? Bring forth therefore fruits meet for repentance" (Matt. 3:5-8).

"Therefore if thou bring thy gift to the altar, and there rememberest that thy brother hath aught against thee; leave there thy gift before the altar, and go thy way; first be reconciled to thy brother, and then come and offer thy gift" (Matt. 5:23, 24).

"Repent ye therefore, and be converted, that your sins may be blotted out, when the times of refreshing shall come from the presence of the Lord" (Acts 3:19).

"And the times of this ignorance God winked at; but now commandeth all men every where to repent: because he hath appointed a day, in the which he will judge the world in righteousness by that man whom he hath ordained; whereof he hath given assurance unto all men, in that he hath raised him from the dead" (Acts 17:30, 31).

"Whereupon, O king Agrippa, I was not disobedient unto the heavenly vision: but shewed first unto them of Damascus, and at Jerusalem, and throughout all the coasts of Judaea, and then to the Gentiles, that they should repent and turn to God, and do works meet for repentance" (Acts 26:19, 20).

5. We must also have faith that God will forgive.

"The just shall live by his faith" (Hab. 2:4b).

"By faith the harlot Rahab perished not with them that believed not, when she had received the spies with peace" (Heb. 11:31).

6. We must confess (testify to) salvation after we receive it.

"Let the redeemed of the LORD say so, whom he hath redeemed from the hand of the enemy" (Psalm 107:2).

"Whosoever therefore shall confess me before men, him will I confess also before my Father which is in heaven. But whosoever shall deny me before men, him will I also deny before my Father which is in heaven" (Matt. 10:32, 33).

"That if thou shalt confess with thy mouth the Lord Jesus, and shalt believe in thine heart that God hath raised him from the dead, thou shalt be saved. For with the heart man believeth unto righteousness; and with the mouth confession is made unto salvation. For the scripture saith, Whosoever believeth on him shall not be ashamed. For there is no difference between the Jew and the Greek: for the same Lord over all is rich unto all that call upon him. For whosoever shall call upon the name of the Lord shall be saved" (Romans 10:9-13).

Salvation, although it is by far the most important thing, is not the only thing. There is more to walking with God than simply being saved. One thing that a Christian should do is to grow in grace.

"As newborn babes, desire the sincere milk of the word, that ye may grow thereby" (I Peter 2:2). "But grow in grace, and in the knowledge of our Lord and Saviour Jesus Christ" (II Peter 3:18a).

But there's a problem: every Christian, at least every one of long-standing, knows that salvation doesn't change quite everything. Some measure of the old sin nature still remains in the heart, even after salvation. Sometimes it takes a while after salvation before a person realizes this. This remaining carnality has given every Christian considerable trouble and difficulty. Some people, once they have realized this, try to grow their way out of the problem. This does not work, although growing in grace may sometimes help a person deal with specific manifestations of the problem.

However, there is good news regarding this situation. God, being a perfect Father, and having perfect knowledge of our condition, has prepared a second gift for us. He has already given us the gift of spiritual life. Now He wishes to give His children the gift of perfect love. This gift takes care of all remaining carnality in a Christian's heart. This gift is the second work of grace.

It is fitting that love is the essence of entire sanctification; for love is the most powerful thing in the universe (see John 3:16; Romans 5:8). Paul tells us—incredible as it might seem—that love is even greater than faith (I Cor. 13:13)!

How do we know that there is a second work? After all, many thoughtful, godly men have said that they could find no proof of one anywhere in the Bible. One way we can know is from the personal history of the apostles.

Opposition to the idea of a second work of grace has a tendency to lead people to absurd lengths and utterly illogical, unscriptural positions. A few people, in their desperation to "prove" that a second work does not exist, have actually claimed that the original disciples were never saved at all until the Day of Pentecost!

Of course they were saved before then—I don't think that any real Christian would seriously question that statement, although reasonable people may differ as to when it happened. My opinion is that it was pretty early in Jesus' earthly ministry. But in the interest of being thorough, here are some passages that prove they (and others of Jesus' followers) were saved before Pentecost.

"And another of his disciples said unto him, Lord, suffer me first to go and bury my father. But Jesus said unto him, Follow me; and let the dead bury their dead" (Matt. 8:21, 22).

"And Simon Peter answered and said, Thou art the Christ, the Son of the living God. And Jesus answered and said unto him, Blessed art thou, Simon Barjona: for flesh and blood hath not revealed it unto thee, but my Father which is in heaven" (Matt. 16:16, 17).

"Notwithstanding in this rejoice not, that the spirits are subject unto you; but rather rejoice, because your names are written in heaven" (Luke 10:20).

"But as many as received him, to them gave he power to become the sons of God, even to them that believe on his name" (John 1:12).

"I have manifested thy name unto the men which thou gavest me out of the world: thine they were, and thou gavest me them; and they have kept thy word. Now they have known that all things whatsoever thou hast given me are of thee. For I have given unto them the words which thou gavest me; and they have received them, and have known surely that I came out from thee, and they have believed that thou didst send me. I have given them thy word; and the world hath hated them, because they are not of the world, even as I am not of the world" (John 17:6-8, 14).

So having laid the background, we now come to the grand event.

"And when the day of Pentecost was fully come, they were all with one accord in one place. And suddenly there came a sound from heaven as of a rushing mighty wind, and it filled all the house where they were sitting. And there appeared unto them cloven tongues like as of fire, and it sat upon each of them. And they were all filled with the Holy Ghost, and began to speak with other tongues, as the Spirit gave them utterance" (Acts 2:1-4).

As we have seen, the men and women in the Upper Room had been saved at some point prior to this. Whatever the reader's specific theological position may be, I think it is undeniably clear that a second **something** happened to these people. But before we delve into this further, let's back up a bit. Why did this happen at all?

The Church has done itself a great disservice by concentrating so much on Matthew's account of the Great Commission, because Matthew tells only half the story. The other half is told by Luke.

"And, being assembled together with them, [Jesus] commanded them that they should not depart from Jerusalem, but wait for the promise of the Father, which, saith he, ye have heard of me. For John truly baptized with water; but ye shall be baptized with the Holy Ghost not many days hence. But ye shall receive power, after that the Holy Ghost is come upon you: and ye shall be witnesses unto me both in Jerusalem, and in all Judaea, and in Samaria, and unto the uttermost part of the earth. Then returned they unto Jerusalem from the mount called Olivet, which is from Jerusalem a sabbath day's journey. And when they were come in, they went up into an upper room, where abode both Peter, and James, and John, and Andrew, Philip, and Thomas, Bartholomew, and Matthew, James the son of Alphaeus, and Simon Zelotes, and Judas the brother of James. These all continued with one accord in prayer and supplication, with the women, and Mary the mother of Jesus, and with his brethren" (Acts 1:4, 5, 8, 12-14).

"And, behold, I send the promise of my Father upon you: but tarry ye in the city of Jerusalem, until ye be endued with power from on high. And he led them out as far as to Bethany, and he lifted up his hands, and blessed them. And it came to pass, while he blessed them, he was parted from them, and carried up into heaven" (Luke 24:49-51).

The more I thought about this passage, the more remarkable it became. You see, the disciples already had power—lots of it. They had far more power than most Christians today. Most if not all Christians today would consider them to be mighty spiritual warriors. They could do amazing things like casting out demons. But we see here an astounding thing—Jesus was telling them that they needed even **more** power before they went out preaching to the world!

They had what I would characterize as outward power—the sort that could force demons to obey, cure sickness, etc.

"And when he had called unto him his twelve disciples, he gave them power against unclean spirits, to cast them out, and to heal all manner of sickness and all manner of disease" (Matt. 10:1).

"And the seventy returned again with joy, saying, Lord, even the devils are subject unto us through thy name. Behold, I give unto you power to tread on serpents and scorpions, and over all the power of the enemy: and nothing shall by any means hurt you. Notwithstanding in this rejoice not, that the spirits are subject unto you; but rather rejoice, because your names are written in heaven" (Luke 10:17, 19, 20).

But they needed inward power—the sort that would offer a stabilizing influence on their hearts and minds.

"Commit thy works unto the LORD, and thy thoughts shall be established" (Prov. 16:3).

"But the wisdom that is from above is first pure, then peaceable, gentle, and easy to be intreated, full of mercy and good fruits, without partiality, and without hypocrisy" (James 3:17).

As Acts 1:8 above says, this power could not come until they had perfectly pure hearts, and they received both the purity and the power at Pentecost. And it changed their lives forever.

No Christian is as powerful and as bold as he can be until he receives the Holy Ghost. Assuming (for the sake of convenience) that there were exactly 120 in the Upper Room, and that there were exactly 3,000 people saved on the Day of Pentecost, then each of the 120 was responsible for 25 people getting saved in one day. How many preachers have a similar record? How many years would it take for the average preacher to accumulate 25 saved souls?

Of all the preachers and missionaries that the average Christian is likely to be aware of, almost all that could come anywhere close to equaling that record on the Day of Pentecost were people who knew that they had received a second, definite work of grace. The "Faith Chapter" Hall of Fame of the Holiness movement would have names such as (but not limited to) John & Charles Wesley, John Fletcher, Adam Clarke, Francis Asbury, Peter Cartwright, Pheobe Palmer, William & Catherine Booth, Dwight L. Moody, A. B. Simpson, W. B. Godbey, Phineas Bresee, Martin Wells Knapp, and A. W. Tozer.

Boldness, in a new and greater way, is another sure sign of the work. The theme of the Holy Ghost, when He indwells the believer, is an intermingled, three-braided strand of POWER, BOLDNESS, and PURITY. The purity is what fuels the power and the boldness. We can see this in the lives of the apostles. Before Pentecost, even though they achieved some things for God, it was as nothing compared to what they did after Pentecost. Before, their successes were often marred by failure; after, they preached to hostile authorities, healed the sick, and raised the dead. Before, they were confined to the Holy Land; after, they traveled over large parts of the Roman Empire, and likely even beyond, preaching with great power and effectiveness as they went. Tradition says that Thomas carried the Gospel into India before being martyred. In just thirty years, there were churches in many of the Roman Empire's major cities. Biblical scholars are nearly unanimous that most of the apostolic epistles to the various churches were written by AD 65, with the rest of the New Testament being written by about AD 95.

The best and most visible example of this is how it changed Peter's life. Compare his actions before and after Pentecost. Peter before Pentecost: "Then began he to curse and to swear, saying, I know not the man. And immediately the cock crew" (Matt. 26:74). Peter after Pentecost: "Then Peter and the other apostles answered and said, We ought to obey God rather than men. And we are his witnesses of these things; and so is also the Holy Ghost, whom God hath given to them that obey him" (Acts 5:29, 32). This is a snapshot of the difference. For the full picture, read all of Acts 3-5.

Some opponents of Holiness doctrine have made much of Peter's sin recorded in Gal. 2:11-14. But they either forget, or else ignore, that that occasion was the one single time AFTER Pentecost that Peter is recorded to have fallen into sin. In the three and a half years of Jesus' ministry, Peter fell multiple times. But in the roughly 30-35 years that Peter lived after Pentecost, he fell only **once**. That fact is proof that the events on the Day of Pentecost had a tremendous, life-long impact on him.

Even Jesus Himself had the help and empowerment of the Holy Ghost during His earthly ministry.

"Now when all the people were baptized, it came to pass, that Jesus also being baptized, and praying, the heaven was opened, and the Holy Ghost descended in a bodily shape like a dove upon him, and a voice came from heaven, which said, Thou art my beloved Son; in thee I am well pleased. And Jesus being full of the Holy Ghost returned from Jordan, and was led by the Spirit into the wilderness" (Luke 3:21, 22, 4:1).

"But if I cast out devils by the Spirit of God, then the kingdom of God is come unto you" (Matt. 12:28).

Before going any farther, I should clarify something here regarding terminology. Sometimes very small details are very important. Baptism "by" the Spirit is something very different than baptism "with" the Spirit. Being baptized "by" the Spirit is equivalent to being baptized "into" God; and it refers to what happens at salvation. "For by one Spirit are we all baptized into one body, whether we be Jews or Gentiles, whether we be bond or free; and have been all made to drink into one Spirit" (I Cor. 12:13). "Know ye not, that so many of us as were baptized into Jesus Christ were baptized into his death?" (Romans 6:3).

Whereas being baptized "with" the Spirit means sanctification. Both John the Baptist and Jesus used "with" when they prophesied about the Day of Pentecost. "I indeed have baptized you with water: but he shall baptize you with the Holy Ghost" (Mark 1:8). "For John truly baptized with water; but ye shall be baptized with the Holy Ghost not many days hence" (Acts 1:5).

Now some people object to all this about Pentecost being such a special event. Some claim that the disciples had already received the Holy Ghost.

"Then the same day at evening, being the first day of the week, when the doors were shut where the disciples were assembled for fear of the Jews, came Jesus and stood in the midst, and saith unto them, Peace be unto you. And when he had so said, he shewed unto them his hands and his side. Then were the disciples glad, when they saw the Lord. Then said Jesus to them again, Peace be unto you: as my Father hath sent me, even so send I you. And when he had said this, he breathed on them, and saith unto them, Receive ye the Holy Ghost" (John 20:19-22).

I agree with some of our opponents that this passage is significant; but not for the reasons that they think. The reason that it's significant is because this point marks the beginning of the transition from the Second to the Third Personages of the Trinity. The dispensation of Jesus was drawing to a close, and the dispensation of the Holy Ghost was about to begin. This transition did not complete until the Day of Pentecost. What Jesus said here was more in the sense of a commission or blessing, rather than an actual giving of the Holy Ghost. We know this because just a little earlier, He had told them that the Holy Ghost would be sent from the Father. "But the Comforter, which is the Holy Ghost, whom the Father will send in my name, he shall teach you all things, and bring all things to your remembrance, whatsoever I have said unto you" (John 14:26).

And Jesus had to leave before the Holy Ghost could come. "Nevertheless I tell you the truth; It is expedient for you that I go away: for if I go not away, the Comforter will not come unto you; but if I depart, I will send him unto you" (John 16:7).

Another objection that sometimes comes up is that the filling of the Holy Ghost is a repeatable thing; i.e., simply a special visitation from God, but not anything like a second work of grace. This next verse is the most commonly used for this point of view.

"And when they had prayed, the place was shaken where they were assembled together; and they were all filled with the Holy Ghost, and they spake the word of God with boldness" (Acts 4:31).

Some think that the 120 were filled with the Holy Ghost a second time. This view is incorrect. For the whole picture, read all of chapter 4. But for now, let's take a closer look at some of the details. This was after Peter and John had healed the lame man at the temple (Acts 3:1-10). This caused such a commotion that the authorities arrested them (4:1-3). Peter, of course, had already been filled with the Spirit, as Luke reminds us: "Then Peter, filled with the Holy Ghost, said unto them, Ye rulers of the people, and elders of Israel" (verse 8). As I mentioned earlier, being filled with the Spirit produces holy boldness. "Now when they saw the boldness of Peter and John, and perceived that they were unlearned and ignorant men, they marvelled; and they took knowledge of them, that they had been with Jesus" (verse 13).

Now let's back up to verse 4: "Howbeit many of them which heard the word believed; and the number of the men was about five thousand." So this was at least a little while after Pentecost, because a separate group of 3,000 believed on that day. Now verse 23: "And being let go, they went to their own company, and reported all that the chief priests and elders had said unto them."

In other words, "their own company"—the assembly of Christians—included people who had gotten saved after the Day of Pentecost. Peter and John reported what had happened, and then had a group session of prayer. After that, the ones who had been saved after Pentecost were filled with the Holy Ghost. The apostles were not included in this particular outpouring, because they had already gotten the blessing (and the boldness) earlier.

Now some people object to all this. They say that the apostles received the Holy Ghost separately from salvation simply and solely because of a unique set of circumstances; and that everybody since then receives the Holy Ghost at the moment of salvation. A close look at the history of the Church in its very earliest years answers this objection.

"Then Philip went down to the city of Samaria, and preached Christ unto them. And the people with one accord gave heed unto those things which Philip spake, hearing and seeing the miracles which he did. For unclean spirits, crying with loud voice, came out of many that were possessed with them: and many taken with palsies, and that were lame, were healed. And there was great joy in that city. But when they believed Philip preaching the things concerning the kingdom of God, and the name of Jesus Christ, they were baptized, both men and women. Now when the apostles which were at Jerusalem heard that Samaria had received the word of God, they sent unto them Peter and John: who, when they were come down, prayed for them, that they might receive the Holy Ghost: (for as yet he was fallen upon none of them: only they were baptized in the name of the Lord Jesus.) Then laid they their hands on them, and they received the Holy Ghost" (Acts 8:5-8, 12, 14-17).

We see in this passage two separate works of grace clearly defined. Philip "preached

273

Christ unto them" (verse 5); they "believed" and "were baptized" (verse 12); the apostles heard about what had happened (verse 14); and only **after** that—at some indeterminate time LATER—did they receive the Holy Ghost (verse 17).

"And Saul, yet breathing out threatenings and slaughter against the disciples of the Lord, went unto the high priest, and desired of him letters to Damascus to the synagogues, that if he found any of this way, whether they were men or women, he might bring them bound unto Jerusalem. And as he journeyed, he came near Damascus: and suddenly there shined round about him a light from heaven: and he fell to the earth, and heard a voice saying unto him, Saul, Saul, why persecutest thou me? And he said, Who art thou, Lord? And the Lord said, I am Jesus whom thou persecutest: it is hard for thee to kick against the pricks. And he trembling and astonished said, Lord, what wilt thou have me to do? And the Lord said unto him, Arise, and go into the city, and it shall be told thee what thou must do. And the men which journeyed with him stood speechless, hearing a voice, but seeing no man. And Ananias went his way, and entered into the house; and putting his hands on him said, Brother Saul, the Lord, even Jesus, that appeared unto thee in the way as thou camest, hath sent me, that thou mightest receive thy sight, and be filled with the Holy Ghost. And immediately there fell from his eyes as it had been scales: and he received sight forthwith, and arose, and was baptized. Then had the churches rest throughout all Judaea and Galilee and Samaria, and were edified; and walking in the fear of the Lord, and in the comfort of the Holy Ghost, were multiplied" (Acts 9:1-7, 17, 18, 31).

Many people claim that Saul didn't actually get saved until Ananias came to visit him at Damascus. However, it is evident that Saul got saved in verse 6. Notice what he says: he addresses Jesus as "Lord." He has just been informed in a very definite, unmistakable way that Jesus is God; and lo! instantly he believes. Next we see Saul's submission: "What wilt thou have me to do?" And his status as a believer is confirmed in verse 17, when Ananias addresses him as a brother in Christ. Also notice at the end of that verse—Ananias tells Saul that he was sent by God, to (among other things) see that Saul was "filled with the Holy Ghost"—just like the original apostles were on the Day of Pentecost.

"There was a certain man in Caesarea called Cornelius, a centurion of the band called the Italian band, a devout man, and one that feared God with all his house, which gave much alms to the people, and prayed to God alway. He saw in a vision evidently about the ninth hour of the day an angel of God coming in to him, and saying unto him, Cornelius. And when he looked on him, he was afraid, and said, What is it, Lord? And he said unto him, Thy prayers and thine alms are come up for a memorial before God. And now send men to Joppa, and call for one Simon, whose surname is Peter: he lodgeth with one Simon a tanner, whose house is by the sea side: he shall tell thee what thou oughtest to do. Then Peter opened his mouth, and said, Of a truth I perceive that God is no respecter of persons: but in every nation he that feareth him, and worketh righteousness, is accepted with him. While Peter yet spake these words, the Holy Ghost fell on all them which heard the word. And they of the circumcision which believed were astonished, as many as came with Peter, because that on the Gentiles also was poured out the gift of the Holy Ghost" (Acts 10:1-6, 34, 35, 44, 45).

We know that Cornelius was saved before Peter visited him. God hears the prayers of the righteous; He does not hear sinners, other than prayers for forgiveness.

"The eyes of the LORD are upon the righteous, and his ears are open unto their cry" (Psalm 34:15).

"If I regard iniquity in my heart, the Lord will not hear me" (Psalm 66:18).

"Then shall they cry unto the LORD, but he will not hear them: he will even hide his face from them at that time, as they have behaved themselves ill in their doings" (Micah 3:4).

"Now we know that God heareth not sinners: but if any man be a worshipper of God, and doeth his will, him he heareth" (John 9:31).

"And Cornelius said, Four days ago I was fasting until this hour; and at the ninth hour I prayed in my house, and, behold, a man stood before me in bright clothing, and said, Cornelius, thy prayer is heard, and thine alms are had in remembrance in the sight of God" (Acts 10:30, 31).

Cornelius was a devout man (10:2), and God heard his prayers. There should not be any doubt in anyone's mind that Cornelius was saved before he summoned Peter.

"Now therefore are we all here present before God, to hear all things that are commanded thee of God" (Acts 10:33b). There is a bit of a side note that I would like to mention here. As I read this verse, it struck me quite forcibly that this sounds for all the world like the attitude of many present-day Christians who want to hear the word of God, when they assemble in church to hear a sermon. What Cornelius said here to Peter could be said, word for word, by many people to their pastor.

"And as I began to speak, the Holy Ghost fell on them, as on us at the beginning. Then remembered I the word of the Lord, how that he said, John indeed baptized with water; but ye shall be baptized with the Holy Ghost. Forasmuch then as God gave them the like gift as he did unto us, who believed on the Lord Jesus Christ; what was I, that I could withstand God?" (Acts 11:15-17).

This is Peter's account of Cornelius. Notice here that Peter equates the Holy Ghost falling on a person with the baptism of the Spirit. There is more than one biblically-valid way of describing sanctification.

"And when there had been much disputing, Peter rose up, and said unto them, Men and brethren, ye know how that a good while ago God made choice among us, that the Gentiles by my mouth should hear the word of the gospel, and believe. And God, which knoweth the hearts, bare them witness, giving them the Holy Ghost, even as he did unto us; and put no difference between us and them, purifying their hearts by faith" (Acts 15:7-9).

Notice that "purifying" is spoken of the second work, not the first. The first work forgives; the second work purifies (see Matt. 3:11, 12). Mind you, this is not to suggest that salvation doesn't purify at all; it does a great deal along that line. But remember (just in case anybody should need a reminder), salvation leaves a certain remnant of the carnal nature in the heart. Sanctification purifies the heart from that remaining contamination.

"And it came to pass, that, while Apollos was at Corinth, Paul having passed through the upper coasts came to Ephesus: and finding certain disciples, he said unto them, Have ye received the Holy Ghost since ye believed? And they said unto him, We have not so much as heard whether there be any Holy Ghost. And he said unto them, Unto what then were ye baptized? And they said, Unto John's baptism. Then said Paul, John verily baptized with the baptism of repentance, saying unto the people, that they should believe on him which should come after him, that is, on Christ Jesus. When they heard this, they were baptized in the name of the Lord Jesus. And when Paul had laid his hands upon them, the Holy Ghost came on them; and they spake with tongues, and prophesied" (Acts 19:1-6).

Again, pay attention to the order of events. These disciples believed on Jesus; they were then baptized; and **only after that** did they receive the Holy Ghost. Notice as well, in verse 2, that Paul clearly expected this order of events: "Have ye received the Holy Ghost **since** ye believed?"

These four passages, by themselves, ought to be enough to show the existence of two separate works of grace. At the very least, they ought to make any opposer of Holiness doctrine stop and think really hard about his position.

Chapter 12

Perfection vs. Sin

Another way that we know that a second work exists is because Christians are commanded to pursue it. Many times, it is referred to as "perfection." God expects us, and moreover commands us, to be perfect.

"And when Abram was ninety years old and nine, the LORD appeared to Abram, and said unto him, I am the Almighty God; walk before me, and be thou perfect" (Gen. 17:1).

"Thou shalt be perfect with the LORD thy God" (Deut. 18:13).

"As for God, his way is perfect; the word of the LORD is tried: he is a buckler to all them that trust in him. God is my strength and power: and he maketh my way perfect" (II Sam. 22:31, 33).

"Let your heart therefore be perfect with the LORD our God, to walk in his statutes, and to keep his commandments, as at this day" (I Kings 8:61). Notice this: "your heart"; not "your head." I talked in chapter 1 about the different kinds of perfection: Divine, angelic, heavenly, human, and Christian. God distinguishes between the different types of perfection, even though many people do not.

"Be ye therefore perfect, even as your Father which is in heaven is perfect" (Matt. 5:48).

"I in them, and thou in me, that they may be made perfect in one; and that the world may know that thou hast sent me, and hast loved them, as thou hast loved me" (John 17:23).

"And he gave some, apostles; and some, prophets; and some, evangelists; and some, pastors and teachers; for the perfecting of the saints, for the work of the ministry, for the edifying of the body of Christ" (Eph. 4:11, 12). These are offices of the Church here on earth, not in Heaven: they were given for perfecting; therefore it is possible to be perfect here on earth.

"All scripture is given by inspiration of God, and is profitable for doctrine, for reproof, for correction, for instruction in righteousness: that the man of God may be perfect, thoroughly furnished unto all good works" (II Tim. 3:16, 17).

The Bible was given for our benefit and for us to use while we are still on earth; therefore, once again, we see that Christian perfection is possible on this earth.

"Therefore leaving the principles of the doctrine of Christ, let us go on unto perfection; not laying again the foundation of repentance from dead works, and of faith toward God" (Heb. 6:1).

"Now the God of peace, that brought again from the dead our Lord Jesus, that great shepherd of the sheep, through the blood of the everlasting covenant, make you perfect in every good work to do his will, working in you that which is wellpleasing in his sight, through Jesus Christ; to whom be glory for ever and ever. Amen" (Heb. 13:20, 21).

"But the God of all grace, who hath called us unto his eternal glory by Christ Jesus, after that ye have suffered a while, make you perfect, stablish, strengthen, settle you" (I Peter 5:10).

Some people may be confused by the mention of "eternal glory," and think that being made perfect will not happen until we get to Heaven. But what about the other things that are mentioned in this verse? There won't be any temptations or battles in Heaven: so why mention the other things—"stablish, strengthen, settle"—in the same breath? The answer is that all four are supposed to happen to us here on earth.

Many people object to this talk of perfection. Many say that the various words that the KJV translates as "perfect" should more properly be translated "mature."

Let's test this hypothesis. "Be ye therefore mature, even as your Father which is in heaven is mature."

I don't know about the reader, but that seems like a definite mis-translation to me. It leaves a bad taste in my mouth. Among other issues, talk of "maturity" necessarily implies a period of immaturity. Has our Heavenly Father ever been immature?

Other people say that the words should be translated as "complete."

This is not the objection that they think it is. They think that this is a counter to the idea of Christian perfection. They seem to feel that it is possible for a Christian to be complete without being perfect. People who feel this way claim that perfection of any sort is impossible here on earth. In actuality, however, the two words sometimes describe the same phenomenon. For example, in II Tim. 3:17 above, we could replace "perfect" with "complete" without changing the meaning one iota.

Consider the task of bleaching cloth. When the process is complete, the cloth is without blemish; it is white all over, or perfectly white. When the Holy Ghost finishes the task of bleaching our hearts from all trace of sin, we are completely pure. Somebody who has perfect love is complete in love; there is nothing more to add. Somebody who follows God perfectly has completely forsaken the ways of sin. When Adam and Eve were created, they were perfect; they lacked nothing.

Again, the idea of completeness takes several forms, and we need to distinguish which form we are talking about. We are currently not complete/perfect in the same manner that we will be once we have glorified bodies, for example.

Regarding God's command to be perfect:

Would God command us to do something that is impossible? What if He did? What then? Paul used this same technique in I Cor. 15:14ff: "If Christ be not risen..."

So let's explore this "If" and see where it goes.

The Bible presents God as a perfect father. "Every good gift and every perfect gift is from above, and cometh down from the Father of lights, with whom is no variableness, neither shadow of turning" (James 1:17). But if it is actually impossible to be perfect while here on earth, then we are faced with the fact that God has explicitly commanded us to do something that is impossible—and not just once, but numerous times. That is not the act of a perfect father, or even a good father. Even a merely bad father probably wouldn't do that. Any very powerful being who knowingly and deliberately and repeatedly commands his followers to do something impossible, would be a psychopathic monster—far worse than any of the gods of classical mythology. Do you see any other conclusion? I certainly don't. So if being perfect is impossible, then the Bible has consistently lied to us about the nature of God. And if THAT is true, then the whole thing falls down—there is not one word of the Bible that we can trust.

So we find ourselves faced with the very extremes of the question: there is absolutely nothing in the middle. Either the God of the Bible is a monster, OR it is indeed possible, in some fashion, to be perfect here on earth.

Now we all know that there are some ways in which being perfect is impossible. Our own experience, the experience of our friends and family, and all of recorded history agree—it is impossible to be humanly perfect. Moreover, nowhere does God command us to be humanly perfect. There is no passage analogous to I Kings 8:61 above wherein God commands us to have perfect minds. So what does that leave us? Once we become Christians, we have something that could be called a dual experience: both the normal, routine things of human existence (work, grocery shopping, etc.), and also a foretaste of the heavenly life, in the form of our personal walk with God. So once we drop the idea of human perfection, we are then left with just one option: the idea of Christian perfection.

Now having said all this, it is true that we are unable to fulfill any Divine command *in our own power*. But God always provides a way. He NEVER gives us a command without at the same time providing a way for us to obey it. He gave the ancient Israelites the system of sacrifices and burnt offerings. In our day, He gives us two things: Jesus' shed blood to wash away our sins; and then the Holy Ghost to provide stabilizing, keeping power, so that we don't have to fall back into sin. Receiving the new nature fundamentally changes us to the point where we *can* obey God's commands.

Another way we know that perfection is possible is because the Bible says that some people had it.

"Now it came to pass in the third year of Hoshea son of Elah king of Israel, that Hezekiah the son of Ahaz king of Judah began to reign. And he did that which was right in the sight of the LORD, according to all that David his father did. He removed the high places, and brake the images, and cut down the groves, and brake in pieces the brasen serpent that Moses had made: for unto those days the children of Israel did burn incense to it: and he called it Nehushtan. He trusted in the LORD God of Israel; so that after him was none like him among all the kings of Judah, nor any that were before him. For he clave to the LORD, and departed not from following him, but kept his commandments, which the LORD commanded Moses" (II Kings 18:1, 3-6).

"In those days was Hezekiah sick unto death. And the prophet Isaiah the son of Amoz came to him, and said unto him, Thus saith the LORD, Set thine house in order; for thou shalt die, and not live. Then he turned his face to the wall, and prayed unto the LORD, saying, I beseech thee, O LORD, remember now how I have walked before thee in truth and with a perfect heart, and have done that which is good in thy sight. And Hezekiah wept sore" (II Kings 20:1-3).

Our opponents would say that Hezekiah was deluded in thinking that he had a perfect heart. But nowhere does God say that he didn't.

This story also shows the difference between types of perfection. Hezekiah had a completely understandable desire to live longer.

"But the high places were not taken away out of Israel: nevertheless the heart of Asa was perfect all his days" (II Chron. 15:17).

There are a great many people who declare that perfection is impossible while here on earth—some hold that position because they honestly don't see how it is possible, while others hold it because they don't wish to give up a favorite excuse for sinning.

Do these people think that God inspired the Bible just for fun? Do they think that some parts of it are trivial and unimportant? If not—and I am confident that many opposers of the second work would be horrified at such a suggestion—then why do they contradict God's Word? Why is it that they don't pay attention to ALL of the Bible? For lo! we see here the inspired pen telling us that Asa had a PERFECT HEART!

Matthew Henry, although in almost all respects an excellent commentator, was an opponent of the second work of grace. To show how far astray opposition to this work can take a person, he says of the parallel passage in I Kings 15, "The perfection which is made the indispensable condition of the new covenant is not to be understood of sinlessness (then we were all undone), but sincerity." Sincerity! It's hard to believe that

Matthew Henry would make such a wild mistake. As numerous people have pointed out over the years, sincerity is no guarantee of anything. Every once in a while, we hear news reports of somebody who accidentally killed a friend or family member, all because of a sincere belief that a gun was unloaded. Or if it's religion you want, it's mighty hard to get more sincere than the radical Muslims who are willing to kill themselves for their beliefs. We see all around us evidence that it is possible to be both perfectly sincere, and perfectly mistaken.

We also see from this verse that a perfect heart does not necessarily protect us from mistakes in judgment. The Bible doesn't tell us why Asa did not remove all the high places. Perhaps circumstances were such that he felt it wasn't necessary. Perhaps he felt unable to, for some reason. Regardless—he had a perfect heart.

This wording is not the sole province of the KJV. Ten other translations render this word as "perfect." This includes Young's Literal Translation. Robert Young was committed to literalness in his translation, even at the expense of making it a clunky read. An additional six translations render the word as "blameless," which tracks well with the idea of Christian perfection.

I would like to give a solemn warning to the reader before moving on. We have, both in this verse and in the parallel passage, a definite statement of fact regarding heart perfection. If you are one of the people who claim that perfection is impossible while we are on earth—STOP! After reading this verse, I don't see how it would be possible to continue to claim that perfection is impossible, *unless you are willing to knowingly and deliberately contradict God.*

It is possible to serve God, at least to some extent, and not be perfect.

"Amaziah was twenty and five years old when he began to reign, and he reigned twenty and nine years in Jerusalem. And his mother's name was Jehoaddan of Jerusalem. And he did that which was right in the sight of the LORD, but not with a perfect heart" (II Chron. 25:1, 2).

"Be watchful, and strengthen the things which remain, that are ready to die: for I have not found thy works perfect before God" (Rev. 3:2).

This does not mean, however, that Christian perfection is some minor thing, or some trivial add-on to the Christian life. On the contrary, in many respects it is second only to salvation itself in importance.

How do we pursue Christian perfection?

"I beseech you therefore, brethren, by the mercies of God, that ye present your bodies a living sacrifice, holy, acceptable unto God, which is your reasonable service. And be not conformed to this world: but be ye transformed by the renewing of your mind, that ye may prove what is that good, and acceptable, and perfect, will of God" (Romans 12:1, 2).

What does this mean?

A very little thought will suffice to show that Paul is not simply talking about our physical bodies. Everybody has some sort of sickness, deformity, or other defect. Even though some people's bodies outwardly appear to be without blemish, such a reading would exclude the old, crippled, and so forth.

Just as Jesus offered Himself to God as a holy sacrifice without sin, so, too, in the same manner we should offer ourselves to God as a sacrifice without conscious sin. Only after we have been washed in the Blood are we an acceptable sacrifice. Only then can we be described, in any sense whatsoever, as holy and without blemish. Matthew Henry says regarding this verse, "*Your bodies*—your whole selves; so expressed because under the law the bodies of beasts were offered in sacrifice, 1 Cor. vi. 20. Our bodies and spirits are intended." Adam Clarke says, "All these phrases are *sacrificial,* and show that there must be a complete surrender of the person—the *body,* the whole man, mind and flesh, to be given to God; and that he is to consider himself no more his own, but the entire property of his Maker."

In addition, I would like to point out that a sacrifice is not a process, but an **event**. It occurs at a specific, identifiable point in time.

This command is aimed at Christians. Sinners are spiritually dead—they cannot offer themselves as a **living** sacrifice. Furthermore, they possess nothing that God would accept as a sacrifice.

This is not the only place where such a distinction is made. "And I will pray the Father, and he shall give you another Comforter, that he may abide with you for ever; even the Spirit of truth; whom the world cannot receive, because it seeth him not, neither knoweth him: but ye know him; for he dwelleth with you, and shall be in you" (John 14:16, 17).

Notice what Jesus says: the world cannot receive the Holy Ghost. That leaves Christians as the only possible ones. Now stop and consider: would we ever say that the world couldn't receive Jesus? Of course not. But for the Holy Ghost, there is a distinction that simply is not present for the other parts of the Trinity.

All this is another way that we can know that a second work of grace exists.

"... present your bodies a living sacrifice, holy, acceptable unto God..."

"If his offering be a burnt sacrifice of the herd, let him offer a male without blemish: he shall offer it of his own voluntary will at the door of the tabernacle of the congregation before the Lord. And he shall put his hand upon the head of the burnt offering; and it shall be accepted for him to make atonement for him. And he shall kill the bullock before the Lord: and the priests, Aaron's sons, shall bring the blood, and sprinkle the blood round about upon the altar that is by the door of the tabernacle of the congregation. And he shall flay the burnt offering, and cut it into his pieces. And the sons of Aaron the priest shall put fire upon the altar, and lay the wood in order upon the fire: and the priests, Aaron's sons, shall lay the parts, the head, and the fat, in order upon the wood that is on the fire which is upon the altar: but his inwards and his legs shall he wash in water: and the priest shall burn all on the altar, to be a burnt sacrifice, an offering made by fire, of a sweet savour unto the Lord. And if his offering be of the flocks, namely, of the sheep, or of the goats, for a burnt sacrifice; he shall bring it a male without blemish. And he shall kill it on the side of the altar northward before the Lord: and the priests, Aaron's sons, shall sprinkle his blood round about upon the altar" (Lev. 1:3-11).

"And if his oblation be a sacrifice of peace offering, if he offer it of the herd; whether it be a male or female, he shall offer it without blemish before the Lord. And he shall lay his hand upon the head of his offering, and kill it at the door of the tabernacle of the congregation: and Aaron's sons the priests shall sprinkle the blood upon the altar round about" (Lev. 3:1, 2).

Notice that these two passages say that the sacrifice is "without blemish." This is not a perfect analogy for our living sacrifice. But such a sacrifice is perfect in that we've gone as far as we can, up to that point: even though we still have remnants of carnality, we have repented of all sin that we're personally responsible for, and we are as pure as we can be under the circumstances.

Also take note of the "living" part. This has a double meaning. I've already mentioned the spiritual aspect. In addition, a physically dead, inert thing is not an acceptable sacrifice. Only a living being, with thoughts, feelings, emotions, and free will, can be the kind of sacrifice that God demands. He wants us to sacrifice ourselves to Him, and allow Him to metaphorically kill us in the sense that we utterly abandon ourselves to His will.

This next verse is one that I already quoted, but I'm quoting it again to make a point.

"And when Abram was ninety years old and nine, the Lord appeared to Abram, and said unto him, I am the Almighty God; walk before me, and be thou perfect" (Gen. 17:1).

The Hebrew word that's translated "perfect" is Strong's #8549. It has the sense of "without blemish, complete, ... without spot"; it is also used in Deut. 18:13 and II Sam. 22:31, 33 (both quoted previously). This same word is translated "undefiled" in Psalm 119:1.

"Blessed are the undefiled in the way, who walk in the law of the Lord" (Psalm 119:1).

"For such an high priest became us, who is holy, harmless, undefiled, separate from sinners, and made higher than the heavens; who needeth not daily, as those high priests, to offer up sacrifice, first for his own sins, and then for the people's: for this he did once, when he offered up himself" (Heb. 7:26, 27).

"For the bodies of those beasts, whose blood is brought into the sanctuary by the high priest for sin, are burned without the camp. Wherefore Jesus also, that he might sanctify the people with his own blood, suffered without the gate. Let us go forth therefore unto him without the camp, bearing his reproach" (Heb. 13:11-13).

"For whom he did foreknow, he also did predestinate to be conformed to the image of his Son, that he might be the firstborn among many brethren" (Romans 8:29).

We have seen that the Hebrew word in Gen. 17:1 and Psalm 119:1 has the sense of being without spot or blemish. Sin, and nothing else, defiles a person: there is nothing else that can blemish us morally. "And when he had called all the people unto him, he said unto them, Hearken unto me every one of you, and understand: there is nothing from without a man, that entering into him can defile him: but the things which come out of him, those are they that defile the man" (Mark 7:14, 15).

This passage tells us that it is sin that defiles us. It should be obvious, through simple logic, that while we are defiled by sin we are not undefiled. Therefore, being undefiled means being free of sin.

Jesus was perfect and without sin. Not only was He without voluntary sin, but He also had no carnality. Christians are supposed to be in His image. Therefore, putting all these verses together, it is clear that the command to "be perfect" means to be cleansed from all taint of sin. This includes both voluntary actions, as well as the inbred sin nature.

God commands us to put away all sin; i.e., be completely pure.

"Seven days shall ye eat unleavened bread; even the first day ye shall put away leaven out of your houses: for whosoever eateth leavened bread from the first day until the seventh day, that soul shall be cut off from Israel. Seven days shall there be no leaven found in your houses: for whosoever eateth that which is leavened, even that soul shall be cut off from the congregation of Israel, whether he be a stranger, or born in the land" (Exodus 12:15, 19).

"Unleavened bread shall be eaten seven days; and there shall no leavened bread be seen with thee, neither shall there be leaven seen with thee in all thy quarters" (Exodus 13:7).

These two passages paint a symbolic picture of a life that is completely divorced from sin in every respect. There are no exceptions here; no room for "small" sins; no room for "involuntary" sins; no room for the sin nature. When God tells us to be pure, He actually means it.

"Thou shalt not offer the blood of my sacrifice with leaven" (Exodus 34:25a).

As the reader might expect by now, our opponents have a different view of the matter.

"Q. 78. *Whence ariseth the imperfection of sanctification in believers?*

"A. The imperfection of sanctification in believers ariseth from the remnants of sin abiding in every part of them, and the perpetual lustings of the flesh against the spirit; whereby they are often foiled with temptations, and fall into many sins, are hindered in all their spiritual services, and their best works are imperfect and defiled in the sight of God" (Westminster Larger Catechism).

Proponents of a sinning religion will always find some way of justifying their views. However, contrary to what they believe, this verse (Exodus 34:25a) tells us that the work and obedience we offer to God should be and can be untainted by sin.

It's one thing if a person honestly struggles against carnality and relies on God's help to consistently gain the victory. But if a person is careless, or deliberately tries to have it both ways, he falls under the curse that God pronounces in Mal. 1:6-14.

"Keep thy heart with all diligence; for out of it are the issues of life. Put away from thee a froward mouth, and perverse lips put far from thee. Let thine eyes look right on, and let thine eyelids look straight before thee. Ponder the path of thy feet, and let all thy ways be established. Turn not to the right hand nor to the left: remove thy foot from evil" (Prov. 4:23-27).

"Wash you, make you clean; put away the evil of your doings from before mine eyes; cease to do evil" (Isaiah 1:16).

And yet Satan has tricked people into thinking that ceasing to do evil is impossible. Who is the liar here—Satan; or God?

"Then Jesus said unto them, Take heed and beware of the leaven of the Pharisees and of the Sadducees" (Matt. 16:6).

"Your glorying is not good. Know ye not that a little leaven leaveneth the whole lump? Purge out therefore the old leaven, that ye may be a new lump, as ye are unleavened. For even Christ our passover is sacrificed for us: therefore let us keep the feast, not with old leaven, neither with the leaven of malice and wickedness; but with the unleavened bread of sincerity and truth" (I Cor. 5:6-8).

"Having therefore these promises, dearly beloved, let us cleanse ourselves from all filthiness of the flesh and spirit, perfecting holiness in the fear of God" (II Cor. 7:1).

"Behold, what manner of love the Father hath bestowed upon us, that we should be called the sons of God: therefore the world knoweth us not, because it knew him not. Beloved, now are we the sons of God, and it doth not yet appear what we shall be: but we know that, when he shall appear, we shall be like him; for we shall see him as he is. And every man that hath this hope in him purifieth himself, even as he is pure" (I John 3:1-3).

Far from sin being inevitable, as our opponents claim, it is clear that God expects our lives to be sin-free.

Regarding the state of an unsanctified Christian: In talking about salvation, we often use the analogy of Jesus standing at the door of a house, knocking and asking to be let in. But after we let Him in, we discover that there is still a part of the house where sin remains. It is true that the power and presence of Jesus often keeps sin subdued, but nevertheless sin, like leaven, keeps trying to expand itself.

Surely nobody would want to live in a physical house that was perpetually dirty and grimy, no matter how often it was cleaned. Suppose somebody came to visit, and remarked on it. You would have to say, "I've tried all the cleaning agents I can think of, but nothing gets rid of all the dirt."

As I ponder this, it seems like many Christians must have a remarkably limited imagination. If you are saved but not sanctified, consider this:

Do you really think that Jesus WANTS to live in a partly dirty house????

Stop and think about it. Don't you think that He would be pleased (just as you would be) to live in a perfectly CLEAN house? If you were renting a room in your physical house to a guest, and the guest told you that he had a cleaning agent that would truly clean the house, and furthermore, could produce testimonials from other people about how well it worked—just imagine how he would feel if you told him that you thought you could just muddle through without it, and you weren't interested in even trying it. Just so it seems to me that Jesus must be terribly unhappy that many of His children refuse to let Him perfectly cleanse their hearts; either because they don't realize His power to do so, or (worse yet) because "I don't believe in that doctrine."

We do not achieve this purification: God does.

"And I will turn my hand upon thee, and purely purge away thy dross, and take away all thy tin" (Isaiah 1:25).

"And he shall sit as a refiner and purifier of silver: and he shall purify the sons of Levi, and purge them as gold and silver, that they may offer unto the Lord an offering in righteousness" (Mal. 3:3).

"John answered and said, A man can receive nothing, except it be given him from heaven" (John 3:27).

At the same time, however, God will not purge and purify us unless we ask Him to, and do what He requires of us. God does not save people against their will; and He does not sanctify people against their will.

I would like to step back for a moment, and take a little time to talk about reconciling Scripture with Scripture. We have just read some commands to be pure/sinless.

Jesus often called Himself the "Son of man." Somebody who doesn't know much about the Bible, or how to study the Bible, might take this self-description to mean that Jesus was just an ordinary man. We see here the importance of reconciling passages that on the surface appear to contradict each other. But this is something that opponents of Holiness doctrine somehow just do not do. They look steadfastly at the few passages that seem on the surface to say that we cannot be without sin, and stubbornly refuse to reconcile them with the vast number of passages that command us to live a holy, righteous, unblemished life while here on earth. Instead, they keep insisting over and over that their own experience and that of a sub-set of Christians trumps what God has explicitly told us to do.

But they're not stupid—just stubborn. They know very well that they have to handle those commands somehow, so many opponents have come up with the weak expedient of shifting those commands in time, and saying that they don't apply until we get to Heaven. Alternately, some claim—contrary to Scripture—that God expects us to fight against the carnal nature in our own power, and therefore fail on a daily basis. Mind you, they won't actually admit that they claim this—but as the saying goes, "Your actions speak so loud that I can't hear what you say." Opponents do say that God is available to help us, but they keep wailing over and over again about how hard it is to fight carnality, and spend so much time on that, that they never get around to actually asking God for help, at least not in any effective way. If they took even a tenth of that wailing time, and instead used it in asking God in faith for help, I truly believe that they would be amazed at the results.

"For sin shall not have dominion over you: for ye are not under the law, but under grace. What then? shall we sin, because we are not under the law, but under grace? God forbid" (Romans 6:14, 15).

Our opponents are forced to admit that there **should** be a distinct difference in a person's life after he gets saved. One part of the difference is that sin has dominion over a sinner's life, whereas it doesn't over a Christian's. So our opponents claim that sin no longer has dominion over them—and yet, in the very next breath, they claim that they can't help sinning! This is a very serious contradiction. It would be like somebody claiming that he is no longer a drunkard, and yet he gets drunk on a regular basis. To admit that there is something that you do frequently, and furthermore to claim that you cannot avoid doing it, and yet at the same time to claim that that thing doesn't have any power over you, is to twist the meaning of language beyond all recognition.

Our opponents contradict Paul on this issue of sinning. Pay attention to what he says, and you can hear Paul thundering down the corridors of time: "GOD FORBID!!!" (Romans 6:2).

But how can we actually put away all sin?

Opponents accuse us of redefining sin as "mistakes." They say that this is the only way we can claim to have sinless perfection.

Much of the difficulty that many people have with this doctrine is due to the fact that they define sin in a very broad fashion; even (dare I say it) an inappropriately-broad fashion. Calvinists, and others who are influenced by that school of thought, tend to define sin as including any sort of mistake or infirmity. All of them say that it includes any and all involuntary transgressions. Some point to Romans 3:23, and even go so far—believe it or not—as to say that **anything** that comes short of God's glory is a sin!

If sin actually included these things, then yes: it would indeed be impossible to live without sin. But as I said, this is an inappropriately-broad definition.

There are two separate things mentioned in Romans 3:23: sinning, and coming short of the glory of God. Opponents of this doctrine conflate the two. We always have come short of the glory of God, and always will, even when we get to Heaven. We come short precisely **because** we're human. We come short even of the glory of the angels, and the angels, in turn, also come short of the glory of God. God gives us a very, very tiny fraction of His glory, (because that's all we can tolerate without physically dying—see Exodus 33:17-23), and we absorb it, use it, and re-radiate it to others. But if we ever stopped coming short of God's glory, we would no longer be human at all, but we would quite literally BE God.

Most people are familiar with the definition of sin as "missing the mark." But what is that, exactly?

For the idea of living a holy life, sin can be defined thusly:

Anything, either commission or omission, that is KNOWN to be contrary to the will of God.

Our opponents tend to scoff at this type of definition. However, it is the only type that takes into account the mercy of God.

Most non-Calvinists believe that children who die before reaching the age of account-ability will go to Heaven, even though they are technically sinners. They do wrong, in a technical sense, but they do not KNOW that in a moral sense: they are not morally responsible for their actions. And knowledge is the key. A person has to know that a target exists before he can even attempt to hit it.

"If I had not come and spoken unto them, they had not had sin: but now they have no cloak for their sin" (John 15:22).

"Therefore by the deeds of the law there shall no flesh be justified in his sight: for by the law is the knowledge of sin" (Romans 3:20).

"What shall we say then? Is the law sin? God forbid. Nay, I had not known sin, but by the law: for I had not known lust, except the law had said, Thou shalt not covet. But sin, taking occasion by the commandment, wrought in me all manner of concupiscence. For without the law sin was dead" (Romans 7:7, 8).

"And I thank Christ Jesus our Lord, who hath enabled me, for that he counted me faithful, putting me into the ministry; who was before a blasphemer, and a persecutor, and injurious: but I obtained mercy, because I did it ignorantly in unbelief" (I Tim. 1:12, 13).

"Therefore to him that knoweth to do good, and doeth it not, to him it is sin" (James 4:17).

If the definition of sin were so broad as to cover involuntary omissions, then this last statement (being so much narrower in scop e), would be both nonsensical and unneces-sary. Everything it covers would already be covered in the broader definition.

How did sin enter the world? Through a choice. We know from Exodus chapters 7 and 8, and Matt. chapter 4 that Satan can work miracles. We know from Gen. 3:1, Matt. 24:24, and II Cor. 11:14 that God's children are in danger of falling prey to his decep-tions. So why did he not simply trick Eve? He could have disguised the fruit so that Eve honestly would have thought that she was eating something entirely different. And such a scenario would have been fool-proof, whereas he couldn't be sure that he would be able to persuade her openly. But he didn't disguise the fruit—because a mistake is not a sin, and Eve would not have been at fault. Such a scenario would not have produced the result that Satan wanted. He had to set up a situation where she would eat the fruit knowing full well what she was doing.

Sometimes we learn that something we've innocently been doing is actually a sin in God's eyes. But God, in His mercy, provides a way to deal with this sort of thing.

"If a soul commit a trespass, and sin through ignorance, in the holy things of the LORD; then he shall bring for his trespass unto the LORD a ram without blemish out of the flocks, with thy estimation by shekels of silver, after the shekel of the sanctuary, for a trespass offering. And he shall make amends for the harm that he hath done in the holy thing, and shall add the fifth part thereto, and give it unto the priest: and the priest shall make an atonement for him with the ram of the trespass offering, and it shall be forgiven him. And if a soul sin, and commit any of these things which are forbidden to be done by the commandments of the LORD; though he wist it not, yet is he guilty, and shall bear his iniquity. And he shall bring a ram without blemish out of the flock, with thy estimation, for a trespass offering, unto the priest: and the priest shall make an atonement for him concerning his ignorance wherein he erred and wist it not, and it shall be forgiven him" (Lev. 5:15-18).

Note that even this deals with conscious knowledge of sin; with a sin becoming known. Otherwise the transgressor would never know that he needed to offer an offering. The ancient sin offering of ignorance is symbolic of increasing light. Once God tells us about something, then it **becomes** sin to us if we do not obey.

Sometimes God speaks to us directly. But many times other Christians are instrumental in showing and teaching us things. "And a certain Jew named Apollos, born at Alexandria, an eloquent man, and mighty in the scriptures, came to Ephesus. This man was instructed in the way of the Lord; and being fervent in the spirit, he spake and taught diligently the things of the Lord, knowing only the baptism of John. And he began to speak boldly in the synagogue: whom when Aquila and Priscilla had heard, they took him unto them, and expounded unto him the way of God more perfectly" (Acts 18:24-26).

Receiving more light can sometimes be a painful process, and a dangerous one, as well. Sometimes people draw back, and don't want to accept the new truth. Sometimes people will say things like, "But what I do is my choice."

True—God gave us the power of choice, and we have the right to use it. But the right of choosing doesn't automatically mean that we will make the right choice. I greatly fear that some people focus so much on *their* choice that they've forgotten to consider *God's* choice for their lives. No Christian belongs to himself. We are God's property twice over: He made us, and He redeemed us.

"For whether we live, we live unto the Lord; and whether we die, we die unto the Lord: whether we live therefore, or die, we are the Lord's" (Romans 14:8).

"What? know ye not that your body is the temple of the Holy Ghost which is in you, which ye have of God, and ye are not your own? For ye are bought with a price: therefore glorify God in your body, and in your spirit, which are God's" (I Cor. 6:19, 20).

"For the love of Christ constraineth us; because we thus judge, that if one died for all, then were all dead: and that he died for all, that they which live should not henceforth live unto themselves, but unto him which died for them, and rose again" (II Cor. 5:14, 15).

"But there were false prophets also among the people, even as there shall be false teachers among you, who privily shall bring in damnable heresies, even denying the Lord that bought them, and bring upon themselves swift destruction" (II Peter 2:1).

I was involved in an online discussion with a few people who opposed this doctrine very strongly. I tried to point out the distinction between sins and mistakes, and the difference between sinless perfection and human perfection. They weren't having it. They accused me of trying to redefine "sins" as "mistakes." They came right out and said that that was the only way that I could claim to have possession of sinless perfection. So I used the following example: "If I park my car on a steep hill, and forget to set the parking brake, thus leading to it rolling into a lake—I count that as a mistake, whereas you folks call it a sin."

And then the uproar began. For some inexplicable reason, they weren't using the word "mistake" literally. I did; when I used the word, I meant exactly that; no more and no less. But I never did figure out just what exactly they meant by it. For some reason, they seemed either unable or unwilling to tell me what they meant by "mistake."

Infirmities are completely different from sins. The Greek word often translated as "infirmity" is Strong's #769: it means "feebleness (of body or mind); ... disease, sickness, weakness." This word is used in John 5:5 and Romans 8:26.

"And a certain man was there, which had an infirmity thirty and eight years" (John 5:5).

"Likewise the Spirit also helpeth our infirmities: for we know not what we should pray for as we ought: but the Spirit itself maketh intercession for us with groanings which cannot be uttered" (Romans 8:26). This verse helps show the difference between human perfection and Christian perfection. What Paul describes here is a human lack of knowledge; nothing more.

"And I was with you in weakness, and in fear, and in much trembling" (I Cor. 2:3).

"And he said unto me, My grace is sufficient for thee: for my strength is made perfect in weakness. Most gladly therefore will I rather glory in my infirmities, that the power of Christ may rest upon me. Therefore I take pleasure in infirmities, in reproaches, in necessities, in persecutions, in distresses for Christ's sake: for when I am weak, then am I strong" (II Cor. 12:9, 10).

Notice that he **glories** in his infirmities! This is a very strong, marked contrast to his attitude towards both sin and temptation. This contrast should be especially strong for our opponents, since most of them believe that the last half of Romans 7 describes Paul's personal struggles with sin. For these readers especially, this one verse ought to be plenty to show that infirmities are not sins.

"Ye know how through infirmity of the flesh I preached the gospel unto you at the first" (Gal. 4:13).

Another mistake that a lot of people make is conflating sin and temptation. Sometimes even Holiness people make this mistake.

"For we have not an high priest which cannot be touched with the feeling of our infirmities; but was in all points tempted like as we are, yet without sin" (Heb. 4:15).

"Does temptation equal desire? If that were true, then the most wicked man ever to walk on the face of the earth was Jesus Christ, who was tempted in all things! ... Yet, we find Christians who always confess their temptations as sin.

"I explained this principle to my wife, who agreed. Then I asked her if she had ever been tempted to commit adultery; she seemed offended as she said, 'What kind of woman do you think I am?' I explained that her response proved that she still believed that temptation equaled desire. Although the enemy can put absolutely any thought into our minds at nearly any time, these do not represent our wishes, but rather his true character" (Michael Wells; *Sidetracked in the Wilderness*).

Temptation, in and of itself, cannot harm us. Our response to temptation is what harms or helps us.

Since Heb. 4:15 mentions multiple things, I would like to briefly go back to the subject of infirmities. This verse is more evidence that a "narrow" (from the Calvinistic perspective) definition of sin is the correct type. One of the great, enduring mysteries of the Incarnation is that Jesus was both fully God and fully man. We do not understand how this was possible, but God somehow made it possible. Make no mistake—Jesus had a fully human nature and human personality and human body. Even though He Himself was sinless, He still had to endure the myriad indignities that come with living in a sin-blighted world. He got tired; He sweated; etc. So if infirmities, mistakes, etc. are sins, then the inescapable conclusion is that Jesus *inherently could NOT have been sinless*!

Another reason for this definition of sin, as opposed to involuntary transgression, is that the conscience—when operating under God's guidance—is a reliable indicator of purity.

"So when they continued asking him, he lifted up himself, and said unto them, He that is without sin among you, let him first cast a stone at her. And again he stooped down, and wrote on the ground. And they which heard it, being convicted by their own conscience, went out one by one, beginning at the eldest, even unto the last: and Jesus was left alone, and the woman standing in the midst" (John 8:7-9).

Their consciences convicted them because they had sin in their lives.

"And herein do I exercise myself, to have always a conscience void to offence toward God, and toward men" (Acts 24:16).

Witness the contrast between this and the previous passage.

"I say the truth in Christ, I lie not, my conscience also bearing me witness in the Holy Ghost" (Romans 9:1). "Unto the pure all things are pure: but unto them that are defiled and unbelieving is nothing pure; but even their mind and conscience is defiled" (Titus 1:15).

I have placed these two verses together to sharpen the contrast. A conscience that bears the witness of God can safely be followed; but a defiled conscience cannot be trusted.

"For rulers are not a terror to good works, but to the evil. Wilt thou then not be afraid of the power? do that which is good, and thou shalt have praise of the same: for he is the minister of God to thee for good. But if thou do that which is evil, be afraid; for he beareth not the sword in vain: for he is the minister of God, a revenger to execute wrath upon him that doeth evil. Wherefore ye must needs be subject, not only for wrath, but also for conscience sake" (Romans 13:3-5).

"Now the end of the commandment is charity out of a pure heart, and of a good conscience, and of faith unfeigned" (I Tim. 1:5).

"Likewise must the deacons be grave, not doubletongued, not given to much wine, not greedy of filthy lucre; holding the mystery of the faith in a pure conscience" (I Tim. 3:8, 9).

"How much more shall the blood of Christ, who through the eternal Spirit offered himself without spot to God, purge your conscience from dead works to serve the living God?" (Heb. 9:14). The power of God reaches the conscience, and makes it a trustworthy guide.

"But and if ye suffer for righteousness' sake, happy are ye: and be not afraid of their terror, neither be troubled; but sanctify the Lord God in your hearts: and be ready always to give an answer to every man that asketh you a reason of the hope that is in you with meekness and fear: having a good conscience; that, whereas they speak evil of you, as of evildoers, they may be ashamed that falsely accuse your good conversation in Christ" (I Peter 3:14-16).

A conscience that always operates under God's guidance will never become dull. It will actually become sharper over time, as a person matures spiritually, and as God gives more light.

But why is a second work needed when God could do everything at once? It turns out that God often does His work in stages.

"If therefore perfection were by the Levitical priesthood, (for under it the people received the law,) what further need was there that another priest should rise after the order of Melchisedec, and not be called after the order of Aaron? For the law made nothing perfect, but the bringing in of a better hope did; by the which we draw nigh unto God" (Heb. 7:11, 19).

"For if that first covenant had been faultless, then should no place have been sought for the second" (Heb. 8:7).

"For the law having a shadow of good things to come, and not the very image of the things, can never with those sacrifices which they offered year by year continually make the comers thereunto perfect. For then would they not have ceased to be offered? because that the worshippers once purged should have had no more conscience of sins. Then said he, Lo, I come to do thy will, O God. He taketh away the first, that he may establish the second" (Heb. 10:1, 2, 9).

There are some symbolic passages, as well.

"Come, and let us return unto the Lord: for he hath torn, and he will heal us; he hath smitten, and he will bind us up. After two days will he revive us: in the third day he will raise us up, and we shall live in his sight. Then shall we know, if we follow on to know the Lord: his going forth is prepared as the morning; and he shall come unto us as the rain, as the latter and former rain unto the earth" (Hosea 6:1-3).

This passage is rich is symbolism. In verse 2 we see two works: first comes the reviving, and then comes the raising up. And at the end of verse 3 we see two separate rains.

"And he cometh to Bethsaida; and they bring a blind man unto him, and besought him to touch him. And he took the blind man by the hand, and led him out of the town; and when he had spit on his eyes, and put his hands upon him, he asked him if he saw aught. And he looked up, and said, I see men as trees, walking. After that he put his hands again upon his eyes, and made him look up: and he was restored, and saw every man clearly" (Mark 8:22-25).

If this man had been like many Christians, he would have stopped at the first stage of healing. Imagine if he had said, "Well, it's disappointing, but we live in imperfect bodies, and this is the best I can hope for. I can't expect to have perfect vision until I get to Heaven. All I can do until then is stumble around and bewail my fate." He would have missed out on the best that God had to offer him.

We see in all these passages a powerful pattern regarding how God works. He does many of His most important things in sets of two. The first part of each set is of necessity "imperfectly perfect," for God deals with man where he is at the time. It takes time for man, both individually and collectively, to reach a state where he is ready for and able to grasp further revelations and/or illuminations of God's will and knowledge. Perhaps it would be better to characterize each first half as incomplete, rather than imperfect.

Everything that comes from God partakes of His perfection, but the first Testament, the first dispensation of Law, and the first work of salvation in a man's soul are incomplete, because that's all that man can handle when he first comes to the knowledge and truth of God.

The second Testament, the second dispensation of Grace, and the second work of completely eradicating sin in the heart all pick up where their first halves left off, and complete the process.

So we have three sets of two works. Call me crazy, but I don't think that that's a coincidence. It certainly shows a pattern.

This is more speculative, but I find it very interesting indeed that a Triune God would create three different sets like that.

Chapter 13

God's Gifts and Expectations

Faith is as necessary for the second work as for the first work. Without faith, nothing will happen.

"He answereth him, and saith, O faithless generation, how long shall I be with you? how long shall I suffer you? bring him unto me. And they brought him unto him: and when he saw him, straightway the spirit tare him; and he fell on the ground, and wallowed foaming. And he asked his father, How long is it ago since this came unto him? And he said, Of a child. And ofttimes it hath cast him into the fire, and into the waters, to destroy him: but if thou canst do any thing, have compassion on us, and help us. Jesus said unto him, If thou canst believe, all things are possible to him that believeth. And straightway the father of the child cried out, and said with tears, Lord, I believe; help thou mine unbelief" (Mark 9:19-24).

God can do things that we cannot: including handling the sin nature. Notice that verse 23 says "all things" are possible—*if you believe*. For those who don't, on the other hand—you may have some blessing from God in your life, simply because His mercy, but you will never have God's full approval and blessing until you pray "help thou mine unbelief."

"And they came to Jericho: and as he went out of Jericho with his disciples and a great number of people, blind Bartimaeus, the son of Timaeus, sat by the highway side begging. And when he heard that it was Jesus of Nazareth, he began to cry out, and say, Jesus, thou son of David, have mercy on me. And many charged him that he should hold his peace: but he cried the more a great deal, Thou son of David, have mercy on me. And Jesus stood still, and commanded him to be called. And they call the blind man, saying unto him, Be of good comfort, rise; he calleth thee. And he, casting away his garment, rose, and came to Jesus. And Jesus answered and said unto him, What wilt thou that I should do unto thee? The blind man said unto him, Lord, that I might receive my sight. And Jesus said unto him, Go thy way; thy faith hath made thee whole. And immediately he received his sight, and followed Jesus in the way" (Mark 10:46-52).

Here is another blind man. This man, too, wanted to be healed. Others told him that he should be content with his condition, but he redoubled his efforts. His efforts and his faith were rewarded: he was healed.

"Therefore I say unto you, What things soever ye desire, when ye pray, believe that ye receive them, and ye shall have them" (Mark 11:24).

"Jesus saith unto her, Said I not unto thee, that, if thou wouldest believe, thou shouldest see the glory of God?" (John 11:40).

"Therefore it is of faith, that it might be by grace; to the end the promise might be sure to all the seed; not to that only which is of the law, but to that also which is of the faith of Abraham; who is the father of us all: he staggered not at the promise of God through unbelief; but was strong in faith, giving glory to God; and being fully persuaded that, what he had promised, he was able also to perform" (Romans 4:16, 20, 21).

This is the opposite of our opponents. God has promised them a FULL deliverance from sin; but they stagger at the promise, and refuse the gift. Unlike blind Bartimaeus, they don't have the faith to be made whole. And because they lack faith, they miss out on the best part of God's glory, as Jesus told Martha in John 11:40 above.

The Bible sometimes treats sin as a disease.

"Ah sinful nation, a people laden with iniquity, a seed of evildoers, children that are corrupters: they have forsaken the LORD, they have provoked the Holy One of Israel unto anger, they are gone away backward. Why should ye be stricken any more? ye will revolt more and more: the whole head is sick, and the whole heart faint. From the sole of the foot even unto the head there is no soundness in it; but wounds, and bruises, and putrifying sores: they have not been closed, neither bound up, neither mollified with ointment" (Isaiah 1:4-6).

Another way we can know the second work exists is because God is a perfect Healer.

I have quoted passages where people were healed of physical diseases. As mentioned earlier, leprosy is a type of sin. Did Jesus only partially heal people who came to Him for physical healing? Did He give them just enough healing to let them sort of stumble through life? No! He healed them **completely**—*as long as they had faith.*

Then why—WHY—do so many people insist that we have no choice but to stumble through life only partially healed from sin? Why do they insist on limiting God in that fashion?

"But he was wounded for our transgressions, he was bruised for our iniquities: the chastisement of our peace was upon him; and with his stripes we are healed" (Isaiah 53:5).

"Heal me, O Lord, and I shall be healed; save me, and I shall be saved: for thou art my praise" (Jer. 17:14).

Notice the absolute certainty here: "I **shall** be healed." Again—when Jesus healed physical diseases, did He partially heal or completely heal?

Another reason for the second work is that everything outside of the will of God should die.

"These are the generations of Noah: Noah was a just man and perfect in his generations, and Noah walked with God. And God looked upon the earth, and, behold, it was corrupt; for all flesh had corrupted his way upon the earth. And, behold, I, even I, do bring a flood of waters upon the earth, to destroy all flesh, wherein is the breath of life, from under heaven; and every thing that is in the earth shall die. And every living substance was destroyed which was upon the face of the ground, both man, and cattle, and the creeping things, and the fowl of the heaven; and they were destroyed from the earth: and Noah only remained alive, and they that were with him in the ark" (Gen. 6:9, 12, 17, 7:23).

This is often described as purifying the earth. Everything that was outside the will of God died. God can purify the human heart just as thoroughly as He purified the earth. It doesn't matter if the problem is sin, or carnality, or the outworkings of either one: all of that is outside of God's will, and it should die.

Another reason that we know the second work exists is because we are commanded to have the spirit of prayer at all times. Sanctification is a tremendous help in keeping the spirit of prayer.

"Praying always with all prayer and supplication in the Spirit, and watching thereunto with all perseverance and supplication for all saints" (Eph. 6:18).

"Continue in prayer, and watch in the same with thanksgiving" (Col. 4:2).

"Pray without ceasing" (I Thess. 5:17).

Can you pray to God while simultaneously rejecting Him by sinning? Sin would have to be a form of prayer!

Yet another reason is because we are commanded to always be joyful and thankful.

"As ye have therefore received Christ Jesus the Lord, so walk ye in him: rooted and built up in him, and stablished in the faith, as ye have been taught, abounding therein with thanksgiving" (Col. 2:6, 7).

"Rejoice in the Lord always: and again I say, Rejoice" (Phil. 4:4).

"Paul is so emphatic about this because the word *rejoice* literally means 'to return to the source of our joy.' ...

"Over the years a similar prayer of rejoicing has kept me, in many situations, from giving in to such temptations as envy, jealousy, fear, and anger. Rejoicing, even in times of testing, is acknowledging that *God* is the source of life. And rejoicing brings us to the place where our lives can be filled by the source of life—God himself...

"Rejoicing begins when we acknowledge that God is the source of all life. In fact, God *is* life, which is why we adore him and sing praises to him. Rejoicing reveals faith, because it demonstrates our expectation that God will reveal to us the depths and heights of his love. All of this is so that we may be filled up to *all* the fullness of God. That's the ultimate in fulfillment!" (Gary Smalley; *Joy that Lasts*).

"Rejoice evermore. In every thing give thanks: for this is the will of God in Christ Jesus concerning you" (I Thess. 5:16, 18).

Think about the times you have fallen into sin. Were you joyful at that moment?

But wait! Perhaps you had the wrong attitude about all this. Perhaps a Christian is supposed to be joyful about falling into sin. Do you think perhaps that that's what the Bible means?

Obviously not. So what conclusion can we draw? If we are supposed to always be joyful, and if sin brings sadness and regret, then I see only one way out of this pickle—and that is, that we are not supposed to fall into sin at all!

An unsanctified Christian is capable of living above personal sin, but it is extremely difficult to do so consistently. The sin nature keeps trying to drag a person down. Sanctification helps wonderfully in this matter as well.

Since God is a perfect Father, He wants to give us an abundance of good things. The "health and wealth" crowd uses this as an excuse for greed. In the material realm, He wants to give us all we need—however much or however little that may be. "All we need" means just that, and nothing more. See Matt. 5:25-34. In the spiritual realm, however, there is a difference: God wants to give us an "abundance of abundance." For instance, He does not want to merely give us just barely enough grace to get us to Heaven, and nothing more. He wants to give us grace abundantly—abundant, enabling, conquering, all-sufficient grace.

"Thou preparest a table before me in the presence of mine enemies: thou anointest my head with oil; my cup runneth over" (Psalm 23:5).

"Thou lovest righteousness, and hatest wickedness: therefore God, thy God, hath anointed thee with the oil of gladness above thy fellows" (Psalm 45:7). Abundance is one of the rewards of righteousness.

"Thou openest thine hand, and satisfiest the desire of every living thing. The LORD is righteous in all his ways, and holy in all his works. The LORD is nigh unto all them that call upon him, to all that call upon him in truth. He will fulfil the desire of them that fear him: he also will hear their cry, and will save them" (Psalm 145:16-19).

"Until the spirit be poured upon us from on high, and the wilderness be a fruitful field, and the fruitful field be counted for a forest" (Isaiah 32:15).

"For I will pour water upon him that is thirsty, and floods upon the dry ground: I will pour my spirit upon thy seed, and my blessing upon thine offspring" (Isaiah 44:3).

"And it shall come to pass afterward, that I will pour out my spirit upon all flesh; and your sons and your daughters shall prophesy, your old men shall dream dreams, your young men shall see visions: and also upon the servants and upon the handmaids in those days will I pour out my spirit" (Joel 2:28, 29).

"In the last day, that great day of the feast, Jesus stood and cried, saying, If any man thirst, let him come unto me, and drink. He that believeth on me, as the scripture hath said, out of his belly shall flow rivers of living water. (But this spake he of the Spirit, which they that believe on him should receive: for the Holy Ghost was not yet given; because that Jesus was not yet glorified.)" (John 7:37-39).

Regarding this passage, let us look at verse 38 in particular—"rivers of living water." First of all, what is a river? Well, it isn't a creek; and it isn't a seasonal stream. Rather, it means a continual flowing of a substantial body of water. This is reinforced by the use of the plural form.

I checked a large number of translations to see how they handle this verse. There is a remarkable degree of uniformity across translations. This tells me that the original Greek is clear and easy to understand.

The wording of this verse implies a strong, continuous, involuntary outpouring. Jesus paints us a picture of a person who is so filled with grace and God's presence that he couldn't contain it if he tried.

But now we move from the theoretical ideal to common reality. And the contrast is very unpleasant, for a lot of Christians do not fit this picture that Jesus painted here. Instead of a continuous flowing, all too many Christians let the riverbed get choked up by the debris of sin—anger, pride, fear of man, and so on. Somebody who allows the ordinary irritations of life to choke off the flow of living water is showing the world a deeply unflattering view of God's grace and power. The world does not need a version of God that works well only when things are going well for His followers. But when we live so close to God, and have so much of His presence, that we show it to the world by not getting angry when things are going badly, or we show it by retaining a humble spirit even when we're praised and exalted, then we become proper examples to the world.

"Hitherto have ye asked nothing in my name: ask, and ye shall receive, that your joy may be full" (John 16:24).

"And God is able to make all grace abound toward you; that ye, always having all sufficiency in all things, may abound to every good work" (II Cor. 9:8).

Mark well what this verse says: "every good work." And not sparingly, or grudgingly, but abounding. If we meet this description, we literally will not have time to sin!

"In whom we have redemption through his blood, the forgiveness of sins, according to the riches of his grace; wherein he hath abounded toward us in all wisdom and prudence" (Eph. 1:7, 8).

"And to know the love of Christ, which passeth knowledge, that ye might be filled with all the fulness of God" (Eph. 3:19).

Mark this well: "filled with **all** the fullness" of God. In sanctification, we are filled with the Spirit.

In ancient times, it was common for kings to be assassinated, often by poison. So let us imagine a teapot that has been specially designed with assassination in mind. It looks normal, both outside and inside. But cleverly hidden inside is a little secret compartment wherein poison can be placed. By pressing a hidden button, the poison can be dispensed into the tea.

Now when the teapot appears to be full, is it actually full of tea? No; part of the space that should be filled with tea is taken up by the poison compartment.

This is a symbol of the heart that is saved but not sanctified. Carnality is poison; it wreaks terrible things. It is flat-out impossible to be COMPLETELY filled with God as long as we still have carnality in the heart, for there is a space that God cannot fill until the remains of carnality are removed.

"And this I pray, that your love may abound yet more and more in knowledge and in all judgment; that ye may approve things that are excellent; that ye may be sincere and without offence till the day of Christ; being filled with the fruits of righteousness, which are by Jesus Christ, unto the glory and praise of God" (Phil. 1:9).

Paul speaks of things that are "excellent"; things which we must have to be "without offence." Is the carnal nature "excellent"? Does having it in the heart make a person "without offence"? If not, then it needs to be gotten rid of.

"Not by works of righteousness which we have done, but according to his mercy he saved us, by the washing of regeneration, and renewing of the Holy Ghost; which he shed on us abundantly through Jesus Christ our Saviour" (Titus 3:5, 6).

"And beside this, giving all diligence, add to your faith virtue; and to virtue knowledge; and to knowledge temperance; and to temperance patience; and to patience godliness; and to godliness brotherly kindness; and to brotherly kindness charity. For if these things be in you, and abound, they make you that ye shall neither be barren nor unfruitful in the knowledge of our Lord Jesus Christ. But he that lacketh these things is blind, and cannot see afar off, and hath forgotten that he was purged from his old sins. Wherefore the rather, brethren, give diligence to make your calling and election sure: for if ye do these things, ye shall never fall: for so an entrance shall be ministered unto you abundantly into the everlasting kingdom of our Lord and Saviour Jesus Christ" (II Peter 1:5-11).

The sort of life that so many Christians lead—continually struggling with inbred carnality, and with one sin after another, and falling into sin so often, and then repenting, only to repeat the cycle again—(A), that is not the life that God wants us to lead, and (B), when viewed through the lens of Scripture, it is a very **abnormal** life.

When something is "purged" (verse 9), it is removed—not suppressed; not left for us to struggle with—but removed.

We are supposed to abound in the fruits of the Spirit. Verse 10 tells us that IF we are properly diligent in our walk with God, we **"shall never fall"** into sin.

Can God's Word be trusted, or not?

Sanctification helps tremendously in the Christian life, but even an unsanctified Christian has both the duty and the ability to live above sin.

The abundance of God includes abundant pardon for sin.

"Let Israel hope in the LORD: for with the LORD there is mercy, and with him is plenteous redemption. And he shall redeem Israel from all his iniquities" (Psalm 130:7, 8).

"Let the wicked forsake his way, and the unrighteous man his thoughts: and let him return unto the LORD, and he will have mercy upon him; and to our God, for he will abundantly pardon" (Isaiah 55:7).

"The thief cometh not, but for to steal, and to kill, and to destroy: I am come that they might have life, and that they might have it more abundantly" (John 10:10).

"Moreover the law entered, that the offence might abound. But where sin abounded, grace did much more abound: that as sin hath reigned unto death, even so might grace reign through righteousness unto eternal life by Jesus Christ our Lord" (Romans 5:20, 21).

Pay close attention to what these passages say: redeemed (or freed) from ALL iniquities; *abundantly* pardoned, which leads to *abundant life*; these are not the actions of a God who pardons and takes care of only a bare minimum of sin and no more. This is a God who not only pardons the sin that we are personally responsible for, but also pardons the sin that we are not responsible for, and thereby removes from the heart all remnants of the carnal nature.

Isaiah tells us that salvation involves *forsaking* the ways of wickedness. Even our thoughts are supposed to be righteous. Is there any room in that verse for being allowed to return to sin? Once again, Christians are not supposed fall back into sin!

One of the good things, specifically, that God wants to give us is perfect peace.

"Mark the perfect man, and behold the upright: for the end of that man is peace" (Psalm 37:37). Notice how peace is linked to perfection.

"Great peace have they which love thy law: and nothing shall offend them" (Psalm 119:165).

"Thou wilt keep him in perfect peace, whose mind is stayed on thee: because he trusteth in thee" (Isaiah 26:3).

This is a promise for anyone who meets the condition—a condition that comes through perfection. Pay close attention to this condition: "whose mind is stayed on thee." But—"A double minded man is unstable in all his ways" (James 1:8). A saved but unsanctified man is an unstable, double-minded man. This should be abundantly obvious to every person who has experienced this position first-hand. One day you're rejoicing in Jesus; the next you're despondent over something. One day you have the victory over sin; the next you're sorrowing because you've fallen into sin. But Isaiah is talking about something very different; a stable condition. The word "stayed" connotates an iron-clad, tenacious, bomb-proof fixity of purpose.

"Draw nigh to God, and he will draw nigh to you. Cleanse your hands, ye sinners; and purify your hearts, ye double minded" (James 4:8).

Notice in the last half of this verse that sinners are a separate group from the double-minded. And what does James tell the double-minded ones to do? Purify their hearts. Refer back to the end of chapter 11, to Acts 15:7-9, where the second work of grace is described as purifying the heart.

"And the work of righteousness shall be peace; and the effect of righteousness quietness and assurance for ever. And my people shall dwell in a peaceable habitation, and in sure dwellings, and in quiet resting places" (Isaiah 32:17, 18).

"O that thou hadst hearkened to my commandments! then had thy peace been as a river, and thy righteousness as the waves of the sea" (Isaiah 48:18).

"Finally, brethren, farewell. Be perfect, be of good comfort, be of one mind, live in peace; and the God of love and peace shall be with you" (II Cor. 13:11).

"And the peace of God, which passeth all understanding, shall keep your hearts and minds through Christ Jesus. Finally, brethren, whatsoever things are true, whatsoever things are honest, whatsoever things are just, whatsoever things are pure, whatsoever things are lovely, whatsoever things are of good report; if there be any virtue, and if there be any praise, think on these things. Those things, which ye have both learned, and received, and heard, and seen in me, do: and the God of peace shall be with you" (Phil. 4:7-9).

"Grace and peace be multiplied unto you through the knowledge of God, and of Jesus our Lord" (II Peter 1:2).

"There is no fear in love; but perfect love casteth out fear: because fear hath torment. He that feareth is not made perfect in love" (I John 4:18).

Thus we see that perfect love is linked to trusting God completely (Psalm 119:165 and Isaiah 26:3 above). Love, peace, and perfection all go together. You can have limited measures of love and peace without Christian perfection, but only limited measures.

Another thing that God wants to give us is rest from unbelief and double-mindedness.

"But with whom was he grieved forty years? was it not with them that had sinned, whose carcases fell in the wilderness? And to whom sware he that they should not enter into his rest, but to them that believed not? So we see that they could not enter in because of unbelief. Let us therefore fear, lest, a promise being left us of entering into his rest, any of you should seem to come short of it. For unto us was the gospel preached, as well as unto them: but the word preached did not profit them, not being mixed with faith in them that heard it. For we which have believed do enter into rest, as he said, As I have sworn in my wrath, if they shall enter into my rest: although the works were finished from the foundation of the world. For he spake in a certain place of the seventh day on this wise, And God did rest the seventh day from all his works. And in this place again, If they shall enter into my rest. Seeing therefore it remaineth that some must enter therein, and they to whom it was first preached entered not in because of unbelief: again, he limiteth a certain day, saying in David, To day, after so long a time; as it is said, To day if ye will hear his voice, harden not your hearts. For if Jesus had given them rest, then would he not afterward have spoken of another day. There remaineth therefore a rest to the people of God. For he that is entered into his rest, he also hath ceased from his own works, as God did from his. Let us labour therefore to enter into that rest, lest any man fall after the same example of unbelief" (Heb. 3:17-4:11).

The land of Canaan is a double-sided type, or symbol. It is a type of Heaven, but that usage does not concern us at the moment.

When the Israelites were in Egypt, they were in bondage. This is a type of sin. Pharaoh, or the Devil, enslaves people and leads them to do all sorts of things that are not exactly in their best interest. But God set them free from that bondage. The time spent in the wilderness is a type of the saved but unsanctified person. Just like James 1:8 tells us, the Israelites were unstable. They would faithfully follow God for a while, and then they would complain that God's yoke was too heavy, and they wanted desperately to be back in Egypt's bondage. Satan is marvelously efficient at convincing people that sin is a lighter burden than righteousness is.

The Israelites could have been in Canaan much earlier than they actually were. It took no more than two years to reach the border, and much of that time was spent before Mt. Sinai, building the tabernacle (Ex. 19:1 & 40:17; Num. 10:11). But since they rejected God's will, they were forced to spend much longer in that unstable state, wandering around in the wilderness.

Canaan is a type of sanctification; a land of abundance. God had set up the land with everything they needed. Yes, there were still battles to be fought, and there always will be until we reach Heaven. But once they entered Canaan, they were home. They were where God intended them to stay from then on. They rested; not in the sense of not having battles to fight, but in the sense of no longer wandering in the wilderness of unbelief.

"Teach me to do thy will; for thou art my God: thy spirit is good; lead me into the land of uprightness" (Psalm 143:10).

"The land of uprightness" is a dwelling place; just like the land of Canaan. Even though it is not a physical place, it is nevertheless a very real place. Once we reach it, God intends us to dwell there permanently. But if you are as yet unsanctified, I say unto you, "There remaineth yet very much land to be possessed" (Joshua 13:1c).

This is what Adam Clarke says at the end of Hebrews chapter 3:

"This whole chapter, as the epistle in general, reads a most awful lesson against *backsliders*, *triflers*, and *loiterers* in the way of salvation. Every believer in Christ is in danger of *apostasy*, while any remains of the *evil heart of unbelief* are found in him. God has promised to purify the heart; and the blood of Christ cleanses from all sin. It is therefore the highest wisdom of genuine Christians to look to God for the complete purification of their souls; this they cannot have too soon, and for this they cannot be too much in earnest...

"Where there are so many snares and dangers it is impossible to be too watchful and circumspect. Satan, as a roaring lion, as a subtle serpent, or in the guise of an angel of light, is momentarily going about seeking whom he may deceive, blind, and devour; and, when it is considered that the human heart, till entirely renewed, is on his side, it is a miracle of mercy that any soul escapes perdition: no man is safe any longer than he maintains the spirit of *watchfulness* and *prayer;* and to maintain such a spirit, he has need of all the means of grace. He who neglects any of them which the mercy of God has placed in his power, tempts the devil to tempt him."

One of the reasons why God wants to give us all these things is because He is our Father; He wishes to supply us with every needed and every desirable thing.

"Wherefore, if God so clothe the grass of the field, which to day is, and to morrow is cast into the oven, shall he not much more clothe you, O ye of little faith? Therefore take no thought, saying, What shall we eat? or, What shall we drink? or, Wherewithal shall we be clothed? (For after all these things do the Gentiles seek:) for your heavenly Father knoweth that ye have need of all these things. But seek ye first the kingdom of God, and his righteousness; and all these things shall be added unto you" (Matt. 6:30-33).

"Ask, and it shall be given you; seek, and ye shall find; knock, and it shall be opened unto you: for every one that asketh receiveth; and he that seeketh findeth; and to him that knocketh it shall be opened. Or what man is there of you, whom if his son ask bread, will he give him a stone? Or if he ask a fish, will he give him a serpent? If ye then, being evil, know how to give good gifts unto your children, how much more shall your Father which is in heaven give good things to them that ask him?" (Matt. 7:7-11).

Would getting rid of the carnal nature be a good thing, or a bad thing?

But we must ask—we don't get it automatically.

"If a son shall ask bread of any of you that is a father, will he give him a stone? or if he ask a fish, will he for a fish give him a serpent? Or if he shall ask an egg, will he offer him a scorpion? If ye then, being evil, know how to give good gifts unto your children: how much more shall your heavenly Father give the Holy Spirit to them that ask him?" (Luke 11:11-13).

Here in the parallel passage, we see that the Holy Ghost is one of those good things that God wants to give us. Notice that using Jesus' analogy, we are **already** God's children, when we ask for the Holy Ghost. Once again, we see that salvation and sanctification are entirely separate things. Some may note that analogies are often imperfect—but the person who accuses Jesus of using a flawed analogy would be a much bolder person than I.

The plain language of the text shows clearly and distinctly that sanctification comes at some point *after* salvation. (Of course, this assumes that we can trust Jesus' accuracy.)

"For the LORD God is a sun and shield: the LORD will give grace and glory: no good thing will he withhold from them that walk uprightly" (Psalm 84:11).

Once again: Is getting rid of the carnal nature a good thing, or a bad thing? If it's a good thing, then behold God's promise, which He cannot break, that "no good thing" will be withheld from those who obey Him.

Why is it that our opponents are so reluctant to take God at His word? They not only hurt themselves by their refusal, but they also do damage to the cause of God, by being unnecessarily flawed examples of God's grace and power.

But to get all these things that God wants to give us, there is a condition: we must hunger and thirst after righteousness.

"Blessed are they which do hunger and thirst after righteousness: for they shall be filled" (Matt. 5:6).

Jesus was not speaking of a polite curiosity. It is not a mild interest. It is a strong, perhaps even violent, longing. Holiness people pursue this with a vigor and passion that seems to alarm and/or offend many others. These same people would have accused Abraham of being a fanatic. They freely admit that it's good to hunger and thirst to a degree. But they say, "Stop! Hold up! You've gone too far. You're hungering and thirsting after righteousness *too much*." And then they accuse us of boasting about it.

How far should we go? David went very far indeed.

"Let not them that wait on thee, O Lord GOD of hosts, be ashamed for my sake: let not those that seek thee be confounded for my sake, O God of Israel. Because for thy sake I have borne reproach; shame hath covered my face. I am become a stranger unto my brethren, and an alien unto my mother's children. For the zeal of thine house hath eaten me up; and the reproaches of them that reproached thee are fallen upon me" (Psalm 69:6-9).

"I opened my mouth, and panted: for I longed for thy commandments" (Psalm 119:131).

Once we have been pardoned and rescued from ALL sin, God expects us to stay that way, not fall back into sin. We are supposed to lead pure, spotless lives.

"Who shall ascend into the hill of the LORD? or who shall stand in his holy place? He that hath clean hands, and a pure heart; who hath not lifted up his soul unto vanity, nor sworn deceitfully. He shall receive the blessing from the LORD, and righteousness from the God of his salvation" (Psalm 24:3-5). Notice that purity of heart is linked with humbleness.

"For I say unto you, That except your righteousness shall exceed the righteousness of the scribes and Pharisees, ye shall in no case enter into the kingdom of heaven" (Matt. 5:20).

"Even as Christ also loved the church, and gave himself for it; that he might sanctify and cleanse it with the washing of water by the word, that he might present it to himself a glorious church, not having spot, or wrinkle, or any such thing; but that it should be holy and without blemish" (Eph. 5:25b-27).

Sin is a blemish on the soul. Sin is unholy.

"Do all things without murmurings and disputings: that ye may be blameless and harmless, the sons of God, without rebuke, in the midst of a crooked and perverse nation, among whom ye shine as lights in the world" (Phil. 2:14, 15).

"For our conversation is in heaven; from whence also we look for the Saviour, the Lord Jesus Christ" (Phil. 3:20).

Our mode of life here on earth should partake of heavenly purity. Will we sin in Heaven? If not, then why should we sin here on earth? What excuse do we have?

"And ye are complete in him, which is the head of all principality and power: in whom also ye are circumcised with the circumcision made without hands, in putting off the body of the sins of the flesh by the circumcision of Christ" (Col. 2:10, 11).

"And the Lord make you to increase and abound in love one toward another, and toward all men, even as we do toward you: to the end he may stablish your hearts unblameable in holiness before God, even our Father, at the coming of our Lord Jesus Christ with all his saints" (I Thess. 3:12, 13).

I would call attention to this phrase: "unblamable in holiness." Sin brings blame. But holiness of heart renders us unblamable. Notice, however, that this is just in a moral sense; God does not call us to be unblamable in knowledge, in wisdom, etc. This is yet more evidence that Christian perfection is not the same as perfection in any other way.

"Abstain from all appearance of evil. And the very God of peace sanctify you wholly; and I pray God your whole spirit and soul and body be preserved blameless unto the coming of our Lord Jesus Christ. Faithful is he that calleth you, who also will do it" (I Thess. 5:22-24).

Every Christian has a measure of the Holy Ghost. This is, after all, only logical, since the Holy Ghost is a manifestation of God. Among other things, the Holy Ghost is a general teacher and guide (see John 16:8-14). But for unsanctified Christians, that is all that He is. It is also true that every Christian is sanctified in the sense of being set apart. (Although some Christians have a hard time acting as if they meant to be set apart.) This is partial, or positional, sanctification. But non-Holiness writers, when they talk about Christians being sanctified, almost invariably mean it ONLY in that sense. There are some verses in the New Testament that talk about sanctification in this sense. I do not intend to quote any of them—every opponent of the doctrine of sanctification as a second definite work can and likely will find such verses on his own.

But this passage talks about entire sanctification—"sanctified wholly." Sanctification, as a definite work, is about purifying the heart. Every Christian necessarily and automatically receives a foreshadowing of that work at regeneration, when he is cleansed from personal sins. Unfortunately, far too many Christians either don't know about the second work, or else they are more or less content with merely the foreshadowing.

Unsanctified Christians are living far below their privileges and responsibilities.

We see God's power here: "who also will do it." This is an iron-clad, first-rate promise. If a person fulfills the requirements for being sanctified wholly, God WILL do it.

"Seeing ye have purified your souls in obeying the truth through the Spirit unto unfeigned love of the brethren, see that ye love one another with a pure heart fervently: being born again, not of corruptible seed, but of incorruptible, by the word of God, which liveth and abideth for ever" (I Peter 1:22, 23).

Another way that we know that God expects us to be sinless and spotless is because we are supposed to follow Jesus' example.

"For whom he did foreknow, he also did predestinate to be conformed to the image of his Son, that he might be the firstborn among many brethren" (Romans 8:29).

So what does this mean? Let us look at Christ's character.

Obedience to God's will

"And he went a little farther, and fell on his face, and prayed, saying, O my Father, if it be possible, let this cup pass from me: nevertheless not as I will, but as thou wilt" (Matt. 26:39).

"For I came down from heaven, not to do mine own will, but the will of him that sent me" (John 6:38).

Humbleness

"Let this mind be in you, which was also in Christ Jesus: who, being in the form of God, thought it not robbery to be equal with God: but made himself of no reputation, and took upon him the form of a servant, and was made in the likeness of men: and being found in fashion as a man, he humbled himself, and became obedient unto death, even the death of the cross" (Phil. 2:5-8).

Note that this is a definite command. We are supposed to have the mind of Christ.

Unselfishness

"We then that are strong ought to bear the infirmities of the weak, and not to please ourselves. Let every one of us please his neighbour for his good to edification. For even Christ pleased not himself" (Romans 15:1-3a).

Righteousness

"Being justified freely by his grace through the redemption that is in Christ Jesus: whom God hath set forth to be a propitiation through faith in his blood, to declare his righteousness for the remission of sins that are past, through the forbearance of God; to declare, I say, at this time his righteousness: that he might be just, and the justifier of him which believeth in Jesus" (Romans 3:24-26).

"But of him are ye in Christ Jesus, who of God is made unto us wisdom, and right-eousness, and sanctification, and redemption" (I Cor. 1:30).

"For such an high priest became us, who is holy, harmless, undefiled, separate from sinners, and made higher than the heavens" (Heb. 7:26).

Purity

"For even hereunto were ye called: because Christ also suffered for us, leaving us an example, that ye should follow his steps: who did no sin, neither was guile found in his mouth: who, when he was reviled, reviled not again; when he suffered, he threatened not; but committed himself to him that judgeth righteously: who his own self bare our sins in his own body on the tree, that we, being dead to sins, should live unto righteous-ness: by whose stripes ye were healed" (I Peter 2:21-24).

Notice that we are specifically called to follow this example.

"This then is the message which we have heard of him, and declare unto you, that God is light, and in him is no darkness at all" (I John 1:5).

How, then, can we fully and perfectly fulfill Romans 8:29 if we still have the carnal nature within us? Reader, is sin darkness? Yes or no?

"And ye know that he was manifested to take away our sins; and in him is no sin" (I John 3:5).

Perfection

"Till we all come in the unity of the faith, and of the knowledge of the Son of God, unto a perfect man, unto the measure of the stature of the fulness of Christ" (Eph. 4:13).

"Though he were a Son, yet learned he obedience by the things which he suffered; and being made perfect, he became the author of eternal salvation unto all them that obey him" (Heb. 5:8, 9).

Now having gone through some of the attributes of Jesus, let us turn our attention back to Romans 8:29. "For whom he did foreknow, he also did predestinate to be con-formed to the image of his Son, that he might be the firstborn among many brethren." I hope that the reader now has a much greater understanding of what this verse entails. There are two things that I especially wish to point out: (A), it means a very great deal to be conformed to the image of Jesus; and (B), we have NO hope of even coming close without help from God.

Furthermore, I maintain, and will continue to maintain with great vigor, that the only way to completely fulfill this verse is to have every last bit of the carnal nature removed. Imagine, if you will, the futility of trying to match perfectly clean paper when all we have at our disposal is partly smudged paper. But it is clear that the Apostle John believed it is possible to imitate Jesus.

"He that saith he abideth in him ought himself also so to walk, even as he walked" (I John 2:6).

There is another thing that enters in to all this: another tool, so to speak, at our disposal. I refer to what is called the fear of the Lord.

"And Moses said unto the people, Fear not: for God is come to prove you, and that his fear may be before your faces, that ye sin not" (Exodus 20:20).

In other words, sufficient fear of God keeps us from sinning.

"The fear of the Lord is the beginning of knowledge: but fools despise wisdom and instruction" (Prov. 1:7).

Since the fear of God is related to knowledge and wisdom, I would like to take a little time to contrast the wise man and the fool. You see, fools sin. Here's an example. "Be not hasty in thy spirit to be angry: for anger resteth in the bosom of fools" (Eccl. 7:9).

A man who doesn't control anger is a fool. Anybody who gets angry is no better, at least in one sense, than an atheist. "The fool hath said in his heart, There is no God" (Psalm 14:1a).

In addition to anger, we are told that fools behave in unseemly ways in general. "Fools make a mock at sin: but among the righteous there is favour" (Prov. 14:9).

Furthermore, anger is antithetical to God's ways. "Wherefore, my beloved brethren, let every man be swift to hear, slow to speak, slow to wrath: for the wrath of man worketh not the righteousness of God" (James 1:19, 20). By contrast, a wise person knows and fears God.

"The fear of the Lord is to hate evil: pride, and arrogancy, and the evil way, and the froward mouth, do I hate" (Prov. 8:13).

How much do you really hate evil if you keep on doing it? To hear some people talk, we sound more like puppets than free moral agents.

"The fear of the Lord is the beginning of wisdom: and the knowledge of the holy is understanding" (Prov. 9:10).

"A wise man feareth, and departeth from evil: but the fool rageth, and is confident. The fear of the LORD is a fountain of life, to depart from the snares of death" (Prov. 14:16, 27).

The fear of God causes a man to depart from evil, not keep returning to it.

"He that refuseth instruction despiseth his own soul: but he that heareth reproof getteth understanding. The fear of the Lord is the instruction of wisdom; and before honour is humility" (Prov. 15:32, 33).

"By mercy and truth iniquity is purged: and by the fear of the Lord men depart from evil" (Prov. 16:6).

"Let us hear the conclusion of the whole matter: Fear God, and keep his commandments: for this is the whole duty of man" (Eccl. 12:13).

Once we have a referential fear of God, then we can grow in the knowledge of God. The two things are linked; refer back to Prov. 1:7 above.

"Grace and peace be multiplied unto you through the knowledge of God, and of Jesus our Lord, according as his divine power hath given unto us all things that pertain unto life and godliness, through the knowledge of him that hath called us to glory and virtue" (II Peter 1:2, 3).

This is the operating factor for the increase of grace and peace in our lives. The knowledge of God refers partly to simply "knowing" God—i.e., being saved. But I believe that it also refers to the closeness of our walk with God. The degree of closeness is, in many cases, the determining factor in our knowledge of God's standards and how He wants us to live our lives. Those of us who have grown up in the Holiness movement have sat under preaching by people who were deeply spiritual, and thereby we gained theoretical knowledge how we should live. But such knowledge doesn't become alive to us until we get saved ourselves.

I would like to point out in this passage that God has given us ALL things that "pertain unto life and godliness." Why don't the opponents of Holiness doctrine take this literally? The carnal nature is death and darkness: it most emphatically does NOT "pertain unto life and godliness." Therefore, it logically follows that the removal of the carnal nature **does** pertain to those things. And since this passage declares that God gives us **everything** that pertains to this, the removal of the carnal nature is most certainly included. I do not understand why our opponents refuse to take God at His word. Instead of heeding His promises, they refuse to accept God's gift of heart-holiness, and then they go through life bewailing their struggles with carnality.

"Yea, if thou criest after knowledge, and liftest up thy voice for understanding; if thou seekest her as silver, and searchest for her as for hid treasures; then shalt thou understand the fear of the LORD, and find the knowledge of God. For the LORD giveth wisdom: out of his mouth cometh knowledge and understanding. He layeth up sound wisdom for the righteous: he is a buckler to them that walk uprightly. He keepeth the paths of judgment, and preserveth the way of his saints. Then shalt thou understand righteousness, and judgment, and equity; yea, every good path" (Prov. 2:3-9).

"Hear the word of the LORD, ye children of Israel: for the LORD hath a controversy with the inhabitants of the land, because there is no truth, nor mercy, nor knowledge of God in the land" (Hosea 4:1).

"For this cause we also, since the day we heard it, do not cease to pray for you, and to desire that ye might be filled with the knowledge of his will in all wisdom and spiritual understanding; that ye might walk worthy of the Lord unto all pleasing, being fruitful in every good work, and increasing in the knowledge of God; strengthened with all might, according to his glorious power, unto all patience and longsuffering with joyfulness" (Col. 1:9-11).

What happens when we don't have the knowledge, or we treat it carelessly and lose it?
"Therefore my people are gone into captivity, because they have no knowledge: and their honourable men are famished, and their multitude dried up with thirst" (Isaiah 5:13).

The last part of this verse points us back to the section on abundance. Go back and re-read Isaiah 44:3, where God promises to pour water (a symbol of the Holy Ghost) on those who are thirsty, and John 7:37-39, where Jesus tells us how to acquire a plenteous, never-ending flow of water.

"For if after they have escaped the pollutions of the world through the knowledge of the Lord and Saviour Jesus Christ, they are again entangled therein, and overcome, the latter end is worse with them than the beginning" (II Peter 2:20).

But this doesn't have to happen. God has plenty of power to keep and protect His followers.

Chapter 14

God's Power

Opponents of Holiness doctrine, almost to a man, have a shockingly low, shallow view of God's power. Oh sure, they admit in the abstract that God has plenty of power: but when it comes to concrete, specific things in their own lives, they just don't seem to understand how God's power could apply to their own lives.

I'm going to re-quote something, because it illustrates this so well.

"Q. 149. *Is any man able perfectly to keep the commandments of God?*

"A. No man is able, either of himself, or by any grace received in this life, perfectly to keep the commandments of God; but doth daily break them in thought, word, and deed" (Westminster Larger Catechism of 1647).

Notice this: "by any grace received in this life." The authors of this document clearly could not conceive of God's power being able to overcome sin in their own lives.

This attitude is very prevalent in our own day as well. Every time that a person claims that it is impossible to have carnality removed, and/or that it is impossible to live a completely sinless life, what he is really saying (whether he realizes it or not) is that it is impossible for God's grace and power to *completely* change his life, and turn him 100% from sin to holiness. But the Bible refutes this view.

"He will keep the feet of his saints, and the wicked shall be silent in darkness; for by strength shall no man prevail" (I Sam. 2:9).

"As for God, his way is perfect; the word of the Lord is tried: he is a buckler to all them that trust in him. For who is God, save the Lord? and who is a rock, save our God? God is my strength and power: and he maketh my way perfect" (II Sam. 22:31-33).

"For the eyes of the Lord run to and fro throughout the whole earth, to shew himself strong in the behalf of them whose heart is perfect toward him" (II Chron. 16:9a). Once again we see the theme of heart perfection.

"Cast thy burden upon the Lord, and he shall sustain thee: he shall never suffer the righteous to be moved" (Psalm 55:22).

Notice that this refers to attacks from the outside: "be moved"—acted upon by an outside agency. We can still move ourselves out of God's will and blessing by choosing to sin.

"When I said, My foot slippeth; thy mercy, O Lord, held me up. But the Lord is my defence; and my God is the rock of my refuge" (Psalm 94:18, 22).

"Every word of God is pure: he is a shield unto them that put their trust in him" (Prov. 30:5).

If we cannot help sinning, what does that say about the quality of God's shield?

This verse also talks about God's purity. How well can we serve a pure God, if we still have a measure of impurity in our hearts? Don't you think that we could serve God better, more thoroughly, and more effectively with a perfectly pure heart?

"Now our Lord Jesus Christ himself, and God, even our Father, which hath loved us, and hath given us everlasting consolation and good hope through grace, comfort your hearts, and stablish you in every good word and work" (II Thess. 2:16, 17).

If we are established in **everything** that is good, then the presence, love, and power of God will fill our lives to the point where they exclude everything that isn't good—including the remnants of the carnal nature.

"But the Lord is faithful, who shall stablish you, and keep you from evil" (II Thess. 3:3)

Mark this well: God is able to keep us "FROM evil." In other words, if we commit sin, not only is it our fault, but also we deliberately cast aside the power of God to keep and protect us. This verse promises that God will establish us in lives of holiness and purity. But we must want it, and do our part to both get and keep it. God is a perfect gentleman; if we choose to sin, He will not override our choice.

"Blessed be the God and Father of our Lord Jesus Christ, which according to his abundant mercy hath begotten us again unto a lively hope by the resurrection of Jesus Christ from the dead, to an inheritance incorruptible, and undefiled, and that fadeth not away, reserved in heaven for you, who are kept by the power of God through faith unto salvation ready to be revealed in the last time" (I Peter 1:3-5).

Pay close attention to verse 5: "kept"; "**kept** by the power of God." Here again the mighty power of God is brought to our attention. Anybody who believes that Christians cannot keep from sinning is either actively spurning the power of God, or (at best) has a very low, shallow view of what God's power can do for a person.

"Now unto him that is able to keep you from falling, and to present you faultless before the presence of his glory with exceeding joy, to the only wise God our Saviour, be glory and majesty, dominion and power, both now and ever. Amen" (Jude 24, 25).

If God is able to keep us from falling back into sin, then why does it happen? Because we *choose* to sin. The fault is entirely ours.

This points back to the definition of sin, among other things. Our opponents claim that sinning is inevitable. If we truly cannot avoid sinning, and if God has the power to keep us from falling, then the only possible conclusion is that He **deliberately lets** us fall!

Speaking of the power of God, He has plenty of power to do the work of sanctification.

"He sent his word, and healed them, and delivered them from their destructions" (Psalm 107:20).

I would like to draw attention to the phrase "delivered from." To hear a lot of people talk, one would think that God just sort of left us to muddle through on our own. Not so. God has both the power and desire to break the power and hold of sin in every aspect of our lives.

But a lot of people talk like they don't have a choice in the matter.

Let's take a trip of the imagination to a place where slavery still exists. You are a slave on the farm of Mr. A_____, a prosperous farmer. However, he treats his slaves extremely poorly. After some time, Mr. B_____, the neighboring farmer, buys you. He tells you that he treats his slaves much better, and the work load is lighter.

At first, everything is like you were told it would be. In fact, you would gladly spend the rest of your life there. But one grim day, farmer A. comes into farmer B.'s field, where you are working, and drags you off to work in his field again. "Did B. sell me back to you?" "No, I just decided that you should work for me today." After nightfall, you escape back to B.'s farm. The next day, the same thing happens again. The third day, as A. comes toward you, you see B. nearby. "At last!" you think. "Finally this will stop!" But to your shock and horror, B. does nothing as A. drags you away.

The next morning, you get a chance to ask farmer B. what's going on. He tells you that he is aware of the situation, but for various reasons, he is not able to stop farmer A.

In this illustration, farmer B. is God. Farmer A. is the Devil. There is a word for people who are forced on a daily basis to do things they don't want to do—"slave." To hear many opponents of Holiness doctrine talk about it, they talk like they don't even have a choice of sinning or not sinning—that old slave-master, the Devil, drags them back into sin every day, regardless of how they feel about it. And to make matters worse, God doesn't seem to have the power to do anything about it. These people are left to fight sin and the Devil on their own.

I'm sure that a lot of our opponents will be horrified by this analogy. Such people should stop and take a hard look at their doctrine, and really think about what it says. In actuality, God can and will intervene in our lives, and help us to overcome sin, if we ask Him to.

"I will also save you from all your uncleannesses" (Ezekiel 36:29a).

Mark this well: "ALL your uncleannesses." Once again we see that little but very important word "all." God promises to save us from ALL forms of uncleanness; this, by definition, includes the remains of carnality in the saved but unsanctified person's heart.

"But Jesus beheld them, and said unto them, With men this is impossible; but with God all things are possible" (Matt. 19:26).

Virtually every single opponent of the second work, regardless of his exact theology, sings from the same song: "It's impossible to be delivered from the carnal nature in this life."

Oops—it looks like Jesus says something different. I'm not sure exactly who should take responsibility for this mix-up of ideas, but I know it's not God.

"Now unto him that is able to do exceeding abundantly above all that we ask or think, according to the power that worketh in us, unto him be glory in the church by Christ Jesus throughout all ages, world without end. Amen" (Eph. 3:20, 21).

Our opponents should pay very close attention to this. They don't think that getting rid of carnality is possible, and therefore they don't ask God to remove it. But God has a message for such people: He has the power to do more—abundantly more—than they "ask or think."

"Who hath delivered us from the power of darkness, and hath translated us into the kingdom of his dear Son: and you, that were sometime alienated and enemies in your mind by wicked works, yet now hath he reconciled in the body of his flesh through death, to present you holy and unblameable and unreproveable in his sight: if ye continue in the faith grounded and settled, and be not moved away from the hope of the gospel, which ye have heard, and which was preached to every creature which is under heaven; whereof I Paul am made a minister; whom we preach, warning every man, and teaching every man in all wisdom; that we may present every man perfect in Christ Jesus" (Col. 1:13, 21-23, 28).

Verse 13 talks about the "power of darkness." Do you suppose that there might—just might—be some degree of darkness in carnality? After all, it's the thing that weakens us in our spiritual battles; it urges us to give in to temptation; regardless of the situation, it always takes the side of Satan. Some people might think it wild and reckless to to call it "darkness"; but, all in all, I think that it's a fairly safe assumption.

But (being serious again) this verse tells us that God *delivers* us from that power. Does God squelch or suppress carnality? No; He removes it entirely. A perfect God can be depended on to provide a perfect deliverance.

I would also like to remark on verse 28. Notice that he talks about preaching, etc. as things to be done *now*, and thereby get people perfected (and ready to present) *now*.

Jesus came to break the chains of sin in every respect. There is more evidence in the Bible that this is the correct view. God has tremendous power, and He strongly desires to use it on behalf of His followers.

"He that committeth sin is of the devil; for the devil sinneth from the beginning. For this purpose the Son of God was manifested, that he might destroy the works of the devil" (I John 3:8).

Surely we can all agree that the sin nature is one of the "works of the Devil." I have a good imagination, but I have a hard time imagining anything else that it could be. But behold—we see here the inspired Word plainly declaring that Jesus came to destroy those works. This is a definite, all-inclusive statement. No exceptions are listed. Let's break this down.

What did Jesus come to do?

To destroy.

And what did He come to destroy?

The works of the Devil.

Therefore, it logically follows that He came to destroy the remaining sin nature in a Christian.

Speaking of the works of the Devil, one thing that he sometimes does is counterfeit God's work, or at least tries to. This is yet another way we know that the second work of grace exists, because Satan tried to counterfeit it in Judas.

"He then lying on Jesus' breast saith unto him, Lord, who is it? Jesus answered, He it is, to whom I shall give a sop, when I have dipped it. And when he had dipped the sop, he gave it to Judas Iscariot, the son of Simon. And after the sop Satan entered into him. Then said Jesus unto him, That thou doest, do quickly" (John 13:25-27).

At some point before the Last Supper, Judas had made the decision of betrayal. In other words, by the time they sat down to eat (if not long before), Judas was a follower of Satan. But lo!—we see a terrible marvel. Matthew Henry says, "Judas was all along a devil (ch. vi. 70), a son of perdition, but now Satan gained a more full possession of him, had a *more abundant entrance* into him... Though the devil is in every wicked man that does his works (Eph. ii. 2), yet sometimes he enters more manifestly and more power-fully than at other times, when he puts them upon some enormous wickedness, which humanity and natural conscience startle at."

Here we see, in Judas, Satan trying to duplicate or counterfeit the second work of grace.

Some people may scoff at the idea that the Devil could or would preemptively counterfeit something. But he's done it before. The Egyptian goddess Isis was in part a preemptive counterfeit of the Virgin Mary. Isis was married, not a virgin, but neverthe-less one of her titles was "mother of god." And Egyptian art sometimes portrays her as nursing her son Horus in a manner that is very reminiscent of paintings of Mary nursing Jesus.

Various ancient gods and goddesses were sometimes called "bringer of light"—some-what like Jesus is portrayed in John 1:5.

And then there is a certain "false counterfeit," for lack of a better phrase. Many people believe that the Mesopotamian goddess Ishtar is the origin of the word "Easter." This connection does not actually exist, but many people believe that it does.

In addition, many people believe that the story of Noah and the Flood was plagiarized from Mesopotamian stories about a flood—stories that were written down centuries before Moses was even born.

So in short, this preemptive counterfeiting is fairly successful. A significant number of people believe that many Christian symbols and practices are plagiarized from pagan sources. Thus Satan was able, in advance, to discredit Christianity in the eyes of many.

Going back to the subject of God's power: as I mentioned in chapter 9, our opponents seem to have a semi-Gnostic view of the body.

However, the God that made the body has power to overcome its shortcomings.

"And Moses said unto the Lord, O my Lord, I am not eloquent, neither heretofore, nor since thou hast spoken unto thy servant: but I am slow of speech, and of a slow tongue. And the Lord said unto him, Who hath made man's mouth? or who maketh the dumb, or deaf, or the seeing, or the blind? have not I the Lord? Now therefore go, and I will be with thy mouth, and teach thee what thou shalt say. And he said, O my Lord, send, I pray thee, by the hand of him whom thou wilt send. And the anger of the Lord was kindled against Moses, and he said, Is not Aaron the Levite thy brother? I know that he can speak well. And also, behold, he cometh forth to meet thee: and when he seeth thee, he will be glad in his heart" (Exodus 4:10-14).

Moses rejected God's help because of unbelief. This is similar to the attitude of our opponents. They agree in the abstract that God has power; but when it comes down to their own lives, they don't call upon that power. And then, like Moses in verse 13, they try to disguise their failures with pious platitudes about "God's will."

The physical body and its desires/appetites can certainly be a source of temptation. But God has power to help us resist temptation; He has power to sustain and keep us.

"And lead us not into temptation, but deliver us from evil: For thine is the kingdom, and the power, and the glory, for ever. Amen" (Matt. 6:13).

The Devil leads us into temptation; but God delivers us from evil. This includes, but is not limited to, the remnants of carnality. Anybody who believes that it is impossible to be delivered from carnality and/or that it is impossible to live without sinning has no business praying this prayer; it is a mockery of sacred things to pray for something that you don't believe can be done.

"Wherefore let him that thinketh he standeth take heed lest he fall. There hath no temptation taken you but such as is common to man: but God is faithful, who will not suffer you to be tempted above that ye are able; but will with the temptation also make a way to escape, that ye may be able to bear it" (I Cor. 10:12, 13).

Mark this well: God will make a way for us to escape any temptation that is too much for us. This means that if we yield to temptation, it is strictly our fault; God will not command us to do something without providing help to obey.

There have been a few times when I felt that a temptation was about to overwhelm me, despite my best efforts to resist. In desperation, I cried out to God for help; and— poof!—the temptation simply disappeared. This has happened more than once.

"The Lord knoweth how to deliver the godly out of temptations" (II Peter 2:9a).

"Satan has gone to great lengths to blind Christians to the complete work of Christ. Many see Him only as the sacrifice for their sins; they don't realize that in receiving His very life and the crucifixion of the old self we can be as free from sin as Christ is...

"One of the problems associated with unbelief is its tendency to protect God. By that I mean if God has spoken on a particular subject, and yet we have not been able to experience it, we cannot admit that the fault lies within us, but neither can we let the blame lie with God. We must, therefore, whitewash what God has spoken and give it an alternate meaning, thus protecting God and at the same time freeing ourselves from the accusation that we might be failing. This is especially true when it comes to the supernatural aspects of our relationship with God" (Michael Wells; *Sidetracked in the Wilderness*).

We have now seen several verses about God's power. As mentioned earlier, our opponents seem to have an astoundingly low, shallow view both of what God can do and what He wants to do for His children.

"Jesus answered and said unto them, Ye do err, not knowing the scriptures, nor the power of God" (Matt. 22:29).

Some verses specifically mention God's power to deliver us from all forms of sin and uncleanness; others talk about His power to keep us from evil, once we have been delivered; others tell us of His power to establish us in lives of faith, purity, and love. So the question then becomes—can we, or can we not, take God at His word? Can we trust what He says, or not?

"Having a form of godliness, but denying the power thereof" (II Tim. 3:5a).

Saying that Christians can't help sinning is another form or version of this verse. Opponents of the second work of grace have a form of godliness, but they deny a large part of its power. Indeed, they go farther, and deny that ANY form of godliness has the power to raise us up above sin, and give us the victory over it on a daily basis.

There are many people who think that we become totally purified only upon death; that being purified is impossible while we are here on earth. I have a simple question for such people. *What is so special about death?* Why (in their opinion) must we wait until then for absolute purity of heart? These people insist with great vehemence that being perfectly pure while here on earth is flat-out impossible; but very, very few of them even *attempt* anything more than a very weak, cursory explanation as to why. Many don't even do that much. They talk as though physical death has a greater cleansing power than Jesus' blood.

Would anyone say that we have to wait until we die in order to receive the work of salvation? I would certainly hope not. The idea is both absurd and unscriptural. Then why do people say that we have to wait for death to get our hearts purified?

It is utterly astonishing to me how so many people fail to recognize God's power.

"For God speaketh once, yea twice, yet man perceiveth it not" (Job 33:14).

"God hath spoken once; twice have I heard this; that power belongeth unto God" (Psalm 62:11).

It is my opinion that these verses are symbolic, as well. We have two different verses; each one mentioning how God speaks twice. There are two separate works of grace; yet non-Holiness Christians "perceive it not."

The Church as a whole, and many individual Christians, would be so much better off if people would just pay attention to what God says, and actually believe His Word. Reader, if you have gone through life up to now, believing that you just have to muddle along with carnality, then I beg you—I implore you—start taking God at His Word!

If you really do believe that God is all-powerful, then do God the courtesy of actually ACTING like you believe it!

Chapter 15

Actions of the Sanctified Life

Entire sanctification touches or influences virtually every aspect of the Christian life. For example, we are commanded to love God without any limit or restriction.

"And thou shalt love the LORD thy God with all thine heart, and with all thy soul, and with all thy might" (Deut. 6:5).

Are we allowed an opportunity to slide by with partial devotion? No. But here is a question for the reader. How well do people really love God, if they disappoint Him daily by sinning in thought, word, and deed? How strong is such love?

Here is another question. If part of the Christian's heart still has carnality in it, then how exactly can such a person obey this command to love God with ALL his heart? Can carnality love God?

"And the LORD thy God will circumcise thine heart, and the heart of thy seed, to love the LORD thy God with all thine heart, and with all thy soul, that thou mayest live" (Deut. 30:6).

Circumcision is a "cutting off." All forms and degrees of sin must be cut off from the heart before it is fit to enter Heaven.

I am not claiming that a person must be sanctified to enter Heaven. Salvation is all that is necessary for that. Sanctification is for our benefit, here on earth.

Now some people may point out (and quite accurately) that there must be some process by which God removes the carnal nature from the soul at some indefinable moment between the point of death and the point at which the soul enters Heaven. We know by simple logic that there must be some non-purgatorial process for doing this, for we are told that sin and its effects will not be allowed into Heaven (I Cor. 15:50-54; Rev. 21:4, 8, 27; 22:3).

To this I reply, with child-like simplicity (Matt. 18:3; Mark 10:15), with a very simple question.

Why wait?

When you KNOW that there is waiting for you the delight of an existence that is untainted by sin in the heart, why in the name of common sense would you wait until you get to Heaven to receive it?

There is a connection between loving God, and keeping His commandments.

"And now, Israel, what doth the LORD thy God require of thee, but to fear the LORD thy God, to walk in all his ways, and to love him, and to serve the LORD thy God with all thy heart and with all thy soul, to keep the commandments of the LORD, and his statutes, which I command thee this day for thy good?" (Deut. 10:12, 13).

When God speaks to us here on earth, and gives us a definite command, you can take it to the bank that there is some way, somehow, to fulfill that command. There is no need to ignore it, and no need to explain it away. Find out how to obey it, and then do so.

Notice, as well, that God says He gives us these commands for our own good. This includes the commands to be spotless and sinless.

"Sanctify yourselves therefore, and be ye holy: for I am the LORD your God. And ye shall keep my statutes, and do them: I am the LORD which sanctify you" (Lev. 20:7, 8).

Man has a part, and God has a part. We must want to be holy, and keep God's commandments. In return, God will help us do so.

"Ye shall observe to do therefore as the LORD your God hath commanded you: ye shall not turn aside to the right hand or to the left" (Deut. 5:32).

"Ye shall walk after the LORD your God, and fear him, and keep his commandments, and obey his voice, and ye shall serve him, and cleave unto him" (Deut. 13:4).

The word translated "cleave" is Strong's #1692: it means "abide fast, follow close (hard after), ... pursue hard." But sin produces separation from God. How can we cleave to God as we should if we still have a measure of separation from Him in our hearts?

"But whoso hearkeneth unto me shall dwell safely, and shall be quiet from fear of evil" (Prov. 1:33).

The last part of this verse means (among other things) that somebody who fully obeys God will not be troubled with the carnal nature, because God will remove it.

"The disciple is not above his master: but every one that is perfect shall be as his master. For a good tree bringeth not forth corrupt fruit; neither doth a corrupt tree bring forth good fruit. For every tree is known by his own fruit. For of thorns men do not gather figs, nor of a bramble bush gather they grapes. A good man out of the good treasure of his heart bringeth forth that which is good; and an evil man out of the evil treasure of his heart bringeth forth that which is evil: for of the abundance of the heart his mouth speaketh. And why call ye me, Lord, Lord, and do not the things which I say?" (Luke 6:40, 43-46).

If there is one thing that every single Christian, regardless of creed or denomination, can agree on, it would be that the Bible contains a vast number of warnings against sin. So if we don't want to hear the question in this passage addressed to us personally, the simple thing (at least in theory) would be—DON'T SIN! Now I fully realize that virtually everybody hasn't found it that simple in practice. But that is our fault, not God's.

I fear that many Christians have never entered into God's presence deeply enough to really FEEL what God thinks of sin. Oh sure, they talk about how terrible it is, but sometimes one gets the sense that their knowledge of sin's nature is partly abstract. It's like they have somehow forgotten how they felt when they were seeking salvation. I have heard multiple people speak of sin in almost a slightly-joking way. Sure, they recognize the fact that they shouldn't sin. But they seem to have a touch of the attitude "Everybody does it." And these were people that I had good reason to believe were real Christians! But their consecration to God was terribly shallow in some respects.

It is EXTREMELY unlikely that we will have or keep a deep consecration to God without receiving the second work of grace. At best, it's likely to be a medium consecration.

"If ye love me, keep my commandments. He that hath my commandments, and keepeth them, he it is that loveth me: and he that loveth me shall be loved of my Father, and I will love him, and will manifest myself to him. He that loveth me not keepeth not my sayings: and the word which ye hear is not mine, but the Father's which sent me" (John 14:15, 21, 24).

The Bible is very clear that we are supposed to avoid all sin; some of the commands that we are expected to obey if we love God deal with this issue.

"Afterward Jesus findeth him in the temple, and said unto him, Behold, thou art made whole: sin no more, lest a worse thing come unto thee" (John 5:14).

Notice that Jesus did not say that this man could not sin any more in the sense of somehow being incapable of sinning; if that were the case, such a warning would be utterly pointless. By the same token, if this man could not avoid sinning, then again, Jesus' warning would be pointless. The Bible contains many examples of God warning people, "IF you choose to do such-and-such, then expect a certain thing as a consequence."

"When Jesus had lifted up himself, and saw none but the woman, he said unto her, Woman, where are those thine accusers? hath no man condemned thee? She said, No man, Lord. And Jesus said unto her, Neither do I condemn thee: go, and sin no more" (John 8:10, 11).

Notice that this is a definite command in verse 11: "sin no more." Jesus expected her to change her life completely. Opponents of sanctification as a second work of grace act as though Jesus said to her something like, "rejoice that your sins are forgiven, but continue to sin in thought, word, and deed every day." Or perhaps they think that He said, "struggle against sin, but you will fail on a regular basis."

I can't help feeling that there is a great gulf between what Jesus taught and what proponents of a sinning religion teach.

"Jesus answered them, Verily, verily, I say unto you, Whosoever committeth sin is the servant of sin" (John 8:34).

The word "committeth" is Strong's #4160 (also found in I John 3:8): Strong contrasts this with #4238, which means "perform repeatedly or habitually"; he says that #4160 "[properly] refers to a single act." In other words, if you commit even a single act of sin, you are the servant of sin.

"Unto you first God, having raised up his Son Jesus, sent him to bless you, in turning away every one of you from his iniquities" (Acts 3:26).

I see no hint in this verse that it is God's will, desire, or plan for us to return to sin after turning away from it.

"Or despisest thou the riches of his goodness and forbearance and longsuffering; not knowing that the goodness of God leadeth thee to repentance? But after thy hardness and impenitent heart treasurest up unto thyself wrath against the day of wrath and revelation of the righteous judgment of God; who will render to every man according to his deeds: to them who by patient continuance in well doing seek for glory and honour and immortality, eternal life: but unto them that are contentious, and do not obey the truth, but obey unrighteousness, indignation and wrath, tribulation and anguish, upon every soul of man that doeth evil, of the Jew first, and also of the Gentile; but glory, honour, and peace, to every man that worketh good, to the Jew first, and also to the Gentile" (Romans 2:4-10).

Notice in verse 8 that disobedience to God's truth is directly connected with obeying sin. You serve whatever it is that you obey.

"Awake to righteousness, and sin not" (I Cor. 15:34a).

This seems like a very simple, straight-forward command. But most of our opponents studiously ignore the existence of this verse. There are a few who mention this verse, or similar ones, but they just wave them away: "sinning is inevitable, so this doesn't actually mean what it says."

"Be ye therefore followers of God, as dear children; and walk in love, as Christ also hath loved us, and hath given himself for us an offering and a sacrifice to God for a sweetsmelling savour. But fornication, and all uncleanness, or covetousness, let it not be once named among you, as becometh saints; neither filthiness, nor foolish talking, nor jesting, which are not convenient: but rather giving of thanks. For this ye know, that no whoremonger, nor unclean person, nor covetous man, who is an idolater, hath any inheritance in the kingdom of Christ and of God. For ye were sometimes darkness, but now are ye light in the Lord: walk as children of light: (for the fruit of the Spirit is in all goodness and righteousness and truth;) proving what is acceptable unto the Lord. And have no fellowship with the unfruitful works of darkness, but rather reprove them" (Eph. 5:1-5, 8-11).

"Nevertheless the foundation of God standeth sure, having this seal, The Lord knoweth them that are his. And, Let every one that nameth the name of Christ depart from iniquity. But in a great house there are not only vessels of gold and of silver, but also of wood and of earth; and some to honour, and some to dishonour. If a man therefore purge himself from these, he shall be a vessel unto honour, sanctified, and meet for the master's use, and prepared unto every good work" (II Tim. 2:19-21).

Pay attention to this command: "depart from" iniquity; not "depart from it but then return to it over and over."

Refer back to John 14:15, 21, 24 in the section above. Combined with the verses we have just seen, wherein God commands us to avoid sin, the meaning is clear. Anybody who loves God in the way that he should **will** refrain from **all** sin. No excuses are permitted.

Why are we supposed to depart from sin? To answer this, let's take a look at what God thinks of people who commit sin.

"I have hated the congregation of evil doers; and will not sit with the wicked" (Psalm 26:5).

The internet makes checking other translations of the Bible very easy. Out of 50 different translations (not counting the KJV), 33 use either those exact words or very similar wording.

Many of the biggest and most strenuous objections to this doctrine come from Calvinists. So let's be generous, and examine this verse from a Calvinistic viewpoint. Since they believe in eternal security, it makes no difference to the Christian's final destination whether he sins or not. But notice—the first part of this verse makes no mention of a person's *moral* state! It does not talk about unregenerated sinners—those who ARE evil. It only talks about those who DO evil! David—a man after God's own heart (I Sam. 13:14)—says here that he hates the company of such people, in much the same language that God uses when He talks about hating sin. Therefore this verse condemns those who believe that Christians *must* sin.

I quoted Romans 2:6 just a bit above, but I wish to re-quote it here: "Who will render to every man according to his deeds."

"The face of the Lord is against them that do evil, to cut off the remembrance of them from the earth" (Psalm 34:16).

This is a very solemn warning. Again pay attention to the fact that this verse (speaking from a Calvinistic perspective) does not address whether such a person is saved, or claims to be saved, or anything like that. It simply addresses, without any distinction, what people **do**.

There are a vast number of people who think that they can do ("do evil") anything they want, and yet God will still let them into Heaven. For some people, this attitude takes the form "God loves me too much to punish me"; for others, it takes the form "I can't lose eternal life; therefore any punishment I get will only be temporary." This verse tells us that such is not the case. This attitude, regardless of what form it takes, is shown to be incorrect.

"But your iniquities have separated between you and your God, and your sins have hid his face from you, that he will not hear. For your hands are defiled with blood, and your fingers with iniquity; your lips have spoken lies, your tongue hath muttered perverseness. None calleth for justice, nor any pleadeth for truth: they trust in vanity, and speak lies; they conceive mischief, and bring forth iniquity. They hatch cockatrice' eggs, and weave the spider's web: he that eateth of their eggs dieth, and that which is crushed breaketh out into a viper. Their webs shall not become garments, neither shall they cover themselves with their works: their works are works of iniquity, and the act of violence is in their hands. Their feet run to evil, and they make haste to shed innocent blood: their thoughts are thoughts of iniquity; wasting and destruction are in their paths. The way of peace they know not; and there is no judgment in their goings: they have made them crooked paths: whosoever goeth therein shall not know peace" (Isaiah 59:2-8).

"And there is none that calleth upon thy name, that stirreth up himself to take hold of thee: for thou hast hid thy face from us, and hast consumed us, because of our iniquities" (Isaiah 64:7).

"They come to fight with the Chaldeans, but it is to fill them with the dead bodies of men, whom I have slain in mine anger and in my fury, and for all whose wickedness I have hid my face from this city" (Jer. 33:5).

"And this is the condemnation, that light is come into the world, and men loved darkness rather than light, because their deeds were evil. For every one that doeth evil hateth the light, neither cometh to the light, lest his deeds should be reproved. But he that doeth truth cometh to the light, that his deeds may be made manifest, that they are wrought in God" (John 3:19-21).

Once again, take note that John talks about what people **do**. He does not address any claims (either true or false) of being saved.

Notice what John says here: that evil doers HATE the light. And remember: God **IS** light.

In other words, the claim that we can't avoid sinning is really another way of stating that we can't avoid hating God! This should show everybody what a terrible thing that claim is.

I'm pretty certain that the previous paragraph will upset some people. Such people should stop and think, and then re-read what John says.

"For the eyes of the Lord are over the righteous, and his ears are open unto their prayers: but the face of the Lord is against them that do evil" (I Peter 3:12).

It should be abundantly obvious that Peter talks about two different classes of people—mutually exclusive classes. The righteous are totally separate from those who do evil. Once again, we see that the Bible teaches the exact opposite of a sinning religion.

There is a saying that used to be quite common, but is no longer used in much of the church world today. My grandmother grew up under preachers who did not hesitate to talk about "the exceeding sinfulness of sin." (This comes from Romans 7:13.) This saying may sound odd to many ears today, but every Christian should think about this sort of thing. I greatly fear that many Christians have an exceedingly shallow view of just how bad sin is. This is actually poor terminology; "bad" doesn't really even begin to cover the nature of sin. There is a stupendously great gulf between the holiness and purity of God on one hand, and the nature of even a "small" sin on the other. And yet some Christians insist that a Christian cannot possibly keep from sinning! This is a terrible (and terribly effective) deception from Satan. In my opinion, anybody who maintains this view cannot possibly have a correct conception of how exceedingly awful sin really is. They may have a partial conception, and they may honestly, genuinely struggle against sin, but if they have ever truly seen sin through the eyes of God, they have somehow forgotten it.

Someone who has been saved, but backslides, is in an even worse state (at least in some respects) than someone who was never saved at all. One reason for this is because the Church is the betrothed spiritual bride of Christ.

"In my Father's house are many mansions: if it were not so, I would have told you. I go to prepare a place for you. And if I go and prepare a place for you, I will come again, and receive you unto myself; that where I am, there ye may be also" (John 14:2, 3).

Jesus was talking to the disciples. This is when Jesus, in effect, proposed marriage to the Church. The language He used was precisely the language that a Jewish man of that time would use after asking a woman to marry him.

A Jewish engagement of that era can be thought of as roughly halfway between an engagement and marriage in our time and culture. An engaged couple was not allowed to have sexual relations; that was supposed to wait until marriage. But unlike our culture, if an engaged person had sex with somebody else, it was considered adultery, not fornication.

The equivalent of marriage between God and the Church will not take place until we all get to Heaven. We are waiting for our Bridegroom to come back, and take us to His Father's house, just like a Jewish man of Jesus' time would do.

"Then shall the kingdom of heaven be likened unto ten virgins, which took their lamps, and went forth to meet the bridegroom. And at midnight there was a cry made, Behold, the bridegroom cometh; go ye out to meet him. And while they went to buy, the bridegroom came; and they that were ready went in with him to the marriage: and the door was shut" (Matt. 25:1, 6, 10).

"Let us be glad and rejoice, and give honour to him: for the marriage of the Lamb is come, and his wife hath made herself ready. And to her was granted that she should be arrayed in fine linen, clean and white: for the fine linen is the righteousness of saints. And he saith unto me, Write, Blessed are they which are called unto the marriage supper of the Lamb. And he saith unto me, These are the true sayings of God" (Rev. 19:7-9).

But in the meantime, every time we sin, we commit spiritual adultery against God. This is one reason why backsliding is such a serious thing.

"And the LORD said unto Moses, Behold, thou shalt sleep with thy fathers; and this people will rise up, and go a-whoring after the gods of the strangers of the land, whither they go to be among them, and will forsake me, and break my covenant which I have made with them. Then my anger shall be kindled against them in that day, and I will forsake them, and I will hide my face from them, and they shall be devoured, and many evils and troubles shall befall them; so that they will say in that day, Are not these evils come upon us, because our God is not among us? And I will surely hide my face in that day for all the evils which they shall have wrought, in that they are turned unto other gods" (Deut. 31:16-18).

Those who do evil will never prosper. Notice in verse 17 that God says He will forsake such people.

"For, lo, they that are far from thee shall perish: thou hast destroyed all them that go a-whoring from thee" (Psalm 73:27).

"Ye adulterers and adulteresses, know ye not that the friendship of the world is enmity with God? whosoever therefore will be a friend of the world is the enemy of God" (James 4:4).

Sometimes the Bible uses the deeds that a person does as a proxy for his moral state; i.e., saved or unsaved.

"Even a child is known by his doings, whether his work be pure, and whether it be right" (Prov. 20:11).

"Ye shall know them by their fruits. Do men gather grapes of thorns, or figs of thistles? Even so every good tree bringeth forth good fruit; but a corrupt tree bringeth forth evil fruit. A good tree cannot bring forth evil fruit, neither can a corrupt tree bring forth good fruit. Every tree that bringeth not forth good fruit is hewn down, and cast into the fire. Wherefore by their fruits ye shall know them. Not every one that saith unto me, Lord, Lord, shall enter into the kingdom of heaven; but he that doeth the will of my Father which is in heaven" (Matt. 7:16-21).

This is not salvation by works; rather, it is a rebuttal to the idea that "what's on the inside is all that counts." Technically speaking, that idea is correct; but many people use it as an excuse to avoid doing the things that God wants them to do. "The truth will out"; whatever is on the inside of a person WILL eventually show itself through the works that they do. If our inner life is righteous, it will invariably show itself through righteous works. If our inner life is sinful, our works will be sinful, even though many such people try to excuse or deny the sinfulness shown. Thus, what is on the outside DOES matter; not necessarily so much in and of itself, but as a sure sign of the inward condition. However, some of God's commands deal with outward things. I will deal with those in another chapter.

"A good man out of the good treasure of the heart bringeth forth good things: and an evil man out of the evil treasure bringeth forth evil things. But I say unto you, That every idle word that men shall speak, they shall give account thereof in the day of judgment. For by thy words thou shalt be justified, and by thy words thou shalt be condemned" (Matt. 12:35-37).

"Even as I have seen, they that plow iniquity, and sow wickedness, reap the same" (Job 4:8).

If you commit wicked acts, it does you no good to claim that you are saved. Unless you repent, God will see that you receive the harvest—eternity in Hell.

"I the LORD search the heart, I try the reins, even to give every man according to his ways, and according to the fruit of his doings" (Jer. 17:10).

"Ah Lord GOD! behold, thou hast made the heaven and the earth by thy great power and stretched out arm, and there is nothing too hard for thee: thou shewest loving-kindness unto thousands, and recompensest the iniquity of the fathers into the bosom of their children after them: the Great, the Mighty God, the LORD of hosts, is his name, great in counsel, and mighty in work: for thine eyes are open upon all the ways of the sons of men: to give every one according to his ways, and according to the fruit of his doings" (Jer. 32:17-19).

"For the day of the LORD is near upon all the heathen: as thou hast done, it shall be done unto thee: thy reward shall return upon thine own head" (Obadiah 15).

"For the Son of man shall come in the glory of his Father with his angels; and then he shall reward every man according to his works" (Matt. 16:27).

"But after thy hardness and impenitent heart treasurest up unto thyself wrath against the day of wrath and revelation of the righteous judgment of God; who will render to every man according to his deeds: to them who by patient continuance in well doing seek for glory and honour and immortality, eternal life: but unto them that are contentious, and do not obey the truth, but obey unrighteousness, indignation and wrath, tribulation and anguish, upon every soul of man that doeth evil, of the Jew first, and also of the Gentile; but glory, honour, and peace, to every man that worketh good, to the Jew first, and also to the Gentile: for there is no respect of persons with God" (Romans 2:5-11).

"For we must all appear before the judgment seat of Christ; that every one may receive the things done in his body, according to that he hath done, whether it be good or bad" (II Cor. 5:10).

"Be not deceived; God is not mocked: for whatsoever a man soweth, that shall he also reap. For he that soweth to his flesh shall of the flesh reap corruption; but he that soweth to the Spirit shall of the Spirit reap life everlasting" (Gal. 6:7, 8).

"And I saw a great white throne, and him that sat on it, from whose face the earth and the heaven fled away; and there was found no place for them. And I saw the dead, small and great, stand before God; and the books were opened: and another book was opened, which is the book of life: and the dead were judged out of those things which were written in the books, according to their works. And the sea gave up the dead which were in it; and death and hell delivered up the dead which were in them: and they were judged every man according to their works" (Rev. 20:11-13).

In the space of a 3-verse passage, we are told twice that we will be judged **according to our works.**

When God repeats something, it behooves us to pay attention.

I suspect that the foregoing made some people uncomfortable. Brace yourselves, for this next part comes even closer home. Not all deeds are external.

"For as he thinketh in his heart, so is he" (Prov. 23:7a).

"But I say unto you, That whosoever looketh on a woman to lust after her hath committed adultery with her already in his heart" (Matt. 5:28).

I would like to draw attention to the word "commit": this is a definite action, but one that is internal rather than external.

"And Jesus knowing their thoughts said, Wherefore think ye evil in your hearts?" (Matt. 9:4).

By combining this verse with Prov. 23:7a above, we discover that a person who entertains evil thoughts IS evil.

We can take this a step further. We can now see that the claim that Christians can't avoid sinning is equivalent to saying that Christians can't avoid **being evil!**

It is fitting to close this particular section with one of the last verses in the Bible.

"And, behold, I come quickly; and my reward is with me, to give every man according as his work shall be" (Rev. 22:12).

This whole concept should be a terribly fearful thing to those who believe that Christians cannot avoid sinning. If I believed that, there would be no way that I could look forward to Judgment Day with anything but dread. Sin MUST be punished, and punished with all the terrible severity that a just and holy God demands.

Once we depart from evil, we are supposed to do good. If we are righteous at heart, that will manifest itself by doing righteously.

"What man is he that desireth life, and loveth many days, that he may see good? Keep thy tongue from evil, and thy lips from speaking guile. Depart from evil, and do good; seek peace, and pursue it. The eyes of the LORD are upon the righteous, and his ears are open unto their cry" (Psalm 34:12-15).

"Lord, who shall abide in thy tabernacle? who shall dwell in thy holy hill? He that walketh uprightly, and worketh righteousness, and speaketh the truth in his heart. He that backbiteth not with his tongue, nor doeth evil to his neighbour, nor taketh up a reproach against his neighbour. In whose eyes a vile person is contemned; but he honoureth them that fear the LORD. He that sweareth to his own hurt, and changeth not. He that putteth not out his money to usury, nor taketh reward against the innocent. He that doeth these things shall never be moved" (Psalm 15:1-5).

"Trust in the LORD, and do good; so shalt thou dwell in the land, and verily thou shalt be fed. Delight thyself also in the LORD; and he shall give thee the desires of thine heart. Commit thy way unto the LORD; trust also in him; and he shall bring it to pass. And he shall bring forth thy righteousness as the light, and thy judgment as the noonday. Rest in the LORD, and wait patiently for him: fret not thyself because of him who prospereth in his way, because of the man who bringeth wicked devices to pass. Cease from anger, and forsake wrath: fret not thyself in any wise to do evil. For evildoers shall be cut off: but those that wait upon the LORD, they shall inherit the earth" (Psalm 37:3-9).

Notice in verse 4 that God "shall give" us what we want. If we really want a pure heart, and fulfill the requirements to get it, God will give it to us. Unfortunately, many people stop at the first part; they're not willing to do what God requires of them, and thus they are forced to go through life with the handicap of carnality.

"Preserve my soul; for I am holy: O thou my God, save thy servant that trusteth in thee" (Psalm 86:2).

The word translated "holy" is Strong's #2623: it means "godly (man), good, merciful, saint." I suspect that many people would balk at applying these terms to themselves simply out of a sense of humility. But humility does not mean a refusal to face facts as they are. Nor is it boasting to humbly make a factual statement. If you cannot honestly describe yourself in this way as David did, then any hope you currently have of getting to Heaven is a delusion.

"Blessed are they that keep his testimonies, and that seek him with the whole heart. They also do no iniquity: they walk in his ways" (Psalm 119:2, 3).

Notice verse 3: "They also do no iniquity." Once again, we see that the idea of a sinning religion contradicts the Bible. The idea of walking in God's ways is intimately and inextricably connected with living a *sinless* life.

"The sinners in Zion are afraid; fearfulness hath surprised the hypocrites. Who among us shall dwell with the devouring fire? who among us shall dwell with everlasting burnings? He that walketh righteously, and speaketh uprightly; he that despiseth the gain of oppressions, that shaketh his hands from holding of bribes, that stoppeth his ears from hearing of blood, and shutteth his eyes from seeing evil; he shall dwell on high: his place of defence shall be the munitions of rocks: bread shall be given him; his waters shall be sure" (Isaiah 33:14-16).

Righteousness is the only defense against the "devouring fire" of punishment.

"What shall we say then? Shall we continue in sin, that grace may abound? God forbid. How shall we, that are dead to sin, live any longer therein? Let not sin therefore reign in your mortal body, that ye should obey it in the lusts thereof. Neither yield ye your members as instruments of unrighteousness unto sin: but yield yourselves unto God, as those that are alive from the dead, and your members as instruments of righteousness unto God. For sin shall not have dominion over you: for ye are not under the law, but under grace. What then? shall we sin, because we are not under the law, but under grace? God forbid. Know ye not, that to whom ye yield yourselves servants to obey, his servants ye are to whom ye obey; whether of sin unto death, or of obedience unto righteousness? But God be thanked, that ye were the servants of sin, but ye have obeyed from the heart that form of doctrine which was delivered you. Being then made free from sin, ye became the servants of righteousness. I speak after the manner of men because of the infirmity of your flesh: for as ye have yielded your members servants to uncleanness and to iniquity unto iniquity; even so now yield your members servants to righteousness unto holiness. But now being made free from sin, and become servants to God, ye have your fruit unto holiness, and the end everlasting life" (Romans 6:1, 2, 12-19, 22).

I wanted to quote all of this chapter, but decided not to because of reasons of space.

"For if the firstfruit be holy, the lump is also holy: and if the root be holy, so are the branches" (Romans 11:16).

A holy heart **cannot** produce sin.

This is a good spot to bring in something else, because this verse is in a sense telling the end of the story.

"Then Jesus said unto them, Take heed and beware of the leaven of the Pharisees and of the Sadducees" (Matt. 16:6).

"Your glorying is not good. Know ye not that a little leaven leaveneth the whole lump? Purge out therefore the old leaven, that ye may be a new lump, as ye are unleavened. For even Christ our passover is sacrificed for us: therefore let us keep the feast, not with old leaven, neither with the leaven of malice and wickedness; but with the unleavened bread of sincerity and truth" (I Cor. 5:6-8).

Paul was addressing Christians who still had carnality in their hearts. That's why they needed to purge out the leaven. Once we have purged out all sin, then the new lump is holy, as described in Romans 11:16 above.

"If ye then be risen with Christ, seek those things which are above, where Christ sitteth on the right hand of God. Set your affection on things above, not on things on the earth. For ye are dead, and your life is hid with Christ in God. Mortify therefore your members which are upon the earth; fornication, uncleanness, inordinate affection, evil concupiscence, and covetousness, which is idolatry: for which things' sake the wrath of God cometh on the children of disobedience: in the which ye also walked some time, when ye lived in them. But now ye also put off all these; anger, wrath, malice, blasphemy, filthy communication out of your mouth. Lie not one to another, seeing that ye have put off the old man with his deeds; and above all these things put on charity, which is the bond of perfectness" (Col. 3:1-3, 5-9, 14).

Notice verse 8: "put off." We put off not just the nature of the old man, but also his deeds.

Paul also mentions at the end the relationship between love and perfection.

"Behold, what manner of love the Father hath bestowed upon us, that we should be called the sons of God: therefore the world knoweth us not, because it knew him not. Beloved, now are we the sons of God, and it doth not yet appear what we shall be: but we know that, when he shall appear, we shall be like him; for we shall see him as he is. And every man that hath this hope in him purifieth himself, even as he is pure. Whosoever committeth sin transgresseth also the law: for sin is the transgression of the law. And ye know that he was manifested to take away our sins; and in him is no sin. Whosoever abideth in him sinneth not: whosoever sinneth hath not seen him, neither known him. Little children, let no man deceive you: he that doeth righteousness is righteous, even as he is righteous. He that committeth sin is of the devil; for the devil sinneth from the beginning. For this purpose the Son of God was manifested, that he might destroy the works of the devil. Whosoever is born of God doth not commit sin; for his seed remaineth in him: and he cannot sin, because he is born of God. And he that keepeth his commandments dwelleth in him, and he in him. And hereby we know that he abideth in us, by the Spirit which he hath given us" (I John 3:1-9, 24).

I have already quoted much of this in an earlier chapter, but it bears repeating. The point needs to be pounded home. A life influenced by sin is a very abnormal life in God's eyes.

If we actually abide in Christ, we will necessarily and automatically partake of His image, and follow His example: a life of victory over sin.

"For though we walk in the flesh, we do not war after the flesh: casting down imaginations, and every high thing that exalteth itself against the knowledge of God, and bringing into captivity every thought to the obedience of Christ" (II Cor. 10:3, 5).

Some people may be confused by the wording here. Paul is using "flesh" in this case to simply mean the physical body. His thought here could be worded like this: "Even though we are human, we do not fight spiritual battles with human weapons."

Mark this well—"every thought." Even our own thoughts are supposed to be obedient to God; in other words, without sin. Yes, it's a high standard. But God gives the grace and the power to maintain it.

Note, however, that we are not responsible for everything we think. Satan is the prince of the power of the air, and he has the ability to put thoughts into our minds as a temptation. But we are responsible for our response; whether we welcome those thoughts, or reject them.

I have already touched on the command to be holy.

I would strongly urge the reader to stop here for a bit and seriously consider this concept. What do you think it means to be holy? How far should we go in our attempts to obey this command? David went far; re-read Psalm 69:6-9 & 119:131.

Now I want to repeat again that every true Christian, no matter how weak or ignorant, has enough of God's holiness to get to Heaven—any other position is preaching salvation by works. But do we want to have simply the bare minimum necessary to reach Heaven? Or do we want to pursue a state of being holy, and not just that, but to pursue it with great vigor? It is sad but true, that many Christians want a measure of friendliness with the world. They want the minimum of separation. They would consider Abraham, David, and Isaiah to be fanatics—"religious nuts." Instead of a double portion of Elijah's spirit, they want to be like Balaam, and die the death of the righteous without making too much effort to live the life of the righteous.

An unsanctified Christian, even though he has the remnants of the carnal nature, will reach Heaven, if he stays true. But, again, should we be satisfied with the bare minimum? Reader, would you agree that getting that carnal remnant removed satisfies the command to be holy in a fuller and more perfect way? If not, why? Be honest with yourself.

As mentioned, many Christians apparently no longer look at sin through God's eyes. Any unforgiven sin, even a very small one, will keep us out of Heaven. One single sin was enough to keep Moses out of the Promised Land. We know this in theory, but all too often people have the attitude, "Well, everybody does it, so it can't be THAT bad." That's an excuse, and a rather poor one. It's really just an adult version of the teenage wail, "But Mom, everybody's doing it!" Firstly, not everybody does it, and secondly, yes, it really is that bad.

Being holy is part and parcel of being made in God's image. If you feel that living a holy life is impossible, then you are not living closely enough to God. Strive with all your might to please God; lean on Him, ask Him for help.

"Be ye holy"—this is a definite command; one that God clearly expects us to obey. But do we? When somebody cuts us off in traffic, and we feel white-hot anger rise up, is that being holy? When somebody praises us, and we feel pride rise up, is that being holy? But this command allows for no exceptions. "But such feelings are inevitable," some might say.

Not quite. Nearly inevitable, perhaps. Very difficult to guard against and prevent, sometimes. But we are told in multiple Scripture passages that Jesus was tempted over and over, yet He never gave in to the temptation. The temptation to sin is inevitable. The giving in to temptation is not inevitable.

I think that everybody would agree that something that made it easier to resist temptation would be highly desirable. And that is exactly what sanctification does. Furthermore, it is impossible to perfectly obey God's explicit command to be holy without the experience of Christian perfection.

Which do you think that God is fully and completely pleased with—perfect obedience, or partial obedience?

"Ye have not yet resisted unto blood, striving against sin" (Heb. 12:4).

Interestingly, even some opponents of Holiness doctrine recognize the importance of living a holy life.

"One principal end of the design of God in sending his Son into the world was to recover us unto that state of holiness which we had lost... To live in known and allowed sin, and yet expect to be saved by Christ is the master deception of Satan... Has he delivered me from the power of Satan and caused me to take *his* yoke upon me? Has his sceptre broken the dominion of sin in me? Am I a loyal subject of his kingdom? If not, I have no rightful claim to a personal interest in his sacrifice. Christ died to procure holiness, not to secure an indulgence for unholiness" (Pink; ch. 3).

This quote is an excellent example of how people are sometimes able to grasp a large portion of the truth, and rise above their "official" theology, while at the same time not quite realizing what exactly they've found. Pink was a hyper-Calvinist; yet he writes here like a thorough-going Arminian.

"Suppose for a moment that you were allowed to enter heaven without holiness. What would you do? What possible enjoyment could you feel there? To which of all the saints would you join yourself, and by whose side would you sit down? Their pleasures are not your pleasures, their tastes not your tastes, their character not your character. How could you possibly be happy, if you had not been holy on earth?

"*Now* perhaps you love the company of the light and the careless, the worldly minded and the covetous, the reveler and the pleasure-seeker, the ungodly and the profane. There will be none such in heaven.

"*Now* perhaps you think the saints of God too strict and particular, and serious. You rather avoid them. You have no delight in their society. There will be no other company in heaven.

"*Now* perhaps you think praying, and Scripture reading, and hymn singing, dull and melancholy, and stupid work—a thing to be tolerated now and then, but not enjoyed. You reckon the Sabbath a burden and a weariness; you could not possibly spend more than a small part of it in worshiping God. But remember, heaven is a never-ending Sabbath. The inhabitants thereof rest not day or night, saying 'Holy, holy, holy, Lord God Almighty' and singing the praise of the Lamb. How could an unholy man find pleasure in occupation such as this?" (Ryle; ch. 3).

"Let me ask everyone who may read these pages, *Are you holy?* Listen, I pray you, to the question I put to you this day. Do you know anything of the holiness of which I have been speaking?

"I do not ask whether you attend your church regularly—whether you have been baptized, and received the Lord's Supper—whether you have the name of Christian—I ask something more than all this: *Are you holy, or are you not?*

"I do not ask whether you approve of holiness in others—whether you like to read the lives of holy people, and to talk of holy things, and to have on your table holy books— whether you mean to be holy, and hope you will be holy someday—I ask something further: *Are you yourself holy this very day, or are you not?*

"And why do I ask so straitly, and press the question so strongly? I do it because the Scripture says, 'Without holiness no man shall see the Lord.' It is written, it is not my fancy—it is the Bible, not my private opinion—it is the word of God, not of man—'*Without holiness no man shall see the Lord*' (Heb. 12:14).

"Alas, what searching, sifting words are these! What thoughts come across my mind, as I write them down! I look at the world, and see the greater part of it lying in wickedness. I look at professing Christians, and see the vast majority having nothing of Christianity but the name. I turn to the Bible, and I hear the Spirit saying, 'Without holiness no man shall see the Lord.'

"Surely it is a text that ought to make us consider our ways, and search our hearts. Surely it should raise within us solemn thoughts, and send us to prayer" (Ryle; ch. 3).

"You may say, 'These are hard sayings: the way is very narrow.' I answer, 'I know it. So says the Sermon on the Mount.' The Lord Jesus said so 1,900 years ago. He always said that men must take up the cross daily, and that they must be ready to cut off hand or foot, if they would be his disciples. It is in religion as it is in other things, 'there are no gains without pains.' That which costs nothing is worth nothing.

"Whatever we may think fit to say, we must be holy, if we would see the Lord. Where is our Christianity if we are not? We must not merely have a Christian name, and Christian knowledge, we must have a Christian *character* also. We must be saints on earth, if ever we mean to be saints in heaven" (Ryle; ch. 3).

"Strive to live a *holy* life. Walk worthy of the church to which you belong. Live like citizens of heaven. Let your light shine before men, so that the world may profit by your conduct. Let them know whose you are, and whom you serve. Be epistles of Christ, known and read of all men—written in such clear letters that none can say of you, 'I know not whether this man be a member of Christ or not.' He that knows nothing of real, practical holiness is no member of 'the church on the rock' " (Ryle; ch. 13).

Ryle was a moderate Calvinist. He talks about "holiness" as a state of being—he didn't realize it, but sanctification is the best way of achieving this goal.

If we live a holy life, we will also live a triumphant, overcoming life.

A friend of mine once said that "everyone who is saved" is an overcomer. He gave the example in his own life of overcoming sin when he got saved. But does this always apply? When we give in to temptation, are we still overcoming sin, or is sin overcoming us?

God wants us and expects us to live a life of victory over sin. Just because we are tempted doesn't mean that we have to sin. Remember, Jesus was tempted.

"The righteous also shall hold on his way, and he that hath clean hands shall be stronger and stronger" (Job 17:9).

"Nay, in all these things we are more than conquerors through him that loved us" (Romans 8:37).

"Be not overcome of evil, but overcome evil with good" (Romans 12:21).

This is the exact opposite of what many people teach. Sure, they claim to believe in living a holy life; but they also claim that being overcome by sin is inevitable.

"Now thanks be unto God, which always causeth us to triumph in Christ, and maketh manifest the savour of his knowledge by us in every place" (II Cor. 2:14).

"I have written unto you, fathers, because ye have known him that is from the beginning. I have written unto you, young men, because ye are strong, and the word of God abideth in you, and ye have overcome the wicked one" (I John 2:14).

"Ye are of God, little children, and have overcome them: because greater is he that is in you, than he that is in the world" (I John 4:4).

We can overcome sin because we have the help of a Power that is stronger than sin.

"For this is the love of God, that we keep his commandments: and his commandments are not grievous. For whatsoever is born of God overcometh the world: and this is the victory that overcometh the world, even our faith. Who is he that overcometh the world, but he that believeth that Jesus is the Son of God?" (I John 5:3-5).

As long as you **consistently** overcome sin and temptation, you can rest assured that you are a Christian. If not—the way back to God lies through repentance.

"He that hath an ear, let him hear what the Spirit saith unto the churches; He that overcometh shall not be hurt of the second death" (Rev. 2:11).

"He that overcometh, the same shall be clothed in white raiment; and I will not blot out his name out of the book of life, but I will confess his name before my Father, and before his angels" (Rev. 3:5).

We know, both from the Bible and from our own experience, that we are unable to do anything good in and of ourselves. The power to do good, and be good, comes from God.

So if you are tired of struggling with sin, and with the carnal nature, why don't you ask for more of God's presence and power? Why don't you ask for God's help in a new and more powerful way?

If we live a triumphant life, we will also live a steadfast life.

"That by two immutable things, in which it was impossible for God to lie, we might have a strong consolation, who have fled for refuge to lay hold upon the hope set before us: which hope we have as an anchor of the soul, both sure and stedfast, and which entereth into that within the veil" (Heb. 6:18, 19).

I hope that every reader who claims to be a Christian has paid close attention to this chapter. The Bible makes it abundantly clear that Christians *will* partake of righteous actions and will *not* partake of sinful actions.

If your life does not measure up to this standard, then I strongly urge you to take a hard look at your life; pray earnestly; and find out how to fix things.

Chapter 16

Righteousness That Permeates

I hope that many readers now see that entire sanctification is a desirable thing, as well as being an attainable thing. But sometimes it is difficult to know how to get the blessing.

This is something of a hard part to write about; the broad outline stays the same from person to person, but the details vary immensely. Some people have needlessly delayed the blessing by insisting that they had to follow the exact same steps as somebody else.

The common part can be summed up thusly: every person who got the blessing hungered and thirsted after righteousness. They weren't satisfied with the status quo. They strongly wanted to have more of God's spirit and presence than ever before. And to get it, they were willing to turn everything over to God.

God leads some people through an agony of crucifixion. (Although in some cases that may be partly self-imposed, through an initial lack of willingness.) Other people experience a much quieter process of total consecration. Some people seemingly start out by having only one thing that they need to surrender; others have many things. For some people, the process takes only a few hours or even minutes of all-out seeking; for others, it takes days, or perhaps even longer.

As Romans 12:1 says, we must sacrifice everything to God.

"Tho' the way seem'd straight and narrow,

All I claimed was swept away;

My ambitions, plans, and wishes

At my feet in ashes lay."

- -"I Will Praise Him," second verse; Mrs. M. J. Harris (also known as Margaret J. Harris)

This results in total, complete submission to God.

"And the king said unto Zadok, Carry back the ark of God into the city: if I shall find favour in the eyes of the LORD, he will bring me again, and shew me both it, and his habitation: but if he thus say, I have no delight in thee; behold, here am I, let him do to me as seemeth good unto him" (II Sam. 15:25, 26).

The reason that many people call this the "death-route" is because a great deal of "dying out" is required. Before a person can be sanctified, he has to die out to all selfish desires, no matter how small. He has to die out to "What will people think?" He has to die out to various modes of dressing and talking. He has to die out to too much love of friends and family. If you want holiness of heart, you need the same attitude that Abraham had when God told him to sacrifice Isaac. Abraham didn't bargain with God, or wail "Why me?" He placed his love for God above his love for his son. Some people, when seeking sanctification, have reported later that God required them to give up a family member. God asked, "Are you willing to give up your child, and let Me take him to Heaven?" If God leads you that way, and you cannot answer that question, you are not ready to be sanctified.

Now I have never heard of a time when somebody was seeking sanctification that God actually took a family member to Heaven—but what matters is not the actual event, but the willingness to make a FULL surrender to God's will, no matter how painful it may be. If you draw back, and say, "But Lord..."; you have not *fully* forsaken everything. You must be willing to be emptied of everything, no matter how small, minor, major, or precious, that is not God. We must be perfectly emptied before we can be perfectly filled with the Holy Ghost.

This attitude is beautifully exemplified in A. B. Simpson's wonderful missionary hymn "The Regions Beyond." In the second verse, he says, "The world may pronounce me a dreamer, a fool, / Enough if the Master I please." Simpson had died out to everything that wasn't God.

I know that some people come up to a certain point, and wonder how in the world they could ever say "Yes" to something like that. It may seem impossible. But there is a way through. "The king's heart is in the hand of the LORD, as the rivers of water: he turneth it whithersoever he will" (Prov. 21:1). God is a perfect gentleman: He will not force us to do anything against our will. But we can give Him permission. When I was struggling with this, my grandmother taught me about a concept that is very important in this type of situation. It is called "being willing to be made willing." If there is something in your life, whether a family member, a habit, a job, etc., that you are not willing to give up, and yet you know that you need to be willing to give it up—there is such a thing as giving God permission to "meddle" in your life, and turn your heart in such a way that you will be willing to give up that thing. You may not have the power in yourself to make a sacrifice of something, but God can give you that power, and if you give Him permission to intervene, He will do so. He will work on your heart until you become willing to give up whatever He demands that you give up.

Once we have renounced everything, and done all that God wants us to do, then God will send the fire of perfect love to burn up all trace of carnality.

"Then said I, Woe is me! for I am undone; because I am a man of unclean lips, and I dwell in the midst of a people of unclean lips: for mine eyes have seen the King, the Lord of hosts. Then flew one of the seraphims unto me, having a live coal in his hand, which he had taken with the tongs from off the altar: and he laid it upon my mouth, and said, Lo, this hath touched thy lips; and thine iniquity is taken away, and thy sin purged" (Isaiah 6:5-7).

"John answered, saying unto them all, I indeed baptize you with water; but one mightier than I cometh, the latchet of whose shoes I am not worthy to unloose: he shall baptize you with the Holy Ghost and with fire: whose fan is in his hand, and he will thoroughly purge his floor, and will gather the wheat into his garner; but the chaff he will burn with fire unquenchable" (Luke 3:16, 17).

Be warned, however: Satan temps us to undo our consecration. "Save thyself, and come down from the cross" (Mark 15:30).

Perfect love is the essence of sanctification.

"And we have known and believed the love that God hath to us. God is love; and he that dwelleth in love dwelleth in God, and God in him. Herein is our love made perfect, that we may have boldness in the day of judgment: because as he is, so are we in this world. There is no fear in love; but perfect love casteth out fear: because fear hath torment. He that feareth is not made perfect in love. We love him, because he first loved us" (I John 4:16-19).

Verse 17 talks about boldness as a result of perfect love; this connects back to how Peter was filled with holy boldness as a result of Pentecost.

Love fulfills the law.

"Love worketh no ill to his neighbour: therefore love is the fulfilling of the law" (Romans 13:10).

The inspired writers of the Bible had a marvelous knack for packing a tremendous amount of meaning into a few words. Henry Drummond wrote an essay describing how love fulfills the law. In it he points out how, if we truly love our neighbor, we will not wish harm of any sort to come to him; therefore (for example) we will not covet his possessions, and thus the commandment against covetousness is fulfilled.

In the Sermon on the Mount, Jesus famously extended the Law's prohibition against wrong actions to the thoughts and desires behind those actions. We do not always have the means or the opportunity to physically commit certain sins, but Jesus makes it clear that desiring to commit sin is every bit as damaging to the soul as physically committing it. Therefore—since love is the fulfilling of the law—as long as we have love to our neighbor, possessing that love makes it truly impossible to commit a whole host of sins. Therefore, perfect love casts out sin.

"For God hath not given us the spirit of fear; but of power, and of love, and of a sound mind" (II Tim. 1:7).

But even before we get sanctified—once we "merely" get saved, we partake of God's righteousness. This is something that our opponents do not seem to understand. Almost unanimously, they focus exclusively on imputed righteousness, and thereby totally ignore imparted righteousness.

Imputed righteousness can be thought of in two different ways. One is the idea of God as a judge; when we get saved, God judicially pronounces us to be righteous. The other way is the idea that God the Father looks at us through the "lens" of Jesus and His shed blood: and thereby sees not our unrighteousness, but rather views us "as if" we were righteous.

"Blessed is the man unto whom the LORD imputeth not iniquity, and in whose spirit there is no guile" (Psalm 32:2). Since God imputes sin to the wicked, it is logical to assume that He also imputes righteousness to Christians. (There are a few verses that mention imputed righteousness, but we don't need them: logic alone suffices in this case.)

But, in addition to that, He also actually imparts (gives) righteousness to us. Otherwise, how exactly would we be a new creation? After all, when God renews the physical creation, and makes a new heaven and earth, it will be purified from the taint of sin.

Some of our opponents argue rather stridently against this idea. I don't know why; it's almost as if the thought of actually *being* righteous, instead of merely being counted as righteous, somehow alarms or offends them.

"For they being ignorant of God's righteousness, and going about to establish their own righteousness, have not submitted themselves unto the righteousness of God" (Romans 10:3). Some use this verse to argue against the existence of imparted righteousness. But it is not *our* righteousness that we are talking about. Rather, God *gives* us **His** righteousness.

"I put on righteousness, and it clothed me: my judgment was as a robe and a diadem" (Job 29:14).

"Hide thy face from my sins, and blot out all mine iniquities. Create in me a clean heart, O God; and renew a right spirit within me" (Psalm 51:9, 10).

This was written after the prophet Nathan confronted him—David had sinned, and once again needed a clean heart. Notice what verse 9 says: "blot out" mine iniquities. This is imparted righteousness, not imputed only—not "declare" or "pronounce" that they're blotted out, but actually **blot** them out.

"Let thy priests be clothed with righteousness; and let thy saints shout for joy. I will also clothe her priests with salvation: and her saints shall shout aloud for joy" (Psalm 132:9, 16).

"O that thou hadst hearkened to my commandments! then had thy peace been as a river, and thy righteousness as the waves of the sea" (Isaiah 48:18).

Pay careful attention to the language used in this verse: "thy"—that's a possessive word; it shows possession of something. This verse talks about two different things: notice that the word construction is identical—"thy" peace; "thy" righteousness. So unless our opponents are prepared to argue that peace, too, is merely imputed to us, instead of actually imparted, they will have to choose between changing their position on this, or else be wildly inconsistent regarding this verse.

"I will greatly rejoice in the LORD, my soul shall be joyful in my God; for he hath clothed me with the garments of salvation, he hath covered me with the robe of righteousness, as a bridegroom decketh himself with ornaments, and as a bride adorneth herself with her jewels" (Isaiah 61:10).

Not that God views us "as if" we're clothed with righteousness; but we actually ARE clothed with righteousness.

"But we are all as an unclean thing, and all our righteousnesses are as filthy rags" (Isaiah 64:6a). I have included this verse to show the continuation of the pattern from several of the previous verses. Before we got saved, our sins were not merely imputed to us, and nothing more; we were actually clothed with sin. But once we get saved, God clothes us with imparted righteousness.

"And I will put my spirit within you, and cause you to walk in my statutes, and ye shall keep my judgments, and do them" (Ezekiel 36:27).

Pay attention to what God says here: He actually puts, or places, "my spirit **within** you." This is not some surface thing; this is not God viewing us AS IF we were righteous; this is an inward change, and an inward possession. God gives us His righteousness. And then it becomes ours.

"Are there yet the treasures of wickedness in the house of the wicked, and the scant measure that is abominable? Shall I count them pure with the wicked balances, and with the bag of deceitful weights? For the rich men thereof are full of violence, and the inhabitants thereof have spoken lies, and their tongue is deceitful in their mouth. Therefore also will I make thee sick in smiting thee, in making thee desolate because of thy sins" (Micah 6:10-13).

Pay careful attention to the question in verse 11: "Shall I count [the wicked] pure?" The answer is "No," found in verse 13, where God says that He will smite and make desolate the wicked, as punishment for their sins. God will not count us pure unless we actually are pure.

This is a good place to bring in a very important point. There is an old riddle, often attributed to Abraham Lincoln: "Q.—How many legs does a dog have, if you count his tail as a leg? A.—Four. Counting his tail as a leg doesn't make it so."

If God simply "counted" or "declared" or "viewed" us as righteous, without actually MAKING us righteous, then God would be claiming something that had no basis in reality. In other words, if God called us "righteous" without actually making us so, **then God would be lying.**

"For I say unto you, That except your righteousness shall exceed the righteousness of the scribes and Pharisees, ye shall in no case enter into the kingdom of heaven" (Matt. 5:20).

Notice this: "your" righteousness; again, a sign of possession.

"And there came a leper to him, beseeching him, and kneeling down to him, and saying unto him, If thou wilt, thou canst make me clean. And Jesus, moved with compassion, put forth his hand, and touched him, and saith unto him, I will; be thou clean. And as soon as he had spoken, immediately the leprosy departed from him, and he was cleansed" (Mark 1:40-42).

Remember, leprosy is symbolic of sin. Jesus did not "declare" or "pronounce" lepers to be clean; that would have been a cruel mockery. He actually, literally made them clean.

"But whosoever drinketh of the water that I shall give him shall never thirst; but the water that I shall give him shall be in him a well of water springing up into everlasting life" (John 4:14). "He that believeth on me, as the scripture hath said, out of his belly shall flow rivers of living water" (John 7:38).

These two verses use the same sort of language. "In" him; "out of" his belly; once again, this is not some surface thing, some outward form of claimed righteousness, but real, inward, actual righteousness.

"Now then we are ambassadors for Christ, as though God did beseech you by us: we pray you in Christ's stead, be ye reconciled to God. For he hath made him to be sin for us, who knew no sin; that we might be made the righteousness of God in him" (II Cor. 5:20, 21).

Mark this well: "made" the righteousness of God: not "pronounced"; not "declared"; not "viewed as"; but really and actually MADE.

"And be found in him, not having mine own righteousness, which is of the law, but that which is through the faith of Christ, the righteousness which is of God by faith" (Phil. 3:9). Once again, we see how the Bible hangs together. Paul follows Isaiah, Jesus, etc. in not trusting to human righteousness: rather, he depends on the fact that God gives us His righteousness and makes us holy.

"I counsel thee to buy of me gold tried in the fire, that thou mayest be rich; and white raiment, that thou mayest be clothed, and that the shame of thy nakedness do not appear; and anoint thine eyes with eyesalve, that thou mayest see" (Rev. 3:18).

The shed blood of Jesus has a two-fold work: it both *covers* our sin, (as symbolized by the shed blood on the original Passover night); but not merely that; it also *cleanses* our sin.

"Wash me thoroughly from mine iniquity, and cleanse me from my sin. Wash me, and I shall be whiter than snow" (Psalm 51:2, 7b).

"Wash you, make you clean; put away the evil of your doings from before mine eyes; cease to do evil" (Isaiah 1:16).

"O Jerusalem, wash thine heart from wickedness, that thou mayest be saved" (Jer. 4:14a).

"Then will I sprinkle clean water upon you, and ye shall be clean: from all your filthiness, and from all your idols, will I cleanse you" (Ezekiel 36:25).

"Know ye not that the unrighteous shall not inherit the kingdom of God? Be not deceived: neither fornicators, nor idolaters, nor adulterers, nor effeminate, nor abusers of themselves with mankind, nor thieves, nor covetous, nor drunkards, nor revilers, nor extortioners, shall inherit the kingdom of God. And such were some of you: but ye are washed, but ye are sanctified, but ye are justified in the name of the Lord Jesus, and by the Spirit of our God" (I Cor. 6:9-11).

"Not by works of righteousness which we have done, but according to his mercy he saved us, by the washing of regeneration, and renewing of the Holy Ghost; which he shed on us abundantly through Jesus Christ our Saviour" (Titus 3:5, 6).

"For if the blood of bulls and of goats, and the ashes of an heifer sprinkling the unclean, sanctifieth to the purifying of the flesh: how much more shall the blood of Christ, who through the eternal Spirit offered himself without spot to God, purge your conscience from dead works to serve the living God?" (Heb. 9:13, 14).

"And having an high priest over the house of God; let us draw near with a true heart in full assurance of faith, having our hearts sprinkled from an evil conscience, and our bodies washed with pure water" (Heb. 10:21, 22).

"Unto him that loved us, and washed us from our sins in his own blood, and hath made us kings and priests unto God and his Father; to him be glory and dominion for ever and ever. Amen" (Rev. 1:5b, 6).

Once our sins have been washed away, we are then "whiter than snow." We, being God's children, and made in His image, directly partake of His holiness. God imparts His righteousness to us, and *makes us* holy in the most literal way possible.

This leads us into another issue.

Almost all the opponents of Holiness doctrine are strong on calling themselves and all Christians "sinners." True, they say, we are sinners saved by grace, but sinners nevertheless. They point to people like John Bunyan, who famously called himself the "chief of sinners." They also point to Paul, who used the same sort of language in I Tim. 1:15, and use him as a major support for their position. Peter, although he never called himself "chief," did once call himself "a sinful man" in Luke 5:8—but that was before Pentecost.

On the other hand, there is a clear distinction between saints and sinners in the Bible. Paul, in thinking about his former sins, quite possibly might have honestly felt that he was the worst of sinners, but he wasn't. There have been people, even in biblical times, who did worse things than he did, and from worse motives. Paul's description of himself is evidence of his humility and humbleness; nothing more.

When we get saved, we receive a new heart; old things pass away. Before, we could not do anything good in our own power; now, the new nature gives us the power to do what is right. When God gives us commands such as "be perfect" and "be holy," He aims those commands at us here on earth. Be holy NOW, not when we get to Heaven, and not at some unspecified time in the future. Be perfect NOW, here on earth, even though we are in imperfect bodies. Don't wait until we get to Heaven. God expects and demands obedience NOW. If we delay; if we spout off excuses why we can't fulfill God's commands while here on earth; if we go through life expecting physical death to be a crutch to somehow help us fulfill those commands; we are likely to be unpleasantly surprised at the outcome.

Saints

"He will keep the feet of his saints, and the wicked shall be silent in darkness; for by strength shall no man prevail" (I Sam. 2:9). Saints can lay claim to God's power to keep and protect.

"Now therefore arise, O Lord God, into thy resting place, thou, and the ark of thy strength: let thy priests, O Lord God, be clothed with salvation, and let thy saints rejoice in goodness" (II Chron. 6:41). We see here one thing that saints do—rejoicing in goodness. By contrast, sinners don't do that.

"O love the Lord, all ye his saints: for the Lord preserveth the faithful, and plentifully rewardeth the proud doer" (Psalm 31:23). Again, saints can lay claim to God's power to keep and protect. Sinners cannot.

"Gather my saints together unto me; those that have made a covenant with me by sacrifice" (Psalm 50:5). We have here a definition of what saints are. Have sinners made a covenant with God?

"Ye that love the Lord, hate evil: he preserveth the souls of his saints; he delivereth them out of the hand of the wicked" (Psalm 97:10). Can we hate evil and still sin every day?

This is actually a very interesting question, so let us pursue it a bit. Calvinists would certainly say we can—and do. I have read some people who seem to view sin as an addiction. Now, there are two ways of looking at addiction. Some view it as a failure of willpower. In which case, it's *still* our fault. On the other hand, some view it as a disease. But if it is a disease, then God can cure it. "If thou wilt diligently hearken to the voice of the Lord thy God, and wilt do that which is right in his sight, and wilt give ear to his commandments, and keep all his statutes, I will put none of these diseases upon thee, which I have brought upon the Egyptians: for I am the Lord that healeth thee" (Exodus 15:26). "Bless the Lord, O my soul, and forget not all his benefits: who forgiveth all thine iniquities; who healeth all thy diseases" (Psalm 103:2, 3). Thus, whether or not sin is viewed as an addiction actually becomes irrelevant; every fork in the argument brings us to the same spot—that God has the power to completely wipe sin out of the believer's life. Thus there is no excuse either way for sin in our lives.

"Precious in the sight of the LORD is the death of his saints" (Psalm 116:15). Let's contrast this with Ezekiel 33:11a: "Say unto them, As I live, saith the Lord GOD, I have no pleasure in the death of the wicked." God views saints and sinners as two entirely different classes of people.

"Let thy priests be clothed with righteousness; and let thy saints shout for joy" (Psalm 132:9). "All thy works shall praise thee, O LORD; and thy saints shall bless thee" (Psalm 145:10). In these two verses, we see different aspects of the lifestyle of saints. Do sinners do these things?

"Ephraim compasseth me about with lies, and the house of Israel with deceit: but Judah yet ruleth with God, and is faithful with the saints" (Hosea 11:12). This is one of the differences between saints and sinners. Saints don't do evil.

"Then Ananias answered, Lord, I have heard by many of this man, how much evil he hath done to thy saints at Jerusalem" (Acts 9:13). In this verse, God's people are explicitly called saints. Imagine, if you can, how strange it would be if this verse read "thy sinners" instead of "thy saints"!

"As for Saul, he made havock of the church, entering into every house, and haling men and women committed them to prison" (Acts 8:3). "And Saul, yet breathing out threatenings and slaughter against the disciples of the Lord, went unto the high priest, and desired of him letters to Damascus to the synagogues, that if he found any of this way, whether they were men or women, he might bring them bound unto Jerusalem" (Acts 9:1, 2). "Which thing I also did in Jerusalem: and many of the saints did I shut up in prison, having received authority from the chief priests; and when they were put to death, I gave my voice against them" (Acts 26:10). The combination of these three verses shows very clearly and explicitly that the saints are God's people—they are "disciples of the Lord." Can we say this about sinners?

"To all that be in Rome, beloved of God, called to be saints: Grace to you and peace from God our Father, and the Lord Jesus Christ" (Romans 1:7). Is anybody "called" to be a sinner?

"I commend unto you Phebe our sister, which is a servant of the church which is at Cenchrea: that ye receive her in the Lord, as becometh saints, and that ye assist her in whatsoever business she hath need of you: for she hath been a succourer of many, and of myself also" (Romans 16:1, 2). Imagine if this read "that ye receive her in the Lord, as becometh sinners"—strange and incongruous at best!

"Paul, called to be an apostle of Jesus Christ through the will of God, and Sosthenes our brother, unto the church of God which is at Corinth, to them that are sanctified in Christ Jesus, called to be saints, with all that in every place call upon the name of Jesus

Christ our Lord, both theirs and ours" (I Cor. 1:1, 2). Again, is anybody "called" to be a sinner?

"Dare any of you, having a matter against another, go to law before the unjust, and not before the saints? Do ye not know that the saints shall judge the world? and if the world shall be judged by you, are ye unworthy to judge the smallest matters?" (I Cor. 6:1, 2). Saints are different from the unjust.

"Now therefore ye are no more strangers and foreigners, but fellowcitizens with the saints, and of the household of God" (Eph. 2:19). There is a clear difference shown here between saints, and strangers to God. Spiritually speaking, saints and sinners are citizens of different countries.

"But fornication, and all uncleanness, or covetousness, let it not be once named among you, as becometh saints" (Eph. 5:3). But sinners do these things as a matter of routine.

"Paul and Timotheus, the servants of Jesus Christ, to all the saints in Christ Jesus which are at Philippi, with the bishops and deacons" (Phil. 1:1). Imagine if this read "sinners in Christ Jesus" – strange and incongruous at best!

"Paul, an apostle of Jesus Christ by the will of God, and Timotheus our brother, to the saints and faithful brethren in Christ which are at Colosse: Grace be unto you, and peace, from God our Father and the Lord Jesus Christ. Giving thanks unto the Father, which hath made us meet to be partakers of the inheritance of the saints in light" (Col. 1:1, 2, 12).

Are sinners "faithful brethren"? Do they have an inheritance in light? No; their inheritance is in darkness. "But the path of the just is as the shining light, that shineth more and more unto the perfect day. The way of the wicked is as darkness: they know not at what they stumble" (Prov. 4:18, 19). "The people which sat in darkness saw great light; and to them which sat in the region and shadow of death light is sprung up" (Matt. 4:16). "Then said the king to the servants, Bind him hand and foot, and take him away, and cast him into outer darkness, there shall be weeping and gnashing of teeth" (Matt. 22:13). "Woe unto them! for they have gone in the way of Cain, and ran greedily after the error of Balaam for reward, and perished in the gainsaying of Core. These are spots in your feasts of charity, when they feast with you, feeding themselves without fear: clouds they are without water, carried about of winds; trees whose fruit withereth, without fruit, twice dead, plucked up by the roots; raging waves of the sea, foaming out their own shame; wandering stars, to whom is reserved the blackness of darkness for ever" (Jude 11-13).

"To the end he may stablish your hearts unblameable in holiness before God, even our Father, at the coming of our Lord Jesus Christ with all his saints" (I Thess. 3:13). "And Enoch also, the seventh from Adam, prophesied of these, saying, Behold, the Lord cometh with ten thousands of his saints" (Jude 14). When Jesus returns to earth, will He come from Hell, with sinners and demons following Him, or will He come from

Heaven, with saints and angels following Him?

Sinner/Sinners

"But the men of Sodom were wicked and sinners before the LORD exceedingly" (Gen. 13:13). Only one small family in Sodom was righteous; just four people (see Gen. 19:15-17). All the rest of the residents were sinners, who were consumed in God's judgment upon them. "And Abraham drew near, and said, Wilt thou also destroy the righteous with the wicked?" (Gen. 18:23). If Christians are still sinners, then Abraham's question makes no sense: it makes a distinction that wouldn't exist.

"Blessed is the man that walketh not in the counsel of the ungodly, nor standeth in the way of sinners, nor sitteth in the seat of the scornful. Therefore the ungodly shall not stand in the judgment, nor sinners in the congregation of the righteous" (Psalm 1:1, 5). These two verses give us a clear distinction between saints and sinners.

"Gather not my soul with sinners, nor my life with bloody men" (Psalm 26:9). If God's people still qualify as sinners, then this verse makes no sense—David would be saying that he doesn't want his soul to end up where God's people are.

"Then will I teach transgressors thy ways; and sinners shall be converted unto thee" (Psalm 51:13). Are saints still in need of salvation? No; only sinners are.

"Let the sinners be consumed out of the earth, and let the wicked be no more" (Psalm 104:35a). Try to imagine God saying this about saints.

"My son, if sinners entice thee, consent thou not" (Prov. 1:10). Again, try to imagine God speaking about His redeemed people in such terms.

"Righteousness keepeth him that is upright in the way: but wickedness overthroweth the sinner. Evil pursueth sinners: but to the righteous good shall be repayed" (Prov. 13:6, 21). Both of these verses were designed to give the clearest possible distinction between saints and sinners.

"For God giveth to a man that is good in his sight wisdom, and knowledge, and joy: but to the sinner he giveth travail, to gather and to heap up, that he may give to him that is good before God" (Eccl. 2:26a, b). Saints, not sinners, are good in God's sight.

"And I find more bitter than death the woman, whose heart is snares and nets, and her hands as bands: whoso pleaseth God shall escape from her; but the sinner shall be taken by her" (Eccl. 7:26). There are two separate classes of people mentioned here: sinners; and those who please God.

"Though a sinner do evil an hundred times, and his days be prolonged, yet surely I know that it shall be well with them that fear God, which fear before him: but it shall not be well with the wicked, neither shall he prolong his days, which are as a shadow; because he feareth not before God" (Eccl. 8:12, 13). Again, we see two classes of people—sinners, who don't fear God; and saints, who do fear God.

"And the destruction of the transgressors and of the sinners shall be together, and they that forsake the LORD shall be consumed" (Isaiah 1:28). "Behold, the day of the

LORD cometh, cruel both with wrath and fierce anger, to lay the land desolate: and he shall destroy the sinners thereof out of it" (Isaiah 13:9). Will Christians be destroyed? Or is that fate reserved for sinners?

"The sinners in Zion are afraid; fearfulness hath surprised the hypocrites. Who among us shall dwell with the devouring fire? who among us shall dwell with everlasting burnings? He that walketh righteously, and speaketh uprightly; he that despiseth the gain of oppressions, that shaketh his hands from holding of bribes, that stoppeth his ears from hearing of blood, and shutteth his eyes from seeing evil; he shall dwell on high: his place of defence shall be the munitions of rocks: bread shall be given him; his waters shall be sure" (Isaiah 33:14-16). Only those who walk in righteousness are safe. Do sinners walk righteously?

"Then cometh he to his disciples, and saith unto them, Sleep on now, and take your rest: behold, the hour is at hand, and the Son of man is betrayed into the hands of sinners" (Matt. 26:45).

"And as ye would that men should do to you, do ye also to them likewise. For if ye love them which love you, what thank have ye? for sinners also love those that love them. And if ye do good to them which do good to you, what thank have ye? for sinners also do even the same. And if ye lend to them of whom ye hope to receive, what thank have ye? for sinners also lend to sinners, to receive as much again. But love ye your enemies, and do good, and lend, hoping for nothing again; and your reward shall be great, and ye shall be the children of the Highest: for he is kind unto the unthankful and to the evil" (Luke 6:31-35). Christians must exceed the good deeds of sinners; the only way to do that is to have Divine love in our hearts.

"I say unto you, that likewise joy shall be in heaven over one sinner that repenteth, more than over ninety and nine just persons, which need no repentance" (Luke 15:7). Sinners need to repent: Christians don't.

"Now we know that God heareth not sinners: but if any man be a worshipper of God, and doeth his will, him he heareth" (John 9:31). We see another crystal-clear difference between saints and sinners.

"But God commendeth his love toward us, in that, while we were yet sinners, Christ died for us. For as by one man's disobedience many were made sinners, so by the obedience of one shall many be made righteous" (Romans 5:8, 19). We know that sinners are not righteous.

"Knowing this, that the law is not made for a righteous man, but for the lawless and disobedient, for the ungodly and for sinners, for unholy and profane, for murderers of fathers and murderers of mothers, for manslayers" (I Tim. 1:9). We see yet another sharp distinction.

"For such an high priest became us, who is holy, harmless, undefiled, separate from sinners, and made higher than the heavens" (Heb. 7:26). Is Jesus separate from Christians? If not, then Christians cannot possibly be sinners.

"Let him know, that he which converteth the sinner from the error of his way shall save a soul from death, and shall hide a multitude of sins" (James 5:20). Sinners have a current and present need to be saved from death; Christians are already saved from death.

"And if the righteous scarcely be saved, where shall the ungodly and the sinner appear?" (I Peter 4:18). Here is another verse that distinguishes between saints and sinners.

When talking about ourselves, if we are Christians, or when talking about another person that we have reason to believe is a Christian, we should be careful in our language. It is inappropriate, inaccurate, and unbiblical to use the word "sinner" to describe any Christian.

The reader very well may have a question at this point: But isn't a person who commits sin a sinner?

Indeed he is. We **were** sinners before being saved. But that changed at the instant God entered our hearts. "Therefore if any man be in Christ, he is a new creature" (II Cor. 5:17a).

Whenever God creates something new, the old version is no longer in effect. We see this not only in the spiritual world, but also in the physical world.

"For, behold, I create new heavens and a new earth: and the former shall not be remembered, nor come into mind" (Isaiah 65:17). "Nevertheless we, according to his promise, look for new heavens and a new earth, wherein dwelleth righteousness" (II Peter 3:13).

Righteousness is an integral part of that new creation.

"For this my son was dead, and is alive again; he was lost, and is found. And they began to be merry" (Luke 15:24). The son "**was** dead" in sin, but now "is alive" again.

We were dead in sin in the past, but are alive in righteousness in the present. Paul also speaks of this, in greater detail.

"And you hath he quickened, who were dead in trespasses and sins; wherein in time past ye walked according to the course of this world, according to the prince of the power of the air, the spirit that now worketh in the children of disobedience: among whom also we all had our conversation in times past in the lusts of our flesh, fulfilling the desires of the flesh and of the mind; and were by nature the children of wrath, even as others. But God, who is rich in mercy, for his great love wherewith he loved us, even when we were dead in sins, hath quickened us together with Christ, (by grace ye are saved;) and hath raised us up together, and made us sit together in heavenly places in Christ Jesus" (Eph. 2:1-6).

There can be no righteousness without genuine repentance. And righteousness should permeate our entire being.

The Bible is very clear that the state of being a sinner is totally incompatible with the state of being a Christian. We cannot be both at the same time.

"No man can serve two masters: for either he will hate the one, and love the other; or else he will hold to the one, and despise the other. Ye cannot serve God and mammon" (Matt. 6:24).

"For do I now persuade men, or God? or do I seek to please men? for if I yet pleased men, I should not be the servant of Christ" (Gal. 1:10).

As we have seen, several passages explicitly draw a clear, sharp distinction between the two. Moreover, God assures us in the clearest possible language that Christians do not sin.

"Even so every good tree bringeth forth good fruit; but a corrupt tree bringeth forth evil fruit. A good tree cannot bring forth evil fruit, neither can a corrupt tree bring forth good fruit. Every tree that bringeth not forth good fruit is hewn down, and cast into the fire. Wherefore by their fruits ye shall know them" (Matt. 7:17-20).

Calvinists, and other people who hold the idea of eternal security (i.e., "1-point Calvinists"), are fond of saying that we aren't sinners because we sin, but rather that we sin because we're sinners. That distinction is entirely true of somebody before he gets saved; we were born with the old nature, and our inherited depravity gives us a bent towards sinning until God comes along and convicts us of our sin. But once we become saints, and are no longer sinners, then it switches around. Once we become saints, we remain saints until we once again commit sin. (Which, unfortunately, virtually every-body does, especially before they get sanctified; we don't have to sin, but it's very, very seldom that one hears of somebody who never backslid. Although many people have testified that they never backslid after getting sanctified.) And then once we do commit sin again, in that instant we once again become sinners. Remember—we CANNOT be a saint and a sinner at the same time.

It's all too common for Christians to get a little careless or a little lazy—although sanctification helps tremendously with that, too. Satan is on the lookout for such occa-sions, and he often attacks when that happens, because in such a case the chances are good that a sudden temptation will catch us off guard, and we will fall. Such a case is very different from somebody who decides that he is tired of the Christian life and de-liberately sets out to sin. Somebody who retains a good attitude towards God will most likely repent immediately, and in many cases will be a sinner for only a very short period of time. But make no mistake—if we fall back into sin, repentance is as necessary as it was the first time around.

Despite the fact that salvation changes a person from a sinner to a saint, that is only the beginning of a person's spiritual journey. We can live above sin, and still have rem-nants of carnality. But as long as carnality remains, we do not and cannot have Christian perfection. Righteousness should permeate a Christian's entire life. But this cannot be done completely until carnality is removed.

I maintain, with great emphasis and vigor, that God's plan for every Christian's life is for us to be as pure as He is. I will not falter from this position; I will not flinch; I will not back down. "BE YE HOLY."

Having finished the main theology, we now turn to the outgrowths and ramifications of entire sanctification.

Conclusion

Chapter 17

Benefits and Results of Sanctification

The work of sanctification has many benefits and results. Many of these are related and correlated, but most of them can be divided into general categories.

There are two core benefits. First and foremost is the actual removal or eradication (both terms are used) of the sin nature in a person. This results in a perfectly pure heart. Everything else springs from this, either directly or indirectly.

"He who begins to give the least way to sin is in danger of final apostasy; the best remedy against this is to get the evil heart *removed*, as *one* murderer in the house is more to be dreaded than *ten* without" (Adam Clarke on Heb. 3:12).

The second item which I would term a core benefit is that it makes resisting temptation so much easier. Before sanctification, we have a "fifth column" of sin in the heart. That old nature works against us, and insidiously (or in some cases, openly and vigorously) undermines our resistance to temptation. As an example, suppose that somebody steps on your foot. In many cases, there is a temptation to anger there. In an unsanctified person, the old nature is there to fan the flames, and sometimes the temptation catches fire almost before the person has a chance to realize what's going on. But once the last bit of the carnal nature is removed, there is no longer anything in the heart to undermine our efforts. Now, certainly, there is still plenty of danger from temptation. But here's the key point—ALL the danger is outside the heart, not within. Those who have never experienced the second work have no way of understanding this, except in a limited, purely theoretical sense. The difference is one of those things that has to be experienced first-hand in order to be fully understood.

Note, however, that this is not to say that resisting temptation will necessarily be easy (although in some cases it is); rather, that it will be significantly **easier** than before. There are times when the battle is still difficult, perhaps even very much so.

I do not intend to list or describe all the outgrowths of sanctification and all the ancillary points of Holiness doctrine; that would be another book all by itself. There are a great many points of difference between Holiness Christians and most non-Holiness Christians.

Some of the other results are the following:

1. A definite dress standard. There are certain modes of dress that every Christian would agree are modest. On the other hand, there are certain modes that probably every Christian would agree are immodest. But between the two, there is something of a gray area. For clothing that falls into this area, I would guess that roughly 70-80% of non-Holiness Christians would say it was modest, whereas at least 95% of Holiness Christians would say that it was immodest.

This standard also includes plainness of dress. Holiness people tend to disapprove strongly of most things whose sole or primary purpose would be ornamentation.

2. A firm line of separation from the world. Non-Holiness Christians sometimes speak about refraining from worldly practices—but most of them do many things that Holiness Christians consider to be worldly.

3. A higher sensitivity towards using everyday life as a witness for God, to show the world that we serve a different master than they do.

Baptism is all well and good, and a fine symbol as far as it goes, but it doesn't go very far. For starters, it's usually a one-time thing (at least in theory). Moreover, nobody carries around a sign "I've been baptized." On the other hand, modest, plain clothing tells a story every day, without needing to say a word. There is a saying in Holiness circles: "You should dress so that all three worlds (Heaven, Earth, and Hell) know you're a Christian."

4. A higher sensitivity (at least seemingly) towards spiritual light, as well as having more light in general. While an unsanctified Christian may be sensitive to all the light that he has, and he may be walking as close to God as he knows how, the mere presence of the carnal nature in his heart inevitably forces a certain distance between him and God. I think about the various Christians I have known over the years, and it seems quite certain that the average sanctified Christian has a deeper and closer walk with God than the average unsanctified Christian. (There are exceptions both ways, of course.) That difference manifests in various ways.

* * * * *

Many, perhaps most, unsanctified Christians are too caught up and entwined with their physical possessions. They don't go so far as to actually be idolaters, but they fail to strike the proper balance. They tend to forget that there is a correlation between their treasure and their heart.

A car is generally regarded as a necessity in America today. For the job that I currently have, it actually is a necessity: the job involves traveling between several different sites. And yet—if God told me to sell my car: once I did the necessary testing, like Gideon, and found that it was really the Lord, I would obey that order as quickly as possible. I have absolutely no clue how God would provide for me in such a case; but I have faith that He would, and probably in a delightfully unexpected way.

I have heard first-hand accounts of people, recounting when they were in a traffic accident, who got terribly angry; and all because their possession was damaged. And these people claim to be Christians. What kind of an attitude is that? It wasn't even about the money, because there was ample insurance to take care of that issue. It was primarily the fact that a physical possession (apparently the apple of their eye) was damaged. Such people do not bother to look at things through the lens of Eternity. Let's assume for the sake of the argument that we will remember everything about life on earth after we get to Heaven. Will we care that things went wrong on earth, that cars or houses were damaged? It's ludicrous to think such a thing. When we see the unutterable glories of Heaven, earthly issues will dwindle into utter insignificance.

But remember: we are citizens of Heaven even now, not citizens of earth. Therefore, does it not behoove us to look at things through God's eyes?

Fairly recently, I was rear-ended while sitting at a stoplight. I wasn't hurt, and there wasn't much damage, but my car did require some repair. Now—this next part is going to seem strange and incredible to most non-Holiness Christians. As I stood there, inspecting the damage, I praised God. Why? Because I felt absolutely no anger at all; not even the tiniest hint. This total lack of anger continued over the next several days, even when I discovered that the man who hit me had lied, and given me fake insurance information.

That, friend, is just one of the many things that the work of sanctification does for a person.

* * * * *

Holiness people, both individually and collectively, just simply seem (on average) to be more closely attuned to God, and His power and presence.

I have attended two non-Holiness churches, and I have visited many others, of various denominations. Sometimes God's presence is noticeable. But I have never felt it the way I have many times in Holiness churches.

I have been in services in Holiness churches, where, even before the service actually started, the presence of God was so obvious and so powerful that seemingly nobody wanted to even move—they were drinking in God's presence with such delight.

Prayer plays a much bigger role in Holiness church services than in non-Holiness ones. Holiness churches generally set aside a spot in their order of worship for congregational prayer. I have never seen a non-Holiness church that did that, nor have I seen a non-Holiness preacher call for a special time of prayer around the altar. In addition, I have never seen a non-Holiness church that conducted an actual altar call for the unsaved. Many of them routinely practice something that they apparently regard as an altar call, but it's a pale imitation of one.

Sometimes the reason why we don't see God move with power is because we don't let Him. It does not do any good to ask God to do great things if there is something known in our lives that hinders the flow of Divine grace and power. We must turn everything over to God first, and do whatever He requires of us, then ask.

When God comes in great power in a church service, human-imposed order goes right out the window. There are three things that generally happen when God really settles down—some people shout for joy; some people walk or run up and down the aisles; and some people weep, either for joy or because they are under conviction. Our family friend Harlie Smith used to say, "I wouldn't give a translucent dime for a dry-eyed religion."

The term has largely died out now, but in decades past, it used to be common for Holiness people to be called "Holy Rollers" as a term of disparagement and derision. This was because Holiness church services tend to be more emotional than most other groups. This was used both by non-religious people, and by worldly religious people.

Despite the great benefits of sanctification, however, I fear that many Holiness people have gotten stuck in a rut. Sure, God comes in our services in a powerful way, and we're thankful for that. But I fear, in many cases, that we have gotten away from expecting God to do much of anything else. I have met Holiness people who seem to have little or no interest in actually going out and talking to people about God. They're so scared of being contaminated by the world, that they seem to forget that they have the shield of God's purity to protect them.

Peter Cartwright (1785-1872), a Methodist circuit-rider for many years, was willing to attempt great things for God. One time he was traveling, and needed a place to spend the night. In those days, travelers often spent the night at private homes. This particular time, he found a hospitable gentleman who was hosting a party that night, but welcomed him nevertheless. The people in that area were extremely ignorant of Divine things.

"A beautiful, ruddy young lady walked very gracefully up to me, dropped a handsome courtesy, and pleasantly, with winning smiles, invited me out to take a dance with her. I can hardly describe my thoughts or feeling on that occasion. However, in a moment I resolved on a desperate experiment. I rose as gracefully as I could; I will not say with some emotion, but with many emotions. The young lady moved to my right side; I grasped her right hand with my right hand, while she leaned her left arm on mine. In this position we walked on the floor. The whole company seemed pleased at this act of politeness in the young lady, shown to a stranger. The colored man, who was the fiddler, began to put his fiddle in the best order. I then spoke to the fiddler to hold a moment, and added that for several years I had not undertaken any matter of importance without first asking the blessing of God upon it, and I desired now to ask the blessing of God upon this beautiful young lady and the whole company, that had shown such an act of politeness to a total stranger.

"Here I grasped the young lady's hand tightly, and said, 'Let us all kneel down and pray,' and then instantly dropped on my knees, and commenced praying with all the power of soul and body that I could command. The young lady tried to get loose from me, but I held her tight. Presently she fell on her knees. Some of the company kneeled, some stood, some fled, some sat still, all looked curious...

"While I prayed, some wept, and wept out aloud, and some cried for mercy. I rose from my knees and commenced an exhortation, after which I sang a hymn. The young lady who invited me on the floor lay prostrate, crying earnestly for mercy. I exhorted again, I sang and prayed nearly all night. About fifteen of that company professed religion, and our meeting lasted next day and next night, and as many more were powerfully converted" (*Autobiography*; ch. 16).

I can easily think of a dozen of Cartwright's contemporaries or near-contemporaries in the Holiness movement who very well might have done that sort of thing. They might not have tried it on their own, but if they felt a leading from God, they would have obeyed without any hesitation. And I have personally known possibly a dozen other people who I believe would obey such a leading without hesitation. By contrast, I can scarcely think of a dozen non-Holiness people over the last 500 years who I can imagine even potentially doing something like that without hesitation.

Another man who achieved great things for God was Charles Finney (1792-1875). In recent years, it has become fashionable in certain circles, especially Calvinistic circles, to scoff at Finney and his methods. It is true that a few areas of his theology were not quite as solid as we might wish. But he was a firm believer in the second work of grace; indeed, he experienced it for himself the evening of the very day he got saved. He had the presence and power of God upon him like very few people before or since; and anybody who criticizes a man such as that without a very good reason plays a very dangerous game.

"Finney received an invitation to preach one night in the village of New York Mills. The building was crowded with people, especially young factory workers. God began to convict the people immediately. The next morning Finney was invited to tour the large cotton mill. He entered one room where the girls at the looms and spinning machines were light-heartedly laughing. As he walked toward the work area, one of the girls looked into Finney's eyes and began to tremble. Her shaking fingers broke the thread and the loom stopped. The girl next to her looked up to see why the loom had ceased. As she saw Finney's face, she also began to tremble and broke her thread. One after another, the looms stopped.

"The owner heard the equipment stopping and came in to see what was going on. When he saw that the whole room was in tears, he told the superintendent to stop the mill, for it was more important for souls to be saved than for the mill to run. Up to this point Finney had not said one word" (Wesley Duewel; *Revival Fire*; ch. 13).

Evan Roberts, who was instrumental in the great Welsh revival of 1904, could not be used the way God wanted to use him until he received the second work of grace. And then God began to move.

"On Friday night [of the second week of the revival] the crowd was larger than ever, with Baptists, Congregationalists, Calvinists, and Methodists present. The service lasted for five hours. Roberts again asked everyone present to repeat the 'chain' prayer, 'Send the Holy Spirit now for Jesus Christ's sake.' Then he started again in the front row and had everyone repeat, 'Send the Holy Spirit now more powerfully for Jesus Christ's sake.'

"Scores fell on their knees so deeply convicted of their sins that they were unable to utter a syllable. Others cried pitifully for God's mercy...

"On Saturday two young women held an open-air evangelistic meeting during the day, while others went to a gypsy camp and won many to the Lord. Many homes in the area held all-day prayer meetings. Girls held open-air services outside of drinking establishments. When the drinkers came outside, they became gripped by the Holy Spirit and were saved. Revival fire began to spread as people read the newspaper reports and came to see for themselves.

"At meeting time there were such crowds that simultaneous services were held in two churches. A well-known singer was so overcome that he stood up in the balcony and began to sing 'Saved by Grace.' The people sang it over and over. At 2:00 A.M. Sunday, both churches were still so crowded that people could not push in or out. People lost all sense of time and had no desire to eat or to go home. One service lasted until 6:00 A.M." (Duewel; ch. 25).

"In 1932 God sent one of the greatest revivals of the twentieth century to the Shantung province of northern China. It began in the North China Mission of the Southern Baptists through the ministry of Miss Marie Monsen, a Norwegian Evangelical Lutheran missionary who was a refugee in Chefoo. The revival spread specifically throughout the Southern Baptist work, but it also spread to a number of other missionary societies and to other provinces of northern China...

The Shantung revival has been reported in some detail by Dr. C. L. Culpepper, respected missionary leader of the Southern Baptist board. The revival was characterized by conviction of sin, confession, clear experiences of the new birth, and emphasis upon a definite experience of the fullness of the Spirit. Like all revivals, prayer abounded, even all-night prayer meetings, as people hungered for the mighty workings of God and the experience of the fullness of His Spirit...

"Miss Monsen's methods were simple. She gave personal testimony and she posed two simple personal questions to everyone: 'Have you been born again?' and 'Are you filled with the Spirit?' Many of the Southern Baptist missionaries had attended a conference in Peitaiho in 1929, where Canadian Presbyterian missionary Dr. Jonathan Goforth spoke. Goforth had been mightily used of God in the North China revivals of 1908-1909. The spiritual hunger of the Chinese people deepened.

"When Miss Monsen met Dr. Culpepper, her first words to him were, 'Dr. Culpepper, have you been filled with the Holy Spirit?' When he stammered an indefinite reply, she told him how 'fifteen years earlier she had prayed for and received the promise of the Holy Spirit as recorded in Galations 3:14.' ...

"[A little while later] Culpepper and two Chinese preachers had agreed to meet Saturday night to pray to be filled with the Spirit. Culpepper had been hesitant and fearful to make a full surrender, but God applied Luke 11:9-13 to his heart. He was able to trust God's promise as he surrendered all. The Holy Spirit flooded his soul, and for half an hour he was 'completely enraptured' in Jesus. 'Human words and man's mind cannot understand nor explain what I heard and saw. The experience is as if it happened yesterday. The Lord became more real to me than any human being had ever been. He took complete control of my soul—removing all hypocrisy, sham, and unrighteousness—and filled me with His divine love, purity, compassion, and power.' It seemed to Culpepper that his heart burst with love and compassion for others: for his wife, children, coworkers, and the unsaved. For the first time he experienced the Holy Spirit powerfully interceding through him" (Duewel; ch. 38).

* * * * *

In 1890, a Methodist preacher named John Wesley Hughes started a Christian school named Kentucky Holiness College, in Wilmore, KY. At some point, apparently fairly early, the name was changed in order to honor Francis Asbury (the first Methodist bishop in America), and the school became famous as Asbury College. In 2010, the name was changed again to Asbury University.

As far as I have been able to tell, the early school leaders were all on fire for God. It is indisputable that for many years, Asbury College unflinchingly maintained a strong emphasis on entire sanctification. It is also indisputable that throughout the majority of its history, the school was tremendously blessed by God; probably more so than any other Christian school in the nation. Great revivals repeatedly swept through the school. We will focus on two of them.

"During early 1950 Asbury College experienced another in the series of revivals

God has sent there since 1905. It continued unbroken for 118 hours. A small group of male students had been praying and fasting for revival every night for many weeks. Often they prayed all night long in the gymnasium and in their rooms. The group kept growing in numbers. Groups of students assembled for fasting and prayer in dormitory rooms, in various chapels, in the gymnasium, and in other places. They claimed God's covenant revival promise in 2 Chronicles 7:14.

"During chapel on February 23, a student arose and testified, and one after another followed. Since an outside speaker was scheduled to speak in the chapel, the chairman interrupted and asked for the message. The evangelist was so overcome by the presence of God that he spoke only briefly. The Holy Spirit came upon the entire college...

"My friend and former teacher, Dr. W. W. Holland, reported, 'So mighty was the presence of the Holy Spirit in that chapel service that the students could not refrain from testimony. Testimonies were followed by confessions, confessions by crowded altars, crowded altars gave place to glorious spiritual victories... Thus it ran for several days.' ...

"An overwhelming sense of God's presence prevailed. It seemed as if a great magnet drew people to the large Hughes Auditorium. Students made phone calls to home churches, parents and loved ones, testifying, asking forgiveness, and reporting on what God was doing. Asbury Theological Seminary, across the street, dismissed classes for a time. Delegations from churches in other places arrived to be present and experience the Lord's blessing.

"The service had begun at 9:00 A.M. on Thursday. It continued uninterrupted throughout the day and night. Few left the chapel. Hundreds prayed all night. Other crowds returned after 6:00 A.M., and thus it continued all Friday, Saturday, and Sunday, when many went to the local Wilmore churches. After midnight Sunday the dean requested the young ladies to retire to their dormitories, where group meetings went on. The young men prayed on in the chapel. It was not until 7:00 A.M. on Tuesday, March 1, that the chapel service concluded, after 118 hours. All the rest of the week capacity crowds filled the auditorium. Hundreds of people sought a spiritual experience from God...

"After five days of continuous services, classes were resumed, but each night crowds of a thousand to fifteen hundred continued to fill the auditorium. Night after night the long ninety-foot altar at the front of the auditorium was filled with people seeking salvation. Revival fires broke out in many sections of the United States when someone from Asbury visited...

"One call came from Jackson, Mississippi, and when the delegation from the college arrived, revival broke out in Methodist and Baptist churches and continued for about a week...

"At the Asbury revival, prayer was given first place. People prayed in relays twenty-four hours a day. Day and night people visited the prayer rooms. Preachers drove for miles to come and receive personal refreshing. It was not a time of religious excitement but a time of great peace and of praise...

"Asbury College president Z. T. Johnson said, 'There was no feeling of elation or boastfulness on the part of any of us. Asbury College feels honored to have had such a gracious outpouring of the Holy Spirit.' Dr. Bob Shuler, Jr., wrote, 'It seemed to be as near to Pentecost as this modern day can come... It was a genuine Holy Ghost revival and nothing less.' Dr. T. M. Anderson has estimated that the total network of revival blessing radiating out from the 1950 revival saw some fifty thousand people find a new experience in Christ" (Duewel; ch. 42).

The year 1970 was notable in two ways: it saw perhaps the greatest of all the great revivals that Asbury College was privileged to witness. It was also, unfortunately, the last of them.

Groups of students had been praying for revival since the previous fall. On Feb. 3, without any warning whatsoever, the floodgates of Heaven were opened. The following paragraphs are excerpts from a collection of various eyewitness accounts and testimonies (*One Divine Moment*; Ed. Robert Coleman), with a little commentary from me.

"Casual chatter occupied the conversation of students as they hurried to the 10 A.M. chapel service... The program that morning did not follow its customary worship pattern. The dean of the college, who was the scheduled speaker, did not feel impressed to preach. Instead, he felt led to have students participate in a testimony meeting... The dean opened the testimony service by sharing his own experience with God. He then invited others to do the same... One recalcitrant senior shocked the audience by confessing, 'I'm not believing that I'm standing here telling you what God has done for me. I've wasted my time in college up to now, but Christ has met me and I'm different. Last night the Holy Spirit flooded in and filled my life. Now, for the first time ever, I am excited about being a Christian!' ...

"No sooner had the invitation [to the altar] been extended than a mass of students moved forward... There was not room for all who wanted to pray at the altar... The presence of the Lord was so real that all other interests seemed unimportant. The bell sounded for classes to begin, but went unheeded."

"Day after day the campus community was absorbed in only one thing: getting right with God and seeking His will. Divine prerogatives transcended all other considerations. Being present at the services seemed to be the most important thing at the moment. Radio, TV, parties, ball games, and other activities did not hold any appeal."

"Deep repentance. Twenty-three at the altar. A minister from Georgia is telling of his filling by the Holy Spirit... Unusual spirit of holiness at this moment. Many souls at the altar. Sobbing."

This is from a student's "diary" of the revival.

"Forty-two souls at the altar. I have just seen a couple arise from the altar after three and one-half hours of prayer. They are victorious."

Take note of how long it took this couple: hours of prayer, not two or three minutes.

Many churches, with their pale shadow of an altar service, would have rushed that couple off after just a few minutes of prayer, and thereby gravely injured their spiritual health. I believe a lot of churches are so shallow that they wouldn't know how to handle somebody who was too deeply convicted of sin to be satisfied with a 5-minute "altar call."

"I have found that Christ gives us as much as we want and are willing to accept in the area of spiritual growth. It just depends on how far out on the limb we are willing to go for Him."

This was the testimony of a student.

"Like many other students at Asbury I had been praying for revival, but had little faith that anything like this would ever take place. When it came, I should have been rejoicing in the presence of God. But my conscience was heavy. God was dealing with me, and at first I did not know why. After spending much time in prayer and introspection, I realized my true inward condition by the faithfulness of the Holy Spirit.

"The Lord had saved me from a life of sin and rebellion against Him my junior year in high school. Since that time, even though my purpose to serve God had remained true, my Christian experience had been quite unstable. I had long heard the doctrine of entire sanctification preached clearly and explicitly. There was no doubt in my mind that this work of grace subsequent to conversion was possible. To me it was evident that if I was ever going to amount to anything at all for God, I must obtain whatever it was that changed Peter on the day of Pentecost from the vacillating character he was into a vessel fit for the Master's work...

"When I arose on Friday, I felt something different was going to happen. My spirit was so heavy and hungry, I knew that for me things had come to a climax. That afternoon as I lay on my bed, my faith somehow caught hold and the Holy Spirit came in His fulness. Those moments are almost too sacred and beautiful to describe. Even after the intensity of God's marvelous revelation has diminished, the experience of heart purity remains a reality in my life."

"The spontaneous revival continued into the chapel period on Tuesday, February 10... The administration decided to resume classes at the end of the period. However, the auditorium was kept open for prayer... Shortly before 3 A.M. on Wednesday morning the last student left the sanctuary. For 185 hours—without any interruption— the services had continued! During all this time there was no pressure, no scheduled meetings, no paid advertising, no offering, no invocation, no prelude or postlude, and no benediction."

One's heart can't help but be stirred when reading such thrilling accounts of God's power. But we should not necessarily want such events as such; we should want to be bathed in God's presence, regardless of what specific form it takes.

* * * * *

Another issue, and in many ways the biggest difference between Holiness and non-Holiness people, is separation from the world.

"Depart ye, depart ye, go ye out from thence, touch no unclean thing; go ye out of the midst of her; be ye clean, that bear the vessels of the Lord" (Isaiah 52:11).

"And be not conformed to this world: but be ye transformed by the renewing of your mind, that ye may prove what is that good, and acceptable, and perfect, will of God" (Romans 12:2).

"Wherefore come out from among them, and be ye separate, saith the Lord, and touch not the unclean thing; and I will receive you, and will be a Father unto you, and ye shall be my sons and daughters, saith the Lord Almighty" (II Cor. 6:17, 18).

"Abstain from all appearance of evil" (I Thess. 5:22).

"And I heard another voice from heaven, saying, Come out of her, my people, that ye be not partakers of her sins, and that ye receive not of her plagues" (Rev. 18:4).

"Depart from... be not conformed... come out... be separate... abstain."

Holiness people take this command, and these verses, very seriously. Doing so helps a great deal with the next verses.

"Ye are our epistle written in our hearts, known and read of all men: forasmuch as ye are manifestly declared to be the epistle of Christ ministered by us, written not with ink, but with the Spirit of the living God; not in tables of stone, but in fleshy tables of the heart" (II Cor. 3:2, 3).

"Whether therefore ye eat, or drink, or whatsoever ye do, do all to the glory of God" (I Cor. 10:31).

Many of our opponents will readily admit that committing sin is not something that glorifies God—yet they keep right on doing it anyhow.

I, along with many other Holiness people, have had occasions where somebody has commented on some aspect of how I live my life, whether something that I do, or something that I don't do. Many of those comments are on how we dress, since that is probably the most readily-visible aspect of our lives. Some comments are hostile/mocking; some are from curiosity; others are appreciative.

Non-Holiness Christians sometimes talk about separation from the world, but very few of them seem to actually understand what it entails.

Let's say that somebody took any typical church-goer from nearly any major group or denomination, and set that person down next to an atheist. They tell you that two people are in a room together; one is an atheist, and the other claims to be a Christian. So you go into the room, and take a look. In the vast majority of cases, you would have absolutely no basis for even guessing which was which.

The way we dress is one of the biggest and easiest ways to show separation from the world.

If you claim to be a Christian, you should dress in such a way that a complete stranger could take one look at you, and say, "I think that person might be a Christian."

This involves two things: modesty, and plainness. Based on what the Bible says, both specifically and in general principles, we can find certain guidelines to follow. These should be tight enough to be a definite dress standard, while at the same time loose enough to allow for individuality and variation.

Women are not supposed to wear pants. There is an old-fashioned name for this: cross-dressing. There is supposed to be a clear-cut distinction between men and women. This distinction takes multiple forms. In Western cultures, one of those distinctions is that men wear pants and women wear skirts or dresses. (Other cultures have their own distinctions.)

"The woman shall not wear that which pertaineth unto a man, neither shall a man put on a woman's garment: for all that do so are abomination unto the Lord thy God" (Deut. 22:5).

Now some women try to argue that they are not wearing men's clothing when they wear pants; that their pants are designed for women, not for men. This is supposed to make everything ok. But pay close attention to what this verse says. It does not simply say that a woman shouldn't wear what "is" a man's, but what "pertaineth unto a man"; i.e., similar to a man's attire. Thus these particular women fall right into the trap which their carnality has so neatly laid for them.

Some people try to argue that this command is part of the ceremonial law. Not so. We can tell this by the language used: an "abomination unto the Lord."

Here are some other things that are abominations to God. This is a partial list, drawn strictly from the Old Testament.

Idolatry	Deut. 7:25; 27:15
Child sacrifice	Deut. 12:31
Witchcraft	Deut. 18:10-12
Shedding of innocent blood	Prov. 6:17
Lying	Prov. 6:17; 12:22
Cheating	Prov. 11:1; 20:10
Pride	Prov. 16:5
Perverting morality	Prov. 17:15

All these things are violations of the moral law. And all of them are specifically described as being abominations to God.

On the other hand, violations of the ceremonial law, such as the clean/unclean animals; tend to read "abomination unto you"; i.e., the person doing it (see Lev. 11).

How are we supposed to treat these things that God declares to be abominations?

"Neither shalt thou bring an abomination into thine house, lest thou be a cursed thing like it: but thou shalt utterly detest it, and thou shalt utterly abhor it; for it is a cursed thing" (Deut. 7:26).

Having said all that, however, if I am in church sitting near a woman, I would almost infinitely prefer that she wear pants rather than a miniskirt. I have seen some women in church, who—as far as I could tell—were there to show off their legs, not there to worship God.

Many non-Holiness Christians talk about dressing modestly; but, again, many of them don't actually understand what it means. Some people dress more or less modestly most of the time, but think that it is ok to expose their bodies while exercising. (Hint: it's not ok.) Others like to swim, so they wear a "modest" 1-piece swimsuit instead of a bikini. In recent years, a niche market of modest swimwear has sprung up, aimed mainly at conservative Muslims. But outside of such specialty items, there is no such thing as a modest swimsuit.

The absolute minimum length of a skirt or dress, for purposes of modesty, is that it should fully cover the knees when sitting down. The preferred length is anything closer to the ankles than to the knees.

But length is not the only issue. There should be a balance between tightness and looseness. A long dress that is very tight is not modest. And a blouse that has a very high neckline, but is loose enough to show cleavage when the wearer bends over, is not modest.

In addition, sleeveless shirts and blouses are not modest. At a minimum, most of the upper arms should be covered. Full-length sleeves are preferred.

Many people are pleased to call all this "legalism." It isn't. It's modesty. I readily admit that dress standards can be over-emphasized, and thus become legalism. But very few people are in serious danger of that. The vast majority of Christians are in danger from being too lax, rather than too strict. They want to be at least a little bit like the world, instead of wanting to be a light to the world and an example of holy living. The common tendency is to ask, "What's the harm in X?" Now, strictly speaking, that's an entirely appropriate question, and one that we should ask about a variety of things. But in most cases, the question is asked from a wrong or impure motive. It should be motivated by caution; by a desire to avoid anything impure. But the way it is often used, it is motivated by carelessness or worldliness.

It's not about the standards themselves (at least in a sense). It's not about rules for the sake of rules. It's about living a holy, separated life.

If anything, the standard of the Holiness movement might actually be looser than the biblical standard of modesty.

"Neither shalt thou go up by steps unto mine altar, that thy nakedness be not discovered thereon" (Exodus 20:26). The altar was fairly tall; but it had a ramp going up to it, instead of steps. If the priests had needed to lift up their feet on a staircase, they might have exposed parts of their bodies that needed to be kept from public view. And this was not a case of the priests wearing robes and nothing else—see Exodus 39:28.

"And in the midst of the seven candlesticks one like unto the Son of man, clothed with a garment down to the foot, and girt about the paps with a golden girdle" (Rev. 1:13).

John goes on to describe Jesus' head, hair, eyes, feet, and hands—because that was all of His body that was uncovered.

Nakedness, in and of itself, is not inherently sinful—see Gen. 2:25. But once sin entered into the world, public nakedness, or even near nakedness, is often connected with shame (Exodus 32:25; Isaiah 47:1-3); punishment (Hosea 2:2, 3); and demon possession and possibly insanity (Luke 8:27, 35).

Most people today, including most professing Christians, think that it is perfectly fine to walk around in public showing parts of their bodies that only their families and their doctors should ever see. The Bible tells us that exposing oneself in that manner is not dressing modestly.

* * * * *

Christians (of either sex) are not supposed to wear jewelry or cosmetics.

"Ye are the children of the Lord your God: ye shall not cut yourselves, nor make any baldness between your eyes for the dead. For thou art an holy people unto the Lord thy God, and the Lord hath chosen thee to be a peculiar people unto himself, above all the nations that are upon the earth" (Deut. 14:1, 2).

We see in this passage the principle of being God's children. As such, we are a holy and separated people. Because of those characteristics, the world also counts us as a "peculiar people" in the modern sense of that word. Part of that peculiarity comes from not doing certain things that the world considers to be a normal part of life.

"Ye shall not offer unto the Lord that which is bruised, or crushed, or broken, or cut; neither shall ye make any offering thereof in your land" (Lev. 22:24).

This is a symbolic passage. The "cutting" can be symbolic of ear piercings. Shall we offer to God our deliberately pierced and mutilated bodies?

"And when Jehu was come to Jezreel, Jezebel heard of it; and she painted her face, and tired her head, and looked out at a window" (II Kings 9:30).

We know very little about Jezebel; the Bible doesn't give us much information. But we do know two things: (A), she was a very wicked woman, and (B), she used makeup.

When a person who is notorious for wickedness engages in a certain practice, it behooves us to take a hard look at that thing, and consider whether we wish to be associated with it.

There is a line of nail polish that is sold under the brand name "SinfulColors." It can be found in many major stores. It is aptly named, for people who like to use that sort of thing are displaying pride, vanity, and a general refusal to be satisfied with the way that God made them.

"And when thou art spoiled, what wilt thou do? Though thou clothest thyself with crimson, though thou deckest thee with ornaments of gold, though thou rentest thy face with painting, in vain shalt thou make thyself fair; thy lovers will despise thee, they will seek thy life" (Jer. 4:30).

Judah is compared here to a desperate woman who resorts to outward beauty and cheap tricks as a last-ditch defense. Anybody who trusts to their own efforts, instead of relying on God for the inner beauty of Divine purity, will face a terrible reckoning.

"The LORD said moreover unto me; Son of man, wilt thou judge Aholah and Aholibah? yea, declare unto them their abominations; that they have committed adultery, and blood is in their hands, and with their idols have they committed adultery, and have also caused their sons, whom they bare unto me, to pass for them through the fire, to devour them. Moreover this they have done unto me: they have defiled my sanctuary in the same day, and have profaned my sabbaths. For when they had slain their children to their idols, then they came the same day into my sanctuary to profane it; and, lo, thus have they done in the midst of mine house. And furthermore, that ye have sent for men to come from far, unto whom a messenger was sent; and, lo, they came: for whom thou didst wash thyself, paintedst thy eyes, and deckedst thyself with ornaments, and satest upon a stately bed, and a table prepared before it, whereupon thou hast set mine incense and mine oil" (Ezek. 23:36-41).

God lists the sins of Aholah and Aholibah—idolatry, child sacrifice, etc. But in verse 40, He goes on to declare that in addition to all that, they used cosmetics and jewelry. To most people, these further charges probably seem like small potatoes compared to the previous ones; and in a way, they are. But the mere fact that God lists all of those in one group shows that every single one of those things is a sin.

"Love not the world, neither the things that are in the world. If any man love the world, the love of the Father is not in him" (I John 2:15).

This verse applies to a great many things. The specific thing that I wish to point out has to do with jewelry. When a woman puts on jewelry, does she do so unwillingly? I suppose that a very few might, out of a carnal fear of man, and what people might think if she didn't. But the vast majority of women wear jewelry because they want to. People generally don't spend money on something, or wear something, unless they like it. This applies to men, too. Some men wear jewelry in the form of an expensive watch, when they would be better off, both financially and spiritually, to wear a cheap watch.

If somebody likes jewelry enough to actually wear it, I seriously question whether that person is heeding this verse. Mind you, it is entirely possible—under certain circumstances—for a person to wear jewelry and still be a Christian. Some people have never been taught very well about how Christians should behave. But even if you are a Christian—if you wear jewelry, you are not walking in all the ways of David your father.

It is possible—unlikely, but possible—to wear jewelry from completely pure motives. There might be sentimental attachment to a piece, and therefore a person might wear it as a means of honoring a relative's memory. Or a young child might present a cheap piece as a gift, and therefore it might be worn as a sign of love for the child. If you carefully and prayerfully examine your heart in the searchlight of God's gaze, and you find absolutely no trace of any impure motive or mixed motives for wearing jewelry, that somewhat alters the situation. But VERY few people can say that.

Even if your motives are entirely pure, I would recommend that you carefully consider I Thess. 5:22, and ponder how it might apply to your situation.

"I traveled in the state of Ohio in 1806, and at a largely-attended camp meeting near New Lancaster, there was a great work of God going on; many were pleading for mercy; many were getting religion; and the wicked looked solemn and awful. The pulpit in the woods was a large stand; it would hold a dozen people, and I would not let the lookers-on crowd into it, but kept it clear, that at any time I might occupy it for the purpose of giving directions to the congregation.

"There were two young ladies, sisters, lately from Baltimore, or somewhere down east. They had been provided for on the ground in the tent of a very religious sister of theirs. They were very fashionably dressed; I think they must have had, in rings, earrings, bracelets, gold chains, lockets, etc., at least one or two hundred dollars' worth of jewelry about their persons. The altar was crowded to overflowing with mourners; and these young ladies were very solemn. They met me at the stand, and asked permission to sit down inside it. I told them that if they would promise me to pray to God for religion, they might take a seat there. They were too deeply affected to be idle lookers-on; and when I got them seated in the stand, I called them, and urged them to pray; and I called others to my aid. They became deeply engaged; and about midnight they were both powerfully converted. They rose to their feet, and gave some very triumphant shouts; and then very deliberately took off their gold chains, earrings, lockets, etc., and handed them to me saying, 'We have no more use for these idols. If religion is the glorious, good thing you have represented it to be, it throws these idols into eternal shade' " (Peter Cartwright; *Autobiography*; ch. 7).

"In like manner also, that women adorn themselves in modest apparel, with shamefacedness and sobriety; not with broided hair, or gold, or pearls, or costly array; but (which becometh women professing godliness) with good works" (I Tim. 2:9, 10).

"Whose adorning let it not be that outward adorning of plaiting the hair, and of wearing of gold, or of putting on of apparel; but let it be the hidden man of the heart, in that which is not corruptible, even the ornament of a meek and quiet spirit, which is in the sight of God of great price" (I Peter 3:3, 4).

As we know, there are two parts to a person, any person: the outward part, which is only temporary, for this earthly existence; and the inner part, which will live forever, somewhere. We are told by Paul and Peter how the inner part should be adorned; good works, meekness, etc.

Isn't this enough? It certainly should be. Why, then, is there such a desire to adorn the outward part—the temporary part? Why do so many people want to adorn the part of themselves that will decay and rot?

The subject of wedding rings is a possible exception to the "no jewelry" rule, but it certainly is not a very good idea to wear one, for several reasons; some of them religious, and some of them pragmatic.

The whole idea of wedding rings is loaded with myths and misconceptions. Sure, it's traditional—but that doesn't automatically mean that it is morally right. If the age of a practice were the only guideline, then the "oldest profession" would have no detractors. At many weddings, I have heard somewhere in the ceremony that a ring symbolizes a couples' love, because it has no beginning and no ending. This idea is idiotic tripe. OF COURSE love has a beginning—and all too often, it has an ending, as well.

Both wedding and engagement rings are often thought of as signifying that the person is "taken." This is not always a good thing. Some women openly admit that they target men who are wearing wedding rings—they take it as a challenge, and they think that it is great sport to seduce a married man.

For what a lot of rings cost, you could buy twenty or more Bibles at retail prices and mail them overseas to a mission field.

Hmmm—this is a hard decision. Should I spend my money on something that is temporary and utterly unnecessary, or should I spend it on something that will almost certainly have eternal results?

Now, I'm not saying that buying a ring is absolutely wrong—still, all things considered, I'd rather not appear before God on Judgment Day having spent money on frivolous stuff like that. I seriously question whether He would consider it to be good stewardship.

If you already have a ring, that's one thing. If you don't, I recommend that you don't buy one. And if you do buy one, the cheaper the better. And if you do insist on buying one, deliberately make it the "wrong" size, so that it can't be worn: make it a purely private symbol of love between you and your spouse.

If the presence of a ring on your finger is the only way, or even the best way, of-showing people that you are married—you should take a hard look at your life, because something about your mindset or behavior is way out of line for a married person. You should be both willing and eager to show that you are married by the way you behave, not by wearing some bauble on your finger.

Some non-Holiness people look at our standards of dress and conduct, and conclude that we think of sin as some external thing. The great pains we take about certain external things are not inherently because they are external; on the contrary, they are a natural outgrowth of internal purity. Our external standards **arise out of** biblical principles regarding a holy life, being separated from the world, obeying God, etc. When somebody who has been brought up in the Holiness movement breaks these rules, it causes great concern and anguish—NOT inherently because of the rule itself being broken, but because it is a readily-visible sign that at least one of the biblical principles is being broken in the person's heart.

Many non-Holiness Christians may feel that our standards are too strict. But this is another area where the study of history is very instructive. Many centuries before the Holiness movement was organized, the early Church Fathers were writing about these things, and in many cases doing so almost word-for-word the way that Holiness people have traditionally taught.

Clement of Alexandria

The Instructor

"If, then, He takes away anxious care for clothes and food, and superfluities in general, as unnecessary; what are we to imagine ought to be said of love of ornament, and dyeing of wool, and variety of colours, and fastidiousness about gems, and exquisite working of gold, and still more, of artificial hair and wreathed curls; and furthermore, of staining the eyes, and plucking out hairs, and painting with rouge and white lead, and dyeing of the hair, and the wicked arts that are employed in such deceptions? ... I admire that ancient city of the Lacedæmonians which permitted harlots alone to wear flowered clothes, and ornaments of gold, interdicting respectable women from love of ornament, and allowing courtesans alone to deck themselves...

"As, then, in the fashioning of our clothes, we must keep clear of all strangeness, so in the use of them we must beware of extravagance. For neither is it seemly for the clothes to be above the knee, as they say was the case with the Lacedæmonian virgins; nor is it becoming for any part of a woman to be exposed. Though you may with great propriety use the language addressed to him who said, 'Your arm is beautiful;' yes, 'but it is not for the public gaze.' 'Your thighs are beautiful;' but, was the reply, 'for my husband alone' " (Book 2, ch. 11).

Notice the connection he makes between prostitution and ornamentation. Notice as well his definition of modesty; arms and upper legs should not be exposed to public view. Probably less than half of one percent of Holiness people would have any clue that the details of our dress standard are so old.

"It is childish to admire excessively dark or green stones, and things cast out by the sea on foreign shores, particles of the earth. For to rush after stones that are pellucid and of peculiar colours, and stained glass, is only characteristic of silly people, who are attracted by things that have a striking show. Thus children, on seeing the fire, rush to it, attracted by its brightness; not understanding through senselessness the danger of touching it. Such is the case with the stones which silly women wear fastened to chains and set in necklaces...

"But these women, who comprehend not the symbolism of Scripture, gape all they can for jewels, adducing the astounding apology, 'Why may I not use what God hath exhibited?' and, 'I have it by me, why may I not enjoy it?' and, 'For whom were these things made, then, if not for us?' Such are the utterances of those who are totally igno-rant of the will of God. For first necessaries, such as water and air, He supplies free to all; and what is not necessary He has hid in the earth and water. Wherefore ants dig, and griffins guard gold, and the sea hides the pearl-stone. But ye busy yourselves about what you need not. Behold, the whole heaven is lighted up, and ye seek not God; but gold which is hidden, and jewels, are dug up by those among us who are condemned to death.

"But you also oppose Scripture, seeing it expressly cries 'Seek first the kingdom of heaven, and all these things shall be added unto you.' But if all things have been con-ferred on you, and all things allowed you, and 'if all things are lawful, yet all things are not expedient,' says the apostle...

"In fine, they must accordingly utterly cast off ornaments as girls' gewgaws, reject-ing adornment itself entirely. For they ought to be adorned within, and show the inner woman beautiful...

"Apelles, the painter, seeing one of his pupils painting a figure loaded with gold colour to represent Helen [of Troy], said to him, 'Boy, being incapable of painting her beautiful, you have made her rich.'

"Such Helens are the ladies of the present day, not truly beautiful, but richly got up. To these the Spirit prophesies by Zephaniah: 'And their silver and their gold shall not be able to deliver them in the day of the Lord's anger [Z. 1:18].'

"But for those women who have been trained under Christ, it is suitable to adorn them-selves not with gold, but with the Word, through whom alone the gold comes to light...

"And let not their ears be pierced, contrary to nature, in order to attach to them ear-rings and ear-drops. For it is not right to force nature against her wishes. Nor could there be any better ornament for the ears than true instruction, which finds its way naturally into the passages of hearing. And eyes anointed by the Word, and ears pierced for perception, make a man a hearer and contemplator of divine and sacred things, the Word truly exhibiting the true beauty 'which eye hath not seen nor ear heard before' " (Book 2, ch. 13).

He goes on in this general vein at great length. In another section he becomes even stronger and more emphatic in denouncing this sort of behavior: he uses language that many people would consider downright rude and offensive. If you want a sermon that will blister your ears, read the whole thing.

"Just as the plastered hand and the anointed eye exhibit from their very look the sus-picion of a person in illness, so also cosmetics and dyes indicate that the soul is deeply diseased...

"Is it not monstrous, that while horses, birds, and the rest of the animals, spring and bound from the grass and meadows, rejoicing in ornament that is their own, in mane, and natural colour, and varied plumage; woman, as if inferior to the brute creation, should think herself so unlovely as to need foreign, and bought, and painted beauty?" (Book 3, ch. 2).

"To such an extent, then, has luxury advanced, that not only are the female sex deranged about this frivolous pursuit, but men also are infected with the disease. For not being free of the love of finery, they are not in health; but inclining to voluptuousness, they become effeminate, cutting their hair in an ungentlemanlike and meretricious [showy or tawdry] way, clothed in fine and transparent garments, chewing mastich, smelling of perfume" (Book 3, ch. 3).

Another aspect of dressing appropriately has to do with the general way in which we present ourselves. Showiness and slovenliness are alike unbecoming to the Christian.

"The Word prohibits us from doing violence to nature by boring the lobes of the ears. For why not the nose too?—so that, what was spoken, may be fulfilled: 'As an ear-ring in a swine's nose, so is beauty to a woman without discretion.' For, in a word, if one thinks himself made beautiful by gold, he is inferior to gold; and he that is inferior to gold is not lord of it" (Book 3, ch. 11).

Tertullian
On the Apparel of Women
"Female habit carries with it a twofold idea—dress and ornament. By 'dress' we mean what they call 'womanly gracing;' by 'ornament,' what it is suitable should be called 'womanly *dis*gracing.' The former is accounted (to consist) in gold, and silver, and gems, and garments; the latter in care of the hair, and of the skin, and of those parts of the body which attract the eye. Against the one we lay the charge of ambition, against the other of prostitution"
(Book 1, ch. 4).
We see again a link between outward ornamentation and other sins.

"What am I to interpret those jewels to be which vie with gold in haughtiness, except little pebbles and stones and paltry particles of the self-same earth; but yet not necessary either for laying down foundations, or rearing party-walls, or supporting pediments, or giving density to roofs? The only edifice which they know how to rear is this silly pride of women" (Book 1, ch. 6).

There are a lot of church-goers today, who, if they were preached to in this manner, would make common cause with the Jews of Thessalonica, and riot, crying, "These that have turned the world upside down are come hither also" (Acts 17:6b).

"There must be no overstepping of that line to which simple and sufficient refinements limit their desires—that line which is pleasing to God. For they who rub their skin with medicaments [nostrums], stain their cheeks with rouge, make their eyes prominent with antimony, sin against Him. To them, I suppose, the plastic skill of God is displeasing! In their own persons, I suppose, they convict, they censure, the Artificer of all things! For censure they do when they amend, when they add to, [His work]; taking these their additions, of course, from the adversary artificer. That adversary artificer is the devil. For who would show the way to change the body, but he who by wickedness transfigured man's spirit? He it is, undoubtedly, who adapted ingenious devices of this kind; that in your persons it may be apparent that you, in a certain sense, do violence to God. Whatever is born is the work of God. Whatever, then, is plastered on, is the devil's work... Shall a Christian be assisted in anything by that evil one? [If he do,] I know not whether this name [of "Christian"] will continue [to belong] to him; for he will be *his* in whose lore he eagerly desires to be instructed" (Book 2, ch. 5).

I would imagine that very few people have thought about the issue in these terms. Once you do, however, the point becomes quite obvious. If your body is in need of artificial beauty, then there must be something wrong with the way that God made it.

"If it is true, (as it is,) that in men, for the sake of women (just as in women for the sake of men), there is implanted, by a defect of nature, the will to please; and if this sex of ours acknowledges to itself deceptive trickeries of form peculiarly its own,—[such as] to cut the beard too sharply; to pluck it out here and there; to shave round about [the mouth]; to arrange the hair, and disguise its hoariness by dyes; to remove all the incipient down all over the body; to fix [each particular hair] in its place with womanly pigment; to smooth all the rest of the body by the aid of some rough powder or other: then, further, to take every opportunity for consulting the mirror; to gaze anxiously into it:—while yet, when the knowledge of God has put an end to all wish to please by means of voluptuous attraction, all these things are rejected as frivolous, as hostile to modesty" (Book 2, ch. 8).

Vanity shows up in men, too.

"For why is the integrity of a chaste mind defiled by its neighbour's suspicion? Why is a thing from which I am averse hoped for in me? Why does not my garb pre-announce my character, to prevent my spirit from being wounded by shamelessness through [the channel of] my ears? Grant that it be lawful to assume the appearance of a modest woman: to assume that of an immodest is, at all events, not lawful" (Book 2, ch. 12).

As I said earlier, Christians should dress in a manner that shows that they are Christians. The next quote continues this theme.

"Perhaps some [woman] will say: 'To me it is not necessary to be approved by men; for I do not require the testimony of men: God is the inspector of the heart.' [That] we all know; provided, however, we remember what the same [God] has said through the apostle: 'Let your probity appear before men [Phil. 4:5; Rom. 12:17; II Cor. 8:21].' For what purpose, except that malice may have no access at all to you, or that you may be an example and testimony to the evil? Else, what is [that]: 'Let your works shine?' Why, moreover, does the Lord call us the light of the world; why has He compared us to a city built upon a mountain; if we do not shine in [the midst of] darkness, and stand eminent amid them who are sunk down?" (Book 2, ch. 13).

Some people have likened how we dress to a military uniform. If we are God's soldiers, why would we wear Satan's uniform?

Commodianus (dates unknown)

I did not include anything from Commodianus in the history section; his work is of uneven quality, and I did not look at all of it. However, he does say a few things about the subject currently under discussion.

He was a poet, and possibly a bishop, somewhere in Northern Africa; we know very little about him. His *Instructions* may have been written around 240-260.

Instructions

"Thou wishest, O Christian woman, that the matrons should be as the ladies of the world. Thou surroundest thyself with gold, or with the modest silken garment. Thou givest the terror of the law from thy ears to the wind. Thou affectest vanity with all the pomp of the devil. Thou art adorned at the looking-glass with thy curled hair turned back from thy brow. And moreover, with evil purposes, thou puttest on false medicaments, on thy pure eyes the stibium, with painted beauty, or thou dyest thy hair that it may be always black... Do ye, O good matrons, flee from the adornment of vanity; such attire is fitting for women who haunt the brothels. Overcome the evil one, O modest women of Christ. Show forth all your wealth in giving" (ch. 59).

It is very interesting that so many people would associate outward adornment with prostitution. This pattern *should* make people today stop and think.

"Hear my voice, thou who wishest to remain a Christian woman, in what way the blessed Paul commands you to be adorned. Isaiah, moreover, the teacher and author that spoke from heaven, for he detests those who follow the wickedness of the world, says: 'The daughters of Zion that are lifted up shall be brought low.' It is not right in God that a faithful Christian woman should be adorned. Dost thou seek to go forth after the fashion of the Gentiles, O thou who art consecrated to God? God's heralds, crying aloud in the law, condemn such to be unrighteous women, who in such wise adorn themselves. Ye stain your hair; ye paint the opening of your eyes with black; ye lift up your pretty hair one by one on your painted brow; ye anoint your cheeks with some sort of ruddy colour laid on; and, moreover, earrings hang down with very heavy weight. Ye bury your neck with necklaces; with gems and gold ye bind hands worthy of God with an evil presage. Why should I tell of your dresses, or of the whole pomp of the devil? Ye are rejecting the law when ye wish to please the world... Thou, although thou mayest be chaste, dost not prove thyself so by following evil things" (ch. 60).

This is a very stiff message indeed, but one that a lot of people need to hear.

Cyprian

"You say that you are wealthy and rich. But not everything that can be done ought also to be done; nor ought the broad desires that arise out of the pride of the world to be extended beyond the honour and modesty of virginity; since it is written, 'All things are lawful, but all things are not expedient: all things are lawful, but all things edify not.' For the rest, if you dress your hair sumptuously, and walk so as to draw attention in public, and attract the eyes of youth upon you, and draw the sighs of young men after you, nourish the lust of concupiscence, and inflame the fuel of sighs, so that, although you yourself perish not, yet you cause others to perish, and offer yourself, as it were, a sword or poison to the spectators; you cannot be excused on the pretence that you are chaste and modest in mind. Your shameful dress and immodest ornament accuse you; nor can you be counted now among Christ's maidens and virgins, since you live in such a manner as to make yourselves objects of desire...

"You say that you are wealthy and rich, and you think that you should use those things which God has willed you to possess. Use them, certainly, but for the things of salvation; use them, but for good purposes; use them, but for those things which God has commanded, and which the Lord has set forth. Let the poor feel that you are wealthy; let the needy feel that you are rich. Lend your estate to God; give food to Christ...

"The characteristics of ornaments, and of garments, and the allurements of beauty, are not fitting for any but prostitutes and immodest women... Thus in the Holy Scriptures, by which the Lord wished us to be both instructed and admonished, the harlot city is described more beautifully arrayed and adorned, and with her ornaments; and the rather on account of those very ornaments about to perish [Rev. 17:1-6]...

"Has God willed that wounds should be made in the ears, wherewith infancy, as yet innocent, and unconscious of worldly evil, may be put to pain, that subsequently from the scars and holes of the ears precious beads may hang, heavy, if not by their weight, still by the amount of their cost? All which things sinning and apostate angels put forth by their arts, when, lowered to the [contagion] of earth, they forsook their heavenly vigour. They taught them also to paint the eyes with blackness drawn round them in a circle, and to stain the cheeks with a deceitful red, and to change the hair with false colours, and to drive out all truth, both of face and head, by the assault of their own corruption.

"And indeed in that very matter, for the sake of the fear which faith suggests to me, for the sake of the love which brotherhood requires, I think that not virgins only and widows, but married women also, and all of the sex alike, should be admonished, that the work of

God and His fashioning and formation ought in no manner to be adulterated, either with the application of yellow colour, or with black dust or rouge, or with any kind of medicament which can corrupt the native lineaments. God says, 'Let us make man in our image and likeness;' and does any one dare to alter and to change what God has made? They are laying hands on God when they try to re-form that which He formed, and to transfigure it, not knowing that everything which comes into being is God's work, everything that is changed is the devil's. If any artist, in painting, were to delineate in envious colouring the countenance and likeness and bodily appearance of any one; and the likeness being now painted and completed, another person were to lay hands on it, as if, when it was already formed and already painted, he, being more skilled, could amend it, a serious wrong and a just cause of indignation would seem natural to the former artist. And do you think yourself likely with impunity to commit a boldness of such wicked temerity, an offence to God the artificer? For although you may not be immodest among men, and are not unchaste with your seducing dyes, yet when those things which belong to God are corrupted and violated, you are engaged in a worse adultery. That you think yourself to be adorned, that you think your hair to be dressed, is an assault upon the divine work, is a prevarication of the truth...

"Are you not afraid, I entreat you, being such as you are, that when the day of resurrection comes, your Maker may not recognise you again, and may turn you away when you come to His rewards and promises, and may exclude you, rebuking you with the vigour of a Censor and Judge, and say: 'This is not my work, nor is this our image. You have polluted your skin with a false medicament, you have changed your hair with an adulterous colour, your face is violently taken possession of by a lie, your figure is corrupted, your countenance is another's. You cannot see God, since your eyes are not those which God made, but those which the devil has spoiled. You have followed him, you have imitated the red and painted eyes of the serpent. As you are adorned in the fashion of your enemy, with him also you shall burn by and by.' Are not these, I beg, matters to be reflected on by God's servants?" (Treatise 2; On the Dress of Virgins).

This is a very solemn warning; one that everybody who claims to be a Christian should take to heart.

Just because a person is wealthy is no excuse for buying unneeded things. A good steward will use what God has given him in a way that benefits God's work.

Constitutions of the Twelve Apostles
[Note: this quote is in regards to men's attire.]
"That beauty which God and nature has bestowed on thee, do not further beautify; but modestly diminish it before men. Thus, do not thou permit the hair of thy head to grow too long, but rather cut it short; lest by a nice combing thy hair, and wearing it long, and anointing thyself, thou draw upon thyself such ensnared or ensnaring women. Neither do thou wear over-fine garments to seduce any; neither do thou, with an evil

subtilty, affect over-fine stockings or shoes for thy feet, but only such as suit the measures of decency and usefulness. Neither do thou put a gold ring upon thy fingers; for all these ornaments are the signs of lasciviousness, which if thou be solicitous about in an indecent manner, thou wilt not act as becomes a good man: for it is not lawful for thee, a believer and a man of God, to permit the hair of thy head to grow long, and to brush it up together, nor to suffer it to spread abroad, nor to puff it up, nor by nice combing and platting to make it curl and shine; since that is contrary to the law, which says thus, in its additional precepts: 'You shall not make to yourselves curls and round rasures.' ... But if thou do these things to please men, in contradiction to the law, thou wilt be abominable with God, who created thee after His own image. If, therefore, thou wilt be acceptable to God, abstain from all those things which He hates, and do none of those things that are unpleasing to Him" (Book 1, sec. 2).

Men, too, must be careful to dress modestly and plainly.

"If thou desirest to be one of the faithful, and to please the Lord, O wife, do not superadd ornaments to thy beauty, in order to please other men; neither affect to wear fine broidering, garments, or shoes, to entice those who are allured by such things. For although thou dost not these wicked things with design of sinning thyself, but only for the sake of ornament and beauty, yet wilt thou not so escape future punishment, as having compelled another to look so hard at thee as to lust after thee, and as not having taken care both to avoid sin thyself, and the affording scandal to others" (Book 1, sec. 3).

⁕ ⁕ ⁕ ⁕ ⁕

A lot of people, when confronted with the Church Fathers on these subjects, try to excuse sin by means of the old chestnut, "But things are different now."

Not so. Fashions and customs may change, but God is still God, and sin is still sin.

"For I am the LORD, I change not" (Mal. 3:6a).

"Every good gift and every perfect gift is from above, and cometh down from the Father of lights, with whom is no variableness, neither shadow of turning" (James 1:17).

The subjects of dress, jewelry, and cosmetics are not the only points of agreement. There are other issues, often relating to separation from the world in general, where the Holiness movement (often unknowingly) has been in virtual lock-step with the early writers.

Chapter 18

Conclusion

I have shown in the history section that Christian writers all throughout history have talked about various aspects of Holiness doctrine, including the idea of Christian perfection.

They did not invent these ideas, but took them from the Bible. I trust that I have made it clear from the Book of Acts that the apostolic Church routinely viewed the baptism of the Spirit as a completely separate thing from salvation.

I have posed questions to the reader regarding certain commands in the Bible—commands which I believe are impossible to obey, at least completely, as long as any trace of carnality remains in the heart.

Many people over the centuries have opposed the idea of a second work of grace based on what they believed to be solid scriptural grounds. But once Scripture is properly reconciled with Scripture, those supposed grounds disappear. I have shown in chapter 2 that the apostles spoke with one voice on matters of doctrine. The Bible was written to us, here on earth, in our present condition. Are we to believe that God would give commands in such a Book as that, written under those conditions, and yet those commands would not apply to us here on earth? The idea is ludicrous and preposterous. And yet that idea is precisely what some opponents of Holiness doctrine have claimed. Yes, they admit, God has commanded us to be holy and spotless—but since they have preconceived notions of what is possible, they shift those commands in time, and say that they truly apply to us only **after** we reach Heaven!

Others deal with the issue by creating a theological split personality. According to them, we are simultaneously saint and sinner; holy and unholy; godly and devilish. Do the saints who have gone to be with God in Heaven still have carnality in them? Do sinners in Hell have any degree of righteousness? If not, then why expect or condone such a mixture here on earth?

As noted earlier, it seems that almost every single person who opposes Holiness doctrine is either a Calvinist, or at the very least holds the doctrine of eternal security. They hold two theological positions which lead them to oppose Holiness doctrine.

First and foremost, is the idea of eternal security. If you truly cannot lose your salvation, then obviously there is no need for a pure heart or a holy life. Such a thing may be considered desirable, but it certainly can't be considered necessary. The better class of people who hold to eternal security do indeed make a sincere effort to lead holy lives, but they are living above and beyond what their doctrine requires.

Their second mistake is their fixation on imputed righteousness, which leads them to ignore imparted righteousness. I have no issue with the idea of imputed righteousness, in and of itself. But our opponents take the idea far beyond where it should go. Again, if God has judicially declared us to be righteous, and if nothing can change our standing before God, then whether or not we actually have a pure heart is irrelevant.

These two ideas, if taken to their logical conclusions, completely obliterate any perceived need of a second work of grace, or of having a holy heart, or of living a holy life.

I have shown that the theme of living a **holy** life is woven all throughout the Bible. In chapter 11 alone, I quote over a dozen Bible verses on this topic, representing ten different books of the Bible. Many of these are definite commands.

The Bible teaches us how to distinguish between sin on the one hand, and infirmities, mistakes, and temptations on the other hand. Chapter 12 talks about the differences.

We are told in several Bible verses that God wants to give us every good and needed thing. The gift of perfect love, and the eradication of carnality, is one of those things. In chapter 14, I talk about how Jesus came to destroy ALL the works of the Devil. God wants us, and expects us, to live a life that is absolutely permeated with righteousness, and absolutely free from all trace of sin and carnality.

I have shown in chapter 10 that opponents of entire sanctification have failed to properly reconcile the Scriptures. Once this has been done, we see that there is absolutely no scriptural grounds for the idea of a sinning religion.

The people who deny the possibility of having the carnal nature eradicated are behaving in a very rude manner to those of us who claim such an experience. The evidence for the second work is exactly the same as the evidence for the first work. In the words of A. H. Ackley: "You ask me how I know He lives? / He lives within my heart."

If the reader were to meet a humble, modestly-dressed man, who told you, "I'm saved, and I know it because I have Jesus in my heart," would you retort, "I don't believe it"? I would certainly hope not. And yet many people who do not understand the doctrine of entire sanctification act in precisely that way towards people who claim that they have received the second blessing.

The Amish say it is presumption to claim we can know for sure that we are saved. Holiness opponents use the same sort of language when talking about the second work.

The evidence for the first work of grace, of KNOWING that we are saved, is precisely the same type of evidence for the second work of grace, of KNOWING that we are sanctified and that the carnal nature is totally eradicated.

"The Spirit itself beareth witness with our spirit, that we are the children of God" (Romans 8:16).

"If we receive the witness of men, the witness of God is greater: for this is the witness of God which he hath testified of his Son. He that believeth on the Son of God hath the witness in himself: he that believeth not God hath made him a liar; because he believeth not the record that God gave of his Son" (I John 5:9, 10).

That's the internal evidence. There is very often external evidence as well, although how noticeable it is varies from person to person. We have probably all heard someone, who, when talking about a certain person who has gotten saved, talks about the noticeable transformation in that person's life. Sanctification also produces some degree of noticeable change. As I said earlier, Peter is a prime example. He had a vastly steadier, more stable, more consistent walk with God after Pentecost than he did before. Untold numbers of people have testified to the same thing. In the history section, I quote a few preachers who found that they had more power for God's service, and more success at winning souls, once they had a completely pure heart. I did not quote D. L. Moody, but he discovered the same thing.

But opponents of entire sanctification use a different standard of evidence. Ironically, however, they are consistent on one point. They claim that it is impossible to live without sin—and they prove it in their own lives by acting in a haughty, proud, arrogant manner towards people that they should be treating with Christian love. They show this attitude by claiming that they know our hearts better than we through the grace of God know them!

This next part may make me rather unpopular with some readers. Even though unsanctified Christians often bewail their carnal nature, and fight against it, it seems to me that in many cases, there surely must be some corner of their heart that feels differently. And here I am not talking about the carnal nature itself, although I daresay that the carnal nature influences this. I am talking about some hidden corner of the heart, that although it is more or less in tune with God, feels that carnality (even though carnality is enmity against God) isn't REALLY all that bad. This is perhaps one manifestation of the double-minded man that St. James talks about. In short, it seems to me that the typical unsanctified Christian must somehow, in some form or another, **tolerate** carnality within his heart, even if he is not consciously aware of that toleration.

Now perhaps I am wrong on this point. I'm largely guessing on this, although I have grounds for feeling that my guess is an accurate one. The unsanctified reader may be feeling right about now that I am definitely wrong. If so, I would request that the reader stop and think about this for a minute. If I am wrong, then just WHY, exactly, *have you never asked God to remove that carnal nature?*

I would strongly encourage you to think, meditate deeply, and pray on this point. If you have never asked God to remove the remnant of the carnal nature from your heart, perhaps you should seek the answer to this question in prayer.

Carnality is dangerous to the soul. Many an unsanctified Christian has started to do something for God, only to have the carnal nature set to work on them. It can be all too easy to let carnality reason us out of giving 100% for God. And if that happens, we miss out on the best that God has for our lives.

When the three Hebrews refused to bow down to Nebuchadnezzar's statue, you can be sure that carnality would have pointed out, with great eloquence and vigor, the foolishness of their decision. But they were resolved to obey God NO MATTER WHAT. If you have that same attitude, you are either sanctified, or else on the path to that blessing.

Now we need to be careful to draw a distinction between carnality and the inherent frailties of the flesh. If God calls a shy or retiring person to do something for Him in public, that is almost certainly going to be much harder for such a person than for somebody who is gregarious and outgoing. At the same time, however, we need to be careful that we do not excuse carnality by calling it human nature, or anything of the sort.

When Jesus was in Gethsemane, it is very clear that (to use a modern turn of phrase) He was not exactly looking forward to the experience that He was about to go through. He wanted very much for there to be another way that God's will could be fulfilled. But even though His humanity trembled under the burden, He did not let either carnal or human reasoning change His path.

"Jesus, I my cross have taken,
　　All to leave, and follow Thee;
Naked, poor, despised, forsaken,
　　Thou, from hence, my all shalt be:
Perish ev'ry fond ambition,
　　All I've sought, and hoped, and known;
Yet how rich is my condition,
　　God and heav'n are still my own!"
- -"Jesus, I My Cross Have Taken," first verse, by Henry Lyte

"Now if any man have not the Spirit of Christ, he is none of his" (Romans 8:9b).

Should we be satisfied with just a little of God's spirit? When Jesus was on earth, did He fight sin, or did He accommodate it?

I know that many Christians maintain an active struggle with their carnality. I have heard them say so, and I have read anguished outpourings on the subject, in various books. I deeply sympathize with those people, especially when they don't know any better.

I hope that nobody will be offended if I switch to tough love mode for a moment. One of the wisest pagans, Marcus Aurelius, said this: "Put an end once for all to this discussion of what a good man should be, and be one." If you are ACTUALLY tired of the carnal nature inside you, then DO SOMETHING ABOUT IT. Humble yourself in the dust before God, and seek purity of heart with all your mind, soul, and strength. Be like Jacob—"I will not let thee go, except thou bless me." Hunger and thirst after righteousness with every fiber of your being; and according to the God which cannot lie, you shall be filled.

Sometimes it can be difficult to know how to put theory into practice. So if you are not sure how to implement this in your own life, try this—pray specifically that God will increase your hunger and thirst.

Don't struggle over words and terms. A. B. Earle (at the beginning of ch. 8) viewed this work of entire sanctification as complete rest and trust in Jesus, rather than as perfection. It would be a terrible tragedy if somebody missed out on the best that God has to offer, simply because a certain term caused him to stumble and reject the whole concept.

But even after we have gone all the way with God, we must be careful and watchful. There are many hindrances to spiritual life. Solomon fell because of an inordinate love of pleasure (I Kings 11). Uzziah fell because of pride (II Chron. 26).

If you want to get (and keep) God's **full** blessing and presence, it is not enough to get rid of everything in your life that is definitely sinful; you must also get rid of everything that is merely dubious.

I have reluctantly concluded that I should give a portion of my personal testimony regarding the work of sanctification. I didn't want to—I would very much prefer to keep myself in the background. Furthermore, I am quite certain that some people who read this book will misinterpret my words. However, I must do my duty and let God take care of the consequences.

There are a great many unpleasant things that happen to us in life. Some of them are transitory; others are longer lasting. I have witnessed the effects of the second work of grace in my life time and time again. Whether somebody cuts me off in traffic; whether I have a stressful day at work; whether somebody says he will do something, and then doesn't do it; all those things affect me only on the surface. Regardless of what happens, I am still—thank God!—conscious of the abiding peace of God deep within my soul. Those outward things do not reach the inner corners of my heart, nor do they affect my relationship with God. Indeed, they cannot, unless I choose to let them. I am sometimes disappointed when certain things happen; occasionally I am alarmed; sometimes I am grieved. Sometimes I am tempted to become angry; but the presence of God in my heart—a presence absolutely unmixed with any taint of sin—gives me strength to resist such temptations.

This works with afflictions as well. The years 2001 and 2002 were unpleasant years for me in virtually every respect. Even now, I do not wish to go into detail—suffice it to say that I went through deep trials during that period. But through it all, God's grace and presence remained. That was the only bright spot during that period. I knew that I *could not* lose God unless I chose to give in to temptation.

There have been many times in my life that circumstances were such that I was tempted to become bitter. Sometimes I was able to shove aside the temptation quite easily; other times I struggled with it. I thank God that there was absolutely nothing in my heart that responded to that temptation—I'm not sure what the outcome would have been otherwise. The attack was all from outside of my heart, not from the inside. This is why absolute purity of heart is a marvelous stabilizing influence in such cases.

Once you have read this book, I sincerely hope that any unsanctified readers will strive for the second blessing. If you have opposed this doctrine in the past, I hope that you will not do so in the future. Opposition to this doctrine is a dangerous thing. There have been many people who have made shipwreck of their faith by such opposition. If you do not fully understand the doctrine, that's one thing—I do not believe that God will condemn opposition based on faulty knowledge. But if you do understand, but oppose anyway because you are not willing to pay the price to give up the carnal nature—be warned. If the finger of God reaches down and touches some item in your life, whether it be a family member, a habit, some article of clothing, or even an attitude, and you are not willing to surrender that—then at that point, that thing becomes an idol to you; and if you do not change your mind, you will sooner or later find it blocking your path to Heaven.

Untold numbers of people have discovered for themselves that it is indeed possible to live a sin-free life; one of purity and perfection of heart. Join us, and discover for yourself how marvelous it is!

For any opponents of Holiness doctrine who have made it this far, I have some questions for you. Ponder these carefully and prayerfully.

1. What does "Be ye holy" really mean?
2. Do you agree that sin defiles everything it touches?
3. Would you say that living a sin-defiled life presents to the world a fair, accurate picture of God's grace and holiness? If not, what do you plan to do about it?
4. Is the carnal nature holy?
5. Can it be holy? If not, what should be done about it?

6. Is the God of Abraham, Isaac, and Jacob a merciful God? Does He want to help His children?

7. Is He also a just God? Will He deal with sin in a way that only a holy God can?

8. How much power does the blood of Jesus have to wash away sin? Is it limited or unlimited?

9. Is God omnipotent? If so, why do you insist on artificially limiting His power (and mercy)?

I don't know whether I am totally correct on every point that I have written about in this book, although I hope I am. I have certainly done my best to be correct. It is of course preferable to be correct on every point of doctrine. However, in some ways, that is a relatively minor issue. Getting to Heaven is the top priority. Once we get there, we will find out what our theological mistakes have been here on earth. In the meantime, I would much rather DO right (and avoid wrong) than BE right.

"But as he which hath called you is holy, so be ye holy in all manner of conversation; because it is written, Be ye holy; for I am holy" (I Peter 1:15, 16).

Living a truly holy, pure, Spirit-filled life is both the privilege and the duty of every Christian. I have shown that it is God's expectation, as well as His command, that we should be holy and righteous in every respect. Moses, David, Matthew, Paul, Peter, and John are just *some* of the writers who touch on this topic. With the work of sanctification, we are living Bibles to a sin-stricken world. Without it, the pages of our lives are smudged and smeared. We are ambassadors of a purified Kingdom, and servants of the most high God, who is glorious in His shining purity. Why should our lives and our hearts reflect anything less than His absolute purity? Why would any person who truly loves Him be satisfied with anything less?

"And thou shalt make a plate of pure gold, and grave upon it, like the engravings of a signet, HOLINESS TO THE LORD" (Exodus 28:36).

"In that day shall there be upon the bells of the horses, HOLINESS UNTO THE LORD" (Zech. 14:20a).

"The LORD bless thee, and keep thee: the LORD make his face shine upon thee, and be gracious unto thee: the LORD lift up his countenance upon thee, and give thee peace" (Numbers 6:24-26).

Appendix A
Novatian on the Holy Ghost

Note: The following is not directly related to the subject of this book, but I wanted to include it, because I enjoyed it so much. Also, since the Holy Ghost is so intimately connected with entire sanctification, it is a good idea to know more about Him.

Novatian (200-258)

Novatian is another early Father who was controversial. The story begins in 250, when the emperor Decius issued an edict that everybody must perform a sacrifice to the Roman gods. Due to the sweeping nature of the persecution that followed, many more Christians were given the choice of sacrificing or martyrdom. Most previous persecutions had been strictly local affairs. All too many denied Christ. The persecution did not last long, but it left the Church with a wide-spread problem of what to do with people who had denied their faith, but now wanted re-admittance into the Church. Novatian took a very hard line on the subject, and thus found himself in conflict with the majority of Church leaders. The disagreement got worse: "Novatian was called a heretic, not only by Cyprian but throughout the Church, for his severe views about the restoration of those who had lapsed in the persecution. He held that idolatry was an unpardonable sin [by the Church, not by God], and that the Church had no right to restore to communion any who had fallen into it" (Catholic Encyclopedia). In other words, Novation was one of those unfortunate people who let their zeal run away with their brotherly love. However, on other points, he held correct beliefs. He wrote a very valuable book regarding the Trinity about 256. Other than the controversy, we know very little about his life.

The following is from chapter 29 of On the Trinity.
Moreover, the order of reason, and the authority of the faith in the disposition of the words and in the Scriptures of the Lord, admonish us after these things to believe also on the Holy Spirit, once promised to the Church, and in the appointed occasions of times given... And He is not new in the Gospel, nor yet even newly given; for it was He Himself who accused the people in the prophets, and in the apostles gave them the appeal to the Gentiles. For the former deserved to be accused, because they had contemned the law; and they of the Gentiles who believe deserve to be aided by the defence of the Spirit, because they earnestly desire to attain to the Gospel law. Assuredly in the Spirit there are different kinds of offices, because in the times there is a different order of occasions; and yet, on this account, He who discharges these offices is not different, nor is He another in so acting, but He is one and the same, distributing His offices according to the times, and the occasions and impulses of things. Moreover, the Apostle Paul says, "Having the same Spirit; as it is written, I believed, and therefore have I spoken; we also believe, and therefore speak." He is therefore one and the same Spirit who was in the prophets and apostles, except that in the former He was occasional, in the latter always. But in the former not as being always in them, in the latter as abiding always in them; and in the former distributed with reserve, in the latter all poured out; in the former given sparingly, in the latter liberally bestowed; not yet manifested before the Lord's resurrection, but conferred after the resurrection... For this is He who strengthened their hearts and minds, who marked out the Gospel sacraments, who was in them the enlightener of divine things; and they being strengthened, feared, for the sake of the Lord's name, neither dungeons nor chains, nay, even trod under foot the very powers of the world and its tortures, since they were henceforth armed and strengthened by the same Spirit, having in them-

selves the gifts which this same Spirit distributes, and appropriates to the Church, the spouse of Christ, as her ornaments. This is He who places prophets in the Church, instructs teachers, directs tongues, gives powers and healings, does wonderful works, offers discrimination of spirits, affords powers of government, suggests counsels, and orders and arranges whatever other gifts there are of charismata; and thus make the Lord's Church everywhere, and in all, perfected and completed. This is He who, after the manner of a dove, when our Lord was baptized, came and abode upon Him, dwelling in Christ full and entire, and not maimed in any measure or portion; but with His whole overflow copiously distributed and sent forth, so that from Him others might receive some enjoyment of His graces: the source of the entire Holy Spirit remaining in Christ, so that from Him might be drawn streams of gifts and works, while the Holy Spirit dwelt affluently in Christ... He it is who...can make us God's temple, and fit us for His house; who solicits the divine hearing for us with groanings that cannot be uttered; filling the offices of advocacy, and manifesting the duties of our defence,—an inhabitant given for our bodies and an effector of their holiness... For our bodies are both trained in Him and by Him to advance to immortality, by learning to govern themselves with moderation according to His decrees. For this is He who "desireth against the flesh," because "the flesh resisteth against the Spirit." This is He who restrains insatiable desires, controls immoderate lusts, quenches unlawful fires, conquers reckless impulses, repels drunkenness, checks avarice, drives away luxurious revellings, links love, binds together affections, keeps down sects, orders the rule of truth, overcomes heretics, turns out the wicked, guards the Gospel... Established in this Spirit, "none ever calleth Jesus anathema;" no one has ever denied Christ to be the Son of God, or has rejected God the Creator; no one utters any words of his own contrary to the Scriptures; no one ordains other and sacrilegious decrees; no one draws up different laws. Whosoever shall blaspheme against Him, "hath not forgiveness, not only in this world, but also not in the world to come." This is He who in the apostles gives testimony to Christ; in the martyrs shows forth the constant faithfulness of their religion; in virgins restrains the admirable continency of their sealed chastity; in others, guards the laws of the Lord's doctrine incorrupt and uncontaminated; destroys heretics, corrects the perverse, condemns infidels, makes known pretenders; moreover, rebukes the wicked, keeps the Church uncorrupt and inviolate, in the sanctity of a perpetual virginity and truth.

Appendix B
Suggested Reading and Other Resources

Internet
hymnary.org
cyberhymnal.org
hymntime.com/tch/index.htm
These three sites have various biographical information on a vast number of hymn writers and composers. Sometimes you can find scans of a particular hymn from a century-old hymnal.

ccel.org
The Christian Classics Ethereal Library has a tremendous number of digitized books available for free download. Many are historical in nature; others are devotional classics, such as the books of E. M. Bounds. There are even a few Christian novelists available, such as George MacDonald.

earlychristianwritings.com
This site has writings from the Church Fathers and biographical information. It also has various apocryphal books, as well as letters, etc. that some people had at one point either falsely or mistakenly attributed to the Church Fathers. There is also information on authors such as Josephus who are tangentially related to early Church history. Note: this is not really a "Christian" website; rather, it is a historical website about Christianity.

archive.org
The Internet Archive contains a treasure-trove of digitized Christian books from previous years. Many of these are available for free download. There are also some newer books that can be digitally borrowed for a length of time.
For example, here is the full URL for a biography of Billy Sunday:
https://archive.org/details/billysundaygoldeoowill
And here is one of E. E. Shelhamer's books:
https://archive.org/details/bibleholinesshowooshel

Books
Some of these are available in digital form from CCEL. Most can be found in physical form from various online sellers.

Revival Fire by Wesley Duewel
Wesley Duewel provides many thrilling stories of wonderful revivals throughout the years. This book should have a place in all Christian homes and schools.

One Divine Moment edited by Robert Coleman
This is the heart-warming account of the 1970 Asbury College revival.

Letters of John Fletcher edited by Edward Cook
The Church world in general has, to its detriment, largely forgotten about John Fletcher. This collection of his letters provides a look into the life of one of the Church's greatest saints.

Autobiography by George Fox
For students of history, this provides a fascinating look into how the Quakers began.

Christian Leaders of the 18th Century by J. C. Ryle
J. C. Ryle provides a heart-warming, sympathetic look at the lives of some of Whitefield's and Wesley's forgotten contemporaries.

The Adornment of the Spiritual Marriage by Jan van Ruysbroeck
This is a truly remarkable book; all the more so, because the author was a Catholic.

Deeper Experiences of Famous Christians by J. Gilchrist Lawson
This book contains stories about many people—George Fox, John Bunyan, Peter Cartwright, D. L. Moody, William Booth, Madam Guyon, etc.—all of whom discovered the secret of a deeper spiritual life, even though some of them did not have any formal doctrine of a second work of grace.

Be Ye Holy by Leslie Wilcox
He goes over much of the theology of sanctification. He also has a section on the history of the Holiness movement.

Hallelujahs From Portsmouth edited by Seth C. Rees, et al.
For many years, starting in the early 1890s, there was a Holiness camp meeting every summer in Portsmouth, Rhode Island. This book is a collection of reports covering 1896-1899.

Clarke's Commentary by Adam Clarke
I HIGHLY recommend it, if you can afford it. It is not as easy to find a complete physical set as it used to be; it is available online in digital form, but the version that I looked at was not quite a completely-faithful rendition. If you buy only one Bible commentary in your life, make this the one.

Appendix C
Selected List of Holiness Hymns and Hymn Writers

A few of these writers may not have been explicitly Holiness in their formal theology, but the hymns listed are thoroughly Holiness in outlook.

Hugh C. Benner (1899-1975); Nazarene (General Superintendent of the Nazarene Church 1952-1968)
   Power in the Blood of Jesus
Frank Bottome (1823-1894); Methodist
   The Comforter has Come
Ida M. Budd (1859-1911)
   Leaving all to Follow Jesus
T. O. Chisholm (1866-1960); Methodist
   Oh, to be Like Thee
Fanny Crosby (1820-1915); Methodist
   Blessed Assurance
J. E. French (dates unknown)
   This is Like Heaven to Me
Charles H. Gabriel (1856-1932); Methodist
   Pentecostal Power (written under the pen-name Charlotte G. Homer)
John Millard Harris (1867-1934)
   My Soul is Filled with Glory
Frances R. Havergal (1836-1879); Anglican
   Take my Life, and Let it Be
Rev. F. E. Hill (dates unknown); Nazarene
   Since the Holy Ghost Abides
Elisha A. Hoffman (1839-1929); Presbyterian
   Is Your All on the Altar?
C. P. Jones (1865-1949); Baptist; founder of Church of Christ (Holiness)
   Deeper, Deeper
Haldor Lillenas (1885-1959); Nazarene
   Glorious Freedom
   Holiness Forevermore
   My Wonderful Lord
Henry F. Lyte (1793-1847); Anglican (wife Methodist)
   Jesus, I my Cross Have Taken
Mrs. C. H. Morris (1862-1929); Methodist (also known as Lelia Naylor Morris)
   A New Touch of Fire
   Holiness Unto the Lord
   Sanctifying Power
   Sweet Will of God
   'Tis Good to Live in Canaan
Johnson Oatman, Jr. (1856-1922); Methodist
   How the Fire Fell
Rev. L. L. Pickett (1859-1928); probably Methodist

It is for Us All Today
Adelaide A. Pollard (1862-1934)
  Have Thine Own Way, Lord
Andrew Reed (1787-1862); Congregationalist
  Holy Ghost, with Light Divine
R. F. Reynolds (dates unknown)
  Let the Holy Ghost Come In
Edgar Page Stites (1836-1921); Methodist
  Beulah Land
Charles Albert Tindley (1851-1933); Methodist
  Nothing Between
Judson W. Van de Venter (1855-1939); Methodist
  I Surrender All
Charles Wesley (1707-1788); Anglican/Methodist
  Love Divine
  Oh, for a Heart to Praise my God!
H. J. Zelley (1859-1942); Methodist
  I do not Ask to Choose my Path
  The Sweet Beulah Land

Appendix D
Selected timeline of quoted writers (individuals only; not anonymous/semi-anonymous books)

1. Clement of Rome (AD 30-100)
2. Ignatius (35-107)
3. Aristides of Athens (dates unknown, but possibly died 133/134)
4. Polycarp (69-155)
5. Justin Martyr (100-165)
6. Tatian (120-173/180)
7. Athenagoras of Athens (133-190)
8. Theophilus of Antioch (115-181/188)
9. Irenaeus (120-202)
10. Clement of Alexandria (150-215)
11. Tertullian (155-225/240)
12. Hippolytus of Rome (170-236)
13. Origen (185-254)
14. Dionysius of Alexandria (190/200-264)
15. Cyprian (200-258)
16. Gregory Thaumaturgus (213-270)
17. Methodius of Olympus (?-311)
18. Lactantius (250-325)
19. Alexander of Alexandria (?-326)
20. Athanasius (296/8-373)
21. Macarius of Egypt (300-391)
22. Gregory of Nyssa (335-395)
23. John Chrysostom (347-407)
24. Augustine (354-430)
25. Sulpitius (or Sulpicius) Severus (363-420)
26. John Cassian (360-435)
27. Leo the Great (390/400-461)
28. Gregory the Great (540-604)
29. John of Damascus (675-749)
30. St. Francis of Assisi (c.1181-1226)
31. Jan van Ruysbroeck (1293-1381)
32. Thomas a Kempis (c.1380-1471)
33. Brother Lawrence (1610/14-1691)
34. George Fox (1624-1691)
35. Philipp Jakob Spener (1635-1705)
36. Robert Barclay (1648-1690)
37. Madame Guyon (1648-1717)
38. Francois Fenelon (1651-1715)
39. August Hermann Francke (1663-1727)
40. Johann Friedrich Starck (1680-1756)
41. Nicolas Ludwig, Count von Zinzendorf (1700-1760)
42. John Wesley (1703-1791)
43. John Fletcher (1729-1785)
44. Adam Clarke (1760/2-1832)
45. J. A. Wood (1828-1905)
46. A. B. Earle (1812-1895)
47. John Hartley (19th century)
48. A. B. Simpson (1843-1919)
49. Samuel Logan Brengle (1860-1936)
50. E. E. Shelhamer (1869-1947)
51. Peter Wiseman (20th century)

Appendix E
List of Quoted Books of the Bible

Genesis
Exodus
Leviticus
Deuteronomy
Joshua
II Samuel
I Kings
II Kings
II Chronicles
Job
Psalms
Proverbs
Ecclesiastes
Isaiah
Jeremiah
Ezekiel
Hosea
Joel
Amos
Obadiah
Zechariah
Malachi
Matthew
Mark
Luke
John
Acts
Romans
I Corinthians
II Corinthians
Galatians
Ephesians
Colossians
I Thessalonians
I Timothy
II Timothy
Titus
Hebrews
James
I Peter
II Peter

I John
II John
Jude
Revelation

Bibliography

Augsburg Confession. 1530.

Barclay, Robert. Apology for the true Christian Divinity. 1st Stereotype ed. 1827. New York: Samuel Wood and Sons.

———. Theological Theses. 1st Stereotype ed. 1827. New York: Samuel Wood and Sons.

Brengle, Samuel Logan. Heart Talks on Holiness. 2nd ed. [1900].

Brooks, John. Scriptural Sanctification. 1902. Nashville: Publishing House of the M. E. Church, South.

Cartwright, Peter. Autobiography. 1856. Cincinnati: L. Swormstedt & A. Poe.

Clarke, Adam. Clarke's Commentary. 1977. Nashville: Abingdon Press.

Coleman, Robert (Ed.). One Divine Moment. 1970. Old Tappan, NJ: Fleming H. Revell Company.

Cook, Edward (Ed.). Letters of John Fletcher. Kingsley Press ed. 2014. Shoals, IN: Kingsley Press.

Discipline of the Methodist Protestant Church. 1830. Baltimore: John J. Harrod.

Duewel, Wesley. Revival Fire. 1995. Grand Rapids, MI: Zondervan.

Earle, A. B. The Rest of Faith. 1871. Boston: James H. Earle.

Encyclopedia Britannica. 11th ed. 1911. New York: The Encyclopedia Britannica Company.

Erb, Peter (Ed.). Pietists: Selected Writings. 1983. Mahwah, NJ: Paulist Press.

Fenelon, Francois. Christian Counsel. Ed. James Metcalf. 1853. New York.

Fletcher, John. Christian Perfection. [c.1775].

Francis of Assisi. Works of St. Francis of Assisi. 1882. London: R. Washbourne.

Gundry, Stanley (Ed.). Five Views on Sanctification. 1987. Grand Rapids, MI: Zondervan.

Guyon, Jeanne. Method of Prayer. Ed. James Metcalf. 1853. New York.

Hartley, John. Chapters on Holiness: Expository and Practical. 1883. London: Hayman Bros. & Lilly.

Henry, Matthew. A Commentary on the Whole Bible. Reference Library ed. 1986. Iowa Falls, IA: World Bible Publishers.

Herman, Nicolas (Br. Lawrence). The Practice of the Presence of God. [1693].

Jones, Rufus M. (Ed.). George Fox an Autobiography. 1903.

Kempis, Thomas. The Imitation of Christ. 1886. London: John C. Ninmo.

Lawson, J. Gilchrist. Deeper Experiences of Famous Christians. 1911. Chicago: Glad Tidings Publishing Company.

Lewis, A. J. Zinzendorf the Ecumenical Pioneer. 1962. SCM Press Ltd.

Mason, A. J. Fifty Spiritual Homilies of St. Macarius the Egyptian. 1921. New York: The Macmillan Company.

Pickett, L. L. St. Paul on Holiness. [no date]. Titusville, PA: The Allegheny Wesleyan Methodist Connection.

Pink, A. W. The Doctrine of Sanctification. Christian Heritage ed. 1998. Fearn, G.B.: Christian Focus Publications, Ltd.

Ryle, J. C. Christian Leaders of the 18th Century. 1885. Aylesbury, G.B.: Hazell Watson & Viney Ltd.

———. Holiness: Its Nature, Hindrances, Difficulties, and Roots. Hendrickson Publishers ed. 2007. Peabody, MA: Hendrickson Publishers Inc.

Schaff, Philip, et al (Eds.). Ante-Nicene Fathers, Volumes 1-7, 9. 1885. Edinburgh: T&T Clark.
———. Nicene and Post-Nicene Fathers, Series 1, Volumes 2, 3, 9-11. 1887. Edinburgh: T&T Clark.
———. Nicene and Post-Nicene Fathers, Series 2, Volumes 4, 5, 9, 11, 12. 1890. Edinburgh: T&T Clark.

Shelhamer, E. E. Sermons that Search the Soul. 1926. Kansas City: Nazarene Publishing House.

Simpson, A. B. The Holy Spirit, or Power From on High; Volumes 1 & 2. 1895-6.

Smalley, Gary. Joy that Lasts. 2002. Grand Rapids, MI: Zondervan.

Underhill, Evelyn (Ed.). Cloud of Unknowing. 2nd ed. 1922. London.

———. The Adornment of the Spiritual Marriage. 1916.

———. The Sparkling Stone. 1916.

Wells, Michael. Sidetracked in the Wilderness. 1991. Ada, MI: Chosen Books Pub Co.

Wesley, John. A Plain Account of Christian Perfection. [1777].

West, Dawn L. Light After Darkness. 1985. Salem, Ohio: Schmul Publishing Co.

Westminster Larger Catechism. 1647.

Wilcox, Leslie. 1965. Be ye Holy. Cincinnati: The Revivalist Press.

Wiseman, Peter. Scriptural Sanctification. 1951. Kansas City: Beacon Hill Press.

Wood, J. A. Perfect Love. 1915. Chicago: Christian Witness Co.

Yrigoyen, Charles, & Warrick, Susan (Eds.). 2005. Historical Dictionary of Methodism. 2nd ed. Lanham, MD: The Scarecrow Press, Inc.

Index